★

*THE ROYALTY
OF THE PULPIT*

★

THE ROYALTY
OF THE PULPIT

A SURVEY AND APPRECIATION OF THE
LYMAN BEECHER LECTURES ON PREACHING
FOUNDED AT YALE DIVINITY SCHOOL 1871
AND GIVEN ANNUALLY (WITH FOUR EXCEPTIONS)
SINCE 1872

BY

Edgar DeWitt Jones

Essay Index Reprint Series

 BOOKS FOR LIBRARIES PRESS
FREEPORT, NEW YORK

Copyright © 1951 by Harper & Brothers

All rights reserved

Reprinted 1970 by arrangement with
Harper & Row, Publishers, Inc.

INTERNATIONAL STANDARD BOOK NUMBER:
0-8369-1979-3

LIBRARY OF CONGRESS CATALOG CARD NUMBER:
79-134105

PRINTED IN THE UNITED STATES OF AMERICA

Inscribed with Lofty Esteem
to
Three Clergymen, Scholars, and Gallant Christian Gentlemen: Dr. Liston Pope, Dean of Yale Divinity School; Dr. Luther Allan Weigle, Dean Emeritus; the late Dean, Dr. Charles Reynolds Brown

CONTENTS

ACKNOWLEDGMENTS ix

FOREWORD by HALFORD E. LUCCOCK xiii

PREFACE xvii

INTRODUCTORY. THE ORIGIN OF THE LECTURESHIP xxiii

THE LECTURERS

I. OLYMPIANS: 3
1. Henry Ward Beecher, 2. John Hall, 3. William Mackergo Taylor, 4. Phillips Brooks, 5. Robert William Dale, 6. Matthew Simpson, 7. Howard Crosby, 8. Ezekiel Gilman Robinson, 9. Nathaniel Judson Burton, 10. John Albert Broadus.

II. TITANS: 57
1. Robert Forman Horton, 2. George Angier Gordon, 3. Charles Edward Jefferson, 4. Frank Wakeley Gunsaulus, 5. John Henry Jowett, 6. Charles Henry Parkhurst, 7. John Kelman, 8. Albert Parker Fitch, 9. Harry Emerson Fosdick.

III. THEOLOGIANS AND PHILOSOPHERS: 108
1. Adolphus Julius Frederick Behrends, 2. Andrew Martin Fairbairn, 3. George Adam Smith, 4. Peter Taylor Forsyth, 5. William Ralph Inge, 6. Reinhold Niebuhr, 7. Herbert Henry Farmer.

IV. PROPHETS OF SOCIAL CHANGE: 151
1. Washington Gladden, 2. Henry Sloane Coffin, 3. Charles David Williams, 4. Francis John McConnell, 5. Ernest Fremont Tittle, 6. Garfield Bromley Oxnam.

Contents

V. EDUCATORS AND SCHOOLMEN: ... 180
1. James Stalker, 2. William Jewett Tucker, 3. Francis Greenwood Peabody, 4. William Herbert Perry Faunce, 5. William DeWitt Hyde, 6. Lawrence Pearsall Jacks, 7. J. Edgar Park, 8. William Learoyd Sperry.

VI. EDITORS AND PUBLICISTS: ... 222
1. H. Clay Trumbull, 2. Lyman Abbott, 3. Charles Clayton Morrison.

VII. MODERN MASTERS OF PULPIT DISCOURSE: ... 237
1. Charles Reynolds Brown, 2. John Robert Paterson Sclater, 3. George Arthur Buttrick, 4. Edwin McNeill Poteat, Arthur Howe Bradford, Elmore McNeill McKee, Wyatt Aiken Smart, 5. Ralph Washington Sockman, 6. Morgan Phelps Noyes, 7. Paul Ehrman Scherer, 8. Harold Cooke Phillips, 9. Leslie D. Weatherhead.

VIII. A PAGEANTRY OF PREACHERS: ... 303
1. William Mackergo Taylor, 2. John Brown, 3. Charles Silvester Horne.

IX. SHEPHERDS OF THE FLOCK: ... 319
1. William Fraser McDowell, 2. William Pierson Merrill, 3. Raymond Calkins, 4. Albert Edward Day, 5. Walter Russell Bowie.

X. CHURCHMEN AND ECCLESIASTICS: ... 343
1. David Hummell Greer, 2. Herbert Hensley Henson, 3. George Wharton Pepper, 4. James Edward Freeman, 5. Edwin DuBose Mouzon, 6. Henry Knox Sherrill.

XI. MEN OF LETTERS: ... 375
1. Henry van Dyke, 2. John Watson (Ian Maclaren).

XII. AFTER EIGHTY YEARS 1871-1951—A JUDGMENT ... 385

APPENDIXES
1. Who's Who in the Lectureship ... 413
2. Bibliography ... 432

INDEX ... 441

ACKNOWLEDGMENTS

The author wishes to acknowledge his debt of gratitude to the seventy volumes on the Yale Lectureship on Preaching—interesting, informative, inspiring—the most noted Library on Preaching in the world. Also:

To the following publishers who have granted permission for the reprinting of extracts from volumes of the Lyman Beecher Lectures, listed on pages 432-36: Abingdon-Cokesbury Press, Fleming H. Revell Co., Harper & Brothers, Hodder & Stoughton, Ltd., Houghton Mifflin Co., Charles Scribner's Sons; to the following persons who hold copyrights to three volumes in the Series, namely, Albert Edward Day, Francis J. McConnell, and John M. Tittle. Other volumes in the Series from which excerpts have been taken are either in the public domain, or the publishers are no longer in business. To Carl Sandburg and Harcourt Brace & Co. for the lines from *Smoke and Steel*; *Christian Century* for the extracts from "A Word About a Friend" by Paul Hutchinson, and the autobiographical papers of Bishop Francis J. McConnell; to *Time Magazine* for the limerick attributed to the late Dr. William Temple.

To the twenty-four living lecturers for prompt and courteous replies to the questionnaire which I sent them with the humble apologies of one who detests questionnaires.

To Dean Liston Pope of Yale Divinity School, Dean Emeritus Luther A. Weigle, the late Dean, Dr. Charles Reynolds Brown, Professors Roland Herbert Bainton, Kenneth Scott Latourette, Librarian, Raymond Philip Morris, and John Clark Archer, for courteous help and patient kindnesses; and especially to Halford E. Luccock, for his characteristic and generous Foreword.

To Paul E. Scherer, who read the manuscript and made important suggestions—a friendly critic of rare artistry.

To the following friends, counselors, and critics, who in one way or another have made me their grateful debtor for informative,

Acknowledgments

suggestive, and constructive aid, mostly by correspondence: The Reverend William Robinson, lecturer in theology at Birmingham (England) University, and editor of the British *Christian Advocate*; the Reverend G. Earl Daniels, St. James' Church, Cambridge, Massachusetts; the Reverend Frederick Keller Stamm, Plumsteadville, Pennsylvania; Dr. Edward Scribner Ames, professor of philosophy, clergyman, author, Chicago, Illinois; Dr. Andrew W. Blackwood, professor of homiletics, Princeton Theological Seminary, Princeton, New Jersey; the Reverend Roger Eddy Treat, minister, Bushnell Congregational Church, Detroit; the Reverend Paul Austin Wolfe, minister, Brick Church, New York City; the Reverend Boynton Merrill, minister, First Congregational Church, Columbus, Ohio; Dr. W. E. Garrison, literary editor, *The Christian Century*, Chicago; Dr. Henry P. Van Dusen, president, Union Theological Seminary, New York; the Reverend Robert Clyde Yarbrough, minister, The Second Church in Newton, West Newton, Massachusetts; the Reverend D. R. Sharpe, executive secretary, Baptist Union, Cleveland; the Reverend G. Merrill Lenox, Detroit Council of Churches; Catherine W. Reynolds, Cambridge, Massachusetts; the late Dr. Joseph Fort Newton, minister, Church of St. Luke and Epiphany, Philadelphia; the Reverend Perry Epler Gresham, minister, Central Woodward Christian Church, Detroit; Professor Edwin E. Aubrey, University of Pennsylvania, Philadelphia; the Reverend Roy Ewing Vale, Tabernacle Presbyterian Church, Indianapolis; Dr. Francis Carr Stiffler, editorial secretary, American Bible Society, New York City; the Reverend Samuel McCrea Cavert, executive secretary, Federal Council of the Churches of Christ in America, New York City; the Reverend Joseph A. Vance, minister emeritus, First Presbyterian Church, Detroit; the Reverend F. E. Davison, First Christian Church, South Bend, Indiana; the Reverend Clarence E. Lemmon, minister, First Christian Church, Columbia, Missouri; the Reverend F. Elwynn Peace, minister and educator, Lafayette, Indiana; the Reverend F. H. Groom, Whittier, California; William Clark, Detroit.

To Mrs. William Clark and Miss Mary E. Oliphant, without whose expert stenographic services and secretarial efficiency I doubt that this book could have been written.

Acknowledgments

To the Reverend Hal Earl Norton, D.D., minister, First Baptist Church, Grinnell, Iowa, long-time collector and student of the Yale Lectures on Preaching, whose knowledge of the Series is well-nigh inexhaustible. To him I am largely indebted for the statistical research which appears in this work; and for counsel, suggestions, and generous use of volumes in his well-stocked library pertaining to this Lectureship; a bookman of parts and best of companions; God love him a lot!

FOREWORD

The Lyman Beecher Lectures on Preaching at Yale University have had to wait a long, long time for any adequate interpretation and evaluation as a whole. But this volume, *The Royalty of the Pulpit*, by Dr. Jones, was well worth waiting for. It does what has never been done before; it sets the whole series of discussion of preaching, given by some, at least, of the notable preachers of their times, in close relation to the varying currents of thought and experience running through seventy-five years of tumultuous history. In addition to that it presents a fascinating gallery of portraits of great personalities. Under Dr. Jones' skillful touch, these masters of the pulpit come alive. A great majority of those who have given the lectures in this series have long since died. With a few notable exceptions, they are almost, if not entirely, forgotten by the present generation. But these are no formal obituaries, or death masks. A child is always more interested in a zoo than in a museum of natural history. A live animal is more fascinating than a skeleton. Dr. Jones is not the curator of a museum. He deals with life. In his skillful evaluation of these preachers, he makes the reader feel that he is not so much seeing words as hearing voices that carry clearly across the valley of the years.

Two things become very clear as we are enabled to look at the whole series of Yale Lectures as it unrolls.

One is the reflection of the changing world which it gives. Certainly no seventy-five years of history has seen as much tremendous revolutionary change in every realm of thought and activity. These lectures have been, to a very real degree, a sensitive plate reflecting the tensions, perplexities, and turmoils of two generations and more. That makes them historically valuable. They register the trends, the changes in mood, the emergence of new interests, the bewildering onrush of new problems.

It was inevitable that preaching, over such a span of years, should change. There is no need to reiterate here the oft told tale of the changed conditions which the preaching of the Christian gospel has had to meet. But just a mere listing of a few of the great issues confronting the Christian Church in these years will help us see the lectures more vividly in relation to their time.

When Henry Ward Beecher gave the first lecture series in 1872, the large part of the battle over Biblical criticism was still ahead. The preacher was still speaking in what was in many evident ways still an "age of faith." The displacing of the exclamation point by the question mark had only begun. But in the seventy-five years ahead came changes in thought and mood which may fairly be indicated by the words of Henry Steele Commager: "It may be doubted whether at any time in three hundred years religion had meant so little to western man as it meant in the first half of the twentieth century." In rough figures, the date 1890 can be used as a great watershed separating an age of confidence in nearly every realm to one of skepticism and disillusion. The immense influence of psychology was still to arrive. In 1872 Freud was only sixteen years old. William James was only thirty. The whole social interpretation of Christianity to meet a new social discontent was still to make its advent. The Haymarket Massacre in Chicago, the Pullman and Homestead strikes, those grim portents of future turmoil, were still to come. This whole realm was first reflected in Washington Gladden's *Tools and the Man*, delivered in 1887.

Along with these fundamental changes, the sermon itself underwent great transformations. In the 1870's there were still sailing the seas, as approved models, many of the old three-decker sermons, formidable frigates and imposing, if difficult to manage. As the series goes on, we can trace the changes from more formal, traditional oratorical forms to direct, conversational speech.

Yet an entirely different impression is gained from Dr. Jones' portrayal of the series through the generations. That is the constancy amid change. The whole series make a moving demonstration of "Jesus Christ, the same yesterday, today and forever." Paragraphs from the early lectures of Beecher and Brooks and even John Hall could be inserted into the lectures of the latest series considered, that of Dr. Leslie Weatherhead in 1949, or many of the most recent ones, without any incongruity. We get a convincing demonstration of the unchanging resources of Christ in a changing world, and of needs the same in a world of atomic energy as in New Haven without streetcars in the 1870's. Just as the human heart felt the same needs under the pyramids of Egypt, as under the smokestacks of Pittsburgh and Detroit.

It is a stirring company of men into which the chapters of this book lead us. There are not only varieties of human nature, but a rich variety of human experience.

Dr. Jones has a remarkable equipment for his task. He has a sure flair for the thing that is alive. He does not need to carry a stethoscope around with him to tell whether an idea or fact is dead. He can detect the details that wriggle with life. He has the nose of a beagle hound for a fox, when it comes to selecting quotations. They are alive. They are notable in themselves and really illuminate the personality he is portraying. He has been a lifelong student of preaching and a notable preacher himself. His long pastorate at the Central Woodward Christian Church in Detroit was a truly memorable one. He has been president of the Federal Council of the Churches of Christ in America, and has played a part in world movements of the Church.

This book is not a bouquet of orchids. There is appreciation in it, inevitably. But there is frankness and discrimination. When a man muffs the ball as completely as Dean Inge did, Dr. Jones says so in forthright fashion. His speculations on men who might well have been invited to give the lectures will be read with great interest.

Dr. Jones deserves and receives the warm gratitude of Yale University and the Divinity School for the great service he has rendered. As the parade of history, which he allows us to review in this volume, passes by, we are moved to wonder if any gift ever paid off such dividends as did the $10,000, given to Yale in 1871 by Henry W. Sage, to establish the Lyman Beecher Lectures on Preaching.

This review of preaching during seventy-five years also stirs to wonder about the future of preaching. Will the multiplication of machinery in the years ahead make it obsolete as a force? Twenty years or so ago, in a series of books which looked into the crystal ball and toyed with the future of the various arts, the volume on preaching had a provocative title, *Eutychus, or the Future of*

Preaching. Eutychus was the young man who went to sleep under the preaching of St. Paul and fell out the window! So, the future of preaching will consist largely of sleep! *The Royalty of the Pulpit* raises doubts about that. It deepens the conviction that, amid many changes, as long as human nature remains the same, the communication of thought and feeling and faith, hot from one mind and heart to another, will be a high and permanent experience of mankind. It moves us to share the faith expressed by Henry Ward Beecher, in the first series of Yale Lectures in 1872, "True preaching is yet to come. Of all the professions for young men to look forward to, I do not know of another one that seems to have such scope before it in the future as preaching."

HALFORD E. LUCCOCK

Yale University Divinity School

PREFACE

I shall long remember the summer of 1948 at Pentwater, Michigan, where I summered with my family. To be sure, one cannot easily forget the wonder of "the million dollar sunsets" that we were privileged to see from our cottage daily, nor the whispering of the wind in the pine trees that nightly soothed us to sleep; but the circumstance that made this particular summer so unforgettable was the fact that I took sixty-seven volumes of the Lyman Beecher Lectures on Preaching with me and read them, every one, in preparation for this book.[1]

I

I thought I knew these volumes fairly well. I had been collecting them for a quarter of a century or more. Some of the books in the Series I knew intimately. I had my favorites as I suppose every disciple of this great Seriate has. I think I could say that up to the summer of 1948 I had a working acquaintance with at least one-third of the volumes in the Series. I often referred to the Lyman Beecher Lectures in addresses to ministers; indeed, I prepared a lecture on the subject which I titled "My Shelf Supreme"—meaning the volumes in the Yale Lectures. I rather thought myself an authority on these books. Often I displayed them to admiring visitors to my study. "See here," I would say proudly, "behold my collection of the volumes in the greatest Lectureship on Preaching in the world!" But this was prior to the summer of 1948.

That summer I really lived with the Yale Lectures. I started at the beginning and reread Beecher, Hall, Brooks, and Simpson, and

[1] At the time I took the Yale Lecture volumes to Pentwater in 1948, the lectures of Niebuhr, Phillips, and Sherrill had not yet come off the press. To date (July, 1950), the number of published volumes in the Series is 70, while the total number of lecturers, exclusive of those who lectured in 1950, with whom I have not dealt, is 75, due to the fact that two courses in the Series were given, not by one lecturer but by several.

found the second reading better than the first, good as it was then. Next I took up volumes whose backs I knew full well but not the contents. I read on and on and, to my dismay, discovered in three of the volumes in my collection uncut leaves. I cut them shamefacedly and read on, day after day, book after book. Thus I came to know Ezekiel G. Robinson, Howard Crosby, Albert Parker Fitch, and others, as I had not known them before or could have in any other way. I simply found myself baptized, and by immersion at that, in a wealth of sermonic counsel and ministerial experience. I had surely launched out into the deep, or, to vary the figure, I had found mines "richer than Golconda."

II

I have reached certain conclusions about this supreme Lectureship in the Christian ministry, namely: it is illuminating, edifying, comprehensive, stimulating, and exhaustive. The seventy-five men who have thus far appeared in the Series comprise some of the Olympians of the pulpit, the craftsmen of sermonic artistry, educators, and philosophers, and at least two who won fame in the literary realm. Practically every phase of the ministerial vocation is given adequate treatment: pulpit and pastoral responsibilities, churchmanship, and the myriad aspects of the preacher's relationship to his church, his study, and the community. Moreover, the authors draw heavily on their wide and varied experiences, which fact makes their lectures all the more important and valuable.

To peruse closely the thousands of pages in these three score and more volumes is to humble even a veteran like myself. As I read on and on I kept asking myself the question, "Am I too a preacher?" How far short I have fallen from the ideals and standard set up and glorified by the knowledge and experiences of these prophets of the Most High, faithful pastors and efficient administrators! I kept speculating what my own ministry might have been could I have been early schooled in these lectures as I now am after a close and intimate study of this preacher library par excellence.

I still have my favorites in this Lectureship—volumes that show much handling, pages plentifully penciled—but I have added to this list appreciably. There are, I hold, but half a dozen volumes that fall below the high level of the Series, just as there are a dozen or so that rise above that high level. The few that suffer when compared with others could be due to the fact that the men who gave them may not have had the literary skill to put their material in arresting form, and it may also be true that they made up for any defect in the printed form by a delivery that was impressive, perhaps captivating. But it should be said that even the few lectures that fall below the general lofty standard contain much of value for the reader.

It is regrettable that the lectures given but not published are not available for study; especially Dean Inge's, about whom more in certain pages that follow.

The minister who has a complete collection of the Yale Lectures on Preaching is to be congratulated and in truth *envied* by his less fortunate brethren. Young preachers do well to procure every volume of the Series available. Some of these are difficult to obtain; for example, that of Howard Crosby, distinguished Presbyterian clergyman, who was the lecturer for 1879-1880. The three single volumes of Beecher published in 1872, 1873, and 1874 are not easy to find; however, the three volumes in one were brought out by Ford, Howard and Hulbert, New York, in 1892, and later by The Pilgrim Press, Chicago. This one-volume Beecher (three in one) should be picked up without much difficulty. Some of the volumes were published in both the United States of America and in Great Britain. A few of the books appear in cheap bindings; others, in attractive format and beautifully printed.

Something should be said of the classification of the lecturers as it appears in this book. Some sort of classifying of the lecturers was necessary. That the one I have adopted will satisfy every reader, not to speak of the lecturers who are still with us in the flesh, could scarcely be expected. Suffice it to be said that the author is fully aware that no complete classifying of these versatile ministers under any one heading is possible. For instance, some of the "Olympians" were "Theologians and Philosophers," just as some who are classified under the latter heading were also superb craftsmen and faithful "Shepherds of the Flock." Still, on the whole, there seemed good reasons for the listings as they appear, and it is no secret to say that the author labored longer and with more anguish of mind and heart over this aspect of his work than on any other detail. Furthermore, he had expert advice in the task, not only from his capable associate, the Reverend Dr. Hal Earl Norton, but from other able men of the cloth and the academic world.

Something also needs to be said in justification of the title of this book. By *The Royalty of the Pulpit* I have in mind the unique nature of the Christian pulpit, the halo of majesty, romance, and noble traditions which crown the preacher's high calling and mission. That there are regal souls in this long list of lecturers is obvious, but so are there regal men of the pulpit not represented here, a veritable host of illustrious servants of the Lord. Some of these were equal to the greatest who appear in these pages, and others superior to some who spoke in the Yale Series. But quite apart from these reflections, *The Royalty of the Pulpit* as an ideal and inspiration, looms a spiritual Mount Everest whose sky-piercing summit no man has reached.

Of the seventy lecturers about whom I have written in this book it has been my privilege to know twenty-seven, and of this number more than half I cherish as friends. Bishop James E. Freeman, Dean Charles R. Brown, and Charles Clayton Morrison have been pulpit guests in the church I served so long in Detroit; and with others of this goodly company I have shared pulpits and platforms on numerous occasions. As a delegate to the World Missionary Conference held at Edinburgh in 1910, I heard Henry Sloane Coffin deliver a notable address; and in 1937, at the World Convocation of the Churches at Oxford and Edinburgh, I had the pleasure of hearing others who were destined later to lecture at the Yale Divinity School. During my presidency of the Federal Council of Churches, Charles P. Taft II headed one of our important committees, and in the presidency of the Council I was succeeded by Dr. George A. Buttrick.

It is not always easy to write about one's friends, but in this instance I have found it a joy.

Edward Gibbon tells us that when he had completed his massive work, *The Decline and Fall of the Roman Empire*, he laid down his pen and took a stroll in his garden. At first his emotions were of elation now that the formidable task was done. "But my pride was soon humbled," he wrote in his memoirs, "and a sober melancholy was spread over my mind by the idea that I had taken an everlasting leave of an old and agreeable companion." When I had completed this heavy though much more modest work, my own emotions were similar to those of Mr. Gibbon. Having finished the last chapter, I heaved a robust sigh of commingled relief and regret, arose, stretched, and—took my dog out for a walk!

EDGAR DEWITT JONES

Detroit, Michigan
July 15, 1950

INTRODUCTORY

THE ORIGIN OF THE LECTURESHIP

The Lyman Beecher Lectures on Preaching, founded in 1871 at Yale University, by Mr. Henry W. Sage of Brooklyn, is the most renowned Lectureship of its kind in the world. It stands alone, dominating the field as does Mt. Everest the mountains of the earth. The peril of using superlatives is not pertinent in this instance. The premier character of the Beecher Lectureship is everywhere acknowledged, and never grudgingly but with enthusiasm and admiration.[1] To be asked to participate in this Series is in many ways the most distinctive honor that can come to a Christian minister.

The story of the origin of this Lectureship can be told in a paragraph or two. In the Record of the Corporation of Yale College for April 12, 1871, the following paragraph appears:

Voted: To accept the offer of Mr. Henry Sage of Brooklyn, of the sum of ten thousand dollars for the founding of a Lectureship in the Theological Department in a branch of Pastoral Theology, to be

[1] "The only lectures on this side in any way comparable are the Warrack Lectures. This originally was a foundation in The United Free Church of Scotland. The Lectures had to be delivered in the three United Free Church Colleges in Glasgow, Edinburgh and Aberdeen. At the Union of the U.F.C. and the Church of Scotland this Lectureship was taken over by the resulting Church of Scotland (established), and the Lectures are still delivered in the three Universities, not as far as I know in that of St. Andrews. Men like Alexander Whyte, James Reid and Arthur John Gossip have delivered them. But these Lectures have never attained the eminence of the Yale Lectures, neither have they cast their net as wide so far as the Lecturers are concerned. As far as I know you would be perfectly safe in saying that the Lyman Beecher are the greatest of their kind in the world, certainly they are greater than the Warrack Lectures. No other Lectureship in Great Britain as far as I know is devoted to the subject of preaching, though some of these Lectureships, like the Hastie Lectures in Scotland, do permit of this subject being dealt with."
—From a letter to the author by the Reverend William Robinson, D.D., principal of Overdale College, Birmingham, England, lecturer in theology at Birmingham University and editor of the British *Christian Advocate*.

designated, "The Lyman Beecher Lectureship on Preaching," to be filled from time to time, upon the appointment of the Corporation, by a minister of the Gospel of any evangelical denomination who has been markedly successful in the special work of the Christian ministry.

In 1882 the Corporation voted with the consent of the Founder to amend the articles so that "henceforth the Lyman Beecher lecturers shall be invited to lecture on a branch of pastoral theology, or on any other topic appropriate to the work of the Christian ministry." Again, in 1893, with the consent of Mr. Sage, the articles were changed so that "if at any time they should deem it desirable to do so, to appoint a layman instead of a minister to deliver the course of lectures on the Lyman Beecher Foundation.

In the lifetime of the Lectureship seventy-five men have participated in the Series of which twenty-seven are living at the time this is written. In seventy-six years the Lectures were omitted but four times, to wit: 1882-1883; 1893-1894; 1900-1901; and 1936-1937. On all four occasions there were sufficient reasons for these omissions which broke the long continuity of the series. The Lectures of 1880-1881, 1884-1885 and 1924-1925 were not published.

In the early years of the Lectureship the attendance was largely drawn from the seminary students, members of the faculty and local clergymen; but with the passing years the Series has attracted ministers from all parts of the country, and taxed the seating capacity of the auditorium where the Lectures were delivered. The more famed the speaker, the greater the attendance, which on at least one occasion was so great as to require the presence of police officers to manage the crowd.

I

The Founder of this notable Lectureship, Henry W. Sage, was himself a notable man, merchant prince, lumberman, captain of industry, and churchman. He deserves to be better known to the preacher fraternity of our day, to many of whom he is but a name. Born in Middletown, Connecticut, January 31, 1814, the better part of his boyhood was spent in Bristol, Connecticut; and in 1827 the family moved to Ithaca, New York. Young Henry had expected to enter Yale and prepare for a professional career, prefer-

Introductory

ably medicine. Circumstances intervened, however, and shaped his course to the business world, where he was from the first successful. In 1847 he took a fling into politics and was elected to the New York Legislature as a Whig.

As his wealth increased Mr. Sage became a benefactor of Cornell University (named for his friend Ezra Cornell) and showered that institution with generous gifts. In 1870 he was elected to the board of trustees, succeeding Mr. Cornell as chairman in 1875. He supplied funds for a chapel, dedicated in June, 1875, established the Sage School of Philosophy at a cost of more than a quarter of a million dollars, contributed $560,000 to the library, as well as other substantial sums to the University. Visitors to Cornell are soon made aware of the Sage benefactions, for his name is not only written in the history of the University, but the chapel which bears his name is also the burial place of Mr. and Mrs. Sage.

There is an interesting paragraph in *The Autobiography of Andrew D. White,* president of Cornell, which is germane to this aspect of Henry Sage's interest in education and his munificent gifts. It appears on pages 398 and 399, and is as follows:

When Cornell University was opened a young woman made application for admission, on a scholarship. She had passed the best examination for the State scholarship in Cortland County, and on this I admitted her. Under the scholarship clause in the charter I could not do otherwise . . . but soon came a peculiar difficulty. The only rooms for students in those days on the University Hill were the barracks filled with young men; and therefore the young woman took rooms in town, coming up to lectures two or three times a day. It was a hard struggle, for the paths and roads leading to the university grounds, four hundred feet above the valley, were not as in these days, and the electric trolley had not been invented. She bore the fatigue patiently until winter set in; then she came to me, expressing regret at her inability to toil up the icy steep, and left us. On reporting this to the trustees, Mr. Sage [Mr. Henry W. Sage] made a proposal. I had expected from him a professorship or a fellowship; but to my amazement he offered to erect and endow a separate college for young women in the university, and for this purpose to give us two hundred and fifty thousand dollars. A committee of the trustees having been appointed to examine and report upon this proposal, I was made chairman; and, in company with Mr. Sage, visited various Western institutions. So Sage College, a part of Cornell University, was founded. The building now has become a hall for women students at Cornell.

Henry W. Sage's interest in Christianity and the churches was on a par with his concern for educational institutions, if indeed the two were not one in his thinking. For seventeen eventful years this influential layman held membership in Plymouth Church, Brooklyn, where he was an intimate friend and fellow worker with its famous minister, Henry Ward Beecher. During the period of Mr. Sage's membership in Plymouth Church it is doubtful if even the humblest of the congregation's multifarious activities was without the benediction of his interest, or the generosity of his purse; very likely both!

Henry Ward Beecher was Henry W. Sage's beau ideal of preacher and platform orator. Each saw in the other what he felt in himself—success, and success on the side of the angels. Picture these two Henrys in the early 1870's. Behold them together, each happy in the company of the other; Beecher short, slightly rotund, smooth-shaven face, full mobile lips, and flashing eyes, long brown hair slightly streaked with gray falling over his coat collar and shoulders, his stout body carelessly yet elegantly attired, exuberant of speech, exuding virility and a gay humor; Sage, sturdy of frame, and taller than Beecher, wearing a full beard, clean-shaven upper lip, firm mouth, and shrewd eyes, his fine figure swathed in a long-tailed frock coat, a high-topped hat on his head or in his hand. What a precious pair they made, this illustrious preacher and his well-to-do parishioner and friend.

Henry W. Sage believed in an educated, well-trained ministry of the Word. So did Henry Ward Beecher. It is likely they conversed on this subject often, and that the idea of a Lectureship which would bring eminent preachers and ministerial students together, the latter to sit at the feet of the masters, emerged from such conversations. Whether the suggestion first came from Sage or Beecher cannot be answered of a certainty. Anyhow, it came, and Mr. Sage offered to make a gift of $10,000 to Yale University for the founding of a Lectureship on Preaching.

There is a story afloat that Mr. Sage wished to name the Lectureship for Henry Ward Beecher, but the loyal and affectionate son said, "No, name it for my father. At his best he was greater than all his children put together." Whether he made this statement about his father's greatness at that particular time or not, he made just such a remark on another occasion. So what was destined to become the supreme Lectureship on Preaching was named for the Rev. Lyman Beecher, D.D.

When Henry W. Sage died in 1897, thirty-four of the series had been delivered, and Dr. John Watson (Ian Maclaren) was the speaker for that year, his subject: *The Cure of Souls*. Thus Mr. Sage lived to see the abundant fruitage of the planting he had done in 1871. Everyone who hears a lecturer in this Foundation, or reads the published volumes, should say a prayer of gratitude for the foresight and churchmanship of Henry W. Sage.

II

A brief account of the life, labors, and personality of the man for whom the Lectureship was named is appropriate here. Lyman, the father of all the Beechers, was born in New Haven, Connecticut, October 12, 1775. His father was David Beecher, called the "learned blacksmith" by his neighbors, and his mother, Esther Lyman, the third wife of David. His mother died at the time of his birth, and he was brought up by his uncle and aunt, the Lot Buntons, on their farm near Guilford, Connecticut. Cheerfully did Lyman bear the yoke in his youth, with its hard work, plain but wholesome fare, and great dreams.

Lyman graduated from Yale College, as it was called in 1797, and was ordained to the Presbyterian ministry the following year. His first pastorate was at East Hampton, Long Island, which lasted two years. In 1810 he transferred to the Congregational ministry, and entered on his sixteen-year pastorate of the church at Litchfield, where he made history and some enemies. The best thing Lyman did as a fledgling parson was to marry Roxana Foote, who bore him eight children. His second wife, Harriet Porter, while a very different person from the sainted Roxana, was a lovely lady, extremely independent of mind, and destined to become the mother of three more of Lyman's children. At the age of sixty-one

Dr. Beecher took a third wife, Mrs. Lydia Jackson of Boston. She bore him no children, and the biographers fail to say much about her.

In the heyday of his career Lyman Beecher was as famous as Henry Ward in his, although the latter eclipsed eventually the fame of all the Beecher family save Harriet and her far-famed *Uncle Tom's Cabin*. Lyman Beecher, as preacher, theologian, reformer, educator, and lecturer, was in the thick of every fight of his generation in behalf of decency, honesty, Christian ideals and practices. He lay about him with the weapon of the Scriptures and prayer, and struck heavy blows against the demon Alcohol, dueling, and every sort of frivolous and questionable amusement. He began as a heretic, then turned his guns as an orthodox clergyman against the Unitarian movement, and rounded out his career still pretty much of a liberal.

Lyman Beecher, if not a Humanist, was a grand human being. He was something of an athlete, loved to hunt and fish; and sometimes he danced (by himself) in his home, and played the fiddle with relish. Shortly after he had become a D.D., Lyman was on his way to church on a Sunday morning, crossed a trout stream, and this is what happened:

Seeing a big trout jump, and remembering he had left a pole and tackle under the bridge, he sprang down the bank, grabbed his pole and landed the trout. Slipping it into the tail pocket of his ministerial coat he ran on to the church and breathlessly mounted to his high pulpit, his clerical necktie all awry, and his handsome ruddy face flushed with exertion, just as the bell stopped tolling. The next Sunday morning when poor Roxana opened the closet door to brush the ministerial coat, she smelt that fish before she found it.[2]

Pastor in Boston, back again to the Presbyterians, he became minister of the Second Church of that denomination in Cincinnati, and president of Lane Seminary in that city. In a day when the typical preaching was stiff, and strongly logical, Lyman Beecher brought dynamic sermons to the pulpit, in the delivery of which he was an animated prophet of a new school. Dr. Lyman Abbott, who knew Lyman Beecher, wrote of him, "He had a delightful,

[2] Lyman Beecher Stowe, *Saints, Sinners and Beechers*, p. 40.

Introductory xxix

naïve, childlike egotism quite free from self-conceit, yet inspiring him with a kind of self-assurance which is often the precursor of victory."

Lyman Beecher had original ideas about the training of young men for the ministry. Thus he once wrote:

> The soul of eloquence is feeling, and in the ministry, holy feeling. But feeling without social excitement is impossible, and all eloquence unprompted by it is but parrot eloquence.... Of all mistakes made by great and good men, that of shutting up theological students on the Sabbath in a chapel to be edified by classical accuracy at the expense of feeling and untrammeled eloquence is one of the greatest.[3]

For the last years of his life old Lyman took a house in Brooklyn so as to be close to his illustrious son. He heard Henry Ward preach as long as he was able to attend services, and sometimes spoke briefly from Plymouth pulpit. On one occasion when Henry had preached a sermon of thrilling power, the venerable Lyman rose to his feet and in impassioned tones reminded the congregation that there would not have been that great sermon to which they had just listened had it not been for him—Henry's father!

On January 10, 1863, as he lay dying, Lyman Beecher quoted from St. Paul, "I have fought a good fight, I have finished my course, I have kept the faith; henceforth there is laid up for me a crown which God the righteous Judge will give me at that day. ... That is my testimony, write it down. That is my testimony." Thus, this warrior who never asked for quarter laid down his armor and his sword, both bearing the marks of much use.

III

A large share of credit for the success of the Lectureship belongs to those upon whom the responsibility to choose the speakers has rested. It has not been an easy task, requiring a wide survey of talent and a heavy correspondence. In later years the burden of this responsibility has fallen on Dean Charles Reynolds Brown, Dean Luther Weigle, and now, on Dean Liston Pope. These three

[3] *Ibid.*, p. 37.

gifted men have served that sacred trust with unflagging zeal and unending labor. In this they were ably assisted by faculty members.

Eighty years is a long life for a lectureship, however ably projected and soundly financed, but this octogenarian shows no visible signs of failing powers. The Lectures got off to a grand start, and while there is some unevenness in the Seriate, it may not be perceptible to the general reader of the Lectures in book form, and not a serious aspect to the more critical students of the Course. High as the hopes of the Founders must have been for the success of the project, it is unlikely that they ever imagined it would gain the prestige and international renown that the Lectureship has attained.

That the ingenuity and versatility of the Yale Divinity School in the choice of the Beecher lecturers has in no wise diminished, was evidenced by the program for the spring of 1950. Six lecturers were announced, namely, Henry M. Wriston, Ph.D., D.Litt., L.H.D., LL.D., president of Brown University, Providence, Rhode Island; Arthur S. Flemming, LL.D., president of Ohio Wesleyan University, Delaware, Ohio; W. H. Auden, B.A., poet, New York City, manuscript read by Norman Holmes Pearson, Ph.D., assistant professor of English, Yale University; Edmund W. Sinnott, Ph.D., D.Sc., director of the Sheffield Scientific School, and Sterling Professor of Botany, Yale University, manuscript read by Ernest W. Muehl, LL.B., assistant professor of public speaking, Yale Divinity School; Miss Helen Kenyon, L.H.D., LL.D., Moderator of the General Council of the Congregational Christian Churches, West Cornwall, Connecticut; Charles P. Taft, D.H.L., LL.D., lawyer and former president of the Federal Council of the Churches of Christ in America, Cincinnati, Ohio. Mr. Auden and Mr. Taft were the second and third laymen in the Course, the first being another lawyer, George Wharton Pepper, in 1915. Miss Kenyon was the first woman to deliver a Beecher Lecture.

Thus the famous Lectureship moves on, gaining momentum, but not losing its distinctive character.

★

THE LECTURERS

IN WHICH THE LECTURERS TAKE THE
ROSTRUM AND SPEAK THEIR MINDS

★

Few speeches which have produced an electrical effect on an audience can bear the colorless photography of a printed record.
—EARL OF ROSEBERRY

I
★ OLYMPIANS ★

A great preacher is not a mere artist, and not a feeble suppliant; he is a conquering soul, a monarch, a born ruler of mankind. He wills and man bows.

—JOHN A. BROADUS

1. HENRY WARD BEECHER

You think that when you preach you must preach so as to touch the top heads in your congregation. Touch the bottom and you will be sure to touch the top. He that puts a jackscrew under the roof is not going to raise the whole building; but he who puts a jackscrew under the sills of the building, and raises them up, will, I think, take up everything that is above them.

—H. W. BEECHER

Henry Ward Beecher! His name stands alone in the annals of the American pulpit—so unique he was, so buoyant of mind and spirit, so unpredictable and so versatile. No one of his pattern was before him; none among his contemporaries; and no one like him has emerged since his passing. For forty years he made Plymouth Church, Brooklyn, a national institution, the pulpit of which was his throne and millions his willing subjects. The choice of the illustrious son of great old Lyman Beecher to open this Lectureship on Preaching which bears his father's name, was a singularly appropriate one. To be sure, Founder Sage was one of Henry Ward's parishioners and his warm, personal friend, but had the choice been put to a popular vote, who doubts but that the result would have been the same?

Much was expected of the minister of Plymouth Church in accepting the invitation to give these Lectures, and he not only measured up to, but surpassed expectations. Of the seventy-five men who appeared in this Lectureship, Beecher was the only one to give three series. These he gave through as many successive years, ten addresses in the first, eleven in the second, and twelve in the third, totaling thirty-three in all. The lectures approximate 5,500 words each, which in round numbers total some 180,000 words, enough to make three volumes of 250 pages each. This, of itself, was no small achievement.

In the preface to the first published volume, Mr. Beecher wrote: "The discourses here given were wholly unwritten, and were familiar conversational addresses rather than elaborate speeches. I have not been able to revise the reporters' notes or to correct the proofs of the printer. If any are offended by literary infelicities, it may placate them to know that I am more annoyed than they can be."

The miracle is that there are few, if any, infelicities in these lectures. The sentences are complete and parsable, the vocabulary choice and opulent. The resources of the speaker seem inexhaustible, fresh, and sparkling, while the whole series is distinguished by what Beecher would call "plain horse sense."

In commenting on Beecher's Yale lectures, Professor William Cleaver Wilkinson, a not wholly favorable critic, wrote:

He [Beecher] took the whole world into his confidence when, in his Yale Lectures on Preaching, he told everything that he knew himself concerning himself as preacher. Never before was genius more communicative as to its own mystery. It was a revelation then to be informed that the mighty madness of Mr. Beecher's pulpit oratory had so self-conscious and so intelligent a method of its own. Genius actually seemed to be reducing itself to the terms of common sense.[1]

Mr. Beecher delivered his opening lecture in the First Series January 31, 1872, being at that time fifty-nine years old and in the full splendor of his glowing ministry. His audience was composed of theological students, visiting clergymen, and members of the faculty. Among the latter were such distinguished scholars as Leonard Bacon, lecturer on church polity, Samuel Harris, professor of systematic theology, George E. Day, professor of Hebrew and Biblical theology, James M. Hoppin, of the chair of homiletics, George P. Fisher, professor of ecclesiastical history, and

---

[1] William Cleaver Wilkinson, *Modern Masters of Pulpit Discourse*, p. 10.

Timothy Dwight, professor of sacred literature—a formidable sextet!

I

No public speaker was ever more at home with his theme, or his auditors, than was the Brooklyn preacher, as he thus began a Lectureship destined to go so far and attain so impressive a reputation.

In his three sets of lectures Beecher covered the entire field of the ministry: the sermon, delivery, pulpit manners, oratory, worship, music, prayer, the Bible, pastoral visitation, revivals, management of a congregation, prayer meetings, personal problems—in short, he laid his skillful hand on every phase of the High Calling, and it was good. In the presence of so much wealth of material, what is one to do, who must deal with seventy preachers in a single volume? It is like a man trying to glean a collection of brilliant stones from "Acres of Diamonds." It is as difficult as to try to pick a number of masterpieces with all the wealth of the Louvre or the Pitti Palace at his disposal. The task is baffling.

I choose to dispose of this vexatious issue by confining the subject to the sermon, to public address, to pulpit power, in which Mr. Beecher had no equal in his day. Thus I have screened his three lecture volumes for the choice nuggets of wisdom bearing on sermonizing and pulpit power:

Great sermons, young gentlemen, ninety-nine times in a hundred, are nuisances. They are like steeples without any bells in them; things stuck up high in the air, serving for ornament, attracting observation, but sheltering nobody, warming nobody, helping nobody.

A sermon is not like a Chinese firecracker to be fired off for the noise which it makes. It is the hunter's gun, and at every discharge he should look to see his game fall.

Don't make your sermons too good. That sermon, then, has been overwrought and overdone which leaves nothing for the mind of the hearer to do.

Let nobody puff you up by saying you are able preachers, because you can preach three or four good sermons. You have three or four tunes; that is all.

I do not believe that any man ever made a great sermon who set out to do that thing. Sermons that are truly great come of themselves.

Eloquence has been defined, sometimes, as the art of moving men by speech. Preaching has this additional quality, that it is the art of moving men from a lower to a higher life.

True preaching is yet to come. Of all the professions for young men to look forward to, I do not know another one that seems to have such scope before it in the future as preaching.

The essential necessity is, that every preacher should be able to *speak*, whether with or without notes. Christ *"Spake."*

Nor can I avoid a feeling of displeasure akin to that which Christ felt when he condemned prayers at the street corners, when I see a man bow down himself in the pulpit to say his prayers on first entering.

The Word of God in the Book is a dead letter. It is paper, type, and ink. In the preacher that Word becomes again as it was when first spoken by prophet, priest, or apostle. It springs up in him as if it were first kindled in his heart, and he were moved by the Holy Ghost to give it forth.

II

One of the most valuable sections of Mr. Beecher's lectures was the Question and Answer period at the close of each of his addresses in the First and Second Series. Here follow a few specimens:

Q. "Suppose you give out a hymn, and there is nobody to sing it?"

Mr. Beecher: "That is a point on which I ought to have spoken. Every minister who is ordained in the Roman Catholic Church is obliged to know music. It is part of the qualifications of the priesthood in that Church, and it ought to be so in all our churches. When you have got through examining a man on all didactic theology, let him sing. It is far more important with us than it is in the hierarchical church, for there the minister intones, and does not sing; but *you* have to sing. When you get to the point where bad rhetoric and bad music meet, there is intoning. Now in all new settlements, in visiting the sick, you will be expected to sing; in your prayer-meetings you will have to 'set the tune.' If you haven't learned how to sing and are going West, or into new settlements, let one of the first things you learn be how to 'raise' a tune. And if you can't sing, 'make a joyful noise.' "

Q. "Can a minister be eminent both as pastor and as a preacher?"

Mr. Beecher: "Yes. It will depend, however, upon how large his pastorate is, and how much he undertakes to do. A man may not be able to take a large care of individual souls and yet study in such a way as to be able to meet the exigencies of a city pulpit, or any labor of that kind which requires exceeding freshness and newness; he must make an average. He must keep up his pulpit, but at the same time he must keep up his knowledge of human nature, and if he can have no substitute or assistant he must do pastoral work. I do very little of it myself, but have many assistants and the work is done."

Q. "Is it not true that Spurgeon is a follower of Calvin? and is he not an eminent example of success?"

Mr. Beecher: "In spite of it, yes; but I do not know that the camel travels any better, or is any more useful as an animal, for the hump on its back."

It is only fair to note just here Mr. Spurgeon's comment when this remark of Mr. Beecher was reported to him.

As a matter of animal physiology the hump on the camel's back was a wise and indispensable provision for making the wearer capable of his great endurance. The hump, instead of being an excrescence only contributing ugliness to the camel's appearance, is a breast of nourishment to maintain the camel's strength.

Spoken as one Olympian to another.

Q. "According to your statement, the half-educated ought to have revivals; but what shall we do with the educated?"

Mr. Beecher: "In the fullest sense of the term 'education,' no man is educated that is not a Christian. A man is not educated who merely has his *knowing* faculties whetted, sharpened. . . . In my parishes in the West, I have seen men who came out from New England, where they had been for more than forty years in churches—and I think a man that has been in a good old-fashioned New England church for forty years, without being converted, is like a side of sole-leather that has been in a tan-vat for ten years; he is so tough that if there is anything that can affect him, it must be divine—and yet I have seen these men melting down like children, and made truly and thoroughly amiable Christian men."

Thus one might go on and on, swimming, diving, or sailing on this ocean of homiletic wisdom. To the young theologue as well as to the mature minister of the Word, this series which inaugurated the Lyman Beecher Lectureship is of endless interest. Admittedly, no one can imitate Henry Ward Beecher. To try to reproduce his method or manner would result in a pale replica of the original. On the other hand, his wholesome philosophy of life, his buoyancy and saving common sense, is a tonic for preachers of all schools of theology and from every type of pastorate.

III

Beecher's sermons are available in many volumes, and they are remarkably fresh and pertinent. As a specimen of his originality and at the same time his daring, here is an extract from a sermon entitled "What Is Religion?" It was preached at the Twin Mountain House, White Mountains, New Hampshire, Sunday morning, August 23, 1874. Lesson: Galatians 5:1-13.

So God created the church; but whether it should be Presbyterian, or Methodist, or Baptist, or Congregational, or Episcopalian, or Roman Catholic—God has never troubled himself about that, though his zealous disciples have. The form of the instrument of religion is not a part of his decrees. He no more ordained that divine worship should be carried on in certain fixed ways than he ordained that men who live by agriculture should harrow or furrow their fields. Agriculture does not stand on the machines which it employs, but on the necessity of men to eat. When God made men hungry he foreordained agriculture. And in the matter of the church, it does not stand on its ordinances.

But do not think that I am speaking contemptuously of these things. What I desire to be understood as saying is, that men have no business to worship an ordinance. I say that men have no right to make an idol of the church, or of Sunday, or of the Bible, or of anything that is in itself an instrument. Religion is something other than the instrument by which it is produced.

Do I say my prayers to the school-house? No. And yet, I believe in intelligence; and the school is simply an instrument by which we develop that intelligence. Do I say my prayers to the arithmetic, the geography, and the grammar? No. I think they are useful; but I would kick them every one out of the house if you were to tell me that I must say my prayers to them. They are my servants, my helps, but not my masters.

Henry Ward Beecher

And so, when men open the doors of the sanctuary on Sunday, the church is not my master: I am its master, for I am a son of God. It is simply the chariot which he has sent to carry me on my journey.

Henry Ward never had any trouble keeping his congregation awake. Plymouth Church in his day was a poor place to go for a nap. He dearly loved to shock his hearers out of their Sabbath somnolency by exploding verbal bombs about their heads. What a charge he let loose that day when at the close of a sermon on "The Love of God," he volleyed:

When I come up before the eternal Judge, and say all aglow, "My Lord and my God," will he turn to me and say: "You did not come up the right road . . . go down"? I, to the face of Jehovah, will stand and say: "God! I won't go to hell; I will go to heaven; I love Thee. Now damn me if Thou canst. I love Thee." And God shall say, and the heavens flame with double and triple rainbows, and echo with joy: "Dost thou love? Enter in and be blessed forever." Let us pray.

It took courage to talk that way from a Congregational pulpit in Beecher's day.

IV

What was Henry Ward Beecher's supreme word on preaching to those who heard him? In the opinion of this writer, Beecher's finest passages occur in the seventh lecture of his Third Series, delivered March 4, 1874, and entitled "Views of the Divine Life in Human Conditions." The paragraphs have with singular fitness this subtitle, "The Preacher's Reward." Hearken ye who preach or plan to preach: hearken and treasure for lonely contemplation:

And, young gentlemen, it matters but very little what titles you get here, what emoluments, what confidence, and what pleasure; for when you shall stand at the coming of the Lord, in the gateway of heaven, saying to him, "Here am I and these whom I have brought," one greeting, one look from him will repay you for every groan, for every sorrow, for every sadness, and for all the waiting that you ever knew upon earth. You are sons of God walking in disguise. What you do now you know not.

I can conceive, since the extension of the use of electricity, of a man, some old Beethoven, deaf, sitting in his room and playing on an instrument half a mile away, by means of wires connecting that instrument with the keys that are under his hand. I can imagine how, as he rolled off wonderful strains of music which he could not hear, an audience, unbeknown to him, might be gathered about that far-off instrument, listening, music-struck.

In this world you are playing on keys whose response is in the heavenly land, where you cannot hear, but angels listen to it; and when you return and come to Zion with songs and everlasting joy upon your heads, you will be among the happiest of all that have lived upon earth—kings and priests unto God.

The Old Maestro had spoken!

Note: I have nowhere seen so complete a pen portrait of Henry Ward Beecher as that which Gaius Glenn Atkins gives in the preface to his chapter on that famous man in *Master Sermons of the Nineteenth Century*. "He had 'everything it takes.' He had a physique nothing could tire. His massive head was set upon broad shoulders by a neck whose ample vessels made it possible for his visceral force to flood his brain with the blood which sometimes ominously flushed his face. He had a voice studiously cultivated, with an organ-like range. He had every art of the actor, every instinct of the dramatist, imagination, wit, humor, and a marvelous faculty to draw his illustrations from the familiar things of life. He played upon the great chords of human emotion, as apt to evoke laughter as tears." P. 32.

II. JOHN HALL

"John Hall!" Fix your eye on the name. How four-square it looks! Speak it. How solid it sounds! Speak it again. What weight it carries! Once more. How evenly balanced it is! Consider it. What freedom from surplusage! What honest scorn of distinction!

—WILLIAM CLEAVER WILKINSON[1]

It was a wise choice that John Hall, minister of the Fifth Avenue Presbyterian Church, New York City, should follow Henry Ward Beecher, in the Fourth Series of the famed Lectureship. The contrast was sharp and impressive. Beecher was volatile and exuberant; Hall stable and reserved. Beecher was daring and a liberal theologian; Hall conservative both in doctrine and in methods. Beecher was dramatic; Hall quiet in delivery but withal pow-

[1] *Modern Masters of Pulpit Discourse.*

erful. Both were men of distinguished appearance. Hall was the taller of the two, a commanding figure on the platform or in the pulpit. What Beecher was to Brooklyn, John Hall was to New York.

Dr. Hall was an Ulsterman by birth, his Scottish-Irish lineage showing in his broad, smooth face and smiling eyes. Courteous of manner, dignified in pulpit and platform decorum, he stood tenaciously for "the elective evangelical Calvinism" in which he was nurtured. He was graduated from the College of Belfast and the Theological Department of the same institution. His early ministry in Armagh and Dublin was conspicuous for sound doctrine, a massive eloquence, and deep interest in the Irish educational movements, in which he was singularly honored by the appointment as Queen's Commissioner.

Dr. Hall was but thirty-eight when he entered upon his long pastorate of the Fifth Avenue Presbyterian Church, a wealthy and socially prominent parish, and in many respects the most notable pulpit in New York City. Great crowds waited upon his ministry, and it was during Dr. Hall's pastorate that the present house of worship was erected at the corner of Fifth Avenue and Fifty-fifth Street, three families contributing $246,000, almost half of the structure's original cost. He was a tireless shepherd of the flock, never neglecting the sick or the lowly, and on Sundays came into the pulpit with a plain, simple, and powerful exposition of the Scriptures. He spoke without notes, and in a strong voice with just a suspicion of the "auld sod" in it—a preacher in whose noble presence and quiet dignity there was a sermon before he opened his lips.

Dr. Hall and Mr. Beecher (Henry Ward declined an honorary degree and did not relish being addressed as "Doctor") were contemporaries for twenty years. Brooklyn and New York City were separate municipalities at that time, and although the two clergymen were acquainted, it could not be said that they were intimate. It is on record that Mr. Beecher expressed admiration "for the young Irishman with the golden mouth," as he once called him. Likewise, Beecher solicited contributions from Dr. Hall for the religious journals which he edited, and Dr. Hall generously complied.

In the biography of John Hall written by his son, Professor Thomas C. Hall, and published in 1901, the author says that his father

both distrusted Mr. Henry Ward Beecher's theology and disliked what he considered Beecher's superficial treatment of the older thought.... They also met occasionally on the platform, and at one such meeting Mr. Beecher took occasion to speak slightingly of Calvin. This gave an occasion for my father to defend in courteous but vigorous language what he considered Mr. Beecher had too lightly defamed. My father was at that time relatively unknown, but many who were present have since told the writer that they never heard a more able and impressive answer, and never saw a great audience, at the beginning hostile, so completely carried off by enthusiasm for that at which a few minutes before they were laughing and jesting under the influence of Mr. Beecher's wonderful powers of banter and attack.[2]

Dr. Hall's single volume, the fourth in the Yale Series, contains less than three hundred pages, and seems to suffer when compared with Beecher's three volumes of cyclopedic scope. Actually it does suffer, but not to the extent many would believe. Dr. Hall's series in the course holds its own, and sounded the note which the conservatives had missed in the unique and witty lectures of Mr. Beecher. There was a humility about Dr. Hall that was engaging. No one can read the modest introductory paragraphs of his first lecture without being drawn to the big handsome Irishman, who had not the slightest notion of attempting to compete with his predecessor in popular eloquence. The very title, *God's Word in Preaching*, mirrors the mind of the author.

The closing paragraph of the first lecture reveals the man, literary style, and theology:

To get then, the mind of Christ, and to declare it, is the primary end of the teaching officers of the church. The living body of sympathetic men, saturated with the truth and feeling of the Book, must bring it into contact with other men, through that marvelous organ, the human voice, and with such aid as comes from the subtle sympathy that pervades assemblies of human beings. And while systematically teaching Christ's truth, as they have learned it by the Holy Ghost, they must never forget the power that moves them, nor fail to honor

[2] Thomas C. Hall, *John Hall, Pastor and Preacher*, p. 236.

John Hall

that Divine Person who not only gives, but has condescended to be a "tongue of fire." This work of speaking the truth is the justification, the "reason to be," of the Christian ministery.

This passage may seem a little heavy and the sentences involved, but the Doctor could be, and was, pithy and sparkling when the spirit moved him; as for instance in these quotable excerpts: "We soon cease to do what we do with difficulty"—"We [ministers] are not, Gentlemen, heathen philosophers finding out things; we are expositors of a revelation that settles things"—"Forego every bottle but the ink bottle"—"No amount of organizing nor skill in creating machinery and manipulation of committees is a substitute for this personal contact. Who feels the power of a tear in the eye of a committee?"

Dr. Hall's wholesome common sense shines through page after page of this book. He is sane and well balanced, as for instance this counsel, which was so pertinent then, and still is, although modern names could be substituted for those used by the speaker:

There are many men undertaking to deal with Darwinism or with the views of Tyndall and Huxley in their pulpits, who seem to be wasting their power. Think, Gentlemen, for a moment of the most intelligent congregations to which we ordinarily preach; how many men are there in them who could intelligently state the philosophical views and scientific opinions of such men as Professor Tyndall? Are there twenty, or fifteeen, or five? In many cases none. It seems to me a waste of energy to be compelled, first of all, to set up a fortification in the name of some man, explain to the congregation what you are hammering at, and then proceed to overthrow it. As a general thing we may allow those things to take care of themselves on their own plane.

Was this a sly poke at his predecessor in the course, who took the evolutionary theory into the pulpit and gave it a Christian connotation? I doubt it. Dr. Hall was above a thing of that kind. He would likely have given this sensible advice to ministerial students in any circumstances.

Times have changed. Listen to Dr. Hall's answer to the question from one of his student audience, "Should a minister entirely avoid theatrical and operatic performances?"

I am a poor authority on this. I never saw a play acted; never was at the opera in my life. I presume there is a difference between the two. I find ministers speaking on both sides of the theatre question in the same sermon. All the evidence I have yet seen is to the effect that—whatever its abstract power might be—the theatre is, in point of fact mischievous on the whole. The best evidence of its effect is that the pure plays can not get players or spectators. Those of Shakespeare are, it is alleged, kept on the stage at a ruinous cost. The average play-goer must have his moral teaching at the theatre highly spiced, and increasingly so from year to year. No, I never go, never advise anyone to go, am sorry when I hear of Christians going, and think a minister's usefulness in danger from going.

So spake the great old Puritan!

On the vexed question of the use of manuscript in the pulpit this sturdy Presbyterian answers with an anecdote. A leading Welsh minister was invited to preach an anniversary sermon before one of the great societies in London. Naturally anxious to disregard no propriety, he consulted the proper authority, the secretary. "Should I read my sermon?" "Oh it is no matter; only bring some of your Welsh fire." "But you cannot, my dear sir, carry fire in paper." "No, that is true, but you may use the paper to kindle the fire!"

Dr. Hall's mighty ministry at Fifth Avenue Presbyterian Church had a lamentable ending. The church divided over his continuing after thirty-one years of successful ministry. Throughout the ordeal the noble Ulsterman bore himself with a high heart, but that same year, 1898, he died in Ireland, the land of his birth. Did the bitter experience through which he passed shorten his life? Some so thought and so said. A servant cannot be greater than his Lord, and somewhere along the way of the most successful ministry, the iron is likely to enter his soul and the experience enable him to understand the fellowship of Christ's sufferings. Like St. Paul, John Hall finished his course triumphant in an unfaltering trust.

Following Dr. Hall's passing, a flood of tributes and eulogies appeared in both the secular press and the religious journals. Later works of a homiletical character assessed his powers as preacher and pastor. In due time the Fifth Avenue Presbyterian Church dedicated a bronze tablet to his memory, accompanied no doubt with tears and sighs, tinged perhaps with vague feelings of remorse.

Note: Along about the decade 1877-1887, New York and Brooklyn were opulent in famous pulpit men, and this was particularly true of Congregationalists and Presbyterians. In Brooklyn Henry Ward Beecher was in the golden afternoon of his ministry at Plymouth Church; in the Church of the Pilgrims, Richard Salter Storrs was pouring forth a stream of Ciceronian eloquence; at Central Church, Adolphus J. F. Behrends, a dauntless liberal, was going strong. Such was Congregationalism in Brooklyn. In New York the Presbyterians took pride in the massive conservative preaching of John Hall at Fifth Avenue Church; Howard Crosby, scholar and reformer, was at the Fourth Avenue Church; Charles H. Parkhurst, destined to trouble the Tammany Tiger, was at Madison Square Church; and young Henry van Dyke was opening up a brilliant ministry at the Brick Church. At the same time, at the Broadway Tabernacle, a sturdy center of Congregationalism, William M. Taylor was preaching to capacity audiences. Significant, too, is the fact that all of these Peers of the pulpit lectured in the Beecher Series except Dr. Storrs.

III. WILLIAM MACKERGO TAYLOR

His [Dr. Taylor's] fruitful industry, his sound discretion, his firm-set orthodoxy, his practical Christian earnestness, his evangelical spirit, his spotless character, are an example and an inspiration to ministers, for which we all have reason to be sincerely thankful.
—WILLIAM CLEAVER WILKINSON[1]

The faculty of Yale Divinity School chose as the third lecturer in the Series another New York Olympian of the pulpit, the Reverend Dr. William M. Taylor, minister of the Broadway Tabernacle. This choice, too, was a "natural." Dr. Taylor was a preacher of power and a prolific publisher of his sermons. For two decades he managed to do an immense amount of work, writing, preaching, lecturing, and caring punctiliously for his numerous parishioners.

Dr. Taylor was a Scotsman by birth and education. The sturdy faith of his people, and the aura that seems to surround the church and the ministerial office in Scottish life and character, never departed from this dominie, who hailed from Kilmarnock and as

[1] *Op. cit.*

a student trod the halls of Glasgow University. A contemporary, writing of Dr. Taylor, said that "his national and his individual identity is far too sturdy, too resistant, to be effaced and conformed by the external influences amid which it happens to be placed. You are stimulated by the encounter of this frank, unapologetic, unyielding, personal difference." Which is to say he was little influenced in thinking and style of preaching by his American residence.

Of a commanding presence, Dr. Taylor's voice was a flexible instrument of melodious power. When he stood up to preach you felt at once that on any occasion a formal introduction must have seemed superfluous—the man spoke for himself admirably, spoke with an endowment of authority given him from on high—and men and women flocked to hear him expound the Word.

In theology Dr. Taylor was resoundingly orthodox, and a Biblical preacher whose highest joy was the unfolding and interpretation of the Scriptures. He was positive. He was sure that God is and a rewarder of them who seek Him. His pulpit style was heavier than that of Dr. Hall and less diverting and entertaining than Beecher's, but it was elevated and dynamic in content and forthright delivery. A contemporary thus describes the sort of sermonic meal Dr. Taylor set before his hearers: "He offers you not the whipped cream and the syllabub, but the solid roast beef of discourse." And the people heard him gladly.

The story of how Dr. Taylor came to Broadway Tabernacle is of absorbing interest. The famous Dr. Richard S. Storrs of the Church of the Pilgrims, Brooklyn, had gone to Europe on a vacation for his health and had procured as supply during his absence the eloquent young Scotsman, the Reverend William M. Taylor. The Reverend Mr. Taylor was at that time minister of the United Presbyterian Church at Bootle, just below Liverpool, where his success had been phenomenal. So impressed were those who heard William M. Taylor at the Church of the Strangers, that the Broadway Tabernacle leaders became interested, and after some persuasion the promising Scottish preacher accepted a call to succeed Dr. Joseph Parrish Thompson as minister of that church.

On the first Sunday in March, 1872, Broadway Tabernacle welcomed the new minister in a memorable service. The installation ceremony took place on April 9, and it was of a nature to inspire the vast congregation, which included representatives of all the Congregational Churches in New York City and vicinity. Henry Ward Beecher preached the installation sermon, and Dr. Leonard Bacon of the Center Church, New Haven, then seventy years old, gave the installing prayer. In June that year Yale and Amherst conferred the D.D. degree upon him, and Dr. Taylor began auspiciously a new career in America.

Dr. Taylor had been in his new field in New York only four years when he was asked to give the Yale Lectures on Preaching. This fact is significant and indicates the high place the Scottish preacher had made for himself in so short a time. Dr. Taylor took for his subject, *The Ministry of the Word*, devoting twelve lectures to his theme. He made it clear in his opening lecture on "The Design of the Christian Ministry," that no one should aspire to the pastoral vocation unless he is willing to work hard, study continuously, and give himself unreservedly to his parish responsibilities. The last place on earth to be carried to heaven on "flowery beds of ease" is the Christian ministry. It calls for self-renunciation, for perseverance. The motto for the man in the pulpit is that which so obsessed St. Paul, namely, "This one thing I do."

Dr. Taylor contends eloquently for doctrinal preaching. Choose great themes. Give your best to the doctrine of the Incarnation and of the Cross. Aspire to be a Biblical preacher. Utilize the time-tested Book, study variety of themes, and cultivate expository treatment of the Holy Scriptures. He enlivens his paragraphs with brief and appropriate illustrations. The names of the famous preachers of the centuries stud his pages like the bright constellations of the night skies.

Dr. Taylor advises the preacher to write, write, write! He thinks it unlikely that the preacher will ever preach a poor sermon if he writes it out not only once but as many times as are required to bring it to the finest completion of which he is capable. He tells us that for ten years he adopted the *memoriter* method and found it good. Yet he abandoned it for the reading of the manuscript, not slavishly, but competently and with ease. That can be done, but only by skillful and scarcely perceptible management of the sheets of paper. Always, the preaching of the Word effectively is the goal, driving home the points, high-lighting them with suitable illustration, and occasionally employing appropriate quotations, the latter to be used sparingly.

In discussing the relative merits of what he terms "free speech" in the pulpit, the *memoriter* method, and reading from a manuscript, Dr. Taylor gives his views in a single paragraph which for clarity and balance has not been surpassed so far as I know by any other lecturer on preaching:

I would say, that *memoriter* preaching is the method which has the greatest advantages, with the fewest disadvantages; extempore preaching is the method in the employment of which success is hardest, and failure commonest; and preaching from a manuscript is the method in which, if he choose to train himself in it, the man of average ability will make, on the whole, the best of his talents, and make the fewest failures.

A bit of autobiography gives Taylor's opinion of the preacher's cluttering up his time with too many extracurricular activities and loading himself down with unimportant parish activities. Thus he says:

Just before I was settled, I was put on my guard against this too common besetment of young ministers, by an aged elder who took a fatherly interest in me. . . . He said, "Keep yourself entirely for your pulpit work until that becomes manageable; then add something else, and when that has begun to sit lightly upon you, a third enterprise may be taken in hand; and so you will go on increasing your influence; but if you begin all these at once, you will inevitably break down, and will have to throw some of them up, thereby giving an aspect of failure to your work, from which it will never recover.

Better advice was never given any young minister than this. Fortunate is the preacher who has in his congregation an elder of such wisdom.

In 1940 there was published a *History of the Broadway Tabernacle of New York City*, by N. Nelson Nichols, Deacon and Chairman of the Historical Committee. It is a valuable book, and generous space is given to the illustrious ministers who served that Church with distinction. Some account of Dr. Taylor's ministry from such a source, and especially that of his closing days, seems appropriate here.

We are told that Dr. Taylor was a wide reader, that his mind was a storehouse from which he could draw copiously. He drew his illustrations from an enormous field of the world's sorrows and joys. He gave his people the best he had in all of the years of his ministry at the Tabernacle, and there seemed to be no end to the rich treasures that emerged from his fertile mind. "In 1876," according to the record, "his Yale Lectures on *The Ministry of the Word* set a new significance to his ability to teach the theological student. Thereafter Dr. Taylor's addresses had the homiletic flavor that greatly pleased young ministers who came to the Tabernacle to study his method. They usually stayed, to fall in love with the sweetness of his character and the joyous exuberance of his mighty physique."

In 1888 his health began to fail, and a trip to Europe did him little good. On March 30, 1892, he sustained a stroke, and on February 8, 1895, he finished his course. His physician and longtime friend, Dr. William Hanna Thomson, was with him when the end came, and paid Dr. Taylor a tribute which might well be his epitaph:

"*He proved the reality of the Christian life as a gift from above more than did his great sermons.*"

IV. PHILLIPS BROOKS

Of oratory, and all the marvelous, mysterious ways of those who teach it, I dare say nothing. I believe in the true elocution teacher, as I believe in the existence of Halley's comet, which comes into sight of this earth once in about seventy-six years. But whatever you may learn or unlearn from him to your advantage, the real power of your oratory must be in your own intelligent delight in what you are doing.
—PHILLIPS BROOKS

The two most written about preachers in America are Henry Ward Beecher and Phillips Brooks. This was true when they were here in the flesh, and it is true today. It is interesting also to note that in the Yale Lectures the preachers oftenest referred to by their fellow lecturers are Beecher and Brooks. It is difficult for some of us in the Christian ministry to talk about Phillips Brooks without becoming lyrical or fulsome. It is doubtful if any other American preacher has left so deep an impression of spiritual power as this huge-bodied, great-hearted preacher of the unsearchable riches of Christ.

Intellectually he ranked with the best of his contemporaries. Beecher was more the unfettered genius and surpassed Brooks in sheer oratorical power. The content of the Bostonian's preaching was the more sustained in native dignity, although it may have lacked the spontaneity which so distinguished the pulpit utterance of the Brooklyn orator.

If Beecher was the Shakespeare, Brooks was the Browning of the American pulpit, with this difference, he is seldom obscure in style or difficult to follow, and Browning often so.[1]

Both Brooks and Beecher were New Englanders, and each came from homes where religion was held in highest esteem. Brooks was of an ancestry in which blue-blooded families contributed a richness of culture, and the legacy left its hallmark on the boy and man. If "lavender and old lace" are not in the picture of his forebears, the Cotton–Phillips–Brooks line, sterling silver, snowy napery, four-posters, and the faint perfume of a noble aristocracy of mind and morals are in his lineage. Yet few men who preached from prominent pulpits were as free from pride or as democratic in spirit as was Phillips Brooks.

The Boston Latin School, Harvard University, and the Theological Seminary of the Protestant Episcopal Church at Alexandria, Virginia, all had a share in the training of this rare youth, whose first parish was the Church of the Advent in Philadelphia. Two years later he went to Holy Trinity Church, also in Philadelphia, and in 1869 he began his long and illustrious ministry at Trinity Church, Boston. "His elevation to the bishopric of Massachusetts," writes Gaius Glenn Atkins, "was only an episode, though one of the few controversial episodes of his life."

Phillips Brooks was forty-two when he lectured in the Beecher Series, and his volume bearing the simple title *Lectures on Preaching,* is one of the most prized and one of the few frequently quoted

---

[1] To Dr. George A. Gordon, Bishop Brooks said with reference to his own preaching: "When I am interesting I am vague; when I am definite I am dull."

from. It is his first lecture on "Two Elements in Preaching" which contains a definition of preaching that has appeared in every important work on homiletics in the past fifty years, and in some of less importance. "Preaching," says Brooks, "is the communication of truth by man to men." Usually and correctly there is added to this sentence the words "through personality," for the paragraph which contains the ten-word definition later adds this amplified definition: "The truest truth, the most authoritative statement of God's will, *communicated* in any other way than *through the personality of brother man to men* is not preached truth" (italics my own). It is not likely that this definition of preaching will be improved upon or stated more concisely.

Perhaps there is no better place than just here to quote an opinion of Brooks' lectures at Yale by one of the keenest and at the same time one of the most candid critics of preachers and preaching, Professor William Cleaver Wilkinson, who says:

Without intending, or desiring to do so, Mr. Brooks addresses the few rather than the many. It is a kind of spiritual elixir instead of common respirable air that he provides for his reader or hearer, to breathe. This is less true of his lectures than it is of his preaching. His lectures on preaching form a volume as replete with practical wisdom as it is instinct with noble inspiration. I wish they could be universally read by ministers. No minister could read them without being helped by them—helped intellectually, helped morally, helped spiritually. I rejoice in such a book. I believe in such a minister as Mr. Brooks sets before his reader, in ideal.[2]

Professor Wilkinson, who had heard both Beecher and Brooks preach, contrasts them thus:

Mr. Brooks is not an orator such as Mr. Beecher was. He does not speak *to* people, *into* people, as Mr. Beecher did; rather he speaks *before* them, in their presence. He soliloquizes. There is almost a minimum of mutual relation between speaker and hearer. Undoubtedly the swift, urgent monologue is quickened, reinforced, by the consciousness of an audience present. That consciousness, of course, penetrates to the mind of the speaker. But it does not dominate the speaker's mind; it does not turn monologue into dialogue; the speech is monologue still.[3]

[2] *Op. cit.*, p. 109.
[3] *Ibid.*, p. 88.

When one opens Phillips Brooks' *Lectures on Preaching* what does he find? I confidently answer—a noble prophet of the Most High aglow with gratitude and enthusiasm for the preacher's exalted vocation; a reverent and humble servant of his Lord, gentle and gracious; a shepherd heart that overflows with love for all mankind; an ambassador of Christ who knew no higher office than that to which he had been called of God. As one reads on and on he has a greatening sense of the nobility of the speaker, a feeling that what this preacher proclaims he has embodied in his own life—a man of God completely furnished unto every good work.

Take his lecture on "The Idea of the Sermon." Alas! too many of us who stand in pulpits week after week have no well-thought-out idea of the sermon in such terms as this Prince of the Church entertained for himself and set forth for all who would preach the Gospel: "Whatever is in the sermon must be in the preacher first; logicalness, vivacity, earnestness, sweetness, and light, must be personal qualities in him before they are qualities of thought and language in what he utters to his people."

This premier preacher holds that no preaching ever had any strong power that was not the preaching of doctrine. But he is quick to add that the notion that faith consists in the believing of propositions has had a bad effect on preaching. He calls this kind of preaching "heresy," because the preacher declares truth for its own value and not with direct reference to its results in life. He argues that the preacher who thinks that faith is the holding of truth must ever be aiming to save men from believing error and to bring them to the knowledge of what is true; while the man who thinks that faith is personal loyalty must always be trying to bring men to Christ and Christ to men. Which is the true idea? The speaker says that it is not for him to discuss; but it is clear that he himself put the emphasis on the faith in personal loyalty to Christ rather than on loyalty to propositional truths about Christ.

The temptation to cull brilliant sentences from the Brooks lectures and include them here is strong, but I am moved to resist, first, because Professor Allen has done this admirably in the biography and, also, for the reason that detached from the rest of the subject matter they give the impression of the brilliance of the author rather than of the solid substance with which they are so closely interwoven. It is somewhat like attempting to separate certain bright strands from the others in some gorgeous tapestry.

After living for many years with this library on preaching, better known as the Lyman Beecher Lectures, talking with numerous preachers, and reading many books bearing on the subject, I conclude that Phillips Brooks' lectures, in sheer nobility of utterance, stand up as no other single volume in the Series. Professor Allen reports that letters poured in upon him from every quarter following the publication of the lectures, and he cites an excerpt from one of these, which he calls a "specimen":

> I believe neither the English language nor any other has anything worthy to stand beside them, treating such a theme—judging the wide reading, the wit, the wisdom, the mental grasp of the problem, the keenness of the analysis, the profoundness of the insight, or the perfect comprehension of the problems of our day. . . . That book I would lay beside the Bible of every young minister today. I would have every preacher read it every year as long as he lives.[4]

On the subject of controversy the lecturer spoke advisedly. He did not disparage controversy. Theology he held must be prepared to maintain her ground against all comers. If she loses her power of attack and defense, she will lose her life, as they used to say that when the bee parted with its sting it parted with its industry and spirit. Not every minister is made for a controversialist, and the pulpit is not made for controversy. The Bishop is emphatic about this. He urged his hearers to preach positively what they believe, and never to preach what they do not believe, or to deny what they believe.

It should be noted here that Brooks regarded the sermons of Frederick W. Robertson as supreme in quality; it is also true that he valued highly the simple evangelistic preaching of D. L. Moody, and supported his revival meetings in Boston, much to the distaste of some of his clerical associates. This is but one of many instances of Brooks' brotherly spirit and freedom from denominational bias.

Professor A. V. G. Allen, in his memorable biography, says that

---

[4] Alexander V. G. Allen, *Phillips Brooks* (one volume edition), p. 299.

Phillips Brooks' *Lectures on Preaching* were written in a state of spiritual excitement, an excellent definition of inspiration, by the way. "So deeply was he moved," writes Professor Allen, "that for some reason he could not bear to make the journeys to New Haven alone, but took with him a relative." His biographer continues: "The great charm of the Yale lectures, from a literary point of view, is that they constitute the confessions of a great preacher. The book is personal throughout."[5]

As for these lectures—no sensitive minister today can read them without being stirred by the reverential spirit of the speaker in regard to the church and her ministry. Dignity is a cold word on the lips of some clergymen. One thinks of pomp, pageantry, "vestments heavy with jewels," "the sacerdotal stole" of Burns' "Cotter's Saturday Night"; but the word "dignity" on the lips or pen of Phillips Brooks implies genuineness, sincerity, and the mind that bows down in awe and contrition before the Eternal.

The clerical jester suffers justly at the hands of Phillips Brooks. He deals with him in a kind of fierce candor. Of him he says: "He is full of Bible jokes. He talks about the church's sacred symbols in the language of stale jests that have come down from generations of feeble clerical jesters before him. . . . There are passages in the Bible which are soiled forever by the touches which the hands of ministers who delight in cheap and easy jokes have left upon them." Yet this giant of the pulpit had a place for humor. "The smile that is stirred by true humor and the smile that comes from mere tickling of the fancy are as different from one another as the tears that sorrow forces from the soul are from the tears that you compel a man to shed by pinching him."

Phillips Brooks had his critics. He was not orthodox enough for some of his brethren. He was certainly not High Church, which fact disappointed others. There are those who say that while he exalted the doctrine of the Incarnation, he dealt too lightly with the doctrine of the Atonement. But surely the Cross was in his preaching and transcendently in his life. If there be spots on the sun of his theology, they are lost in the splendor of the light which lightens the souls of men and casts about this man a radiance that shineth more and more unto the perfect day.

Despite the honors which fairly rained upon Phillips Brooks,

[5] *Ibid.*, p. 296.

honors which came unsought, he was a lonely man, without wife or child. Whether his celibate state was from choice or through disappointment we may not know. Dr. Gaius Glenn Atkins has a penetrating paragraph in his introduction to a sermon by Bishop Brooks in his praiseworthy volume, *Master Sermons of the Nineteenth Century*. Of Brooks he writes:

> He delighted in travel and had every opportunity, for his parishes were generous in putting money and time at his disposal. No one could have wanted more than life gave him. In the portraits of his early middle life he is a figure of radiant happiness, but his later portraits beginning at fifty, show deepening lines. A year later he is an old man. I know nothing like this in any other series of portraits, as though beneath all his fullness of apparently untroubled success the price and passion of the Cross had its way with him.[6]

Well, life is like that. Study a series of portraits of Abraham Lincoln and see what the presidency and a dreadful internecine war did to him. The photographs taken that spring "when lilacs last bloomed in the dooryard" show a man of sorrows and acquainted with grief. Always it must be that a servant can never be greater than his Lord or escape the law of his Savior's Cross.

Phillips Brooks could not escape that Cross, nor wished to do so. The thing to remember is that he glorified the Cross steadily through bright days and dark.

So must we all, if we are to partake of Christ's passion!

On the day of Phillips Brooks' death, which was January 23, 1893, his brother, the Reverend Arthur Brooks, said: "God be praised today! From God he came; with God he walked; God's world he loved; God's children he helped; God's church he led; God's blessed Son he followed; God's nearness he enjoyed; with God he dwells."

Note: The sermons of Phillips Brooks are available in sets and single volumes. Especially commended is a volume published by E. P. Dutton & Company, New York, 1949, entitled *Phillips Brooks: Selected Sermons*, edited and with an Introduction by the Rt. Rev. William Scarlett, D.D., Bishop of Missouri. It contains 31 Sermons, the very cream of Bishop Brooks' preaching. The Introduction by Bishop Scarlett, though brief, is valuable. His estimate of Brooks as a preacher—"Never in the history of the Protestant Episcopal Church has there been such sustained preaching as this"—is something more than a well-balanced sentence.

[6] P. 191.

V. ROBERT WILLIAM DALE

In choosing the fifth lecturer in this Series on Preaching, the fame of which had traveled far, the faculty of Yale Divinity School turned to England and surveyed the Olympians of the pulpit there. The lot fell on Robert W. Dale, minister of Carr's Lane Congregational Church of Birmingham. The choice was inspired. In church circles of Great Britain "Dale of Birmingham" was a shining name, distinguished alike for his brilliant scholarship, preaching power, and activities in civic affairs.

The biography of Dr. Dale by his son, Sir A. W. W. Dale, published in 1898, is a formidable volume of 771 pages. In the appendix to this work no less than eight pages are devoted to Dr. Dale's literary output, which is also formidable. Books, pamphlets, magazine articles, sermons, and material edited, total 128 items. Not all of the famed pulpit men were theologians in the technical sense of the word, but Robert Dale was a theologian whose conclusions in the *Queen of Sciences* still rank high and are quoted with respect and admiration.

Dr. Dale was an exceptional youth, a precocious lad; some would call him a prodigy. He began to preach at the age of sixteen and published his first book at seventeen. He became co-minister at Carr's Lane at twenty-four and minister of that noted church at thirty, continuing in this capacity until death in 1895—thirty-six wonderful years. Nor was this all; Dr. Dale was a leader in the Free Church circles, chairman of the Congregational Union, editor of *The Congregationalist*, and active in politics as a member of the Liberal party, friend of Gladstone and of Joseph Chamberlain, served on the Birmingham School Board, and was a member of the Royal Commission on Elementary Education. Still, it is doubtful if his study habits suffered through these responsibilities, so well did Dale know how to husband his time.

There were other honors and distinctions that came to Dr. Dale, but his throne was the pulpit at Carr's Lane, from which across the years he poured forth a steady stream of sermons, lectures, and addresses of a literary, historical, and political nature. The church at Birmingham was great when he took it, and far greater when his remarkable ministry came to an end.

Dr. Dale was an impassioned orator when the occasion so demanded, and always he was a lucid, fluent speaker, a personable gentleman whose courage was never questioned and often demonstrated. He confessed a fear that his preaching might be too intellectual for the working people, and his concern may have had validity.[1]

Sir W. Robertson Nicoll, editor of *The British Weekly*, bookman of note, and admirer of Dr. Dale, in a tribute he wrote following the latter's death, expressed the feeling that this minister of Carr's Lane seemed too successful. Things hard to others came easy to him. Honors multiplied, plums were his for the reaching and taking. This is an interesting comment, but a study of Dr. Dale's life shows that he too had his difficulties and disappointments as must all men. Success is ever costly and it was so in Dr. Dale's case. A reading of his letters as they appear in his biography reveals that there were times when this resolute soul knew days that were dark, but with no complaint, only a wistful questioning. To quote Sir W. Robertson Nicoll again, "Not without tears was the New Testament written, not without tears can it be understood."

Dr. Dale took high rank as a theologian. His work on *The Atonement*, published in 1875, was shortly translated into French and German. It is doubtful if any man can preach or write helpfully on Divine Forgiveness who is not himself sensitive to the exceeding sinfulness of sin. Dr. Dale dealt with the problem of sin and forgiveness often and powerfully in sermons and addresses which did not perish with their delivery. Of Dale as a theologian Dr. A. M. Fairbairn, who was well qualified to express an opinion, wrote:

On the whole, when we survey Dale's work as a theologian, we are forced to say that our generation has had no abler interpreter of Evangelical thought. His conspicuous merit was a depth that was

[1] A. A. Kimball, at that time a student at Yale, gave a vivid account of Dale's lectures. "At the start-off the Doctor, who spoke without notes, hemmed and 'ahed' and floundered after the most approved fashion. But soon we saw a miracle.... The language soon rolled out in a volume that was absolutely astonishing."

never narrow and a breadth that was never shallow. He was manysided, rich in his interests, vivid in his speech, clear and compact in his thought, masterly in his collective influence. Were we to select a word to express his most distinctive quality, we should say he was *massive*; but his massiveness was homogeneous, expressing a rare unity and integrity of nature, and representing in its outward being the character and the convictions of as honest a man and as distinctive a thinker as these later times have known.[2]

I

How describe Dale's Yale lectures as a whole? Nine in number, they are skillfully and solidly written. One critic thinks them "diffuse." Possibly so, but not thereby losing in effectiveness. He begins each lecture with the courteous salutation "Gentlemen," and is much more formal in manner than, say, Dr. Burton or Mr. Beecher. There is an English flavor to his style of speech which contributes a quality of elegance. Careful preparation, long familiarity with his theme, and years of research distinguish the lectures. No rehashing of old speeches here; instead, a series written for the high occasion and worthy on every count the man and the event.

Dr. Dale advised delay in preaching on new subjects, theological or otherwise. He says:

We shall not be able at once to do justice to our new discovery. At first we shall not handle it firmly and with any freedom. The kind of mastery over doctrine which is absolutely necessary to effective exposition can only come when by repeated and prolonged meditation we have made it perfectly familiar to us. Let us recommend you, therefore, to build up your theology in private, and not to perplex your congregations with speculations which are only half finished, with theories which are in process of formation. Let the walls of the building be dry before you ask people to come and live in it. Even when you think you have made sure of the new truth, or have constructed a more complete and philosophical exposition of a truth already acknowledged, do not be in a hurry to preach it. There is no need for being in a hurry. Do not be afraid that some one will get out a patent before you. The world can wait for your discovery a

[2] A. W. W. Dale, *Life of R. W. Dale of Birmingham*, pp. 721-722.

week or two longer after waiting for it for so many centuries; and perhaps the delay of even a few months will do mankind no harm.

Consider such thoughts as these, selected at random:

If a minister forgets that he has to preach to a congregation, the chances are that he will soon have no congregation to preach to.

Gentlemen, I decline to believe that dullness is necessary to dignity. The dignity of the pulpit is derived from the grandeur and glory of the truths which the preacher has to illustrate and from the solemnity of the duties which he has to enforce; from the infinite issues which depend upon the manner in which the truths are received and the duties discharged by the people that listen to him.

For myself, I like to listen to a good preacher, and I have no objection in the world to being amused by the tricks of a clever conjurer; but I prefer to keep the conjuring and the preaching separate: conjuring on Sunday morning, conjuring in church, conjuring with texts of Scripture, is not quite to my taste.[3]

On the other hand there is considerable risk in choosing a text in which a great truth is stated with such sublimity and grandeur, or in which the deeper spiritual affections are expressed with such vehemence and energy, or in which there is so powerful an appeal to the imagination, that the text creates expectations which the sermon cannot fulfil. What can any man say after reading the words of St. John, "God is love"? . . . What power of lyrical eloquence ought a preacher to have who ventures to write a sermon on Luke 2:13, 14, "Suddenly there was with the angel a multitude of the heavenly host praising God, and saying, Glory to God in the highest, and on earth peace, good will toward men"?

What about works on homiletics? Dale replies:

Some men speak contemptuously of lectures on preaching and treatises on the science or art of rhetoric. For myself, I have read scores of books of this kind, and I have never read one without finding in it

---

[3] The Reverend George Barber, one-time assistant to Dr. Dale in Birmingham, in his *Reminiscences*, recalls how Dr. Dale disliked "fancy sermons." "We had been speaking of various kinds of preaching, and I had suggested a certain text as a good one for a sermon. He was not a little amused, and replied: 'Yes, it would make a good "fancy sermon," but "fancy sermons" are useless things.' . . . Once I told him of a striking and brilliant sermon I had heard from a popular preacher; he listened as I described it, and then said with considerable warmth: 'Yes, I used to preach like that when I was a young man; but now, thank God, I have more sense.' "

some useful suggestion. I advise you to read every book on preaching that you can buy or borrow, whether it is old or new, Catholic or Protestant, English, French, or German. Learn on what principles the great preachers of other churches as well as of your own, of other countries as well as of your own, of ancient as well as of modern times, have done their work. If your experience corresponds with mine, the dullest and most tedious writer on this subject will remind you of some fault that you are committing habitually, or of some element of power which you have failed to use.

Dr. Dale agrees with Phillips Brooks that the preacher's vocation is an exalted and noble one into which there must not come anything common or unclean. A man should come to the preacher's task as a groom to his bride with commingled awe and devotion. Those who heard Dr. Dale in these lectures must have felt themselves on the one hand ready "to take the veil," and on the other to spring into the arena fully panoplied for the conflict. Evangelistic zeal and scholarship do not always go hand in hand, which fact makes the following paragraph all the more remarkable:

It is not possible—it is not desirable—that you should always preach under the strain of that agony of earnestness with which I trust you will be sometimes inspired. There are hours when the true minister of Christ is conscious that the celestial splendors are shining and glowing around him; and there are hours when every fibre of his nature shivers with terror at the prospect of the indignation and wrath, tribulation and anguish, which menace the finally impenitent. Such hours, I trust, will come to you. When they come, you will preach as if the fate of every irreligious man in your congregation were to be determined at once—determined by a single sermon—determined by the vehemence with which you denounce sin; the tenderness with which you speak of the infinite mercy of God; the fidelity with which you reaffirm the certain destruction of all who persist in their revolt against God's authority; the rapturous confidence with which you dilate on the glory, honour, and immortality which are the inheritance of all who trust Christ and keep His commandments.

The mind of "Dale of Birmingham" never stopped expanding and deepening. Sir W. Robertson Nicoll, who knew and loved him, wrote in *The British Weekly* at the time of Dale's passing: "His experience of life yielded readily a stock of instances on which he was wont to expatiate. But he tolerated no slovenliness, or imperfection, and if at first he was too turgid, the study of the masters, especially of Burke, soon educated him to one of the most perfect styles in the whole range of literature."

So passed one of God's anointed, and his works do follow after him!

Note: Yale bestowed the honorary degree of Doctor of Divinity on Dr. Dale unaware of his objection to Divinity degrees. In a letter to Mr. E. A. Lawrence, dated July 31, 1893, Dale wrote: "Your letter would, I think, give an inaccurate impression of the reason why I have not used my Yale degree. It was not because it came from America, but because I have a sentimental objection—perhaps it is something more—to Divinity degrees. If it had been Doctorship of Laws, I should have used it as I use my Glasgow degree. My American friends have been rather pained by my not using it, and they have complained because they thought I did not value it because it was American. I have tried to remove this error, but I am afraid not very successfully."—*Life of R. W. Dale of Birmingham*, by his son, p. 314.

VI. MATTHEW SIMPSON

This generation of Americans know little or nothing (and eight million Methodists do not know as much as they should) about a preacher second only to Henry Ward Beecher in fame and eloquent speech. In truth, there are some writers, contemporaries of these silver-tongued preachers, who put Simpson on an equality with Beecher, despite the fact that Simpson never held a pulpit of such commanding eminence as Plymouth Church, Brooklyn.

Physically these masters of assemblies were unlike. Beecher was short and rotund; Simpson tall and spare. Beecher exuded radiant health; Simpson battled long with weak lungs, and at one period his life hung in the balance. Yet his capacity for work seemed inexhaustible, and he lived to be seventy-three, dying in 1884. Simpson was a Bishop in a church of centralized government; Beecher a free-lance in a church of Congregational polity. Both men were friends of Abraham Lincoln and stout-hearted defenders of the Federal Union.

Born in Cadiz, Ohio, of English-Scottish ancestry, Matthew was self-educated, being one of three speakers in the Lyman

Beecher Lectureship who were not college graduates. Yet he was destined to be president of two institutions of learning. By his own efforts he was as accomplished a linguist as another self-taught celebrity, Elihu Burritt, "the learned blacksmith." He early acquired a working knowledge of Latin, Greek, and Hebrew, and was able to read the German Bible without a dictionary. As one writer put it, he was "self-educated by absorption." He read prodigiously and his choice of books was discriminating. Thus he became in the course of the years, pastor, professor, college president, and Bishop. But it was as a preacher that he won enduring fame.

Dr. Lewis O. Brastow, one-time professor in Yale Divinity School and an authority on preaching, says in his book, *The Modern Pulpit*, that Simpson "was the great preacher of his church in the last century." Not even Beecher won such demonstrations from his audiences as did Simpson. Under the spell of his eloquence men shouted, sprang to their feet, or pounded the floor with cane and umbrella. Women threw their fans or parasols into the air and, strange as it may seem, sometimes shrilled like nowadays bobbysoxers. These demonstrations usually occurred when Simpson was lecturing on patriotic subjects, but not always. His church audiences frequently broke into applause.

The Bishop's style was oratorical, but it was more than vivid rhetoric; it was closely packed with logic, and revealed a mind well-stocked with not only the flowers but also with the fruits of literature and Biblical lore. There was an element of majesty in his spoken word. He chose great themes and the range of his thinking had a grand sweep of force and vision. One of his famous sermons was on "God's Reign on Earth," a theme in which he was much at home, and his hearers in their interest lost track of time and place. He had vast liberty of utterance, and rarely used manuscripts or even notes.

Bishop Simpson was the sixth man in the Course at Yale, and his discourses bear the informal title of *Lectures on Preaching*. In the preface to this volume the Bishop refers modestly to his lectures, saying: "The writer has been during the preparation and delivery so constantly pressed with ecclesiastical duties, that he has had little time to seek authorities or to cultivate elegance of style."

Matthew Simpson

Such humility is becoming, but there was no cause for apology. The lectures are in the great traditions of preaching, are self-supporting, and can stand alone. The style is warm, often colloquial, and autobiographical to a delightful degree. This is well, since almost everybody is interested in learning how a celebrity does the things that won him fame.

Young preachers will find much to encourage them, and especially so if they suffer from any handicap. Simpson's lungs and voice were weak, but by struggle and discipline both grew strong. The tale of his early privations and itinerant preaching, told simply yet realistically, is thrilling, and rings true. Life was simple in those early days, but hard; no luxuries, and few conveniences. A preacher on horseback, his belongings in his saddlebags, along with Bible and hymn book, is part of the American Dream; in truth, he helped to make that dream come true.

Unless I am mistaken, passages from some of Simpson's great sermons are woven into certain of his lectures. On pages 209-214 I discover what might be called an epitome of the Bishop's famed sermon on "The Vision of Ezekiel" or, as perhaps it was sometimes entitled, "The Valley of Dry Bones." Naturally the lecturer is a trifle restrained, and holds himself in before an audience of professors and ministerial students, but I seem to feel the heart-throb of a powerful sermon in the pages to which I have alluded. I seem to hear the preacher's voice and glimpse the church crowded with attentive listeners, tear-moist eyes, and the eager, wistful expression on many faces. It is difficult to fence a real preacher in; he is almost always sure to leap the barriers, whatever they are.

Bishop Simpson was, for his day (the year was 1879), an open-minded independent, with a liberal outlook. Thus in his final lecture, in discussing "The Warfare Between Science and Religion," the Bishop I imagine went out on a limb in the minds of some of his conservative contemporaries. This is what he said:

> I can accord to the scientist nearly all he can claim, without in the slightest degree affecting the foundations of my faith. Does he tell me this universe was created millions of ages ago? I do not deny it, for my Bible tells me it was "in the beginning," which may have been long before the millions of ages which he claims. Does he tell me

that the laws which are in operation to-day have been in operation for millions of years? I admit it; and only add, that the great Lawgiver existed before these laws. Does he tell me of the boundlessness of space, of the infinitude of worlds? I rejoice the more, for all are the work of my Father's hands. Does he tell me that the laws of evolution show a development from the less to the greater? I accept all that, for, under the Gospel, from a sinner I became a saint, and from a saint I shall be exalted above the angels, and shall sit down with the Saviour on his throne. I believe in the survival of the fittest, for the Christian shall survive "the wreck of matter and the crash of worlds." Does he tell me that this evolution dispenses with the Creator? I say not so. There are many things which are claimed in evolution, to which I must give the verdict of the Scotch jury, "Not proven." Yet, were I to admit them all, they would not affect my faith in the wisdom and skill and power of the great Father.

On the management of a parish Simpson warned that the minister "will need great wisdom and tact in his intercourse and councils with his Church officers, whether they be called elders, deacons, trustees, vestrymen, class leaders, or stewards." "Great wisdom," yes, and great courage too, for a blustery church official by any name sounds ominous to a newly-come minister, especially if it be his first pastorate. In this connection, Bishop Simpson recalled hearing Mr. Spurgeon say that there was one difference between deacons and the Devil. "The Scripture says, 'Resist the Devil, and he will flee from you.' 'But,' said he, 'resist the deacons, and they will fly at you!'"

This humorous strain relieves, at intervals, the Bishop's serious trend. For example, in advising the seminary students to avoid wresting Scriptures from their true significance, he said, "I know a minister, who selected the word 'one,' and preached on one God, one baptism, and one hell. He said many good things, but he did not give the sense of the passage." He knew another who preached on "There appeared a great wonder in heaven: a woman." "I once heard of a man, very illiterate, who fixed on the passage of bringing into the church 'damnable heresies.' Mispronouncing the word, he announced for his text 'damnable hearsays'; and proceeded to give a very proper reproof to the gossip and slanderous stories of the day, which after examination turned out to be only 'hearsays.'" Quoth the Bishop, "he got nearer the fact, in truth, than do many of these fanciful speakers."

Matthew Simpson

In reading Bishop Simpson's Yale lectures, I can believe that those who heard him failed to hear the Bishop at his best. The surroundings were not such as to inspire his stirring oratory. He needed a congregation met to worship God, the singing of the great old hymns, the mystic moments that come and go and tarry in a gathering of what we call ordinary men and women, bringing to a common altar a common faith for renewal and the healing of their hurts in mind and spirit. This impression finds confirmation in a long paragraph which appeared in one of Dr. Gunsaulus' lectures delivered in the same Course thirty-two years later. The quotation is taken from his second discourse which is on the theme *The Spiritual Life and New Viewpoints*. I have italicized the pertinent sentences:

> I once heard Bishop Simpson touch upon an experience of years, which he afterwards related as a student of psychology—for he was a teacher before he was a preacher, and always studied the phenomena of preaching and its results from the point of view of a teacher which he continued to be, in spite of his eloquence. I had seen, as he had, his whole great audience electrified in an instant, at the appearance of something which he seemed, not at all at the beginning, or even in the midst of his discourse, to be preaching or even thinking about. He had superior powers of wooing from the crypts of his memory personal figures who walked forth as if, on some fresh resurrection morning, they had escaped death. But this was not a memory. I can feel and hear the sentence, though I cannot quote it. It was a reason for a reason, urged in behalf of the supremacy of our moral intuitions. It was indeed a stormy moment in the history of the man, for he was grappled by and was grappling with tremendous currents of thought and feeling. *He was very far from being eminently the thin and so softvoiced prelate who once read lectures which I heard here, and which were created in an atmosphere as different from the atmosphere of this sermon, as the atmosphere of the architect of a life-saving ship is different from that of the master of the crew in a crisis of the tempest off Gay's Head. The lift and altitude of his conscious activities; the quick, splendid realization of the currents which flowed within sight of everyone so grandly, were as nothing, in comparison with the message from underneath. It seemed a voice from out of the eternity of the man's ageless spiritual life. He was advancing upon his subliminal self—speaking out of his subconscious life.*[1]

---

[1] F. W. Gunsaulus, *The Minister and the Spiritual Life*, pp. 81-82.

In concluding this chapter on Bishop Simpson I can but marvel at the man's humility. His hearers at Yale must have known that he had been a close friend of the immortal Lincoln and had indeed been chosen to give the funeral address at Springfield. It would have been easy to have brought this association into the lectures in some perfectly natural way. The temptation would have been too strong for some big-name preachers to resist, but not Bishop Matthew Simpson. He was absorbed in the much greater purpose —the making friends of God through Jesus Christ, his Lord and ours!

VII. HOWARD CROSBY

There were giants in those days in New York City when Dr. Crosby flourished—pulpit giants—and he was one of them. He was, to be sure, overshadowed by Beecher in Brooklyn, and in a lesser way by John Hall at Fifth Avenue Presbyterian Church and William M. Taylor at the Broadway Tabernacle, Congregational. But in scholarship he was the peer of any preacher of his day, and far superior in this respect to some of his contemporaries.

One of my correspondents, writing of Crosby, says that "he often quoted his text from the original Greek in his exegesis of it and had his congregation so trained that they liked it." This is an enlightening comment, and it is confirmed in Dr. Crosby's lectures at Yale, in the first of which he employs Greek words and phrases ten times, Hebrew and Latin once each. Unquestionably Crosby was a ripely trained scholar, a graduate of New York University at eighteen and a professor in the same for eight years. Later he taught at Rutgers, and in 1861 was ordained to the Presbyterian ministry. After a short pastorate in New Jersey, Crosby entered on a ministry of eighteen years at the Fourth Avenue Presbyterian Church, New York City.

Dr. Crosby was known as a "born fighter," deeply interested in social reform, temperance but not prohibition, and withal a courteous gentleman. President Lincoln offered Dr. Crosby the post of minister to Greece, but he declined. As further evidence of

Crosby's scholarship, recall his service as a member of the New Testament Revision Committee which prepared the American Revised Version of the Bible.

I

This was the man who gave the Yale Lectures in 1880, and surely one of the "Olympians" of the period. As was to be expected, Crosby's series is pitched to a high, even level of excellence. In print, the discourses give the impression of a stately intellectual presentation, coldly correct, and mildly austere. In delivery, this impression must have been dissipated by the charm of the speaker's personality. Dr. Crosby deals with the preacher himself, and he begins with his "Physical Prerequisites." No physical weaklings, he holds, should go into the ministry. The physical standards set up by Crosby would equal those required by West Point and Annapolis. Dr. Crosby may be right, but here, as usual, the rule has its exceptions. What about Robert Murray McCheyne, Richard Baxter, and Robertson of Brighton, to recall but a few who were either physically handicapped or of frail physique? Still, a sound body is a royal asset in any vocation. Many of the great preachers have had sturdy bodies and nerves of steel. Think of Beecher, Hall, Brooks, Taylor, and Spurgeon.

Dr. Crosby is just as exacting in the standards he exalts for the *mental prerequisites* of the preacher. The lecturer is not impressed with "self-made" men in the ministry, and thinks "their capacity for doing harm is immense." "What about Spurgeon?" This question would not disturb Dr. Crosby in the least. The exception, he would contend, that proves the rule. And it is believable that a college education would have added to Spurgeon's power—an "if" of history that must forever remain a conjecture.

Still, the high standard demanded for men in the ministry by this lecturer has everything to commend it. The students who first heard these discourses must have thought, "Who and what am I to dream of a vocation that requires so much and I seem to have so little?" The story is oft repeated of Rubinstein, who, when asked—I think it was during an engagement in New York City— if he wished to attend church, replied, "Yes, if you can take me to hear a preacher who will tempt me to do the impossible." Is it not well that instructors of young men for the Christian ministry demand of them the impossible? Dr. Crosby thought so, and there are those who agree with him.

Dr. Crosby objects to the *cloistered* life of seminary students. The "ordinary minister comes out of the seminary an imbecile," he declares, and goes on to remark: "He may be a good scholar, an able reasoner, a devoted servant of God, but his place is still in the seminary, not in the seething cauldron of the world." The doctor would heartily approve, we are sure, the present practice in many seminaries of permitting students in their senior years to have regular preaching appointments, and in some instances the pastorate of a church. Crosby reflects in a striking manner the great traditions of the Presbyterians' insistence on an educated ministry.

Reviewing Dr. Crosby's series, it belongs, I venture to say, alongside those of Drs. Dale and Robinson in intellectual content and smooth, precise style in which there is little or no anecdotal material. The fairly numerous Greek phrases seem a trifle pedantic today but may not have so impressed those who heard them at Yale. Quotations in Greek, Latin, or other languages appear in this series as in no other in the Lectures to date, and probably never will again. All the same, the preacher who is unable to read his Greek New Testament is thereby sadly impoverished whether he knows it or not.

Across the years we salute this preacher-scholar who closed his dissertations on *The Christian Preacher* with these wise, warm, and tender words:

Be strong and of a good courage. Keep your life in that spiritual sphere, where your hopes and encouragements will be ever before your eyes, and where consequently weariness and despondency will be never known. Walk closely with God, so that the guidance and protection of His holy arm may be ever felt. Avoid and despise the maxims and methods of the world, while you fill your soul with the principles and power of the sacred Word, and then, when the short campaign for Christ's truth is over and you are summoned to the triumph and the home eternal, you will enter the heavenly gates neither unknown nor alone, your way heralded by those angelic hosts who have been your unseen helpers through your earthly labors, and your train composed of those ransomed souls who received from your lips the message that enfranchised them.

II

In volume VII, *The World's Great Sermons*, compiled by Grenville Kleiser, there is a sermon by Dr. Crosby on "The Prepared Worm," from Jonah 4:7, "But God prepared a worm when the morning rose the next day, and it smote the gourd that it withered." There are four main divisions, namely: I. God Is the Author of Affliction; II. He Uses the Natural Laws of this World as His Agents in Afflicting Us; III. God Is Just in Afflicting Us; and IV. God Afflicts Us in His Love. Next Dr. Crosby notes "some inferences from the subject under consideration":

First. If God afflicts, how foolish it is to go to the world for relief. Is the world greater than God? We may be sure that any comfort the world can give, as against God's affliction, must be dangerous. It is a contest with God, which God may allow to be successful, but only for the greater condemnation thereafter. The world's relief is not a cure but an opiate. It stupefies, but does not give health and strength. The world's relief is a temporary application—a lull before a fiercer storm. The world's relief is a determination not to heed the lesson God sends us; it is the invention of frivolity, and not the device of wisdom. More slumber, more pleasure, and more worldly care are three favorite medicaments the world uses in these cases—anodynes which only weaken the system and prepare it for more fearful suffering. God wishes to awaken the mind by affliction, and man immediately prescribes a narcotic. The great Physician brings the affliction for our good; we turn to quackery to destroy the effects of the divine medicine. Ah! the day is coming when God shall appear as no longer our Savior but our Judge, if this be our treatment of His love. "Because I have called and ye refused; I have stretched out my hand and no man regarded; but ye have set at naught all my counsel, and would none of my reproof; I also will laugh at your calamity; I will mock when your fear cometh; when your fear cometh as desolation, and your destruction cometh as a whirlwind."

Secondly. If God prepares worms, then worms at once form an interesting study for us. We cannot see a caterpillar upon the leaf, but we know God has a mission for that worm. He is an ambassador of the Most High on his way to perform his Master's will. The headache, which unfits us for our ordinary occupation, is more than a headache. It is the voice of our God. Let us listen to the next headache and hear what God would have us learn. Every bird and beast, every raindrop and sunbeam, every breath of wind, and every event, however small, are the writings of a heavenly scribe. Let us study God's providence. It is all a message of love to us. We shall find out infinitely more in this study than in deciphering the hieroglyphics of Egypt. We shall find correction, expostulation, comfort, encouragement and instruction; and the more we look, the more we shall see. We shall become adepts in the high art of interpreting the acts of God toward us, and in this, as in prayer, hold constant communion with our divine Redeemer.

Of its type this sermon is a vivid example of the conservative theology of Dr. Crosby's day, of which he was a powerful preacher. He died in 1891.

VIII. EZEKIEL GILMAN ROBINSON

We have inherited a government that was founded on strong moral and religious convictions. It will endure only as these convictions are kept fresh in the popular mind. To keep them fresh there must be growing intelligence. To guide the intelligence there must be enlightened conscience; to enlighten conscience there must be an intelligent pulpit.

—E. G. ROBINSON

The Reverend Ezekiel G. Robinson was the first Baptist to appear in the Lyman Beecher Lectureship. No better selection could have been made from that virile and aggressive denomination. Dr. Robinson, with the possible exception of Dr. John A. Broadus, was the dean of American Baptist preacher-educators whose chief contribution to their day was made as college and university professors, yet who never forgot or abandoned their first love—the ministry of the Word!

The late Professor Arthur S. Hoyt, who spent his life teaching young men how to preach, says in his *The Pulpit and American Life*:

> Dr. Ezekiel G. Robinson, first professor of theology at Rochester and later President of Brown University, had few equals in his day as a platform speaker. He has a subtle, sensitive nature that interpreted common thought, especially of critical hours, and a magnetic personality that charmed and swayed a multitude by his thought. The older citizens of Rochester have never forgotten his inpromptu speech on the assassination of Abraham Lincoln and speak of it as one of the great experiences of their lives.

Robinson was indeed a striking personality. Tall and slightly stooped, he was capable of erecting himself to his full height when an "air of high command" was warranted. His mental processes were finely organized, so much so that he had little patience with persons satisfied with mediocrity or given to slovenly habits of mind and speech. His own pulpit style was terse, precise, accurate, and distinguished by a sedate elegance. That there was something professorial in his manner is probably true. That sharpest of ministerial critics, the sometimes pedantic Professor W. C. Wilkinson, who was a pupil of Robinson at Rochester and devoted to him, was not blind to certain defects in his beloved preceptor's preaching. "Dr. Robinson's equipment," he says, "was too predominantly of the intellectual, rather than of the heart, to constitute him the ideal orator."

This is a neat criticism, for Ezekiel Robinson was an exponent of the extemporaneous method of preaching, gloried in it, and consistently practiced it himself. Reading a sermon, to him, was anathema and an abomination to the Lord. He was hard also on the *memoriter* preacher, and it is strange that in his advocacy of extemporary preaching he seemed to overlook Chalmers, Brooks, and scores of others who mastered the art of manuscript preaching and left a mighty legacy of sermonic riches.

Since this preacher-professor was so adamant in his stand against reading sermons from the pulpit, it is pertinent that we hear again, and more at length, from his devoted admirer and former student, the doughty Professor Wilkinson, that sermon taster par excellence, and see what happens. In a chapter on his mentor in

Modern Masters of Pulpit Discourse Dr. Wilkinson describes a series of sermons he heard Dr. Robinson deliver in Rochester, New York, and observes:

The discourses thus recalled were, like Dr. Robinson's discourses in general from the beginning to the end of his conspicuous career, delivered *ex tempore*. And now I must say something which, save to the most thoughtful, will seem like derogation from the praise that I bestow; to some it will seem, on the contrary, enhancement rather than diminution, of eulogy. Brilliant, then, as those discourses were, and powerful, they yet fell something short of that decisively triumphant effect in oratory of which the speaker seemed all the time tantalizingly capable. This was, I think, the case with Dr. Robinson's public discourse generally. There was a certain lack of *abandon*, a certain self-checking refusal on the part of the preacher to trust himself wholly to the sweep of the inspiration that was perpetually swelling within him almost, but not *quite*, to the volume and the head that would burst every barrier and pour forth eloquence in an irresistible torrent, in an overwhelming flood.[1]

Now a manuscript preacher can "let himself go," as we well know from the study of the great preachers of the Christian centuries. Let me add a personal testimony. I have heard Charles Clayton Morrison, using manuscript deftly, all but lift me from my seat by thunderbolt after thunderbolt of eloquence. Since throughout the Series on Preaching the vexed question, which is the best method of sermon delivery, manuscript, *memoriter*, or extempore, comes up time after time to be argued pro and con, a scriptural answer might suffice, "Let each man be assured in his own mind." One of the best answers to this question I have heard is that from a woman who in her time had heard many sermons. Said she, "I prefer extemporaneous preaching, but I'd rather hear a good sermon read than a poor one delivered extemporaneously." Who wouldn't?

Dr. Robinson's Yale lectures were of a high order and deserve to be better known to student-preachers and ministers generally. There is a quality of aloofness about them, an air of austerity. The objectivity is marked and sustained. Anecdotes and humor are almost wholly absent, and there is a minimum of biographical

[1] P. 436.

references. The high seriousness of the speaker is marked, and his sentences are of marvelous clarity.

Dr. Robinson's third lecture, the "Relation of Preaching to Free Institutions," is especially valuable and as timely today as when it was delivered. The thesis of this chapter is the powerful influence of the Protestant pulpit on free institutions. Previous lecturers had referred to this fact; Dr. Robinson elaborated on it. Put into a pamphlet and widely circulated today, this lecture would bear fruit. Take a memorable incident cited by the lecturer. A sermon preached by Jonathan Mayhew, in his thirtieth year, in Boston, 1756, the speaker says "not only aroused all Massachusetts but reached the ears of all the other colonies." Mayhew's lengthy subject was: "A Discourse Concerning Unlimited Submission and Non-Resistance with Some Reflections on the Resistance to King Charles I." The discourse, which found its way across the Atlantic, assailed the doctrine of the divine right of kings and defended the diviner right of conscience. Incidentally, Mayhew's sermon won him a Doctor of Divinity degree from the University of Aberdeen.

The lecturer ties together incidents like the Mayhew discourse with many others of a similar nature. He instances also the Puritan and Pilgrim contribution, plus the rise of the Dissenter movement in America in which the Baptists had a lusty part.

Robinson, whose familiarity with American history was on a par with his encyclopedic knowledge of the Bible, history, and literature in general, contends that religion, in short Christianity, had a major part in the making of our Republic. This is old news and good news, and it is certainly *new* news to some of the writers of historical textbooks used in the public schools of today. An inspection of some of these modern textbooks of American history would have the reader believe that religion had little or nothing to do with the origins of this Republic—that there was no *Kingdom of God and the American Dream,* to pilfer Sherwood Eddy's title to an excellent book.

Still again, in this fine chapter the lecturer deals with an issue that is so alive today that it is *hot*—the relation of State and Church. "Nothing was further from the minds of the colonists, whether at Jamestown, at Plymouth, or at Boston, than a separation of church and state." Then what changed the minds of the colonists on this subject? Dr. Robinson had the answer.

Some of the chief of these ideas (about human freedom) were embodied in that compact of the Pilgrims on the Mayflower, just prior to the disembarkation at Plymouth. They were the ideas which in the end gave to New England its free civil government and the independence of both its state and its churches. And so also in the compact of the colonists at Boston. Mixed as were their motives at the first, of the relations of the state to the church, and subordinate as they made the civil to the ecclesiastical authority, they nevertheless held principles both religious and civil which were sure to bring forth what in due time came to pass.

Dr. Robinson was never more eloquent and convincing than in this fine sentence:

And if our Republic was worth the prayers and the tears that it cost to found it; if it was worth the prayers and the tears and the treasures and blood of the fathers and brothers who twenty years ago laid down their lives to perpetuate it, then it is worth-while for the Christian minister so to preach the gospel as still to preserve it.[2]

On this high patriotic note we take leave of Ezekiel Gilman Robinson, a gallant fighter for the faith once for all delivered to the saints.

IX. NATHANIEL JUDSON BURTON

When Dr. N. J. Burton, then minister of the Park Church, Hartford, Connecticut, gave the Lyman Beecher Lectures it probably never occurred to him that he was doing a series radically different from those who had preceded him and those who were to follow. Or, if questioned about this later, he might have replied

[2] To those who would welcome a recent book which traces the religious influence in the history of our Republic, *This Nation Under God*, by the Hon. Elbert D. Thomas (New York: Harper & Brothers, 1950), is enthusiastically recommended. It is an important volume to have at hand, since it charts over 30,000 facts of our national life.

as did Wendell Phillips when complimented on a certain speech, "I took it for granted you wanted me to bring myself."

Dr. Burton brought himself to Yale Divinity School in a set of lectures which, for originality of treatment and delightful informality, stand unrivaled in the noble Lectureship. True, the eloquence of a Beecher is not here or the solid dignity of a John Hall; the stately diction of a Phillips Brooks is missing and likewise the scholarly style of a Dr. Dale. But Dr. Burton's message is just as important and interesting as that of these famous preachers whose names were once household words. The series is uniquely refreshing and immensely entertaining.

There are twenty-three chapters in *In Pulpit and Parish*, the volume which contains his lectures, and one surmises that when delivered they were reduced in number by combining the chapters, otherwise a week would not have afforded sufficient time for their presentation. As it is, the second edition comprises 376 pages of closely packed material. This second printing, which appeared in 1925, was hailed by so competent a judge as Dr. Charles E. Jefferson, with this congratulatory letter to the publisher:

I am glad you are reprinting Nathaniel J. Burton's Lectures on Preaching. I have always considered his lectures one of the very best courses in the entire Lyman Beecher series. I was fortunate enough to come upon these Burton lectures near the beginning of my ministry, and they left a mark on me which abides to this day. One cannot read them and ever forget them. They were juicy when they were delivered, and at the end of forty years, they are juicy still.

I

The Burton lectures give the impression of extempore delivery, taken down in shorthand and revised by the author. But this was not the case. The lectures were written and read by him, and there is reason to believe read with a kind of infinite zest filtered through a vivacious personality. Alas! how hard it is to recapture the impression a speech makes on its hearers long after the event is history. This is true when one has been present; how much more so when he was not there and seventy years have intervened between the time the speech was delivered and the time of writing about it.

A fair introduction to Burton's piquant style is discernible in this extract from his lecture on "The Call to the Ministry":

> If a man has gifts, he may be a minister—and examining committees always feel bound to start the question of gifts. Has the candidate any intellect, and has the moral region of his head any size? Can he think? And when he thinks does he produce anything, ordinarily? Is there any ethical sound to the movement of his mind? Does he know anything? Can he tell to other people what he knows? Can he tell it in an engaging manner, so that if we start him out as a preacher, somebody will be likely to want to hear him?
>
> And then passing from his mind to his exterior make-up, what physical gifts has he? Is he a person whom one can look at with any comfort? What sort of a voice has he? Has he lungs, and a degree of digestion, and an affirmative physique all around, rather than a physique negative and peeping?
>
> These, and the like, are the endowments that we like to see in a young man who begins to surmise that the Christian ministry is his proper pursuit.
>
> At the same time, in order that we may not be too knowing in this matter, and may not fall into the delusion that God is shut up to ten-talented people, for the accomplishment of His works, behold what mighty men some weak men are, in His kingdom and work-field.

Dr. Burton goes on to give examples of men weak physically who were used of God victoriously because they had spiritual power and quick minds plus a grand component of common sense. His conclusions set one's mind in motion and speculations ensue. Paul seems to have been weak physically, but about this we may be mistaken; Simon Peter, "the big fisherman," strong as an ox; John, "the beloved," was probably an aesthete, and Apollos an athlete. Who knows definitely? Nobody, but it is pleasant to speculate. There have been some able preachers, perhaps a few geniuses, who all their days battled with grievous ailments. Granting this, it still remains true that, usually, sound minds travel in sound bodies, and Beecher had something when he said that it is a sin to be sick.

Burton lays stress on the need of imagination in preaching, as do others in this notable Series. But this lecturer gets at the subject, as he does at other subjects, in his own novel way. He holds "that

Nathaniel Judson Burton

imagination is necessary in order to the interpretation of the imaginative parts of the Bible and a clear hold on the realities that lie back of its oftentimes poetic vocabulary." Seldom does one find so much wisdom in so brief a statement. It will bear further scrutiny and much pondering. To illustrate:

How often in that Book is God spoken of as angry, as revengeful, as impatient, as punctilious and easily affronted, as blood-thirsty, as treasuring up a personal insult for many generations, and as being many things a man certainly never ought to be. And the prose man —the unmitigated prose man—thinks there must be some element of literality in this,—that God has in His mind, something like those several inclemencies. But the poetic theologian knows that these mighty adjectives are but the tumultuation of the imagination, piling up her sensational images—to express something to be sure; something, but, of a truth, not this—that God actually has in His feeling the literal counterparts of those awful human terms. God is infinitely genial. God is uniformly and eternally genial. God never had a first flutter of impatience. God never stands on His dignity and resents insults. God never in one instance laid an affront away in His memory and watched for an opportunity to get in a killing return stroke. And, how could His creatures survive another minute if He were such a terrific being as that. But in the way God enforces laws throughout His dominions, we have a state of things as though all those adjectives about Him were true words. When we transgress law we smart for it and it hurts us and frightens us, as though back of the law were some great personal anger. When the misdoings of some ancestor of mine report themselves in my diseased body, it is as though God had remembered those misdoings of his back there, and now has a chance to gratify His revenge.

Practically, this New Englander is a more rational theologian than some other Yankees with tough minds and vitriolic vocabularies; and the idealism is here, too, and in plenitude and in power. Give mind to this passage from the chapter on *"Extra-Parishional Faithfulness"*; don't miss the significance of the title, for it is rich in suggestion:

After all, Brethren, the whole end of Theology is love. It seems hard to realize that that is so, but so it is. If your theology does not make you loving, it has not Christianized you, and to that extent is not a Christian theology. . . . Preach the truth in love, and for the development of love. . . . Robert Burns wrote an address to the Devil, which ends up with the following bewitching touch of benevolence. Burns had spent some nineteen verses, giving his Majesty a plain statement of his mean opinion of him, ending with this irreverent snapper:

> An' now, auld *Cloots*, I ken ye're thinkin,
> A certain *Bardie's* rantin, drinkin,
> Some luckless hour will send him linkin,
>   To your black pit;
> But faith! he'll turn a corner jinkin,
>   An' cheat you yet.

But, suddenly now, from that height of impiety the Bardie drops to this flow of the heart:

> But fare-you weel, auld Nickie-ben!
> O wad ye tak a thought an' men'!
> Ye aiblins might—I dinna ken—
>   Still hae a stake—
> I'm wae to think upo' yon den,
>   Ev'n for your sake![1]

Including this bit o' Burns here may necessitate driving some reader to a glossary of the Scottish bard's works, but it's fu' worth it!

II

None of the lectures in this Course, as I recall them, is quite so tantalizingly quotable as Dr. Burton's series. Almost every page fairly bristles with sentences that seem to say, "Here, take me," or "Don't you overlook me. I belong in that book you are writing." Or again, a paragraph shouts this to me: "Dr. Burton won't rest easy in his grave if you don't take me and use me too." Well, now, there is a limit to quotations in any book, and there must be a limit in this one. But the humor of this lecturer must not be overlooked, nor a sample of it omitted. How I love this from the lecture on "High-Heartedness in the Ministry." The Doctor is dealing with the flies

---

[1] *The Complete Poetical Works of Robert Burns* (New York: Thomas Crowell & Co., 1900), "Address to the Deil," p. 15.

in the sermonic ointment (this phrase is mine, not his), the little flaws, mannerisms, habits that subtract from a preacher's effectiveness in the pulpit. Dr. Burton puts the "snapper" (I got this word from him) with this incident:

> When I heard Cardinal Manning and listened to the victorious and far-reaching sniff that he gave whenever he made a thoroughly good point, I thought that for a settled preacher in a first-class position, he would hardly answer. A sniff is nothing. It does not disprove a person's character. It does not show that he is not learned, able and godly enough to be a Cardinal; but it might prevent his being a Cardinal, if the duties of that great office required him to stay on one spot forever, among the same set of people and in such close quarters that they could hear and could not fail to hear, every sniff he put forth—thousands in a year, perhaps.

This reminds me—Dr. Burton's lectures are always reminding me of some person or of some incident—of a minister I once knew, a college president too, whose mannerism was not a sniff, but a snort. When he made a good point he snorted and, while this idiosyncrasy was not objectionable the first time I listened to him preach—I fancied he was troubled with a cold in the head—the second time I heard him punctuate his sermon with a snort at certain intervals, the thing became, I am ashamed to say, vastly amusing, and uncontrollably so when in his desire to celebrate a particularly good point he snorted *twice!*

Do my ministerial brethren grow weary in sermon-making? Well then, the undying fire of Dr. Burton's enthusiasm will revive their drooping spirits:

> I wrote a sermon the other day on Rebecca and Isaac, confining myself to the simple old story of how Isaac got Rebecca—and I could hardly live through it, the whole thing was so fresh, dewy, self-evident and sufficing; so heart-to-heart with all hearts that know what a heart is. And all through the Bible you find quantities and quantities of the same sort of thing—that something or other which makes the Book the spokesman of the human family; the interpreter of the soul of man, man's congenial other self, the Book that finds him, warms him, strengthens him, goes into his circulation and makes his blood red, virile, and copious.

Thus might I go on quoting this dear, beloved fellow preacher of the Everlasting Mercy; but, fortunately, this second printing of his volume of the Yale Lectures is available and easy to procure, which unfortunately cannot be said of some of the books in this highly-prized Series. This is one of the most readable of the numerous works on preaching I have on my shelves: human, wise with a wisdom that has grown with the years of its author, and as refreshing as the shower which follows a hot, dry spell.

X. JOHN ALBERT BROADUS

The first time I heard the name of John A. Broadus was in a dentist's office, in a little town in northeast Missouri, in the year 1895. The dentist, a Kentuckian, called my attention to a recent copy of *The Louisville Courier Journal*, which reported the death of Dr. Broadus in an elaborate article, with his picture conspicuously displayed on the front page. "A great man, and a powerful preacher," remarked the dentist with feeling as he put the newspaper in my hands. Little did I dream, as I read then of Dr. Broadus, that three years later I, a student in the College of the Bible, Lexington, Kentucky, would have as my textbook in homiletics, Dr. Broadus' *On the Preparation and Delivery of Sermons*.

A Virginian by birth, Dr. Broadus was graduated from the University at Charlottesville, June 29, 1830, was pastor of a church there for eight years, professor in the Baptist Seminary, Greenville, South Carolina, some eighteen years, and for as many more years professor in and president of the Southern Baptist Theological Seminary at Louisville. Throughout these years Dr. Broadus was in constant demand as a preacher, supplying conspicuous pulpits and preaching on notable occasions. In 1870 he published his *On the Preparation and Delivery of Sermons*, the best known and most widely used treatise on homiletics written by an American. This book passed through numerous editions. It was revised by Dr. E. C. Dargan in 1898. The bibliography was revised and

John Albert Broadus

amplified by Dr. C. S. Gardner in 1926, and the work "completely revised" by Dr. J. B. Weatherspoon in 1943.[1]

It is difficult for this generation of ministers and churchmen to realize the conspicuous position Dr. Broadus occupied throughout the South in his day, and the esteem and affection in which he was held by Baptists everywhere. This was due in part to his fame as a preacher and also to his gracious personality and unimpeachable integrity. No king upon his throne had more loyal and willing subjects than did this preacher-professor and courteous Southern gentleman.

Professor W. C. Wilkinson, so often quoted in these pages, a warm, personal friend of Dr. Broadus, has given us what is doubtless the most complete pen portrait and character analysis of his great fellow Baptist in existence. Dr. Wilkinson has a chapter on Broadus in his *Modern Masters of Pulpit Discourse,* which is almost but not quite free from the critical thrusts for which the Professor was noted. In his opening paragraphs this Sargent of preacher-portrait-word-painters says:

I have named in my title a man with every natural endowment, every acquired accomplishment, except, perhaps, plenitude of physical power, to have become, had he been only a preacher, a preacher hardly second to any in the world.

A conjectural judgment like the foregoing, it is, to be sure, almost always unwisely bold and hazardous to put forth. I simply record the impression which, after some familiarity acquired with the man himself, seen and heard both in public and in private, and after no little conversance with his productions in print, I find fixed and deepening in my mind concerning Dr. Broadus.[2]

This is superlative praise and, from Dr. Wilkinson, it is unusual.

---

[1] I am basing this chapter on the 1898 revised edition of Dr. Broadus' *On the Preparation and Delivery of Sermons* largely but not altogether for reasons of sentiment, since it is the edition I studied in seminary days at Lexington, Kentucky, and with which I am very much at home. However, the latest edition brought out in 1944 by Harper & Brothers, "completely revised" by Dr. Jesse Burton Weatherspoon, is in every way the edition which ministers should procure, no matter what previous editions of this notable work they may have on their library shelves. A host of us will agree with Dr. Weatherspoon when in his preface he expresses the belief "that a revised Broadus will have greater worth for the next generation than a new book."

[2] P. 344.

Furthermore, his judgment, so well expressed above, is confirmed by others well qualified to speak, both in and outside the Baptist churches. Our interest, however, is not only in Broadus the man, but primarily, perhaps, with his famous treatise entitled *On the Preparation and Delivery of Sermons*. It was in 1889 that Dr. Broadus gave the Lyman Beecher Lectures at Yale. It is cause for regret that we do not have a transcript of those lectures, which were delivered from notes and not written out in full. But we do have the subjects of his eight Yale lectures, to wit: I. The Young Preacher's Outfit; II. Freshness in Preaching; III. Sensational Preaching; IV. Freedom in Preaching; V. The Minister's General Reading; VI. The Minister and His Hymn Book; VII. The Minister and His Bible; and VIII. The Minister's Private Life. These subjects read well; how much better they must have sounded on the lips of such a master of the preaching art!

Dr. Broadus' *On the Preparation and Delivery of Sermons* was a success from the first. It has been adopted as a textbook in scores of theological seminaries from coast to coast and from the Great Lakes to the Gulf of Mexico, and where it is not a textbook, it is required collateral reading. In all, it has passed through twenty-five American editions; and separate editions were published in England. It has been translated into Portuguese for the Protestant missions in Brazil, and enjoyed a similar use in Chinese and Japanese.

The edition of 1898 is a big book, almost too big for use as a textbook. (Dr. Weatherspoon's revision has corrected this flaw.) Following a preface by Dr. E. C. Dargan, who succeeded Dr. Broadus in the chair of homiletics at the Southern Baptist Seminary, is the author's "Preface to the First Edition," dated July, 1870, which covers seventeen pages. The volume falls into five parts: I. Materials of Preaching; II. Arrangement of a Sermon; III. Style; IV. Delivery of Sermons; and V. Conduct of Public Worship. The treatment is full and detailed, and couched in dignified and concise diction. It would probably be described as heavy reading for present-day students, when the style in textbooks is simpler, lighter, and enlivened by much illustrative matter. The reader gets the impression as he leafs through this book that preaching is an exalted and exacting privilege which carries with it the weightiest of responsibilities. The scope of the work is immense, the authorities cited are myriad, are drawn from many cultures, and embrace the Christian centuries with a fullness that is amazing. The elevated style is relieved occasionally by incidents and quotations of a humorous nature, but these are subordinated to the general theme and are embodied in the text as illustrative material, carefully chosen and always with a delightful pertinency. In short, the treatment is the most exhaustive of any work done in this country, with perhaps the exception of Professor Austin Phelps' homiletic treatise of an earlier date, a work, by the way, to which there are eleven references in Broadus' book.

It can be said in passing, that the judgment expressed in *On the Preparation and Delivery of Sermons*, on the various aspects of the preacher's mission, is sound and beyond praise. The young and inexperienced minister who seeks to follow counsel of Dr. Broadus cannot go astray, although he may and probably will find the road rugged at times, and the ideals difficult to reach as he doggedly sets out to "follow the gleam." Take, for example, this advice on good taste:

> Even the most earnest and successful preaching is sometimes such, despite, and never because of, bad taste. And no man can be his own sole judge in matters of taste. He must consider his church, and the community in which he lives. Now with different churches and communities tastes also differ, and a preacher in going from one charge to another, should try to find out the standards of taste prevalent about him, and adapt himself in a reasonable degree to their requirements. No man can be long or really useful in any community whose taste he offends in his preaching. He may shock and startle, and even draw large crowds; but he will also annoy and repel, and good people will grow weary of him. Consultation with judicious friends of both sexes, and a reasonable and manly deference to their opinions, will enable the preacher to keep within the bounds of good taste without losing anybody's respect, and without sacrificing one element of real timeliness and power in his preaching.

Does this sound prim and slightly puritanical to our modern ears? Perhaps. But the gist of the paragraph is the essence of common sense and good breeding. A genius may discount such advice. Catherine Beecher once remarked that her brother, Henry

Ward, often offended in this respect. Nevertheless, the judgment of Dr. Broadus as expressed in the above quotation is as impeccable as the best of human judgments can hope to be. Always there is the danger that when a celebrity is imitated it is his faults or defects which the imitator is prone to copy. Why? Possibly because of that thing called "human nature."

When a man achieves distinction in any art, his own practice of that art naturally becomes a matter of absorbing interest; we want to see how well he lives up to his teaching on the subject. This being true, it should be profitable to study Dr. Broadus in the pulpit. Take now the introduction to a noble sermon on "Justification by Faith":

The doctrine of justification by faith is simply one of the several ways in which the Gospel takes hold of men. You do not hear anything of that doctrine in the Epistles of John. . . . I think sometimes that Martin Luther made the world somewhat one-sided by his doctrine of justification by faith; that the great mass of the Protestant world are inclined to suppose there is no other way of looking on the Gospel. There are very likely some here today who would be more impressed by John's way of presenting the matter; but probably the majority would be more impressed by Paul's way, and it is our business to present now this and now that, to present first one side and then the other. So we have here before us today Paul's great doctrine of justification by faith, in perhaps one of his most striking statements, "Therefore, being justified by faith, let us have peace with God through our Lord Jesus Christ."[3]

The candor of this statement excites admiration and is commendable in every way. How many sermons are preached on Bible doctrines that not only present but one side of the shield but seem to imply there is but one side. A contemporary, writing about Dr. Broadus, observes: "Moderation of tone, conscientious carefulness of statement, sound and vigilant scholarship, are additional, though still kindred characteristics of Dr. Broadus' work. . . . He is a true interpreter of texts, and not a mere user, far less, as many a preacher thoughtlessly is, an abuser of them for homiletic purposes." Dr. Broadus meets the test: what he taught about preaching he applied and used in his own preaching.

[3] *Broadus' Sermons and Addresses*, p. 86.

How vividly I recall a passage in Broadus' volume on imitative gestures, as I sat in the class on homiletics and heard our instructor refer to it. Yes, more, he rose from his desk, which stood on a small platform, and acted this incident for us:

A really good man, in preaching at a University, once said: "You shut your eyes to the beauty of piety; you stop your ears to the calls of the Gospel; you turn your back," etc., and in saying it, shut his eyes, stopped his ears with his fingers, and whirled his broad back into view. Alas! for the good done to the students by his well-meant sermon. In "suiting the action to the word" he "o'erstepped the modesty of nature." Even lifting the eyes toward heaven, or pointing the finger toward it, or pressing the hand upon the heart, etc., though allowable, are sometimes carried too far, or too often repeated.

Something should be said of the note of sympathy and understanding that runs through *On the Preparation and Delivery of Sermons*. There is a complete absence of the cutting and sarcastic comments that creep into the pages of some works on the same subject. Scorn, satire, irony, cynicism, or anything of a mordacious nature are not in Dr. Broadus' book. Instead, the qualities of kindness, urbanity, understanding, and sympathy abound. It could not be otherwise, for did not this gallant Virginian once say: "If I were asked what is the first thing in effective preaching, I should say sympathy; and what is the second thing, I should say sympathy; and what is the third thing, I should say sympathy."

Only when the occasion condoned it did Dr. Broadus let his deep sympathetic nature overflow in a flood tide of emotion. During his professorship in the Southern Baptist Theological Seminary, Louisville, Kentucky, there died a young colleague to whom he was deeply attached. In a memorial discourse, which those who heard it could never forget, occurs this passage:

Eight years ago we buried with the deepest sense of loss our oldest professor, who had been with us from the beginning. What a shock, that the next to pass away should be our youngest! We cannot but feel like parents grown gray when called to bury a son in all his youthful prime. It is a mournful experience. God help us. And can I more say? Three years ago the orange blossom, and now these flowers, that vainly essay to smile upon a scene too full of sadness. O pitying heavens, drop down the dews of your consolation; O pitying angels, doubtless ye care, but ye know not, O angels, the sweet, sweet human love, the bitter, bitter human sorrow. O sympathizing Savior, thou didst weep with sisters beside a brother's grave, and thou knowest, thou knowest, O Savior, that here is a grief still harder to bear. O Holy Ghost, the Comforter, come now and comfort. O God and Father of our Lord Jesus Christ, the Father of mercies and God of all comfort, the Father of the fatherless and the widow's God, come guide and uphold one who strives to be brave and calm as she leads forth into life the tottering steps of her fatherless little boy.[4]

As one tiptoes from out a sacred place with voice hushed and yearning to be alone to muse and dream and pray, so now we withdraw, hallowing the memory of John Albert Broadus.

[4] W. C. Wilkinson, *op. cit.*, p. 361.

II
★ *TITANS* ★

> *We do not treat a preacher fairly when we judge him by his statements, logic, anecdotes, or phrases. We must judge him by his positive and effective message.*
>
> —P. T. Forsyth

I. ROBERT FORMAN HORTON

Robert Forman Horton takes rank with the very greatest of those preachers who have held, in the noble words of John Robinson of Leyden, that "God has yet more light and truth to break forth from his Holy Word." And for him the Word of God is heard, not only in the Scriptures which he loves, but in the songs of poets, in the dreams of artists, and in every wise and loving thought which has flowered in the hearts of men.

—Ernest H. Jeffs[1]

The author of the above tribute to Dr. Horton is one of England's noted journalists who specialized in religious events, sermons, and pulpit personalities. He knew intimately the leading preachers, ecclesiastics, and churchmen of his day and wrote about them intelligently and brilliantly. Mr. Jeffs belonged to that small group of religious journalists in England which included Sir W. Robertson Nicoll, Jonathan Brierley ("J.B."), Arthur Porritt, and Basil Mathews. Those who read Jeffs' *Princes of the Modern Pulpit in England,* will recognize the quotation at the top of this page which was taken from that volume. We do not have in America newspaper men who are trained for this kind of reporting. The "church editors" on our great dailies are efficient in garnering and arranging routine news of the churches and give a competent coverage to important religious events and meetings, but they lack

---
[1] Late of *The Christian World,* London.

intimate acquaintance with ministers, hear few sermons, and of the various schools of theology know practically nothing and, perhaps care less.

I

Dr. Horton was of that highly educated and distinctive company of English preachers who glorified the clerical scene in Great Britain, say, from 1875 to the first quarter of the present century. He was an Oxford man who made his mark as a scholar there and, had he gone with the Anglicans, might have won signal honors in the Established Church. Instead of yielding to what must have been a strong temptation, Horton took a small church at Hampstead in 1880, served it fifty years, and made it a famous center of nonconformity. It was not that he loved Oxford less but that he loved more passionately a preaching ministry and the freedom of the Congregational Church polity.

Early in his ministry Dr. Horton began to write books, and in his biography by Sir John Marriott, some fifty-four publications are listed, which do not include "all his published sermons, lectures, addresses, and articles." Having accepted the "assured results" of the modern school of Biblical scholars, his preaching reflected this fact, as did also his first book of merit, entitled, *The Inspiration of the Bible*, which sold widely and brought the author a barrage of criticism from conservatives in all the denominations. In constant demand as preacher and lecturer, Horton's fame grew apace, and his name became a familiar one to readers of religious journals and the big city dailies.

From humble beginnings Dr. Horton built up a congregation which, at its peak, numbered 1,276 members, besides hundreds of others who attended his services but were not enrolled as members. A new and spacious edifice costing $100,000 was dedicated July 3, 1884, with Dr. Fairbairn preaching the sermon. The Lyndhurst Road Church was the name it bore from then on, and among the notables who worshiped there were Dr. A. E. Garvie, H. H. Asquith, later Prime Minister; the celebrated and eccentric Professor John Stuart Blackie, Dr. Walter F. Adeney, and other widely known educators, ministers, and literary men.

II

Dr. Horton gave the Yale Lectures in 1892, being but thirty-seven years old, in the glory of his prime and of his ever widening renown as a preacher. He spoke on the subject *Verbum Dei* and delivered nine lectures of exceptional merit, the workmanship well-nigh perfect. His discourses followed in part the pattern of those who had preceded him, but only in part. The topics he discussed were: I. The Theme; II. "The Word of the Lord Came"; III. The Word in the New Testament; IV. The Bible and the Word of God; V. The Word of God Outside the Bible; VI. On Receiving the Word; VII. The Logos; VIII. The Preacher's Personality; and IX. Methods and Modes.

"My doctrinal views," wrote Dr. Horton, "are summed up in the words 'Jesus Christ,' but I can only preach what has become vivid and real to myself." And a contemporary wrote of him, "The central *emphasis* of Dr. Horton's teaching . . . is placed neither on the 'Jesus of history' nor the Christ of the formal theologies." This fact accounts for his facility in putting, not only new wine in old bottles but also old wine in new bottles, and managing both feats skillfully. On one subject, namely, that of the direct inspiration and empowerment of the preacher today, exactly as it was with the apostles, Horton stood quite alone, although possibly there were isolated Conservatives who held the same view with modifications. Under fire both in England and elsewhere because of this interpretation, Horton held to his position tenaciously and argued for it enthusiastically, drawing copiously from the Scriptures to prove his case. What is more to the point, Horton's long and successful ministry was closely geared to this theory of the preacher's inspiration for his work. His diaries abound with references to his wrestlings in prayer that he might be receptive to the Spirit of Empowerment in preaching the Word. In Lecture III, "The Word in the New Testament," he sets forth his views in this particular, and the passages that follow, taken from that lecture, are relevant and characteristically presented:

It is of course true to say that holy men of old spoke as they were moved by the Holy Ghost, and even more specifically "searched what manner of time the Spirit of Christ which was in them did point unto" (1 Pet. i. II), but the signal baptism of the Spirit which followed the departure of Christ from the earth was distinguished from those earlier movements of the Spirit in two ways. First, it was, as the prophets themselves had foreseen, for all flesh, and not for a favoured few only; second, it had a specific function and mode of working. It was the result of the exaltation of the victorious Saviour, and itself resulted in presenting the Saviour to the hearts of men, the Saviour in all His fulness, as the rightful Lord of the human heart and of the human race, the Sovereign to whom all knees should bow.

Accordingly the Apostles thus baptized from on high manifested a new and remarkable power, which is thus described: "They were all filled with the Holy Ghost, and they spake the word of God with boldness."[2] The precise nature of that word is presented to us not only in their speeches, but in the results of that Spiritual ministry; and it is very instructive to notice how the phrase "the word of God" is used in the narrative of the Acts of the Apostles. The apostles regard themselves as entrusted with a διακονίᾳ τοῦ λόγου τοῦ θεοῦ, a service of the word of God, which they must prosecute with the closest attention, free from the ordinary distractions of business.[3] No one who pays attention to the subject matter of the Bible can suppose that by "the word of God" is here meant the Old Testament Scriptures. The whole story shows that what the apostles intended was, that close relation to God which would enable them to receive the things of Christ as a speaking message, and to present them with boldness, i.e., with the freedom and force of a communication coming direct from God to the people. The word of God was, to put it briefly, the witness to Jesus, as one of the earliest New Testament writers expresses it, the one "who bare witness of the word of God and of the testimony of Jesus Christ, even of all things that he saw."[4]

The two paragraphs which conclude this lecture summarize Horton's position on a subject which made him the target of numerous critics, some of whom unfairly judged him to be fanatical on the subject:

Born again, cleansed, surrendered, enlightened, they were able to receive the Word of God in their hearts, and to deliver it with astonishing results, of which the Acts of the Apostles preserve some striking examples, and to which the Epistles of St. Paul give a con-

[2] Acts 4:31.
[3] Acts 6:2, 4.
[4] Rev. 1:2, 9; 6:9; 20:4.

stant witness. Signs and wonders were wrought. God-filled men were able to bring the powers of God into contact with death and disease, with doubt and opposition, with sorrow and shame and sin, and to show that in all these things God in them was the Conqueror.

Now, without pressing any further this illustration of our theme, derived from the New Testament writings, it is legitimate to observe, and indeed no one will be inclined to dispute, that the one condition of success in all the ministry of the Word to-day is the repetition of the experience which the first apostles enjoyed. We must not allow ourselves to be misled by the wholly unscriptural dogma that what happened to the apostles must not be expected to happen to us. Their own words are a sufficient refutation of this baseless and ignoble theory: they desired that we should be imitators of them, and that we should be in all points such as they, because they knew that the continuance of the work after their death would entirely depend on other men arising—successors to the apostles indeed—who would press as they had done into the inner circle of the oracle, who would receive as they had done the authentic word of God from God Himself, and would declare this Word of God, as they had done, not in the deadness of the letter, but in the fulness of the spirit, that it might "grow and be multiplied" (Acts xii. 24), each new believer becoming a new organ of the Spirit, and each new preacher receiving the office of a prophet. In this way they had learned Christ, the perfect Word of God, not as a peculiar treasure for themselves to possess and to manipulate, but as a vast treasure open to all, a living source of life and instruction and power which every believer might humbly approach and appropriate, and every veritable preacher might administer and dispense.

Gentlemen, I would commend to you this Apostolic Succession.

III

Dr. Horton's personal life was of a singular and transparent simplicity. There seemed to be no grossness in his nature. The English journalist, Arthur Porritt, once wrote "Reginald John Campbell, John Clifford, Charles Gore and Robert Forman Horton, are sufficient repudiations for me of Mr. Bernard Shaw's dictum that 'There has been only one Christian and they hanged Him.'" Shortly after rising it was Horton's habit to begin the day by spending an hour in prayer. "Prayer as a life force," was not a theory with him but a power to be used. In the index to Albert Peel's and Sir John Marriott's biography of Dr. Horton there are sixteen references to the prayer habits of the minister of Lyndhurst Road Church. Here are certain extracts from his prayers which relate to his preaching: an affinity of which he never doubted:

My Lord, suffer me not to rest until my faith has gone the length of sharing Thy crucifixion. Teach me how to say for myself: "It is no longer I that live, but Christ that liveth in me." . . . Dost Thou crucify, or must I crucify myself? Explain to me; that on this I am set that I may be dead to the Law, to the World, to the flesh, and may live in Christ and Christ in me! Accomplish it, O Lord. (Lugano Feb. 9, 1903)

Lord, help me to gain the note of authority in preaching. May the Gospel of redeeming Grace stand out in its clear objective reality, and may I be so captivated by it and so vibrating with its message that my hearers will be constrained to yield heart and will to it for Christ's sake. (Oct. 12, 1905)

Lord, Who dost not desert us in old age, renew my strength and purpose in such a way that I may start out again in Thy service at the beginning of 1920, 1921, 1929, with as much faith and energy and hope as I did in 1880. Again Feb., 1934.[5]

Horton's study habits were as exacting as his habits of prayer. He disciplined himself to painstaking research, reading, and composition. He wrote rapidly with little need for revision. Despite his devotion to his library, where he spent long hours, he was a faithful and gentle shepherd of the flock. Pomp and ceremony were distasteful to him. He requested his people not to call him "Reverend" or "Doctor" but simply "Mr. Horton."

He loved books, music, flowers, pictures, and little children. Perhaps he remained too long in his fifty years' ministry at Hampstead. Possibly forty years in the active service with that church were sufficient. His audiences fell off in the last decade of his pastorate, although he still preached with much of his early power. Even during his four years as minister emeritus, he continued to write, lecture, and preach acceptably. His bodily strength failed gradually while his mental health still remained good.

Albert Peel and Sir John Marriott close their life story of Robert

[5] Albert Peel and J. A. R. Marriott, *Robert Forman Horton*, p. 225.

Forman Horton in a manner which must have pleased many who read these words:

> The last entry in his diary is March 29th, 1934. "United Communion. Eve of the Passion." For that communion he had prepared but was not destined to share it with the living. In the Passion (the last word he ever wrote) of his Lord he did. The 30th was Good Friday. On that day Horton "was not; he was not, for God took him." Like Enoch of old he had from boyhood "walked with God." Like Enoch "by faith he was translated that he should not see death."

Exactly fifty years earlier (March 30, 1884) Robert Horton had written to his sister: "I should like to work up to the last day of my life, and if I might choose I would die either on leaving my pulpit, or from a disease caught at the bedside of some poor soul to whom I was ministering." His wish was fulfilled. On the very last Sunday of his life he was preaching: to the sick in soul or body he had never ceased to minister, and lovingly ministered on the day before his death.

II. GEORGE ANGIER GORDON

Somewhere I read of a hard question once put to an old scholar and bibliophile. It was this: "If you had to part with all your books but were permitted to keep just one volume, what would your choice be?" I forget the old scholar's answer, but if such a question were put to me and I was limited to the autobiographies of famous preachers, I might answer: "Dr. George A. Gordon's *My Education and Religion*." What Charles E. Jefferson said of Nathaniel J. Burton's volume in this Series on Preaching could also be said of Dr. Gordon's autobiography, to wit: "a juicy book," and it is also solid, high-spirited, and delightfully human. Then too, such a stock of quaint stories! How Lincoln would have reveled in the anecdotes which sprinkle the pages of this noble man and preacher.

There is something in this saga of a Scottish lad, born in a stouthearted, devoutly religious family of Aberdeenshire, that is singularly appealing. It was such a human family withal, and quite free from the taint of the "unco' guid." The author's descriptive passages are done with deep feeling, to which is added a charm of artistry: lo! the misty mountaintops, the well-tilled valley fields; the banks and braes by gently flowing streams; the wild winds blowing in from the boisterous sea; the weird stories of ghosts, witches, and devils told around the countryside; the rural schoolteachers who heeded the scriptural injunction, "spare the rod and spoil the child," with tireless zest; the coming of the Sabbath with everybody going to church, and long, long sermons . . . the scene shifting to a brave, new world to which that "lad of parts" ventured and where, through pluck and toil, he climbed to undreamed of heights of power and influence. Such is an all too prosaic epitome of the contents of Dr. Gordon's *My Education and Religion.*

I

Ultimate Conceptions of Faith was Dr. Gordon's subject for the Yale Lectures in 1903. One of my confreres pronounced these discourses "heavy reading." Possibly so, since they deal with great themes, and he who spoke was theologian, philosopher, and a ripe scholar. Certainly Dr. Gordon's material was not "milk for babes," but "strong meat," as St. Paul put it centuries ago. Unlike Dr. Gordon's biography, which teems with humor, there is scarcely a smile in all these lectures, and of personal experiences none at all. There is a time to laugh, but not for him in a series of addresses of this character. The discussion moves along a majestic range of ideas, exposition and argumentation. As for the man himself, he looked as massive as his material; rugged of countenance, shaggy of brow, and with the frame of an athlete.

Glance at the subjects Dr. Gordon used at Yale. Do they not march in sturdy phalanx? I. The Preacher as a Theologian; II. The Quest for a Theology; III. The Categories of Faith; IV. The Individual Ultimate: Personality; V. The Social Ultimate: Humanity; VI. The Historical Ultimate: Optimism; VII. The Religious Ultimate: Jesus Christ; VIII. The Universal Ultimate: The Moral Universe; IX. The Absolute Ultimate: God.

Obviously not all this material was used by Dr. Gordon at the Divinity School. In his preface he writes:

The first and third chapters were not given as lectures; but they are deemed essential to the course of thought; and of the remaining chapters only about two thirds could be read within the reasonable limit of time prescribed. While the book was originally written for publication, and substantially as it stands, it owes its existence wholly to the invitation with which its author was honored as Lyman Beecher lecturer.

Attempting to do justice to this set of lectures, or any other series, by quoting passages at random, is pretty much like picking a few jewels from a necklace in order to impress someone with the splendor of the ornament in its shimmering entirety. Yet this is a method I am obliged to use. It was difficult with most of the lecturers, and it is more so with the theologians and philosophers, and especially so with Dr. Gordon. Therefore the excerpts will not be numerous though they may be a little longer than most of the quotations in my other chapters. From Chapter 1, this:

Two men, both preachers, have had a very wide influence on theology in this country. Channing was a preacher, and his doctrine of man, his anthropology, has had through his teaching and through the men whom he inspired an immense influence. It has been a precious influence. It has held on its way because it was truth, and because no weapon formed against it has been able to prosper. Channing's doctrine of man, his prevailing teaching about man, is the teaching of Jesus; to Channing more than to any other single influence we are indebted for the revival of the New Testament interpretation of human nature. And on the same level as a popular theologian must be placed Henry Ward Beecher. He did more than any other teacher to break up and abolish the Calvinistic Moloch. He pled for the Infinite Father of mankind when all the seminaries of the land, with their prestige, their learning, their opportunity and power, were putting first God the Sovereign, God the Moral Governor of the world. It was an immense battle, like that of David and a host of Goliaths. Men in middle life will recall the opinion industriously disseminated, that Beecher was no theologian. It was said that the great preacher was neither a scholar nor a consistent thinker. The indictment drawn by a whole generation of scholars and teachers seemed strong enough to send the great commoner into speedy and everlasting oblivion. Contrary to all expectation the professionals failed. As in the case of the shepherd lad in the day of battle, the simple apparatus of the preacher, the sling and the five smooth stones from the brook, the insight and passion and eloquence of Beecher the great pulpit humanist of his time, backed by the sympathy of the Lord of Hosts, prevailed. Greater influence upon the religious belief of the people of the United States has been exerted by none than by William Ellery Channing and Henry Ward Beecher. Both are examples of the good work which the non-professional theologian may do for his generation.

On immortality, Chapter 6:

Unquestionably death is one of the hardest facts with which optimism has to deal. By itself it seems to me fatal. Death as a finality is the supreme sarcasm of life. Everything withers in its presence; its shadow darkens the universe. It involves a contradiction of individual aptitude and desire such as to take the heart out of life. It carries with it a sacrifice of affection that must, on the supposition of its finality, either paralyze or brutalize mankind. It is an engine for the destruction of human values and high moral worth so absolute in its operation as to create the denial of God, and to carry it into overwhelming power. Death as a finality is the *reductio ad absurdum* of all faith in the moral character of the universe, the exposure of the futility of optimism, the terrible irony that turns to vanity and nothingness man's best effort and spirit, the brutal power that quenches in the one black abyss of oblivion the treason of Judas and the love of Jesus. The complete statement of the negation of God and the worth of existence involved in death as a finality opens the door out of this horror. The point of extreme distress is the point of saving help. The annihilation of our human world cannot without protest be permitted. The conception that involves this annihilation cannot be valid. Whatever inverts the order of the world is thereby branded with discredit.

And from the profound Chapter 9 on Deism and Theism:

Deism interprets the universe according to the same human standard; but the man of deism is more of a man than the pale abstraction of atheism. The deistic man is an individual being with intelligence, moral feeling, and will; and therefore the God of deism is a thinker, somewhat of a lover, and an eternal doer. He is the individual human being plus infinity. He is not the mere shadow of reality, a will emptied of all purpose, divorced from all intelligence, and reduced to blind power. He is living and real. Both from the scientific and philosophic points of view deism is a vast improvement upon materialism or atheism. The human standard, the deistic man, is real and so far undistorted; and to a given limit deism is true to its own principle of procedure. Man is the guide to God; and man is an individual being. . . . Still deism is an inconsistent position. It is a half-way house between atheism and Christian theism. Like atheism, deism employs only an emaciated man. The deistic man is a Melchizedek. He has no ancestry and no posterity. He is an individual thread taken out of the social fabric in which he is found, and in which his life has its meaning. Eliminate from man his social nature, and the result is a part and not the whole, a residuum that is not man. And the God of deism is conceived in accordance with this human Melchizedek. He is an infinite Melchizedek. He is not a father, he is not a son, he is not a holy community in himself. Such a God is unintelligible save through his human type. Deism is constructed upon a monstrous man, and Unitarianism when taken at its word is built upon the same foundation.

Christian theism tries to be faithful to the whole man in its endeavor through man to find God. With atheism and deism it is eager to pass over the incidental and to fix attention only upon the essential in man. But against atheism it keeps together will and intelligence and real being; against deism it refuses to separate the individual man and the social man. Man is man only in society. Parenthood, sonhood, and the essential social relations are part of man's being. Without them he could not be; in them he is what he is. And it is precisely this social man who needs God, for whom God has moral meaning. This man with ancestry, with posterity, with a life that is a life in humanity, seeks for an adequate foundation of moral life, and for the eternal ground of it. If God is man plus infinity it must be the social man carried to his highest. Eternal fatherhood, eternal sonhood, eternal love must be the truth of the Godhead; there must be in God the archetype of humanity. The whole man is man in society, and if the human principle is faithfully used, the whole God must be a God with an ineffable society in himself.

II

George A. Gordon and Phillips Brooks were close friends, and mutually admirers each of the other. Francis G. Peabody was another intimate, and dedicates one of his books to the minister of New Old South Church in these lines:

> Still at your post you stand, high in the lighthouse tower,
> Guarding the way of life, speaking the word of power;
> Resolute, tender, wise, full of the love of truth,
> Tending the flame of Christ as it marks the channel of youth.

Mr. Arthur Porritt tells this interesting event in Dr. Gordon's life:

New Old South Church had been seeking a minister for some time, when the name of a young preacher somewhere upstate was mentioned—this was in 1884—as possible minister. George A. Gordon—for it was he—agreed to preach "with a view," and the widow of the previous minister of Old South, who made it her duty to make every minister who preached there feel at home, had her daughter meet him at the station and convoy him to his host's house. Naturally she was eager to hear all about the young preacher-candidate, and when her daughter got back from welcoming the visitor the mother asked: "What is he like?" The daughter threw up her hands: "Oh, Mother," she replied, "he's a regular micky—" (New England equivalent for our word hobbledehoy). But uncouth appearance notwithstanding, George A. Gordon was invited to New Old South and accepted the invitation. In due course too, the young lady who had called him a "micky" became Mrs. George Gordon.

Dr. Boynton Merrill, minister of First Congregational Church, Columbus, Ohio, and Dr. Gordon's fourth and last associate, thus wrote of his one-time Chief:

I loved him, and he stamped my ministry with dear things I shall always cherish. He was the scholar and the orator: in both of these he was dedicated to the cause of Christ.

He was powerful in the pulpit, of course, but far more effective when he preached from his little card with brief outline than when he used his manuscript. I find, still, that to read him is a great intellectual and spiritual experience; for, in his way and field, I believe he has not been equaled in this country.

He was a beautiful guide and friend to young men. Students were his idealized hope of the world. They came by the thousands. How many got his personal ear I would not know—but those who did must have had an unforgettable half hour.

He wrote beautiful and dearly cherished letters to the bereaved and on all sorts of personal occasions. They were brief but beautifully phrased and obviously lovingly sincere.

"My beloved Associate" was the way Dr. Gordon referred to Boynton Merrill.

III. CHARLES EDWARD JEFFERSON

Some years ago in writing an estimate of Dr. Jefferson, who was living at the time, I expressed the opinion that he was the most envied of American preachers by the preaching fraternity generally. I stand by that opinion although Dr. Jefferson has now gone to his long home. I hasten to explain that in using the word "envied" in this connection I would drain the word of all sinister implications. What I meant to convey was that a great cloud of witnesses, ministers of all denominations, in high and lowly parishes throughout America, looked upon Dr. Jefferson with awe and admiration; perhaps *wonderment* is the fitting word to describe what was in my mind. For I was one of this goodly company. I kept nearby my desk the choice little books, *The Minister as a Shepherd, The Minister as a Prophet,* and *Quiet Hints to Growing Preachers,* the last described by Joseph Fort Newton as "a series of familiar talks in the study, telling things that laymen need not hear." It was a day to canonize when the Doctor's Yale lectures, *The Building of the Church,* arrived, and I dropped everything to read it through at one sitting, only to take it up to read again and again through the years to come.

I cherish the memory of the one and only time I heard Dr. Jefferson in his pulpit at Broadway Tabernacle. It was a night service in early spring as I now recall. The church was comfortably filled, and he preached on "Giants and Grasshoppers," an odd theme, yet he put into it much wisdom, a cutting wit, and a dash of pleasantry, the latter to my surprise, since it was, I think, exceptional, though in this I may be mistaken.

Dr. Jefferson in his day was described by the New York newspapers as austere, a Puritan, and given to setting up exacting standards for those who would follow the Great Galilean. There is some truth in this inadequate description, but certainly not all the truth. Dr. Jefferson was a Puritan in character and Christian ideals. A penetrating seriousness is traceable through all his preaching and his published works. The King's business requires seriousness as well as haste; life itself is serious, and perhaps no Christian minister surpassed Dr. Jefferson in the high seriousness he brought to his preaching mission.

"They err who think him stern, cold, or unbending; though as he sits in the pulpit, his appearance gives one an impression of firmness, if not austerity, but as he begins to speak his rugged face is illumined by an inner brightness, and one discovers that it is the firmness of strength, of poise, of serenity suffused by a great gentleness, and touched by that elusive magnetic quality, so impossible to define." So Dr. Joseph Fort Newton wrote in 1923, after listening to a sermon by Jefferson in his Broadway pulpit.

Dr. Jefferson was a man of the study and he achieved his terse epigrammatic style by the hardest kind of work. His habits of preparation, as told me by a former assistant, were rigid. He shut himself up with his books and away from annoying disturbances. I gather from those who should know that, while courteous and kind, Dr. Jefferson was not ordinarily given to lighter social affairs, such as the delightful occasions when preachers foregather, converse at length, and relax in joyous camaraderie. One does not think of Dr. Jefferson as "a clubbable man." Arthur Porritt, the English journalist, in his delightful *More and More of Memories*, tells of being hospitably entertained by Dr. Jefferson in his New York apartments, and comments thus: "A more gracious host could not be imagined, though Dr. Jefferson rarely entertained any one, and had the reputation in New York of isolating himself, even from his ministerial *confrères*." Perhaps here we have a secret of the Jefferson sermonic excellence.

Dr. Jefferson's "occasional preaching" was superb. Returning to Arthur Porritt, who was adept in reporting important religious meetings and expert in his sketches of famous preachers, here is a paragraph referring to Dr. Jefferson too valuable to overlook. He wrote:

Dr. Charles E. Jefferson, who preached the inaugural sermon at the Copenhagen Conference of The World Alliance for Promoting Friendship Through the Churches, was a shy, retiring man, austere in appearance, a New England Puritan in outlook; but a very charming and affectionate man when once his rather chilly reserve had been penetrated. No sermon, I imagine, preached in our time ever had such international publicity as that of "The Spirit of Christ" which he preached in Roskilde Cathedral. It was translated into about twenty languages and sent by delegates at Copenhagen to the religious newspapers in twenty-four countries they represented, and the editors generously found space for a sermon well worthy of a very great occasion.[1]

One could go on almost endlessly quoting from competent witnesses of Dr. Jefferson's pulpit power, but it is time to consider his *The Building of the Church*, one of a dozen in the Series which stand out and above the others like mighty oaks above their fellows.

Dr. Jefferson approaches the preacher through the Church, as Dr. Fosdick does through the Bible, and Dr. Sclater through public worship. It is lamentably true that ministers generally do not exalt the Church, the body of Christ, the community of believers, the ground and pillar of truth, with anything like the noble adequacy which it deserves. For the Church is greater than the best of preaching, greater than its liturgy however impressive, greater than anything we usually associate with its life. The Church is all of these plus something still greater and grander. "The Church Building Idea in the New Testament" is the subject of the first lecture, and in the discussion of St. Paul's idea of the Church, occurs this typical passage which fairly shouts to be quoted:

From that hour [his conversion] to his death Paul knew but two sovereign themes—one was Jesus Christ, the other was the Church. The only sin whose memory burned like fire in his heart was the sin which he had committed against the Church. When you find him with his face in the dust, it is his persecution of the Church which he is bewailing. When he declares he is the Chief of Sinners and that he is not worthy to be called an apostle, it is because the recollection of his sin against the Church rolls over him like a flood. When you seek him at his highest, jubilant and enraptured, you find him thinking of the Church. It is a subject never absent from his mind. He ransacks his vocabulary in search of figures by which adequately to image forth his idea of the Church's character and mission. Sometimes he thinks of it as the household of faith—the family of Jehovah. At other times he sees it as the temple of God, the very seat and shrine of the Eternal. Again it presents itself to him as the body of

[1] Arthur Porritt, *More and More of Memories*, p. 197.

Christ, the organism in which Christ's spirit operates, the instrument by which the soul of Christ works. Still again it rises before him beautiful and radiant as a woman in the hour of her greatest loveliness, the bride of the world's Redeemer. Now and again he sees it lifting itself—superbly as the pillar and ground of the truth, holding aloft in the eyes of the nations the mystery of Godliness—Jesus. ... To regret that Paul has so much to say about the Church is to repine that Christianity is not other than it is.

One is at a loss which to admire the more: the faultless diction of the quotation, or the resolute way in which the Apostle's conception of the Church is stated so fully and in so small a compass. Dr. Jefferson's manner of speech was one long triumph of assiduity over verbosity.

This Church Building idea in the New Testament persists throughout the series and is developed, enriched, and illustrated by a master of assemblies.

The other chapter headings are as alluring as the first, possibly more so because of their practical connotations, thus: "Building the Brotherhood"; "Building the Individual"; "Building Moods and Tempers"; "Building Thrones"; "Building the Holy Catholic Church"; "Building the Plan"; and "The Building of the Builder." The minister who can look at this list of topics and not get excited has missed his calling. In short, Jefferson's Yale lectures are among the twelve "greats" of the Course.

My copy of *The Building of the Church* shows the marks of usage. In the book are two letters from Dr. Jefferson, one thanking me for a piece I wrote about him, and the other in reply to a letter in which I inquired as to his manner of pulpit preparation when I was gathering material for my *American Preachers of Today*. These letters are the soul of courtesy and brotherliness, but I displeased him when in the book referred to above I wrote this sentence: "Here is an outline of a sermon by Dr. Jefferson prepared for his own use, taken into the pulpit and only glanced at now and then in the course of a half-hour's delivery." He said this was not "scientific," that he did not take notes into the pulpit. So be it. I'd rather be chided by Dr. Jefferson for that small error, than to be flattered by almost any other preacher of like fame.

To my beloved Detroit fellow minister, the Reverend Roger

Eddy Treat, D.D., one-time associate of Dr. Jefferson, I am indebted for the following critique of his honored Chief, which he prepared at my request:

Few would question the fact that Dr. Charles E. Jefferson was one of the greatest of the American preachers throughout all the years of his ministry at the Broadway Tabernacle. People who expected him to deliver the spectacular, scintillating, pyrotechnic sermon, commonly associated with "pulpit orators," were certain to be disappointed. More than a few persons have testified to this fact. A Connecticut lawyer-judge once told me of going to the Tabernacle to hear Dr. Jefferson for the first time and wondering how the preacher had won his wide acclaim. There was so little of the dramatic in the man, so much directness and simplicity in his manner, as well as in the sermon itself, as to make such a chance and curious visitor wonder how or why the preacher had become so famous. The one thing that then impressed the stranger from Connecticut was the fact that the sermon filled almost an hour! Dr. Jefferson did not believe in treating high themes with either indifference or brevity.

But on looking back across forty-five years of acquaintance with him, I can see that this "Prophet of Broadway" never dealt with any person or event superficially or carelessly. Dr. Jefferson took all his living, as he took all his preaching, seriously. Even when he played tennis, he put no more effort into the game than was nicely calculated to meet its requirements in victorious fashion. There was nothing wasted and nothing withheld. Here you had the man who had spent all of his conscious years disciplining his body, mind and spirit in order to make them obedient, effective and worthy instruments of high religious purpose. All his thoughts, as well as all his personal habits reflected this disciplined control. I never saw him needlessly excited, although many times I have sensed that his feelings were intense. But they were always held in leash by a level head and an iron will. Thus, Dr. Jefferson was free from the erratic and the fanatical and foolish. His ideas, like his words, were like skillfully fashioned and carefully chosen arrows, sped by strong bow and almost perfect aim to their appointed mark with the ease of effortless artistry.

Dr. Jefferson got his sermon-ideas, sermon-seeds, he called them, as do all preachers, from many sources. But beyond many, he spoke "out of life to life." He wrote painstakingly during much of his ministry. Never, however, did I see him take a manuscript with him into the pulpit until failing memory forced him to do so or the sermon contained facts and figures calling for absolute accuracy. He always spoke of his ability to do "mental-writing," as with an invisible stylus upon the tablet of his memory. The opening and closing sentences of his sermon, at least, were worked out in full and final detail. How important it was, he said, to win your congregation from the first syllable and then to know just how, as well as when, to stop! So completely did Dr. Jefferson master this method of sermon prepapation and delivery as to be able to dictate both of his Sunday sermons to a stenographer on Monday precisely as they had been preached the preceding morning and evening.

For simplicity of structure and directness of delivery, Dr. Jefferson's sermons will long be remembered by those of us who heard enough of them to sense where their great power lay. A minimum of gestures and movements characterized his delivery. So frequently the preacher's hands were folded upon the top of the open Bible. Who of his congregations ever heard him shout, even when his soul was burning at white heat? Yet the voice was full and strong, speaking crystal-clear ideas in one- or two-syllable words, which were never slurred and never clipped. And throughout all of the discourse ran the red thread of an outline, tied inseparably to the text, with inexorable reasonableness, logic and appeal, which you might have expected from one who started to be a trial lawyer, became a minister and was one of the great expositors and defenders of the faith and a spokesman for God in our times.

Selah!

IV. FRANK WAKELEY GUNSAULUS

The persuasive eloquence of Henry Ward Beecher, William M. Taylor, and Matthew Simpson returned to the Yale Lectureship in 1910, when Dr. Frank W. Gunsaulus gave eight addresses on *The Minister and the Spiritual Life*. Those who heard these lectures saw a mountain-of-a-man stand up to pour forth a tide of stirring oratory, warm, tender, and thrilling. Some of his sentences were hard to parse but easy to understand. There was poetry in his prose, music in the lilt of his rolling periods, and an artistry of color spread upon a huge canvas by a master word painter.

Frank Wakeley Gunsaulus

I

The comment of Professor Louis O. Brastow, in his *Modern Pulpit*, on Dr. Gunsaulus' manner of speech is worth noting. "His style of preaching," says Dr. Brastow, "is more impassioned, both in rhetoric and oratory, than that of Dr. Storrs, and one may venture to suggest that he discloses the beneficent results of early nurture in the Methodist Church. His familiarity with poetic literature and his own aptitude for poetic expression are marked, and he may be called much more of a rhetorician than an orator." This is an illuminating comment, yet it is not always easy to say where the rhetorician ceases to be such and becomes the orator. That there is a distinction I admit, but most rhetoricians are orators. Surely Ingersoll was both and likewise Gunsaulus.

Joseph Fort Newton, himself a preacher of rare gifts, had spent much of his literary life analyzing and appraising preachers and their homiletic art, and he had this to say of Dr. Gunsaulus:

Poet, artist, scholar, educator, author, statesman, and above all, a God-endowed preacher whose mysticism was at once the inspiration and illumination of his multifarious activity—it is a story of which America ought to be proud. He was the first citizen of his city—if not the most distinguished—the incarnation of its genius and the prophecy of its future, uniting the fine, firm qualities of the Puritan with the glow, color, and tropical richness of Spain. He also joined the skyey vision of the poet with the practical acumen of a man of affairs. Words are the daughters of earth, deeds are the sons of God, and both were wedded in his life.

Unfortunately for me, I failed to hear Gunsaulus until the closing years of his life and then not in a sermon but a lecture. His voice I can never forget. It had a haunting quality, the sound, at times, of mating birds, and again, the sonorous roll of thunder, peal followed peal. I observed as he came upon the platform that he limped as he walked, and I recalled how that limp came about.

It was in those earlier years at Chicago when he had his church with the great downtown Sunday night service; his duties at the Armour Institute; responding to myriad calls for lectures, writing, much traveling; and the result, the man of iron broke. For six months he lay in agony. No sermons came from the preacher then, no books; only a poem. That poem revealed his intrepid and unconquerable spirit:

> I care not that the furnace fire of pain
> Laps round my life and burns alway;
> I only care to know that not in vain
> The fierce heats touch me throughout night and day.[1]

II

Dr. Gunsaulus' Yale lectures make a good-sized book, just under four hundred pages. The lectures are full, detailed, solid, and must have required an hour in delivery. To say they are eloquent seems both trite and superfluous. How could they be otherwise since Gunsaulus wrote and delivered them? They classify naturally with those of Beecher, Taylor, Brooks, and Simpson in the same series. The Titan is at home with the Olympians, and *The Royalty of the Pulpit* was in evidence from first to last.

The names of the great characters about whom he lectured so ably appear in these pages: Savonarola, Wendell Phillips, Gladstone, Lincoln, and the preachers too, whom he knew and honored—Beecher, Bushnell, Taylor, Brooks, Spurgeon, Simpson, Martineau, and Joseph Parker, comrades of the High Calling; they are all here, woven into the tapestry of his rhetoric, vivid, now full of fire; again, gentle and tender, a shepherd of the flock.

For a characteristic Gunsaulian passage take this one which, even with the huge form, flashing eyes, and marvelous voice missing, vibrates deep chords of emotion:

Once on a doleful day, when the great President's soul was sorely burdened, and various members of the cabinet were looking in vain for him in the White House at Washington, Mr. Lincoln's little boy, called Tad, came into the presence of Secretary Chase and said: "I want my father." The boy was in trouble for he had been badly used by a belligerent child in a physical contest. Now suppose Chase, with his Olympian forehead, had said to him, with the patronage which we sometimes visit cruelly upon those who would be helped, albeit without circumstance and the pomp of learning, "My little fellow, I will tell the Chief Executive of the nation, who will soon prove himself to me, his servant, as the master of unparalleled diffi-

---

[1] Joseph Fort Newton, *Some Living Masters of the Pulpit*, pp. 250-251.

culties in finance, that you wish him." It would have been a true statement, but the boy would have said to the Secretary of the Treasury again, "I want my father." Little Tad encounters Seward with a cry straight from his heart, "I want my father." Suppose Seward had said, "I will get for you the most remarkable diplomatic mind who ever warded off from a young nation in sore straits, the attack of the British Empire. The Secretary of State would have told the truth. The boy, however, wipes the blood and the dirt away and says, "I want my father." The redoubtable and proud Stanton, Secretary of War, hears this boy's appeal and tells him, "I will get for you the Commander in Chief of the Armies of the United States." Stanton knew Abraham Lincoln in this capacity. He was telling the truth about Lincoln, but it was not the boy's truth. Lincoln's child's truth was heard in the sob, "I want my *father*."

Could anything of the kind be more complete, touching, and beautiful?

During the Columbian Exposition held in Chicago in 1893 a visitor heard Dr. Gunsaulus preach from the text in Exodus 4:4, "And the Lord said unto Moses, Put forth thine hand and take it by the tail. And he put forth his hand and it (the serpent) became a rod in his hand." Now what kind of a sermon could be made out of such a text? The big man in the pulpit knew how to handle it. "The fleshly appetites and hot passions of a man, like snakes, coil, hiss, and wriggle at his feet, until at the command of God, he grasps them firmly and they lose their power to do him harm." To write this down is one thing; to hear this powerful preacher deal with this subject, and to see him in action in a mighty drama—aye, that is another and a far different thing—a master pulpit genius preaching an unforgettable sermon.

Passages, even outlines, often thinly veiled, from Dr. Gunsaulus' sermons, are woven skillfully into these lectures, some of them from his volume *Paths to Power*; for instance, the famous one on Andrew and Simon Peter, thus: "There are three stages in the process with Andrew, and there will be these three for you and me:

(1) *Finding.* "He first findeth his own brother Simon." (S. John 1:41)
(2) *Saying.* "And he saith unto him, We have found the Messias." (S. John 1:41)
(3) *Bringing.* "And he brought him to Jesus." (S. John 1:42)

These three points he expounds at length; in truth most of this powerful sermon appears in Lecture Six on "The Spiritual Life and the Minister's Message." It is an evangelistic sermon preached with zest and conviction, and in the closing section of this sermon the preacher gives some sound advice:

Never surrender that advantage when you go out to bring Simon. Never drop the weapon of your fact to argue with your bird on the wing, but fire! Skepticism is like a bright lawyer with a poor case; it is better on argument than on facts. Evangelism, true and thorough, is not a debater, but a witness; it does not argue, it testifies. Sad is the caricature which appears, when any man who has such a fact as "the Messias," engages to debate Simon to Jesus. It was the factualness of the man once blind which counted in widening the Gospel's realm of victory. . . . This one thing I know, that whereas I was blind, now I see.

III

Many are the stories of Dr. Gunsaulus that go the rounds of ministerial groups—stories of his gifts of speech and also of his generous nature. Two are worthy of repeating here. Dr. Gunsaulus delivered the funeral oration over Eugene Field, the poet. He and Field were "rare book brothers," according to Opie Read in his autobiography entitled, *I Remember*. The poet and the preacher loved rare bindings, and set store upon errors in first editions. Read wrote: "Often a song, far off somewhere in the night, brings back to me the first words of the memorable oration. Gunsaulus raised his clasped hands, looked down upon the coffin, and burst forth into a chant: 'O, thou melodious dust!' "

When Charles Clayton Morrison was the youthful minister of a small church in Chicago he engaged Dr. Gunsaulus to preach the evening sermon on the day the building was dedicated. The church was crowded, and the sermon one of the famed preacher's best, and the congregation sat almost breathless under the spell of the impassioned eloquence. The sermon over, Dr. Morrison took his pulpit guest into the pastor's study and bade him be seated. After thanking Dr. Gunsaulus profusely for coming and the noble sermon he had preached, young Morrison said: "Dr. Gunsaulus, I am authorized by my official board to pay you any sum you may name, the treasurer is waiting to make out the check." The big man eased his lame leg, settled back comfortably in his chair and beamed upon the young preacher as he replied:

"Morrison, yours is a young, struggling church. You have plenty of places to put money. Give me the pleasure of making this small contribution of my time and sermon to your church. I'd love to do it."

So spoke a gentleman of the School of Christ!

V. JOHN HENRY JOWETT

"Mr. Jowett," said his principal, the formidable Dr. A. M. Fairbairn, when this promising student had preached in "sermon class," "your gestures are most ungraceful. It seems as if you have a semi-circular row of lighted candles in front of you which you proceed to extinguish, moving your hand from the candle at one end to the candle at the other. Mr. Jowett, we must strive to avoid all mannerisms."

That was good advice, and "Mr. Jowett" followed it so assiduously that "he became," to quote Ernest H. Jeffs, London journalist, "the master of a perfect pulpit manner—graceful, easy, dignified—and with his gift of language improved by study into a mastery like that of a trained musician over his keys or strings." Then Jeffs adds this important sentence: "Theologically, although that was a period of intense unrest in religious thought, Jowett stood like a rock on the enlightened Evangelicalism of the ministry under which he had grown up."

Grace of manner and beauty of speech do not always go hand in hand with a sturdy, unabashed, rocklike proclamation of Biblical doctrines, but they certainly did so in the case of "Jowett of Birmingham." He was one of the most talked and written about, praised and admired preachers in Great Britain and, indeed, in the English-speaking world, and which is more significant, his popularity never knew even as much as a temporary eclipse in a ministry of thirty-four years. This is a record achieved by only a few men of the modern pulpit. In England, Spurgeon and Parker surpassed it, as did Beecher and Brooks in this country. As for the "runners-up," they are an elect company on both sides of the Atlantic, but as for the pinnacle, how few retain popularity to the end.

It was inevitable that Jowett should have his critics. Who among the elect escaped? Not Beecher, or Spurgeon, or Brooks, or any other man who preaches the Word. "To some who heard Jowett," writes Mr. Jeffs, "the art seemed too obvious, the technique almost too perfectly finished. Others gave themselves up freely to the appreciation of the finished canvas. Jowett's art lay in the exquisite use of words and in the infinite variety of his illustrations." We have had no one in the modern American pulpit who resembled Jowett, although Joseph Fort Newton approached him in the chaste beauty of his sermonic style. Fosdick, he of the grand yet down to earth manner, was capable of more powerful and more daring speech; Hillis was more pictorial but of less substance; Gunsaulus more oratorically impressive, and Buttrick more intense. Jefferson, on the other hand, would be placed above Jowett by some because of the rich substance of his sermons and the deep seriousness of the man as he gave his "finest wheat" in a style so crisp, so laconic, and so telling, that no one has been able to imitate it successfully.

Why go on? Although the subject is enchanting to preachers the world over, one star differs from another in glory; besides, there is glory enough to go around. Dr. Jowett was not merely a pulpit star, but a constellation which shone not only on Sunday but weekdays as well. Wherever he preached he strengthened saints and humbled sinners. Behold Birmingham's Carr's Lane Church! He found much there when he went to it, and when he left it was a stronger church than ever before. This, good brethren of the Majestic Fraternity, this is the acid test!

Dr. Jowett lectured at Yale in 1912, when he was in the second year of his ministry at Fifth Avenue Presbyterian Church, New York City. He was the most publicized preacher in America at the time, his name on myriad lips. Almost every Sunday ministers were in his congregation who had journeyed from afar to hear him. Editor Ernest Jeffs, who knew him intimately, says of his New York pastorate: "Surrounded by the aura of public curiosity he declined utterly to play up the part of a great public figure. He preached the gospel of the Grace of God to his New York plutocrats just as he had preached it to his middle-class independents at Birmingham. From the spectacular point of view this was a disappointing ministry; but of its real success and happiness and influence there is no manner of doubt."

Dr. Jowett called his Yale Lectures *The Preacher and His Life Work,* and delivered a series of solid material which, in form and beauty of phrasings, was in keeping with his vast reputation. The titles of the lectures are models of their kind, being short and clear. Moreover, the subtitles, which are scriptural texts and italicized, add to the attractiveness of the title page: I. The Call to Be a Preacher, *"Separated unto the Gospel of God";* II. The Perils of the Preacher, *"Lest I myself should be a castaway";* III. The Preacher's Themes, *"Feed my sheep";* IV. The Preacher in His Study, *"A wise master builder";* V. The Preacher in His Pulpit, *"The service of the sanctuary";* VI. The Preacher in the Home, *"From house to house";* VII. The Preacher as a Man of Affairs, *"Like unto a merchantman."*

Unlike many of his predecessors in the Course, Dr. Jowett, did not take up any time to explain his embarrassment at having to follow the "Princes of the Church" who had preceded him, though it is understandable and proper enough so to speak. Instead, he plunged into the first lecture with a prefatory word of a different character, to wit:

I have been in the Christian ministry for over twenty years. I love my calling. I have a glowing delight in its services. I am conscious of no distractions in the shape of competitors for my strength and allegiance. I have but one passion and I have lived for it—the absorbingly arduous, yet glorious work of proclaiming the grace of our Lord and Savior, Jesus Christ. I stand before you, therefore, as a fellow-laborer, who has been over a certain part of the field, and my simple purpose is to dip into the pool of my experiences to record certain practical judgments and discoveries, and to offer counsels and warnings which have been born out of my own successes and defeats.

So he was off to a good start. And for the "good ending" he made, peruse his final paragraph:

My brethren, you are going forth in a big world to confront big things. There is "the pestilence that walketh in darkness," and there is "the destruction that wasteth at noonday." There is success and there is failure, and there is sin and sorrow and death. And of all pathetic plights surely the most pathetic is that of a minister moving about this grim field of varied necessity, professing to be a physician, but carrying in his wallet no balms, no cordials, no caustics to meet the clamant needs of men. But of all privileged callings surely the most privileged is that of Greatheart facing the highways of life, carrying with him all that is needed by fainting, bruised and broken pilgrims, perfectly confident in Him "Whom he has believed." Brethren, your calling is very holy. Your work is very difficult. Your Savior is very mighty. And the joy of the Lord will be your strength.

Dr. Jowett seemed to be aware of that lively curiosity his brethren of the ministry show respecting the manner in which master preachers go about "getting up a sermon." The passage showing this awareness occurs in his lecture on "The Preacher in His Study," for here we are permitted to see Jowett in his study preparing to preach:

If I may give you my own experience, I have been following this practice for many years. I ask—how would Newman regard this subject? How would Spurgeon approach it? How would Dale deal with it? By what road would Bushnell come up to it? Where would Maclaren take his stand to look at it? Where would Alexander Whyte lay hold of it? You may think this a very presumptuous practice, and I have no doubt some of my conclusions would horrify the saintly men whose heart-paths I have presumed to trace. But here is the value of the practice. It broadens and enriches my own conceptions of the theme, even though I may not have correctly interpreted the other man's point of view. I have looked at the theme through many windows, and some things appear which I should never have seen had I confined myself to the windows of my own mind and heart. . . . But while I am advising you to consult other minds, I must further advise you not to be overwhelmed by them. Reverently respect your own individuality. . . . Without being angular believe in your own angle, and work upon the assumption that it is through your own unrepeated personality that God purposes that your light should break upon the world.

If anyone has thought of Jowett as a preacher only, and not as a shepherd of the flock, he has but to read the chapter on "The

Preacher in the Home," to discover that this "pulpit-great" was also faithful in his parish calls. After reciting the account of a visit to one of his prominent members who was "giving way to drink," and the struggle it cost him, and the good results of the visit, he says:

Gentlemen, it seemed as though I could preach a sermon and never meet a devil; but as soon as I began to take my sermon to the individual the streets were thick with devils, and I had to be like the armed man in *The Pilgrim's Progress* who, after he had received and given many wounds to those that attempted to keep him out, cut his way through them all and pressed forward into the palace! But I will say again, "The fear of man bringeth a snare."

Did Dr. Jowett, this man of the faultless pulpit style of speech, ever fail? That is a fair question. The likelihood is that not only he, but other masters of pulpit discourse sometimes fell below their best and were only too conscious of the painful fact. Mr. Ernest H. Jeffs, who was a reporter of sermons and a writer about preachers, in a sketch of the Reverend J. D. Jones of England (Jones of Bournemouth, he was called), makes this statement: "I have heard Parker fail, and Parker knew he was failing and fought desperately to retrieve his failure. I have known Horne to be too noisy, and Jowett too artificial, and Inge too casual, and 'Dick' Sheppard too childlike, but I have never known 'J.D.' to fail in the presence of an audience." Now "J.D." was a manuscript preacher par excellence. Does that fact help to explain his unique record?

Joseph Fort Newton told of a day when Dr. Gunsaulus preached for him in City Temple, London, and made a "gorgeous failure." Well now, that is the way every preacher who fails would like to fail: "gorgeously." Actually, when most of us fail in the pulpit the Lord knows it, our people know it, and we know it ourselves by "certain infallible signs." What happened, we resolved, must not occur again, and so take fresh courage for another try.

In the pulpit Dr. Jowett rarely drew a smile from his audience, but in a social circle or among his preacher-friends he told or listened to a story with relish. In his letters he was often delightfully witty. A capital example of epistolary gayety is in a letter he wrote to a friend after being made a Doctor of Divinity by the University of Edinburgh:

Eh! it's grand to be a doctor. The "elevation" it gives you is fine. Since I got it the Malverns have shrunk into molehills. As for the Welsh hills, I "havena seen 'em." Everybody seems to be looking at me, I walk wi' such dignity! and all so natural like. The D.D. gets at once into your legs; they say it mounts at last into your "nut." ... Meanwhile I have been thinking of my deacons,—words fail me! They look like ants! I am just amazed at the revelation. For fifteen years I've been deluding myself thinking they were men; man, they're just midges. Doctors of Divinity call them "ephemera," and that's just what they look like.[1]

Those of us who went through a revival with Billy Sunday find ourselves strangely and snickeringly reminiscent when we read Dr. Jowett's comments after attending one of Billy's meetings. It is told in his biography by Arthur Porritt. Addressing an old friend in Birmingham, Dr. Jowett wrote:

As I have just been to hear Billy Sunday, the cultured evangelist, and as he addressed me as a "white-livered black-hearted mug," I think I'll pass the compliment on to you. His tabernacle holds twenty thousand, and the ministers are penned in an enclosure immediately on Bill's right, and as he knows where we are, he fires his torpedoes at us before we even show a periscope. He lets go a shot at us and then retires across his huge platform making silent nods at us. At one moment, observing one or two of us looking slightly resentful, he raced toward us shouting, "I don't care whether your collar's at the front or back." That was too much for me, and if I hadn't a collar around my neck the style of a Jaeger belt [Dr. Jowett wore habitually a wing collar] one of Billy's audience would have gone to pieces and would have been seen no more.[2]

Dr. Jowett returned to England in 1918, and was welcomed by the great of state and church. He was invited to preach in Durham Cathedral and accepted—"the first time since the days of Cromwell that a nonconformist had been admitted to a cathedral pulpit." He led the crusade of the British Free Church for world peace, and his voice was raised in other important councils. It was a new Jowett, writes Jeffs, "who had left his quiet study for the dust of the arena at the call of great issues in a crucial hour. . . .

---

[1] Ernest H. Jeffs, *Princes of the Modern Pulpit in England*, p. 65.
[2] Arthur Porritt, *John Henry Jowett*, pp. 246, 247.

Only for a moment were we given a glimpse of the massiveness of the pillars around which he had delighted to carve the 'lilywork of his exquisite meditations.'" But the time was short. He was stricken in the midst of his activities, resigned his pastorate of Westminster Chapel in 1922, and on December 19, 1923, at the age of sixty, Dr. Jowett died.

VI. CHARLES HENRY PARKHURST

Those of us who were reading the newspapers along about 1892 to 1896 will recall how often Dr. Parkhurst's name and picture appeared in them. He was then engaged in his spectacular fight against crime in New York City, which meant an assault upon Tammany and the accumulated political power it represented. The Doctor, who always wore clerical attire, was regularly caricatured in *Puck* and *Judge*, famous periodicals in those years. Later he became a columnist for the Hearst newspapers, which provoked criticism from some of his clerical brethren; but the noted Presbyterian was used to that and probably thrived on it.

Dr. Parkhurst was a New Englander by birth, a graduate of Amherst, and spent some years in the University at Halle, Germany. He was ordained to the Congregational ministry in 1874, and after a six year pastorate at Lenox, Massachusetts, entered on his long and conspicuous ministry at Madison Square Presbyterian Church, New York City; thirty-eight years the active pastor and fifteen years emeritus, fifty-three years in all.

In *Our Fight with Tammany*, Dr. Parkhurst tells how he came to assume the presidency of "The Society for the Prevention of Crime" in New York City, and to carry on a vigorous and relentless campaign against organized and officially supported vice in the metropolis. "Somewhat prior to my first connection with the Society," he writes, "I had become knowing to a condition of things throughout the city of which during all the years of my residence in town up to that date I had been ignorant, and of which, except for a special cause, I should probably have continued ignorant." Thus it happened that Dr. Parkhurst had the distinction of being the most widely known preacher-reformer in the Beecher Lectureship.

I

The Pulpit and the Pew was Dr. Parkhurst's subject at Yale and, contrary to the expectations of some, he kept close to his subject, with but one lecture devoted to "Ministerial Responsibility for Civic Conditions," and another to the "Responsibility of the Church to the Life of the Town." Not only so, but he does not make as much of his long and hard conflict with the powers of evil in New York City as his hearers might have expected. If he did not play down the part he had in improving the moral climate of his city, he certainly did not play it up, which fact redounds to his credit, since he might have done so *in extenso*, and few would have found fault.

The Parkhurst diction is terse and crisp, with short sentences abounding. Proficient as a manuscript speaker, he used it effectively at Yale, never permitting the pages to get in his way. Perhaps his experience as a daily columnist had something to do with his ability to condense; certainly he wasted no space foolishly. It required but one hundred and ninety-five pages for Dr. Parkhurst to complete his eight lectures, with no dull paragraphs to provide good skipping. There follow three paragraphs which serve not only as a fair specimen of his use of English but as an indication of his knowledge of the subject matter, acquired at no small cost:

Virtue cannot ordinarily be relied upon as confidently as vice, to maintain its interest in the cause it is devoted to. So far as relates to civic matters Christians are Christians only during the months of September and October, and the first week in November. Politicians are politicians all the year around. "Patience in well doing," is a text that it is becoming to use with a good deal of freedom and frequency.

Few people seem able to keep holy indignation steadily in stock. Indignation is exceedingly tiring and consuming. It is only the saints that require to have inculcated the doctrine of perseverance. There are a great many graces and potencies of character that have a very direct relevancy to public matters, and the pulpit will leave part of its duty undone save as it publishes those graces and potencies in their distinct relation to such matters.

On a critical day in the history of a town or city, virtue is more afraid of getting wet than iniquity, more susceptible to atmospheric changes. Vice will go to the polls on foot; virtue waits to be carried. Christians think as much of their religion as sinners do of their commodity, but are more economical in their use of it.

The lecturer gave the newspapers a sharp piece of his mind. He held that it is unusual for a newspaper to decry what is bad simply because it is bad, or to eulogize what is good simply because it is good. It is rare to find one that measures men, or estimates events, from the frank standpoint of absolute righteousness. He states,

That is a function of which the pulpit has the almost exclusive monopoly. Even the best journalistic endeavors in that direction are almost certain to be in some degree thwarted by the prejudice of political partisanship. If you vituperate Democratic wickedness, Republican journals will support you and say all manner of pleasant things about you. If you attack Tammany, in whichever of the two parties the Tammany spirit happens to be incarnated, the anti-Tammany papers will idolize you, not necessarily because they hate iniquity,—for there may be the same amount of iniquity on their own side, although of a more reputable kind perhaps,—but because they hate Tammany. Pulitzer backed me in '94, not because he loved me, or was interested in the Decalogue, but because he hated Dana. [Dana was editor of the New York Sun at that time.]

II

This preacher-reformer has much to say about preaching and the preacher's mission. In six of the lectures, bearing these titles, "The Preacher and His Qualifications," "Pulpit Aims," "The Pulpit's Estimate of the Pew," "Love Considered as a Dynamic," "Dealing with the Fundamentals," and "The Sanctuary and Sanctuary Service," he ranges the wide field of ministerial activity with pithy observations, many of which are quotable. Such sentences as these are characteristic:

I know of a theological seminary where, since the establishment of a fellowship entitling the first scholar in the class to two years abroad, almost every fellow has finally issued as a professor rather than a preacher.

To insist upon the doctrine of verbal inspiration, or upon any doctrine that approaches thereto, seems to be quibbling with a reality that is too immense to deserve handling in any so paltry a way.

Preaching is not the retailing of other men's visions. Inspiration is always original. Lecturing is not preaching. Socrates was not satisfied to be a lecturer; he wanted to be a preacher. Aristotle was satisfied to be a lecturer.

Jesus Christ never lectured. What he said, so far as it has been preserved to us, was distinctly sermon. His pastorate lasted about three years. He was crucified for being a homiletical irritation, nuisance, if you please.

Stephen, the proto-martyr, was stoned. His pastorate was only a brief one. So far as we are informed, he preached but once, but it was preaching. . . . Without that sermon there might have been no Paul.

"The wicked flee when no man pursueth," and they make still better time when somebody is after them.

Dr. Parkhurst published his autobiography in 1923, with the title *My Forty Years in New York*. It is divided into two parts: I. Experiences; II. Reflections. The first section is by far the more interesting. In it we learn that, for one of his vocation, he was a mountain climber of distinction. His chapter on "Mountaineering" is vastly interesting and in parts thrilling. Monte Rosa, the Weisshorn, the Matterhorn—Dr. Parkhurst made the ascent of all three. Of this vigorous kind of exercise he wrote: "Personally I find mountain work intoxicating. It results in sleeplessness. It gives my nature a kind of thrust that keeps me going when my legs stop functioning. . . . An undevout mountaineer is mad!"

Dr. Parkhurst lived to the ripe age of ninety-one, an active, useful life. He fulfilled his ministry and made it felt in a city that has been called "The graveyard of ministers," a cliché that has lost its luster, if it ever had any.

VII. JOHN KELMAN

It has been my privilege to hear many of the preachers of my day, on both sides of the Atlantic, but John Kelman was not one of them. I am the poorer because of this fact and all too conscious of it. I have read his sermons, and their structure, dignity, and other fine qualities fascinate me. Moreover, I happen to know several of Dr. Kelman's friends, fellow ministers, who knew him intimately, notably, Dr. J. R. P. Sclater, of old St. Andrews, Toronto, who could not say enough in praise of Dr. Kelman, his character, and preaching genius. For this preacher belonged to that small and elect company who are the product of rich, cultural traditions, and are trained for their task as only the seminaries at Edinburgh, Glasgow, and Aberdeen can train students who choose the ministerial vocation.

I

The title of Dr. Kelman's lectures given in 1919, *The War and Preaching*, was not one that commended itself generally to the public. The people had been surfeited with books on war, and a reaction had set in. Actually, there are only two lectures in the Course which deal specifically with World War I, namely, "Then Came the War" and "The Soldier's Creed." The others treat superbly with the "art of preaching," a phrase which Dr. Kelman does not like and condemns in strong terms, yet nevertheless he uses occasionally, being careful however first to define the term, saying that art should be a secondary consideration of the sermon-maker and never primary.

In addition to his international reputation as a powerful preacher, Dr. Kelman had two other assets that contributed to his lectures at Yale. One of these was his long experience in speaking to college students, and another his personal experiences in sharing the lot of the "Tommies" in World War I. Some able preachers are not adept in addressing young people, but Dr.

Kelman was at home with an audience of students or a group of soldiers in earshot of the firing line. Has anyone written more feelingly and dramatically of battlefields, and youth facing death thereupon, than this preacher, in the excerpt taken from his lecture on "Then Came the War":

I have seen two great nations going into this war. In Chicago, on 31st March 1917, just before the Declaration of War in Congress, I sat behind the speakers on the platform of that vast gathering which gave expression to the pent-up emotions of the multitude. Great men spoke that night, and the things they said were great. The audience rose to its feet over and over again, its soul moved and swung passionately to and fro, like the innumerable flags that it waved wildly in the air. But as I gazed, my eyes filled with tears, and the magnificent spectacle grew blurred and indistinct. Instead of it I saw the darkened streets of a town in France, where, under a lashing rain, a regiment of British boys was marching to the railway station, *en route* for their first going up to the front. And then I stood upon that low hill in Flanders where, on the Christmas Day of 1916, I had first caught sight of the Line—the long, irregular, loose-flung stream of faint sedge colour, along which the men of two hostile nations watched each other, and in whose strip of No Man's Land they met. I saw again the blood-red sun of Ypres setting behind a network of blasted trees, till night fell, and far and near the horizon was illuminated by countless lights that soared and floated over the opposing trenches. Since then I have been with the armies at almost every point of the British front. I know the weird city of the trenches, with its named streets of underground habitations, its stores and forges, its manifold life and labour, its watching sentries and homeless dreams of home. From the Hill of Kemmel I watched the battle that we fought for Holebeke. Hour after hour we waited in the dark, the silence broken only by an occasional sporadic gun. Then, at the appointed moment, the signal flamed out in crimson, the barrage thundered, and the whole earth seemed on fire, until the dawn stole away the brilliance and the battle raged on through drizzling rain. Then, for days and nights, we received the walking wounded, weary lads who had been in the shell-holes drenched with rain for one day, two days, three days and nights. We saw the operating tables of the theatres in the clearing stations just behind the line, where surgeons raced with death and gambled against terrific odds for men's lives. I dwelt among the wooden crosses, and never a walk but led me from wayside grave to wayside grave. I saw little companies of men with the red hackle on their bonnets, watching a cinema through a winter's evening across a pool of water in a flooded tent. I have seen the Virgin of Albert, on the spire of "La Basilique Martyre," lying along gigantic and horizontal, as if to force her Child to turn His eyes downward from the sky and see for Himself the miseries of the earth He came to save. I can hear now, and shall evermore hear, the voice of the Great War. At the sea, amid the broken clay of the breastworks, a cry; on the crests of the long ridges from Passchendaele to Vimy a shout of victory; and the spacious fields of the Somme, where Nature had thrown its green mantle over the shell-holes of the tortured earth, and the flowers that sprang from that wide and level lawn were the white crosses of the dead, a silence, in which there was more of triumph than of sadness.

The lecture on "The Soldier's Creed" is singularly tender, combining, as it does, emotion and realism. The lecturer steers expertly a middle course between those writers who thought they found a revival of religion in the trenches and those who were sure they found none. He tells how the brave boys met danger and faced death, of the fatalism that so many of them naturally embraced, of their loneliness, heroism and spirit of sacrifice, mysticism, and even their profanity. "Tommy swore infernally—not all of him, but a very large number. It is certainly a very regrettable fact, but to its severest critics one is inclined to reply that if they were in his circumstances some of them would swear too."

Before leave is taken of this section of Dr. Kelman's lectures, while discussing "The Soldier's Creed," he gives what I feel sure to be the shortest sermon ever preached. Dr. Kelman relates: "A chaplain, on a day of storm and heavy rain, had to conduct parade service with troops in the open. He knew his business, and his address was short: 'No man but a fool would detain you on such a day. My text is "What think ye of Christ?" and my sermon is "What think ye of Christ?" Dismiss.'"

II

One often hears it said that the great sermons of famous preachers of past generations would not interest a modern congregation. Dr. Kelman tells of an experiment he tried.

There is a sermon on "God the Lord is a sun and shield," published half a century ago by a distinguished predecessor of my own, of whom I had heard it said that his sermons could not be preached and would not be listened to today. Preaching from the same text, I introduced a page from his book, and it held the congregation listening intently. The real secret lies in expressing oneself so that one's words find an answer in the spirits of the people. Those who fail to arrest attention do so because they are out of touch with facts. Bishop Phillips Brooks has described them in a memorable sentence as "neither high enough to hear the calling of the stars, nor low enough to hear the grumbling of the earthquake." In other words, the preacher must be in touch with either the heights or the depths of his hearers' experience, or at least with some phase of it which they recognize.

In this connection I recall a similar experience I had in reproducing a sermon preached nearly ninety years ago by Henry Ward Beecher, with Abraham Lincoln in his audience. The sermon, which I published in the appendix of my *Lincoln and the Preachers*, is as fresh and down to date as the ablest sermons preached by our best preachers of today. This is not alone my opinion but that of others who have written or spoken to me about the Beecher sermon.

The fifth lecture is especially valuable, although there is not one in the entire series that does not contain strong meat for either the young or mature ambassador of Christ. For example, here is a paragraph that rings true and speaks to the conscience of every loyal member of the High Calling:

The "art of preaching" is a phrase which makes me shudder. Sometimes in proposing a vote of thanks after an address, in which one has poured forth his soul in unreserved and passionate appeal, a kindly chairman will speak of one's words as "eloquent." No epithet—I had almost said epitaph—could possibly grieve one more, or brand one's earnestness with the mark of failure. The only consolation is that the chairman may have had a limited vocabulary, and may have been in the habit of using "eloquent" to characterise all kinds of praiseworthy discourse. If the word was really meant, the speaker may well examine himself: for any preaching which makes upon any man the general impression chiefly of eloquence, is bad preaching. Preaching is indeed an art, but of all arts it is the one of which the maxim is most true, *Summa ars celare artem*. Any art that there is in preaching can only be tolerable as a means to an end, and the test of it is the measure in which the means is concealed and the end made prominent. "Show me your muscles," says Epictetus. "Here are my dumb-bells," replies the athlete. "Begone with your dumb-bells," replies Epictetus; "what I want to see is not them but their effect."[1] Thus "the teacher must begin where he must end, with practice."[2] Otherwise his utterances will not be "the spontaneous outflow of a prophet's soul, but the artistic periods of a rhetorician."[3]

About the preacher's books the lecturer has this wise word for us:

It is well worth while to consider seriously what books we should read. His message will be given to a man, in part at least, by his studies; and still more it will take its general tone, style, and character from these. Above all, of course, there is the Bible itself, and no preacher can without peril neglect its systematic study. But in an age like this we need to read much else besides. "No man," says Matthew Arnold, "who knows nothing else, knows even his Bible."[4] But as God's messenger comes forth from his Bible to his other books, it seems to me as if all the mighty spirits who wrote the Bible were following him with their dreadful searching eyes, to see what books he will supplement them with. Such books should be in themselves great and vital. Further, they should be suggestive books, quickening his own mind to activity rather than merely supplying him with passages or thoughts which he may borrow. The standard classics of literature, the great commentaries, the living books of theology and religion—these are the stuff for inspiration. To neglect these, and simply sit down and copy the division of a text into heads, out of some of the volumes known as "Aids to Preachers," is to sell your birthright. If your reading has been vital, you can divide the text far better for yourselves, if you will take the pains to try. I would even venture to warn you against the undue use of volumes of other men's sermons. These may become a temptation, and some students have made shipwreck of their character, and have even thrown away their power of honest work, by yielding to that temptation. Printed sermons may be useful if they are read after, not before, you have

[1] Hatch, *Hibbert Lectures*, vi.
[2] *Ibid.*, vii.
[3] *Ibid.*, xii.
[4] *Culture and Anarchy*, ch. v.

constructed the framework of your own discourse. It is a mistake to imagine that they teach the art of preaching to any great extent. If any of you find that you have been relying upon them too much, I would advise you to sell three-quarters of your stock of other men's sermons, and to buy books.

What of "political preaching"? On "The Preacher as Statesman," the author states his convictions:

Yet there have always been those who would exclude the Church from all intermeddling with statesmanship and secular affairs. Melanchthon, in his commentary on 2 Timothy ii. 4, says, "So he wishes the minister of the gospel to serve in his own vocation unreservedly, and not to engage in outside affairs, in political management. Let not the minister of the gospel have one foot in the temple and the other in the *curia*." To few readers will this appear a convincing exegesis of the text, "No man that warreth entangleth himself with the affairs of this life." Yet many will justly remind us of the dangers which beset preaching when it ceases to be individualistic and begins to deal in public affairs. Whatever a man's own political views may be, he is not called to be the minister either of the Republicans or the Democrats, either of the Conservatives or the Liberals in his congregation, as an agent in party propaganda. The unfairness of any such course is manifest in an assembly where there is no right of reply. The questions which divide the members of any congregation into different political parties are open questions, on which it is admitted that men of the highest principle and integrity may support either of the rival sides. And, as a matter of fact, it will be found that most men claim the right to do their political thinking and voting for themselves, and to choose for their leaders in these departments others than their religious guides.

The Reverend Paul Austin Wolfe, now minister of the Brick Presbyterian Church, New York City, was associated with John Kelman in his ministry at the Fifth Avenue Presbyterian Church, and of his illustrious Chief he writes:

As a Churchman John Kelman was a preacher, not an administrator or organizer. Perhaps if he had set his mind to be an administrator he could have done it, but administration did not interest him. He was a poet, a mystic, deeply rooted in our Greek-Hebraic inheritance.

He turned over the Sunday School and the Church organizations to me. Mrs. Harkness had recently given the Church $750,000 toward a Parish House provided the Church would raise $250,000. John Kelman let the Church Committee and the assistant minister do the raising. Most of his time he wrestled with his sermons, spending much time in study and lecturing a good deal on Matthew Arnold, Browning, Stevenson.

I had the impression that he focused on his sermons with great difficulty. He used to warn me never to be a preacher. He would stay up half the night trying to get a point to where it could be understood by his congregation and clear to himself. In the morning he would appear all drawn and haggard. But once in the pulpit all signs of weariness left him. His mind seemed freed of encumbrances. He was clear, earnest, sincere, convincing.

He was not, however, popular. I think this was very hard on him. At Free St. George's in Edinburgh there had been long queues outside the Church whenever he was announced as preacher. His thought was too rare and too impersonal to bring success in New York City. . . . New York was not prepared for his thoughtful literary preaching.

"Dear John Kelman." In this affectionate manner a friend so refers to him. He had his great day and it was all too short, as judged by our poor human view of life. Kelman lived a full life, left a precious legacy in his writings, and made many of us his grateful debtors.

VIII. ALBERT PARKER FITCH

Usually when a new volume of the Yale Lectures falls into my hands I drop everything and proceed to devour it with relish and dispatch. But the day Dr. Fitch's *Preaching and Paganism* arrived at my study I gave it only a casual inspection and then stood the book up alongside its royal fellows of the "Glorious Company." And now to account for this act of *lèse-majesté*. For one thing, I did not know much about the author at the time; for another, the title did not appeal to me; and for a third, I was just beginning my Detroit ministry and beset behind and before by those inevitable distractions which such a resettling entails.

It was not until the summer of 1948, at beloved Pentwater on Lake Michigan, that I discovered the "brilliant, scintillating, provocative" mind of Albert Parker Fitch. Beecher and Brooks I knew, or thought I knew; Dale, Simpson, Watson, van Dyke, and others, I thought I knew; but I did not know Fitch previous to that golden summer when on a memorable day I read his *Preaching and Paganism* and, having finished the book,

> I felt like some watcher of the skies
> When a new planet swims into his ken.

And I changed my opinion of the title. None other could have been so appropriate.

I

It became necessary that I find someone who knew Dr. Fitch intimately, and I was fortunate in finding that person in Dr. Henry Pitney Van Dusen, president of Union Theological Seminary. The subject of this chapter fully warrants the reproduction here of much of Dr. Van Dusen's fine and informative letter:

Albert Parker Fitch was a most unusual man. To begin with, he was exceptionally blessed by nature. He stood six feet or more in height, with a robust frame, and a leonine head of impressive size and strength. His voice was one of the most remarkable in its depth, resonance and power which I have ever listened to, and he had mastered its use to perfection; one could only think of a great organ under the fingers of a skilled musician. He came of old New England stock and always cherished his ancestry and his rootage in the soil of Vermont. I am told that during his undergraduate years at Union, although Harry Emerson Fosdick and not a few other outstanding leaders of the pulpit were his contemporaries, Fitch towered above his generation of fellow students in speaking ability and promise. This promise was apparently fulfilled in his pastorate of the Mount Vernon Congregational Church in Boston. I know nothing of the chapter of his life as President of Andover Seminary, although I suspect that he did not show at his best in administrative responsibility. He went to Amherst in 1917 as an ardent follower and friend of Alexander Meiklejohn, fought through the Meiklejohn controversy with passionate devotion to his chief, and left Amherst when Meiklejohn was forced out. The professorship at Carleton College was something of an exile for him. I visited him there in his home which Mrs. Fitch and he had made a place of exquisite beauty and charm. He enjoyed the experience in the Middle West but longed to return to the Eastern Seaboard.

I was surprised to have him indicate an interest in returning to the parish ministry. Some years earlier I had asked him why he had left preaching for the college classroom. His reply from anyone else would have suggested insufferable egotism; in Albert Fitch it revealed acute self-knowledge. He said that he found that he had completely mastered the work of the pulpit, that he could do anything he wanted with a congregation through preaching, and that the role of teacher where he could not use his amazing oratorical powers and had to submit himself to the free give and take of student questioning and criticism intrigued him. I believe he felt that, at Andover and Carleton, he had mastered to his own satisfaction the skills of teaching; in any event he longed to get back to the pulpit and to intimate pastoral contacts, as well as to the East. With this knowledge, I took the initiative in suggesting his possible availability to the Park Avenue Presbyterian Church in New York. That was then a very tiny congregation, but worshiping in one of the most glorious of Ralph Adams Cram's Gothic churches with a beautifully appointed manse next door. The Park Avenue Church could hardly believe that a man of Fitch's eminence would consider a call as their minister. But the total situation of this church, located on Park Avenue, appealed to him, and he accepted. I used to see him often during the four years when he was there. . . .

. . . In any event, Fitch suffered a stroke in 1932 and was compelled to retire to his home in Windsor, Vermont. His condition slowly worsened, and about 1940, he moved to Englewood, New Jersey. As it happened, my family and I were then living in Englewood, and during the next two or three years of his life I was again brought into very intimate touch with him. I shared with three other younger ministers in his funeral service.

Taken all in all, he was a brilliant, scintillating, provocative and most lovable man.

Dr. Fitch is one of the few in the "Foundation," as he called it, who gave the impression of having read most of the lectures which preceded his own. Thus, he refers by name to Brooks, Gladden, Coffin, Brown, and Peabody. There is further evidence of his familiarity with the subject matter of his predecessors as he blazed for himself a trail for a new and original treatment of the general theme. Observe the sheer artistry of his titles: I. The

Learner, the Doer, and the Seer; II. The Children of Zion and the Sons of Greece; III. Eating, Drinking and Being Merry; IV. The Unmeasured Gulf; V. Grace, Knowledge, Virtue; VI. The Almighty and Everlasting God; VII. Worship as the Chief Approach to Transcendence; VIII. Worship and the Discipline of Doctrine.

Now some preachers fail to live up to their sermon titles, but not Dr. Fitch. Talking with Dean Weigle about Fitch's Yale engagement, he told me that of all the lectures on preaching at the Divinity school he had heard, three of Dr. Fitch's stood out as the most exciting and rhetorically effective. There are similar reports abroad about this preacher-educator. He had a reputation for capturing audiences by a tour de force, both by the power of his speech and by the audacity of his ideas.

II

Preaching and Paganism reflects the disillusionment of spiritual leaders of World War I and the failure of the Peace. As the lecturer saw it, his contemporaries preached to a generation largely and unashamedly pagan. His disappointment with theological liberalism in a way forecast the Neo-orthodoxy which was to speak to Europe through Barth, Brunner, and others, and in this country principally through Reinhold Niebuhr. Dr. Fitch's arraignment of Humanism as inadequate and powerless to save this bedeviled world was a vivid feature of his series. Thus in speaking on "The Children of Zion and the Sons of Greece," he says:

Humanism has made Jesus obvious, hence, relatively impotent. With its unified cosmos, its imminent God, its exalted humanity, the whole Christological problem has become trivial. It drops the cosmic approach to the person of Jesus in favor of the ethical. It does not approach Him from the side of God; we approach nothing from that side now; but from the side of man. Thus He is not so much a divine revelation as He is a human achievement. Humanity and Divinity are one in essence. . . . So runs the thrice familiar argument.

Some see the influence of Humanism upon our preaching in the relinquishment of the goal of conversion. We are preaching to educate, not to save; to instruct, not to transform. . . . Hence we blur the distinction between the Christian and the non-Christian. Education supplants salvation. We bring the boys and girls into the church because they are safer there than outside it; and on the whole it is a good thing to do and, really, they belong there anyway. The church member is a man of the world, softened by Christian feeling. He is a kindly and amiable citizen, and an honorable man, and he has not been saved.

In general, then, it seems to me abundantly clear that the humanistic movement has both limited and secularized preaching. It dogmatically ignores supersensuous values; hence it has rationalized preaching; hence it has made provincial its intellectual approach and treatment, narrowed and made mechanical its content. . . . What then has been the final effect of Humanism upon preaching? It has tempted the preacher to depersonalize religion, and since love is the essence of personality, it has thereby stripped preaching of the emotional energy, of the universal human interest and prophetic insight which only love can bestow. Over against this depersonalization we must find some way to return to expressing the religious view and utilizing the religious power of the human spirit.

Dr. Fitch told the seminarians at Yale that "religious preaching begins with two things: man's solitary place in nature, and man's inability to hold that place alone." "Hence," he said, "two more things are necessary as essentials of great preaching in a pagan day: The clear proclamation of a superhuman God, the transcendent Spirit who is able to control and reinforce the spirit of man. . . . It is clear that preaching must deal again, never more than now, with the religion which offers redemption from sin." And what pathos in this passage: "Oh how many sermons since, let us say 1890, have been preached on the text: 'He that hath seen Me, hath seen the Father,' and how uniformly the sermons have explained that the text means not that Jesus is like God, but that God is like Jesus—and we have already seen that Jesus is like us, and that one only has to state it all to see beneath its superficial reasonableness its appalling profanity."

The artistic sensitivity of Dr. Fitch was often a subject of comment on the part of his friends. That quality is surely in evidence in his sixth lecture on "The Almighty and Everlasting God." There he expresses his passion for beauty in this passage of haunting loveliness:

Recall the splendors of the external world, and that best season of our climate, the long, slow-breathing autumn. What high pleasure we take in those hushed days of mid-November, in the soft brown turf of the uplands, the fragrant smell of mellow earth and burning leaves, the purple haze that dims and magnifies the quiescent hills. Who is not strangely moved by that profound and brooding peace into which Nature then gathers up the multitudinous strivings, the myriad activities of her life? Who does not love to lie, in those slow-waning days upon the sands which hold within their golden cup the murmuring and dreaming sea? The very amplitude of the natural world, its far-flung grace and loveliness, spread out in rolling moor and winding stream and stately forest marching up the mountain-side, subdues and elevates the spirit of a man.

How easily the lecturer passed from this prose poem in praise of nature's beauty to preaching. Thus:

Preaching today is not moving on the level of this discussion, is neither asking nor attempting to answer its questions. Great preaching in some way makes men see the end of the road, not merely the direction in which it travels. The power to do that we have lost, if we have lost the more-than-us in Jesus. Humanity, unaided, cannot look to that end which shall explain the beginning. And does Jesus mean very much to us if He is only "Jesus"? Why do we answer the great invitation, "Come unto me"? Because He is something other than us? Because He calls us away from ourselves? back to home? Most of us no longer know how to preach on that plane of experience or from the point of view where such questions are serious and real. Our fathers had a world view and a philosophy which made such preaching easy. But their power did not lie in that world view; it lay in this vision of Jesus which produced the view. Is not this the vision which we need?

When a great teacher can reason so cogently, powerfully and Scripturally, it seems nothing short of a tragedy that he should have been cut down just as the shadows began to lengthen toward the east. He was but sixty-seven when he died. Still, in this we may be wrong, since, "he most lives, who thinks most,—feels the noblest,—acts the best." Think of Stephen, of Frederick William Robertson, of Henry Drummond, of Percy Ainsworth and, in our own generation, of Peter Marshall; and as we think of these and of others who perished in their prime, how fitting for us to pray:

> O God, speak to these curious hearts of ours and teach them to be still![1]

IX. HARRY EMERSON FOSDICK

> ... the essential nature of a sermon as an intimate, conversational message from soul to soul, makes it impossible for printing to reproduce preaching, and, unlike the traditional child, sermons should be heard and not seen.
> —HARRY EMERSON FOSDICK, in the Foreword to
> *The Hope of the World,* his first volume of sermons (1933)

Dr. Fosdick is the only one of the living lecturers in the Yale Series included here among "The Titans," and few will question his right to be in this classification. As I conversed once with a distinguished editor, publicist, and churchman on the American pulpit, he remarked: "Harry Emerson Fosdick is the Henry Ward Beecher of our day." Many will agree with this statement, including some who fail to see eye to eye with Dr. Fosdick and his theology. Not, of course, that he resembles the renowned Brooklyn preacher in temperament, method, or extraordinary oratorical power, although this Titan of the pulpit is an effective public speaker of distinctive style.

My editor-friend went on to say that just as Beecher influenced the preaching of his day for good, making it more human and sentient, so had Dr. Fosdick bettered the pulpit of our day both in sermon content and delivery. This observation makes sense. Consider the ramifications of his ministry at Riverside Church, New York City. His published sermons, seven volumes in all, besides his other books, outsell, I have been informed, those of any other contemporary American preacher. They are also read and prized in Great Britain, on the Continent, in Australia, and in other countries abroad. The peoples of other countries think of Dr.

---

[1] From "The Burial of Moses," by Mrs. Cecil Frances Alexander.

Fosdick as first among American preachers, just as they think of Dr. Niebuhr as first among our theologians.

While yet a fledgling in the ministry Dr. Fosdick set up for himself an exacting standard of preaching excellence and, come rain or shine, he has maintained that standard for nearly half a century. His sermons follow an orderly construction, and abound in quotable sentences often of an epigrammatic flavor. Notwithstanding the touch of grandeur that distinguishes the Fosdick pattern of speech, and the lofty plateau upon which his preaching moves, he is not averse to a colloquialism or a humorous chuckle. His vocabulary is ample but not lavish. He rarely uses an exotic word, although he probably knows a lot of them. Instead, good, strong, lusty words are this preacher's delight. His sentences, long or short, are clear; the illustrative material fresh, and the realms of literature, art, and music are drawn upon with discriminating nicety.

There is also a down to earth quality in Fosdickian preaching. Who could imagine a Phillips Brooks preaching "On Catching the Wrong Bus"; but Dr. Fosdick did, and with zest. The sermon appears in his *On Being Fit to Live With*, and even in print it is warm, human, sagacious. Not even Beecher so much as dreamed of preaching on "The Decisive Babies of the World," but one of Dr. Fosdick's finest sermons is on this theme. That he was indebted to the historian, Creasy, for the inspiration, in no way detracts from the sheer genius of substituting "Babies" for "Battles." Every alert preacher who reads this sermon wonders why he was too dumb to perceive the fine gold in that homiletic hill. Still, all may not be lost to the hard-pressed pastor. It will be recalled that Oscar Wilde, dazzled by a phrase on the lips of his friend, Whistler, the painter, sighed and remarked, "I wish I'd said that," and Whistler replied, "You will, Oscar, you will."

I

In answer to my questionnaire which I sent to all the living lecturers in the Lyman Beecher Lectures, Dr. Fosdick said in part:

I have no idea, either, how much time I spent in immediate preparation. For years I had been giving at Union Theological Seminary a year-long course on the same subject I used at Yale. What I did, therefore, was to take advantage of the lectureship at Yale to arrange, condense, write out carefully and prepare for publication, the material I had been working on for a long time.

So it happens that to date Dr. Fosdick is the only lecturer in the long list to devote his series to the Bible exclusively, as Dr. Jefferson did in 1910 on the Church. Many of the other lecturers gave space both to the Bible and to the Church; uniquely Drs. Jefferson and Fosdick deal solely, one with the institution, and the other with its text book. I think it was a source of disappointment that this master preacher did not choose to take preaching as his subject at Yale. Later he was pressed to return for another series of a homiletical nature, but he could not find the time for the kind of preparation he always gives to the task ahead.

It turned out, however, that the interest in the Fosdick series on *The Modern Use of the Bible*, was marked and sustained. So great were the throngs which came to hear him, that officers were detailed to keep the crowd from storming the chapel when the doors were thrown open. This thing of policing a throng waiting to hear a Lyman Beecher lecturer had never occurred before, nor since, although capacity audiences have greeted several of the lecturers, and in a few instances standing room was at a premium.

The fact that the Fundamentalist-Modernist controversy was rampant at the time, and that Dr. Fosdick was in the center of it and subject to heavy attack, naturally added interest to the occasion and helps to account for the intense interest in the course.

Dr. Fosdick's lectures appeared in book form the year they were delivered, 1924, and enjoyed a huge circulation. The volume belongs in that comparatively small list of the published lectures which deserve classification as "best sellers." The chapters were read from manuscript by Dr. Fosdick, who is adept in that method of preaching. Up to that time only one lecturer in the Course had dealt with the Bible from the modern critical view, and then with only a part of it—Dr. George Adam Smith, whose subject in 1889 was *Modern Criticism and the Preaching of the Old Testament—*

a fact which Dr. Fosdick commented on in the opening paragraph of his first lecture.

Rereading these lectures twenty-five years after their delivery, they appear as fresh, crisp, and pertinent as on that day I first opened the book and read far into the night that followed. As I read I glanced occasionally toward my book shelves, and my gaze fell on Dr. William Newton Clarke's *Sixty Years with the Bible*, a volume which came to me when I needed the reflections of that great yet humble scholar. These two books have much in common, and it is good news to some of us that Dr. Fosdick looked upon Dr. Clarke as a "saint."

There is a paragraph in Dr. Fosdick's first lecture which goes to the heart of the matter, thus:

> The man who ministers . . . must have an intelligible way of handling the Bible. He must have gone through the searching criticism to which the last few generations have subjected the Scriptures and be able to understand and enter into the negations that have resulted. Not blinking any of the facts, he must have come out with a positive, reasonable, fruitful attitude toward the Book. Only so can he be of service in resolving the doubts of multitudes of folk today. If they can see that the Bible is not lost but is the more usable the better it is understood, that the new knowledge has not despoiled it but has set its spirit free for its largest usefulness, that its basic experiences are separable from its temporary forms of thought, and that in its fundamental principles of life lie the best hopes of the world today, they are set at liberty from a great fear that their faith is vain. In the end, like many of us, they may see more in the Scriptures now than ever they saw under the old regime.

Dr. Fosdick is a constructive critic always, and employs a method that is direct, honest, and courageous. But one may follow such a plan and still deal solely with negations. It is different with this New York preacher-professor. He places the emphasis on the affirmative, and holds that liberalism by itself or as a cult is not enough. Neither liberalism nor conservatism availeth anything but a new creature. Take his subjects in order: I. The New Approach to the Bible; II. The Old Book in a New World; III. The Ancient Solution; IV. Abiding Experiences in Changing Categories; V. Miracle and Law; VI. Perils of the New Position;

VII. Jesus, the Messiah; VIII. Jesus, the Son of God. Now, controversial issues emerge in every one of the eight chapters. He meets them head on, but always with humility and a total absence of intellectual pride and doctrinaire vanity. Thus he speaks in a passage which is of the pattern of the whole:

> Here, then, is the first essential of intelligent Biblical preaching in our day: a man must be able to recognize the abiding messages of the Book, and sometimes he must recognize them in a transient setting. No man will ever do this well if he does not divest himself of vanity and pride and clothe himself with humility as with a garment. He must see that many of our ways of thinking are very new; that they, too, are transient, and that many of them will soon be as outmoded as our forefathers' categories are.

If any theological student sitting through the first five lectures found himself heady with the new wine of interpretation from new bottles, the sixth lecture on "Perils of the New Position" must have had a sobering effect upon him. "Now abide three perils of liberalism—irreverence, sentimentality, and ethical disloyalty to Jesus—and the greatest of these is ethical disloyalty to Jesus." Thus endeth the chapter on the perils of the position for which the lecturer had so ably argued.

What Dr. Fosdick taught the theological students at Yale he taught the congregation to whom he preached, and the standards he set up for the young men at New Haven, he, himself, lived by. In this set of lectures delivered six years after World War I, and seventeen years before America's entrance into World War II, Fosdick declared: "The late war violated everything Jesus taught and, pouring the whole world into almost irremediable confusion, has provoked widespread impatience with purely theological speculations about Christ."

In July, 1928, Dr. Fosdick wrote an article which appeared in *Harper's Magazine* on the subject, "What Is the Matter with Preaching?" It attracted wide attention and elicited many comments, most of them favorable. Among other things he said:

> Recently, in a school chapel, so I am told, the headmaster was only well started on his sermon when a professor mounted the pulpit beside him and offered a criticism of what he was saying. Great ex-

citement reigned. The headmaster answered the objection, but the professor remained in the pulpit, and the sermon that day was a running discussion between the two on a great theme in religion. To say that the boys were interested is to put it mildly. They never had been so worked up over anything religious before. It turned out afterward that the whole affair had been prearranged. It was an experiment in a new kind of preaching, where one man does not produce a monologue but where diverse and competing points of view are frankly dealt with.

Any preacher, without introducing another personality outwardly in the pulpit, can utilize the principle involved in this method. If he is to handle helpfully real problems in his congregation, he must utilize it. He must see clearly and state fairly what people other than himself are thinking on the matter in hand. He may often make this so explicit as to begin paragraphs with such phrases as, "but some of you will say," or "Let us consider a few questions that inevitably arise," or, "Face frankly with me the opposing view," or, "Some of you have had experiences that seem to contradict what we are saying." Of course, this method, like any other, can be exaggerated and become a mannerism. But something like it is naturally involved in any preaching which tries to help people to think through and live through their problems.

A publisher of New York City, whose friendship I prize, once described to me the first time he heard Dr. Fosdick preach, and the effect of the sermon upon him. He was a graduate student at Chicago at the time, and Dr. Fosdick was the preacher at the Sunday Evening Club. Orchestra Hall was packed, and although the youth came early, he had difficulty in finding a seat. "For the first time in my life," the publisher said, "I was to see the man who had written *The Meaning of Prayer*, a book that had meant much to my college roommate and me, and to hear the preacher whose name like Abou Ben Adhem's, led all the rest. Even though I was ready for the unusual I didn't expect the extraordinary. Here were ideas presented so cogently and vigorously that my mind could not hold them all, so like a torrent they came. The choice of words was often so apt that it was sheer delight to sense how apposite to the idea was the word chosen to express it. This aesthetic pleasure I remember having experienced years earlier when as a boy I had heard William Jennings Bryan lecture from a Chautauqua platform. The title of Dr. Fosdick's sermon I heard in Chicago I have long since forgotten but I shall never forget the impact made by his preaching."

I have recalled this conversation from a memory still aglow with the enthusiasm of the publisher describing to me the experience. If anything, my account of the incident has lost, not gained, in vividness.

Exciting preaching which is not merely emotional but also highly intelligent and spiritually powerful never lacks for a hearing. Already the name of Fosdick is being ranged alongside the names of Henry Ward Beecher and Phillips Brooks on this side of the Atlantic, and with Frederick William Robertson on the other. Riverside Church, New York City, is destined to take its place in the history of preaching with Plymouth Church, Brooklyn, Trinity Church, Boston, and Trinity Chapel, Brighton, England.

Dr. Fosdick is now minister emeritus of Riverside Church. In semiretirement he is still a busy person. His latest book, *The Man from Nazareth*, is enjoying a wide and enthusiastic reading.

III

THEOLOGIANS AND
★ PHILOSOPHERS ★

A little philosophy inclineth man's mind to atheism, but depths in philosophy bringeth man's mind about to religion.
—FRANCIS BACON

1. ADOLPHUS JULIUS FREDERICK BEHRENDS

In my student days at Lexington, Kentucky, 1898-1900, I chanced to read an Associated Press dispatch under a New York City dateline. It impressed me and I am sure I give it almost verbatim:

The Rev. A. J. F. Behrends from his pulpit in Central Church, Brooklyn, said Sunday: "Bring all the man-made creeds, confessions of faith and the like to a big bonfire. Touch a match to the mass and don't call out the fire department."

This was the extent of my acquaintance with this minister until I read his Yale lectures, given in 1890, on *The Philosophy of Preaching*. Then I began to look into his career.

Born in Holland, March 18, 1839, in a Lutheran parsonage, he came with his family to Ohio at the age of five. Graduating from Denison University in 1862, he completed his seminary course at Rochester Theological Seminary in 1865, and became the minister of Warburton Baptist Church in Yonkers, New York, and from there he went to the First Baptist Church of Cleveland, Ohio. In that pulpit he opposed "close communion" in a sermon that provoked criticism and led to his resignation in 1876. This proved to be a turning point in his life, and shortly before his death in 1900 he said that when he had cut loose from the Baptists, he stood ready for an open door and determined to accept the first call. It came from the First Congregational Church of Providence,

Adolphus Julius Frederick Behrends

Rhode Island. In 1883 he began the ministry of Central Church (Congregational), Brooklyn, which continued up to the time of his death. This church had not then attained the commanding position which it did under his headship. In those days Behrends had to meet the competition of Beecher, Storrs, and Talmage, and he stood up well to the test. An editorial in *The Outlook* of June 2, 1900, characterized him as "one of the not large number of truly great preachers." In 1886 he gave a course on "Socialism and Christianity" at Hartford Theological Seminary, and shortly before his death he gave the course at Yale Divinity School.

In his prefatory note to *The Philosophy of Preaching*, Dr. Behrends says:

There has been no citation of authorities, for the simple reason that none were consulted and used. The views here presented had slowly taken form during a ministry of twenty-five years, and they have at least the merit of profound personal conviction, which the author has been encouraged, by friends in whose critical judgment he has great confidence, to believe may be of service to a wider circle than the one to which they were first given.

This extract, brief as it is, indicates the independence of the lecturer and also his self-assurance, quite characteristic of the man and often in evidence in his ministry.

I

The Behrends lectures are compact, direct, clear, and contain a minimum of quotations, either poetry or prose. As a specimen of terse, tight writing, with few rhetorical embellishments, the addresses stand quite apart in the Lectureship. Dr. Behrends drew little from his own experience and, while there is wit, it is subtle and occurs but infrequently. The mind and habits of a scholar are revealed in the handling of his themes, and an orderly arrangement of his material. The volume is the smallest, physically, in the Course with the exception of that of Dr. L. P. Jacks' and much more meaty than his.

In his first lecture the speaker sees "one large, earnest, aggressive section of the Christian church, whose piety and consecrated zeal are beyond dispute," as maintaining, "that preaching should not only be evangelical, but evangelistic." He sees another section "in sharpest contrast with the evangelistic conception of preaching," which he ventures to call "evolutional." He finds merit in each of these schools, but neither taken by itself is satisfactory.

Of the "evolutional" theory of preaching he states:

It assumes that the religious life is germinally and potentially present in every human soul. It substitutes culture and development for conversion. It addresses every man as a son of God and an heir of heaven, and endeavors to stir within him the recognition of these prerogatives. It makes the sermon a pious meditation, a devotional monologue, an emotional deliverance. . . . Men are asleep, not dead. They need waking up, not resurrection from a moral grave.

While giving the evangelistic theory of preaching its just deserts and conceding that they are large and precious, Dr. Behrends holds that:

the evangelistic theory of preaching is partial. It fails to reach all classes, and it cannot long hold those whom it does reach. It has no meat for strong men. It is too exclusively emotional, dealing only with the rudiments of religious truth. It fails to touch the intellectual and social life of man at a thousand points. . . . The evangelistic theory of the sermon is faulty in another respect. When the aim of preaching is regarded as inciting men to believe on Christ, that they may be saved, a twofold danger is imminent. Salvation is apt to be regarded as synonymous with future and eternal blessedness, and the relation of faith to such blessedness assumes a mechanical aspect. . . . The Biblical emphasis is on holiness, not on happiness, on a present and progressive purity of life; and faith is the soul's habitual fellowship with God in Christ, by whose Spirit renewing and sanctifying energy is imparted.

Praising the evangelistic preaching as necessary, Behrends cites its limitations:

Under such a theory preaching becomes hortatory. It never passes beyond the rudiments of religious instruction. It may make use of the Pauline epistles, but it cannot move in their deep and broad grooves. . . . It counts the converts, it neglects to weigh them. Its ammunition is speedily exhausted, and it can live only by frequent change of place. It is ill adapted to long pastorates, which demand a wider range of instruction.

Returning to the "evolutional" theory of preaching, Dr. Behrends "finds its most illustrious advocate and exponent in Schleiermacher, and in the German pulpit its influence has been marked and salutary." "Maurice, Kingsley, and Robertson," he cites as "notable representatives of the same school, and this form of the sermon is characteristic of Broad Churchmanship. . . . Whatever judgment may be passed upon this theory of preaching, the earnestness and power of its exponents cannot be called in question. They have sapped and undermined the movement toward Unitarianism."

Dr. Behrends also declares:

Schleiermacher's theory of the sermon grew out of his theological system, so far as he had any. It is difficult to class him. He was a pantheist in philosophy, a Calvinist in his doctrine of decrees, a Universalist in his conception of the scope of redemption. The incarnation was the historical emergence and expression of a universal fact. The mediation of Christ involved a universal restoration to holiness. . . .

With such a philosophical basis, the sermon could be nothing else than a gentle, persuasive appeal to the muffled inner man. . . . Christlieb pronounces it an ideal conception, something to be earnestly and devoutly hoped for and kept in view, but he insists that the aggressive and missionary vocation of the Church demands also the evangelistic form of preaching, with its pungent and urgent summons to immediate repentance. But all men need to hear and heed that call. The new birth is a universal necessity.

II

Can these two theories of preaching be combined? Behrends thinks not.

A double, or twofold theory of preaching discredits itself, for unity is the test of philosophical analysis; and a theory which makes preaching a separating or sifting agency, intent upon the enlargement and edification of the Christian Church, surrenders the universality of its outlook, and proclaims itself to be simply an instrument of ecclesiastical proselytism. And for myself, I want both unity in the philosophy, and universality in the outlook.

In the lecture that follows the above statement, Dr. Behrends sets forth his own philosophy of preaching in detail. He rests his case thus:

In a word, *the historical triumph of Christianity* is the immediate and practical result designed to be attained by the preaching of the Gospel. We make the world's evangelization, the discipling of all nations, incidental and subordinate; it is, in reality, supreme and exclusive. The present prosaic earth is the territory which we are summoned to subdue to the obedience of Jesus Christ. Here, where sin threw down the gauge of battle and made man an exile from Paradise, the conflict is to be fought out to its bitter end, until Eden comes back with a fairer and a perennial beauty. What socialism blindly aims at through revolutionary and anarchical measures, Christianity is fitted and destined to accomplish for man. The cry of the poor is to be answered. Every burden is to be loosed, every yoke of oppression is to be broken. Ignorance is to be supplanted by the wisdom whose beginning is the fear of the Lord. Drunkenness is to be exterminated, and Sabbath desecration is to cease. The monster of lust is to be cast into the bottomless pit. The meek are to inherit the earth.

There is more of this; too much to be included here. Dr. Behrends expounded in his first and second lectures the philosophy of preaching that has largely dominated the theology of many of the best minds in the Christian pulpit since the Protestant Reformation. Moreover, there is good reason to believe that the philosophy he so ably set forth still finds favor with the majority of the older ministers and is still held by many of the middle-aged preachers in this country. But this is not generally true of the seminary-trained ministers who have turned to the Neo-orthodox school for a radically different philosophy of preaching. In that school of theology these students have been taught that moral man in an immoral society is quite helpless to save society, and that the once popular slogan "Mankind upward and onward forever," is a delusion.

Professors Barth, Brunner, Niebuhr,[1] and their associates may not have found the final solution to the awful problems that vex our age, but they have certainly shaken the complacent belief that

---

[1] It is but fair to Dr. Niebuhr to state that he repudiates the term "Neo-orthodox" as applied to him.

"God's in His heaven—all's right with the world"; "right," as we liberals believed, because God's children are hard at work rebuilding this bedeviled world, and given time they'll succeed. For answer the Neo-orthodox prophets point to a world crushed and broken by two colossal wars and no lasting peace in sight. In Behrends' generation the new day did seem to be breaking over the world, and the signs of the times were propitious. We must judge him by his day, not ours. He had a hopeful answer to the "obstinate questioning" of his day. The Barths and Niebuhrs have an answer to the baffled liberals of this generation. It may not be a final answer, but it has revived the doctrine of "the exceeding sinfulness of sin," and that is a revival long overdue. There is reason to believe, however, that the philosophy of preaching so ably presented in Behrends' lectures is not outmoded, although it may be outdated temporarily and destined to be qualified not a little by the teachings of Barth, Brunner, and Niebuhr. This leads logically to the expectation that someday the philosophy and theology of the Behrends school and that of the Neo-orthodox will achieve a synthesis of the two viewpoints, much to the good of Christian theology generally.

II. ANDREW MARTIN FAIRBAIRN

This famous theologian and powerful preacher was the lecturer in the Course at Yale in 1892, his subject: *The Place of Christ in Modern Theology*. The edition of this book which I have was published by Charles Scribner's Sons, New York, in 1912, and contains, including the index, 526 pages. Obviously not all of this massive material was given at Yale but much of it was. This learned professor was not only celebrated for his superior mind, which was of encyclopedic range, but also for his lengthy lectures and sermons of an hour or more in duration.

The volume which includes Fairbairn's Yale lectures merits further comment. The table of contents consumes thirteen pages, and is divided and subdivided some sixty-three times. Only eight pages are required for the index, but every page of it is crowded with references, figures, and names. The preface, however, is surprisingly brief for a Fairbairn script, being only four pages in length. Before such erudition as this Scottish scholar possessed one bows in awesome respect and admiration. I venture to paraphrase Robert G. Ingersoll on Shakespeare, "Fairbairn's mind was a theological ocean whose waves touched all the shores of Christian thought."

Little more than a hint of Fairbairn's prodigious labors can be chronicled here. He served on the Royal Commission on Secondary Education, along with the Right Honorable Viscount Bryce and other notables; he took part in the agitation for University Reform and was active in behalf of the "passive resistance" movement against the Education Bill of 1902; he gave both the Hibbert and Gifford Lectures, two of the most highly prized honors in Great Britain, which can come only to a few scholars in a single generation. His correspondence was immense, and a Fairbairn letter could be as long as some chapters in a book. At Oxford he shone not only as a brilliant scholar and lecturer but, also, as an admirable host. Together with his wife and daughters he kept open house, where he dispensed a generous hospitality. As for his headship of Mansfield College, the story of his success there is written in letters that have not faded with the passing years. Such was the man who came to Yale in the spring of 1892 and was welcomed with high honors and unending courtesies.

If at times Dr. Fairbairn gave the impression of egotism, few minded it, since it was but a fleeting trait and forgotten in the wealth of kindness with which his nature overflowed. He could be, and sometimes was, abrupt and blustery, as was, also, great Dr. Sam Johnson when he lorded it over his convivial friends, comfortably seated in some congenial tavern of old London town, in the second half of the eighteenth century.

I

Mr. Arthur Porritt, British journalist, wrote entertainingly of Dr. Fairbairn in a book which I have several times referred to in these pages entitled *The Best I Remember*:

He required a solid hour at least. He would approach Milton, for example, by a comprehensive sweep over Greek thought, and lead up to Cromwell by a survey of the theory of government starting with Plato's *Republic*. At the end of forty minutes he would amaze his hearers by hinting that he was nearing the suburbs of his central subject. His oratory was magnificent. He could "splash at a ten league canvas with brushes of comets hair," so opulent were his historical resources and so wide his horizons. I once saw him fail in ghastly fashion. He was preaching at one of the Tuesday dinner-hour services for city men at Bishopsgate Chapel. The service begins at 1:15 and must end a few minutes before two o'clock so that the men can be back at their offices and warehouses punctually. Dr. Fairbairn, wholly unaccustomed to the tyranny of a clock, found himself with seventeen minutes for his sermon. Given seventy minutes he might do himself justice; but seventeen minutes! He gave a sort of a prelude to his introduction to a massive discourse; but he was desperately uncomfortable and quite ineffectual. As it was he went on till perilously near two o'clock, and might have even passed the hour, but one by one the city men "folded their tents like the Arabs and as silently stole away." Dr. Fairbairn accepted the closure.

Also amazing is the fact that Fairbairn usually spoke without manuscript. A professor in Chicago University, now retired, who heard this theologian lecture there in 1895, related to me the following incident. For nearly an hour before his lecture was to be given, the restless Scotsman paced up and down, back and forth over the University campus, alone, preoccupied, no doubt, with his subject. Then, when the time came for him to speak, he entered the hall and without so much as a scrap of notes, poured forth a swift, deep stream of facts, names, dates, and the conclusions he had reached through years of study, research, and contemplation. The friend who told me of this episode, himself a scholar and author, said he had never witnessed before or since such an astonishing feat of memory.

The year following the delivery of his lectures at Yale, Fairbairn published his book, *The Place of Christ in Modern Theology*, and within four years it passed through twelve editions. His biographer, Professor W. B. Selbie, regards this book as the most representative and in some respects his best. It had been a long time in course of preparation, and embodies his mature thought on many of the subjects with which he had previously dealt in a more tentative fashion. Writes Dr. Selbie:

> The book starts from what he calls the new feeling for Christ, and is in no sense a system of theology. Its author did not so regard it. He described it as "an endeavor through a Christian doctrine of God at a sketch of the first lines of a Christian theology." . . . The dominant note of the book, as its title indicates, is the recognition of Jesus Christ as the original and determinative factor in Christianity. Fairbairn's theology is always theo-centric, God as Father, and man as child of God are the two foci of his thought. But we know God in Christ, and it is the Fatherhood of God as interpreted by the consciousness of Jesus which he here sets forth, or as he puts it, "This theology must, to use a current term, be as regards source Christo-centric; but as regards object or matter theo-centric: in other words, while Christ determines the conception the conception determines the theology."[1]

II

What of Fairbairn as a theologian, and the effect upon his day and ours as a thinker in his chosen field? Following the publication of his *The Place of Christ in Modern Theology*, Dr. Peter T. Forsyth wrote of the work in the *Evangelical Magazine* for May, 1893:

> The work will change and color our theology for many a day. We hope it may restore public interest through history to dogmatics. It is an extraordinary combination of readability and profundity, of sparkle and depth, of epigrams which open vistas, and thoughts "which broke through language and escaped." But we all know that skilful lucidity, that genial sympathy, that sanguine note, that keen dialectic, that informed eloquence, that sustained march of the whole army of thoughts carrying without disorder its small brisk counter-marches of antithesis, and its excursions into the locality it may pass. Without Newman's ethereal haze, it has more than Newman's brilliancy, more than his critical acumen, much more than his philosophic power, and a light worn wealth of knowledge, both philosophic and historic, which makes the father of modern Anglicanism by comparison a jungle of ignorance crossed by streaks of insight and pricked with spots of light.

[1] W. B. Selbie, *Life of Andrew Martin Fairbairn*, p. 229.

In the same month of the same year Dr. A. B. Bruce wrote in the *Contemporary Review* as follows:

> When a man of Principal Fairbairn's standing, ability, learning, earnestness, and undoubted loyalty to the faith makes an appeal to his fellow Christians to the effect that theology requires revision and reconstruction on the basis of Christ's idea of God, it cannot reasonably or safely be put aside. Its claim to attention is strengthened by the perfect courtesy and good temper with which the writer's views are stated, even when as in the case of the Church question his attitude is most uncompromising. Dr. Fairbairn's theological position is by no means revolutionary. He discards no recognized theological categories and he adds no new ones. He aims only at revision and correction, and above all at the breathing of Christ's spirit into theology. The fault of the book in the eyes of many will be that it alters so little. It will much help all who accept the Catholic faith, but it will disappoint those who wish forever to be rid of the miraculous and the transcendental in religion, and to have a creed based on thoroughgoing naturalism.

For a modern appraisal of Dr. Fairbairn's theological position it is good to turn to Dr. Edwin E. Aubrey, professor of religious thought at the University of Pennsylvania. In a letter bearing the date of May 22, 1950, he wrote:

> Fairbairn was one of the most popular theological writers at the turn of this century. He is best known for his two books, *A Philosophy of the Christian Religion* and *The Place of Christ in Modern Theology*. (The former went through four printings in a year.) Today he is little used. This may be due to the fact that he addressed himself to the special problems of his own day, and because in writing on them he often passed over important critical questions which did not seem to him to be crucial for belief in his time. He has therefore been accused of dogmatic dismissal of issues without proper examination; but this may reflect the academic rather than the general Christian mind. Since the theological situation has changed and new issues have appeared or older issues have been revived, his approach seems often "dated."
>
> His style is always lucid and interesting, with an intuitive element that is often quite daring, and sometimes the passages of his prose are fit for use as devotional reading. There is therefore a tendency at times to let eloquence override critical precision, and this exposes him to the criticism of the professional scholar in the field.

He possessed a great range of knowledge spreading over the history of religions, of art, of social thought, of philosophy and theology, and of literature. This helped to make his writing attractive to ministers, but it also distracted attention at times from the close reasoning that some of his discussions required.

The philosophical basis of his system is clearly Idealist: ideas are primary, order is due to mind, the Absolute is expressed most completely in a Person, the unity of history is achieved by an immanent teleology and this is incarnate in Christ, and self-realization is the law of human progress. But he is opposed to Hegel at many points and undertakes in several places to criticize him, especially his a priori rationalism.

Fairbairn was, however, an evangelical Free Churchman, opposed to unreasoning dogmatism of the creeds and to Humean skepticism that undercut the basis for religion and morality alike. He was always alive to the religious temper of his day, and saw the religious problem as one of dealing with certain antitheses that threatened to tear faith apart. The nineteenth century had seen the translations of the Sacred Books of the East under Müller's editorship, and the corresponding tendency to regard one religion as just as good as another. Hegel's attempt to show the supremacy of Christianity as the absolute religion had been rationalistic rather than historical. Fairbairn undertook in his Haskell Lectures to show the supremacy of Christianity on historical grounds. The Tübingen School of New Testament scholarship had applied the methods of historical criticism along Hegelian lines with results culminating in Ferdinand Baur's finding that the Christian experience of Paul was more fundamental than the life of Christ. Fairbairn sought to show, against the background of an extended treatment of the history of Christology, that it was the historical Jesus whose life shaped the experience of the apostles and that in the experience of Christian followers the meaning of Jesus Christ came to be understood as nothing less than God incarnate.

In the controversy between Kantian ethics and the evolutionary ethics of Spencer, Fairbairn stands close to Kant and is critical of Spencerian evolutionism, but once again roots ethics in the Incarnation.

Against the materialism of late nineteenth-century thought Fairbairn set his idealism, though he underestimated the strength of the arguments of the materialists and thus failed to meet them adequately.

One of the puzzling aspects of his writing is his complete ignoring of Ritschl's great work on *Justification and Reconciliation* which had been published in 1870-74, while he mentions the latter's works on early church history. Whether this was due to the Ritschlian break with Hegelianism, and the accompanying tendency to historical positivism, is hard to say; but there are points in common in the moral emphasis that would have led one to expect more attention to this German author.

I suppose that it is the decline of Hegelianism that accounts in part for the fact that Fairbairn's work is largely forgotten today. It may also be that the general point of view he expounded with the vigor of new discovery is now fairly generally absorbed into theological scholarship.

III

A reference to Fairbairn's huge correspondence has already been made here, but something needs to be said of the nature and variety of his letters. Dr. Selbie's biography contains extracts of many of the weighty letters in his correspondence and also the more tender and intimate. In the biography of Fairbairn's friend, Dr. Robert W. Dale of Birmingham, written by Dale's son, there are numerous letters which passed between these two theologians. But a different kind of letter and one that belongs here by "certain inalienable rights," is the following, which Dr. Fairbairn wrote from New Haven to his wife on April 1, 1892:

Last night a great reception in my honor; saw all the professors; everyone quite gracious; a mathematician, Newton by name; an engineer, who wrote on theology; a botanist, who knew the older men, but not Vines—fine art, philosophy, and science professors without end. On Wednesday I attended a club of the professors, and had to give an account of Mansfield and Oxford—all very interested. Ray Palmer and daughter were here; she very sorry Barbara was not with me. I have had yesterday and today to answer seven letters of invitation to various places, Philadelphia, Boston, Northampton, and places you never heard of—plenty to keep me going till autumn. One of the queerest was a letter from an old Scotsman, who knew Byres, Bathgate, etc.; was married to a Marion Shields; a man Inglis by name; and was very anxious that I should visit him; but Fisher has asked him to come to lunch. I was rather hoping to get a little quiet, as the grind of continual lecturing, with the necessary intervals of meals, fills up all my time. Yet my health is splendid; the weather is splendid, simply perfect; and all as gay as may be. Today I walked with Dr. Munger, a local minister, a little way into the country; everything was lovely; air clear as crystal, to breathe it and look through it a pleasure, yet though stimulating it is not strengthening, so little calculated to encourage walking. Though the sunshine is so bright, not a leaf is out, nor a promise of one appearing. No top-coat is needed, save as it draws towards evening; when the sun goes down the air is very chill. I write in haste; the post goes earlier than I expected; so best love to all.[2]

In his autobiography, *My Education and Religion*, page 272, Dr. George A. Gordon tells of an eight-day visit Dr. Fairbairn made in the Gordon home in the autumn of 1889. "We were delighted with him, and especially delighted with him was our daughter of four years of age," writes Dr. Gordon. "She waited patiently outside his bedroom door every morning till he appeared, that she might be carried shoulder high to the dining room." On the return voyage to England Dr. Fairbairn wrote this letter:

H.M.S. Majestic
Sept. 27, 1889

DEAR MRS. GORDON:
Here I am with my face homeward, but my thoughts turned backward to all the happy days spent in your home and the gracious hospitality which made them so delightful.
The visit to Wellesley was most interesting and enjoyable, and the journey to New York as pleasant as and no more restful than a night's journey usually is.
Tell Ruth I do not forget her. Her last kiss still lingers on my lips. The very memory of it is fragrant.
My love to dear Brother Gordon; and when next he comes to Oxford, he must come to us, and not come alone.
With best regards and thanks that cannot be written,
Ever yours,
A. M. FAIRBAIRN

There are many letters of this scholar which reveal his mind. This one, and there are others like it, gives a glimpse into the heart of one who was as gentle as he was great.

[2] *Ibid.*, pp. 329-330.

Writing about Dr. Fairbairn in the middle nineteen twenties, Arthur Porritt said:

I doubt if his books are read today. I asked one of his old students once if he thought Dr. Fairbairn was living in his books. He told me that whenever he went into an old Mansfield man's library and took down Fairbairn's books, he generally found the historical introductions thumb-marked as if they were well read, but when he turned to the pages that contain Dr. Fairbairn's original contribution to the subject the pages were seldom cut, and if cut, looked quite clean.

Sic transit gloria mundi!

The closing paragraph of the last chapter in *The Place of Christ in Modern Theology* deserves to be quoted here. It is altogether likely that his audience heard it at Yale in 1892:

From the strife of the sects we would return into the calm and gracious presence of Him who is at once the Head and the Heart of His Church. He has given us His peace, and it abides with us even amid the collisions and contradictions of men. These are but of time, while He is of eternity. And in His presence we may not meet negation with negation, and affirm of those who say that there is no church but theirs, that theirs is no church of Christ; on the contrary, we shall draw no narrower limits than those traced by the hand of the Son of man: "Whosoever shall do the will of My Father which is in heaven, the same is My brother, and sister and mother."

On May 19, 1919, full of faith and of years, Andrew Martin Fairbairn died, and was buried in Wolvercote cemetery near his old friend, Dr. Legge. A great cross of Aberdeen granite marks the place where he lies.

III. GEORGE ADAM SMITH

None of my predecessors has attempted a full exposition of the material which the Old Testament offers to the Christian preacher. This fact alone might have determined the subject of the following course; but at the same time, as everyone is aware, there is no part of the preacher's field or material which has been the object of more industrious research or of more unsparing criticism than the several Books of the Old Testament, and the national history of which they form the record.

—GEORGE ADAM SMITH[1]

Those of us who were ministerial delegates in attendance at the meeting of *The League to Enforce Peace* in Music Hall, Philadelphia, the spring of 1918, will not forget seeing and hearing Sir George Adam Smith. He appeared on the program along with Lord Reading, Senator John Sharp Williams, William Howard Taft, and other celebrities. His brief speech was grave, earnest, and prophetic, as he attempted to forecast the difficulties of a just and enduring peace. He was in the uniform of a chaplain of His Majesty's army, and we learned, though not from him, that he had lost two sons in the war that was then still raging. My companion, a Presbyterian minister, and I tried to meet Sir George, but in vain; the throng about him was too dense.

Sixteen years later, when motoring through Scotland, and in Aberdeen for a night and a day, I lingered for a time in the vicinity of Sir George's residence trying to work up sufficient courage to knock at his door and ask the boon of clasping his hand. But having learned somewhere about the city that he was not in robust health, I decided not to obtrude myself upon his seclusion. Perhaps it is gratuitous to mention this episode here, but I offer it as further evidence of my propensity for hero worship when it comes to great Christian scholars and giant preachers of the Word.

Sir George Adam Smith's life was one long series of successes in that inclusive field of scholarship where accuracy is as much prized as brilliance, and in some instances possibly more so.[2] Sir

[1] From the introduction to his lectures at Yale Divinity School.

[2] "Dr. Smith was from the first something of a cosmopolitan. He was taught from the beginning to appreciate excellence of every kind. He learned to combine an enthusiasm for literature and learning with a deep evangelical fervor. We believe he himself ascribes the most definite of his early religious experiences to meetings held during the Moody revival. For Mr. Moody he has always cherished a warm admiration and reverence, and higher critic though he is, he was able to work with Moody on his last visit to America, and wrote a heartfelt tribute to his memory as a preface to Professor Drummond's essay. Dr. Smith took his early training at the high school and University of Edinburgh. It was when he went to the New College, however, that his bent

George Adam Smith

George was both accurate and brilliant, nor did he at any period of his illustrious career dwell in an ivory tower of academic aloofness. In addition to his professorial years at the United Free Church College, Glasgow, and at the University of Aberdeen, where he was vice-chancellor and principal, he served as moderator of the United Free Church, and was knighted by King George V the same year.

"He leaped into fame," wrote Sir W. Robertson Nicoll, longtime editor of *The British Weekly*, "as the author of his great commentary on Isaiah." His monumental work on *Jerusalem* is still authoritative, although written many years ago; and his *Historical Geography of the Holy Land* was used by staff officers in the Allenby campaigns of World War I and also in the late war.

Principal William Robinson of Overdale College, Birmingham, England, says of Sir George:

He stood in the front rank of Old Testament scholars along with Driver and Peake and his older colleague, Robertson Smith, to whom he owed much. It is to his credit that he stood by his namesake in his famous heresy trial in 1881. . . . Like Peake, he was a man of strong evangelical fervor, and people knew that, in spite of his critical approach, he was sound in the faith.

As a preacher Dr. Smith was Biblical, expository, and exegetical. There was clarity and simplicity in his discourses, the illustrative material was choice, and he was equally at home in a rural church or on a university occasion. Despite the fact that he had won renown in the Old Testament field, much of his preaching was based on New Testament scripture. In his volume entitled *The Forgiveness of Sins and Other Sermons*, of the fifteen sermons, eleven are from New Testament texts. The sixth sermon is on "The Two Wills" and is based on Matthew 27:12-14, 20-23. The segment that follows is an excellent specimen of Dr. Smith's literary style and exegetical skill:

---

developed. He was strongly influenced by Professor A. B. Davidson, a man of whom it has been truly said that in his quiet way he has done more to influence theological thinking in Scotland during the last thirty years than any other. Smith took to Hebrew and the study of the Old Testament."—W. ROBERTSON NICOLL

Nothing is clearer from the Gospels than this: that it was Christ's own will to die. He had long set His face steadfastly to Jerusalem. While others still deemed it impossible, His soul lay already under the Shadow of the Cross.

Some men make up their minds to die, when they feel the stress of circumstance bearing in that direction. And, indeed, he is invested with a certain sacredness, however mean in soul he may be, whom we see delivered to death by events over which he has no control. But Jesus felt no outward circumstance compelling Him to death. Circumstance, in truth, was much the other way. Humanly speaking His Cross was not inevitable. There were moments when He might have escaped. But He stirred up the Pharisees, disappointed the people who would have made Him King, bade Judas do his business, and, last of all, was silent before Pilate.

It is no less clear that He did this in order to fulfil a mission laid upon Him by His Father. He regarded opportunities to escape as temptations. The lips of flesh would be excused from touching that burning cup and prayed: *Father, if it be Thy will, let this cup pass from me.* But he added, *Nevertheless not my will but Thine be done.* Because it was His Father's will He set His face to the Cross.

He also declared why He must suffer. This was not for martyrdom alone. He had come to bear witness to the truth among a people who, as He pointed out, had with tragic consistency slain their prophets. Yet the burden of truth He brought from heaven was not the only burden He carried. He found another awaiting Him on earth in the sins of men; and this, though sinless Himself, He stooped to bear in all its weight. For, besides meeting temptation in its force, as only He could who fought it to victory, and enduring in all its rigour the moral warfare appointed to every man; He had lifted the burden of the miseries which sin has brought upon the world. Sinless Himself, He had felt the shame and the guilt of sin as never the best or the worst of men had felt it. He had confessed it for others; He had borne it in prayer to God. He had proclaimed its forgiveness. And finally He had connected His Death with that forgiveness. *I give my life,* He said, *a ransom for many.* This is the New Covenant in my blood, shed for many, for the remission of sins.[3]

The preface and introduction to *Modern Criticism and the Preaching of the Old Testament,* delivered at Yale in 1901, are written by the author, and are of such value as to warrant a careful

---

[3] *The Forgiveness of Sins and Other Sermons,* pp. 107-9.

reading before one tackles the eight lectures which follow. For instance this paragraph:

The objects of the Lectures are, in the main, three: a statement of the Christian right of criticism; an account of the modern critical movement so far as the Old Testament is concerned; and an appreciation of its effects upon the Old Testament as history and as the record of a Divine Revelation. Obviously eight Lectures cannot provide an exhaustive treatment of these themes; but the lectures contain, I trust, enough to serve their purely practical aim, and to exhibit to students and preachers the religious effects of the critical interpretation of the larger half of the Scriptures of the Church. In the Fourth Lecture the line of argument is intended for believers in the Christian doctrine of Revelation. I have always felt that for those who believe in the Incarnation the fact of a Divine Revelation through the religion of early Israel, as critically interpreted, ought not to be unintelligible. If we recognize that God was in Christ revealing Himself to men and accomplishing their redemption, it cannot be difficult for us to understand how at first, under the form of a tribal deity—the only conception of the Divine nature of which at the time the Semitic mind was capable—He gradually made known His true character and saving grace.

There is a particularly fine passage in Lecture I, into which Sir George brings the name of his beloved friend, Henry Drummond. The paragraph is too good to omit.

Like every man who has read a little and thought a little, I was aware of this great and tragic commonplace of our day. But during the last year I have come across so many instances of it—each the story of a human soul that it has become vivid and burning in my mind. It has been my privilege to go carefully through the correspondence of one who, probably more than any of our contemporaries, was consulted by persons of the religious experience which I have described. Many address him from the silence and loneliness of those far margins of our world where men have not yet largely settled, and the few who come have leisure and detachment enough to think freshly upon the old ways in which they have been trained; but others are residents of the centers of civilization, and their words are heavy with what I feel to be the greatest pathos of our life—the hunger of souls starving unconsciously within reach of the food they need. One and all tell how the literal acceptance of the Bible—the faith which finds in it nothing erroneous, nothing defective, and (outside of the sacrifices and Temple) nothing temporary—is what has driven them from religion. Henry Drummond was not a Biblical scholar; he was not an authority on the Old Testament. But the large trust which his personality and his writings so magically produced, moved men and women to address to him all kinds of questions. It is astonishing how many of these had to do with the Old Testament: with its discrepancies, its rigorous laws, its pitiless tempers, its open treatment of sexual questions, the atrocities which are narrated by its histories and sanctioned by its laws. Unable upon the lines of the teaching of their youth to reconcile these with a belief in the goodness of God, the writers had abandoned, or were about to abandon, the latter; yet they eagerly sought an explanation which would save them from such a disaster.

To the charge that modern criticism of the Old Testament is a movement of recent growth, Dr. Smith replies:

The modern criticism of the Old Testament may be said to have begun in 1680. In that year a French priest called Simon drew attention to the fact that within the book of Genesis the same event is often described in different words. He emphasized especially the two accounts of the Creation, which lie side by side in the opening chapters, and the two accounts of the Flood which are fused together in chapters vi-ix. For these Simon suggested different authors, whose writings Moses had put together. Such was the beginning of the criticism of the Pentateuch.

To that large number of ministers who struggle in privacy and often "in lonely contemplation" over the difficulties of the Old Testament these lectures come with a double blessing. They not only help to dissolve doubts and difficulties which rise from reading the Old Testament, but at the same time exalt the importance of this older section of the Bible in preaching. Professor Smith refers to the Old Testament lying "not *under*, but *behind* the New"—a nice distinction. He holds to what he calls "the abiding value of the Old Testament for the life and doctrines of the Christian Church. That which was used by the Redeemer Himself for the sustenance of His soul can never pass out of the use of His redeemed."

Dr. Smith observes: Schleiermacher is the only great preacher of the century who would have nothing to do with the Old Testament, judging it to stand to Christianity in the same relation as paganism does. "For our ethics," he says, "the Old Testament is entirely superfluous." We perceive the historical injustice of such a view; but Dr. John Ker has also remarked its evil effect upon Schleiermacher himself as a preacher. "One cannot but see that Schleiermacher's style has suffered from his neglect of the Old Testament." How much of force and charm, of passion and poetry, have all other great preachers derived from the Hebrew Scriptures!

So much for the lectures—all too little it is true; so much for the scholar, the critic, the author, and the teacher. Something now needs to be said of the man, the preacher, devout servant of his Lord. For this we turn to one who knew him intimately and loved him much.

Dr. George Adam Smith is one of the most brilliant men of the day. . . . With all his width of range, his varied interests, his many friendships, he has kept in close touch with forlorn and friendless humanity. It is characteristic of the man that in Glasgow he is not connected with any great or wealthy congregation, but is an elder in a humble mission church, to which he gives much of his strength and time. He has retained through all his successes his charming modesty, his unfailing sympathy, his affectionate concern in all the joys and sorrows of his friends. Above all things, he has recognized that he is not merely a scholar, but a minister of the Word of God, and that as a minister of the Word of God he is bound to see that scholarship does not confuse and weaken but rather strengthen and gladden the Church of Christ.

So wrote Sir W. Robertson Nicoll at a time when George Adam Smith seemed to be at the peak of his powers. Actually, he was to win still greater honors and, also, to know greater sorrows, before which he bowed but did not break. For he could say with Browning:

> . . . we are in God's hand.
> How strange now looks the life He makes us lead:
> So free we seem, so fettered fast we are:
> I feel He laid the fetter, let it lie.

IV. PETER TAYLOR FORSYTH

Dr. Forsyth's volume of lectures delivered at Yale in 1907 is one of the fattest, physically, in the Series. In making this observation I am not forgetting the sturdy volume of Dr. Broadus' *On the Preparation and Delivery of Sermons*, which is a huge amplification of the lectures he gave in 1888-1889. Then there is the corpulent volume of Dr. Fairbairn, lecturer in 1892. In the preface to his *The Place of Christ in Modern Theology* (American Edition 1912), he says: "This book appears as the Morse Lecture, but it contains matter that was delivered in *The Lyman Beecher Lectures* at Yale, besides much matter that has never been delivered at all." In Dr. Forsyth's preface to *Positive Preaching and the Modern Mind*, he writes:

May I remind those who honour me by looking into this book that it consists of lectures, and that I have been somewhat careful not to change that form in print. Also, as the audience consisted chiefly of men preparing for the Ministry, it was inevitable that I should speak chiefly *ad clerum*. I trust this may help to excuse a shade of intimacy that might not befit address to a wider public, possibly something of a pulpit style at times, and a few repetitions. I need hardly add that the lectures were abbreviated in delivery.

A "fat volume physically," might not mean much. There are some big books that are unimportant and some small books that are immortal; it is the nature of the contents that is important; and these three bulky volumes in the Yale series are classics of their kind.

I am indebted to the Reverend William Robinson, D. D., former principal of Overdale College, Birmingham, England, and editor of the *Christian Advocate*, for the piece of portraiture that follows:

Peter Taylor Forsyth was born at Aberdeen in 1848 and died in 1921. He came of Norse stock as his name implies. He was educated at Aberdeen University where he took first class honours in classics.

He then studied under Albrecht Ritschl at Göttingen and later at New College, London (Congregationalist Seminary). He held pastorates in Congregational Churches in Shipley (Yorkshire), Hackney (London), Manchester, Leicester and Cambridge. In 1901 he became Principal of Hackney College, London, the Congregational Seminary associated with New College which was then under Dr. A. E. Garvie, another Scotsman Congregationalist. The Congregationalist Churches in Scotland are small, but they have produced for English Congregationalists two of their greatest Principals, and three if we include Fairbairn, first Principal of Mansfield College, Oxford. In 1905 he was Chairman of the Congregational Union of England and Wales, and in 1907 was Lyman Beecher Lecturer at Yale when he produced his famous *Positive Preaching and the Modern Mind*. Forsyth was a giant among pigmies and little heeded in his day, especially amongst his own people. He was a prophet before his time. Perhaps his only real disciple was an Anglican, the late Canon J. K. Mozley, who wrote two obituary articles for *The Expositor* when Forsyth died. To-day he is recognized as perhaps the one great theologian the Free Churches produced in the nineteenth and twentieth centuries and all his books are being reprinted by the Independent Press (Congregationalist). I first heard of Forsyth when I was a student in Mansfield College, Oxford, in some not very complimentary remarks away back in 1918. That drove me to read Forsyth and at that early date I realised that he had something unique to say. He has been described as the Browning of Theology, largely due to his rugged style. One writer has said that reading his books is like "walking on cobble stones" and that may well be, but they are worth reading even if the effort is painful. If Forsyth had been known, Barth, Brunner and Niebuhr would have become irrelevant. I do not think he was acquainted with Kierkegaard, but all the deep insights which are in him, are to be found in Forsyth without the pathological elements. When I took over the Principalship of a theological college in 1920 I used to get all my students to read two theologians, Forsyth and von Hügel, the Roman Catholic layman. I still do. In many ways they are similar and were certainly aiming at the same thing. The thing that makes them of value is that they both saw the flimsy character of the Harnackian reconstruction of the Gospel with its subjectivity. Forsyth's philosophical acumen led him to the goal of the objective-subjective. So he deals with the Doctrine of the Atonement in *The Work of Christ*, the Doctrine of the Person of Christ in *The Person and Place of Jesus Christ*, the Doctrine of Immortality in *This Life and the*

Next, and the Doctrine of Providence in *The Justice of God*. We are now quite accustomed to the idea of paradox in theology. Forsyth's works are full of paradoxes, but they are paradoxes of *mobility*, not static paradoxes. One word was never off his lips, the word "dynamic." He saw so clearly that the idealistic philosophy which had prevailed for so many centuries was incapable of bearing the Gospel of the *Living* God. It was far too static resulting in a theosophical kind of theology out of harmony with the Biblical concepts. To read Forsyth to-day is to be made aware of how securely he anticipated many of the results of later scholarship with which we are familiar, even in the field of Form Criticism. His insight was amazing. Forsyth was the First Free Churchman to recover a sound doctrine of the Church and Sacraments after it had been lost in the nineteenth century. He was by his brethren suspect of Catholic tendencies! This must have caused him some merriment to assuage the disappointment, but so far as the theologians of the British Free Churches are concerned he has certainly entered into his own in our day: "his works do follow after him." True, he was a High-Churchman and a sacramentalist. Strange as it may seem to some, his High-Churchmanship was born of his studies under Ritschl. His understanding of the Church and the sacraments, whilst it was as "high" as the highest of Catholics, was something quite different. Catholic sacramentalism, he regarded as theosophical with its emphases of "presence" and "substance." For him the Gospel was dynamic and Church and sacraments must be understood in the realm of *action*, which meant the realm of ethics. His book *The Church and the Sacraments* is one of his greatest contributions to theological thought.[1]

I

Dr. Forsyth's subjects are as massive as his material: I. The Preacher and His Charter; II. The Authority of the Preacher; III. The Preacher and His Church; IV. The Preacher and the Age; V. The Preacher and Religious Reality; VI. Preaching Positive and Liberal; VII. Preaching Positive and Modern; VIII. The Preacher and Modern Ethic; IX. The Moral Poignancy of the Cross.

Obviously anything like a just appraisal of these powerful lectures in a single chapter, necessarily brief, is not possible. It is like attempting to photograph Mount Everest by sections. It

---

[1] From a letter to the author.

cannot be done successfully and I am painfully aware of that stubborn fact. The Forsythian style is rugged and some of his paragraphs are enormous. Often he gives the impression in print of a turgid, swift-flowing river, hurrying to hurl itself over some lofty precipice, midst showers of spume. His comparison between preaching and oratory takes a long paragraph, nevertheless I deem it too good to omit:

> Preaching (I have said), is the most distinctive institution in Christianity. It is quite different from oratory. The pulpit is another place, and another kind of place, from the platform. Many succeed in the one, and yet are failures on the other. The Christian preacher is not the successor of the Greek orator, but of the Hebrew prophet. The orator comes with but an inspiration, the prophet comes with a revelation. In so far as the preacher and prophet had an analogue in Greece it was the dramatist, with his urgent sense of life's guilty tragedy, its inevitable ethic, its unseen moral powers, and their atoning purifying note. Moreover, where you have the passion for oratory you are not unlikely to have an impaired style and standard of preaching. Where your object is to secure your audience, rather than your Gospel, preaching is sure to suffer. I will not speak of the oratory which is but rhetoric, tickling the audience. I will take both at their best. It is one thing to have to rouse or persuade people to do something, to put themselves into something; it is another to have to induce them to trust somebody and renounce themselves for him. The one is the political region of work, the other is the religious region of faith. And wherever a people is swallowed up in politics, the preacher is apt to be neglected; unless he imperil his preaching by adjusting himself to political or social methods of address. The orator, speaking generally, has for his business to make real and urgent the present world and its crises, the preacher a world unseen, and the whole crisis of the two worlds. The present world of the orator may be the world of action, or of art. He may speak of affairs, of nature, or of imagination. In the pulpit he may be what is called a practical preacher, or a poet-preacher. But the only business of the apostolic preacher is to make men practically realize a world unseen and spiritual; he has to rouse them not against a common enemy but against their common selves; not against natural obstacles but against spiritual foes; and he has to call out not natural resources but supernatural aids. Indeed, he has to tell men that their natural resources are so inadequate for the last purposes of life and its worst

foes that they need from the supernatural much more than aid. They need deliverance, not a helper merely but a Saviour. The note of the preacher is the Gospel of a Saviour. The orator stirs men to rally, the preacher invites them to be redeemed. Demosthenes fires his audience to attack Philip straightway; Paul stirs them to die and rise with Christ. The orator, at most, may urge men to love their brother, the preacher beseeches them first to be reconciled to their Father. With preaching Christianity stands or falls because it is the declaration of a Gospel. Nay more—far more—it is the Gospel prolonging and declaring itself.

"The Bible," Dr. Forysth declares: "is still the preacher's starting point, even if it were not his living source." And he goes on to say:

The public soon grow weary of topical preaching alone, or newspaper preaching, in which the week's events supply the text and the Bible only an opening quotation. And the New scholarship is making the Bible a new book, a new pulpit for the old Word, a new golden candlestick for the old light. Preachers are inspired by the historic freshness of it, as the public are interested by its new realism. It is a great recent discovery that the New Testament was written in the actual business and colloquial Greek of the day. And less than ever is the textual style of preaching like to die, or the Bible to cease to be the capital of the pulpit. Preaching has a connexion with the Bible which it has with no other book. For the Bible is the book of that Christian community whose organ the preacher is. Like the preacher, it has a living connexion with the community. Other books he uses, but on this he lives his corporate life. It is what integrates him into the Church of all ages. Preachers may, for the sake of change, devote their expositions on occasion to Tennyson, Browning, or Shakespeare. They may extract Christianity from modern art, or from social phenomena. They may do so in order to lay themselves alongside the modern mind. But they will be obliged to come back to the Bible for their charter, if they remain evangelical at all. If they cease to be that, of course, they may be driven anywhere and tossed.

II

Perhaps Forsyth's greatest lecture is his last, on "The Moral Poignancy of the Cross." Surely it is an important one, on a subject to which the noblest theologians have given their best and yet felt it to be inadequate. Here, Dr. Forsyth rises to vast heights of what Principal Robinson calls "amazing insight." After due deliberation, I present this as perhaps his greatest deliverance in this remarkable chapter:

It is not enough, therefore, to emphasize the person of Christ, to set it again in the centre as modern theology was bound to do, and has done ever since Schleiermacher, in order to repair much historic neglect. We may dwell on the person of Christ and mean no more than a perfectly saintly soul reposing in God. But this is a conception too sabbatic for a universe which is an act, and whose energy runs up into human history. Christ's person has its reality in its active relation to other persons—God or men. We must find the key to it in something Christ did with His entirety, and did in relation to that holiness of God which means so much more than all Humanity is worth.

The true key to Christ's person is in His work. It lies not in a miraculous manner of birth, nor in a metaphysical manner of two co-existent natures, but in a moral way of atoning experience. It lies in His personal action, and in our experience of saving benefits from Him. It lies not in His constitution but in His blessings. His love to us is not the image, the reflexion, or even the result of God's love, it is a part of it, the very present action of it. We feel this particularly when we are forgiven. It is only the holy love we have so wronged that has the right to forgive. And the forgiveness we take from Christ is taken directly from the hand and heart of God, immediately though not unmediated. Christ is God forgiving. He does not help us to God, He brings God. In Him God comes. He is not the agent of God but the Son of God; He is God the Son. As we must preach Christ and not merely about Christ, so Christ does not merely bring access to God, He brings God. God is Love only if Jesus is God. Otherwise Jesus would become our real God. God's love then is love in holy action, in forgiveness, in redemption. It is the love for sinners of a God above all things *holy*, whose holiness makes sin damnable as sin and love active as grace. It can only act in a way that shall do justice to holiness, and restore it. Short of that, love does no more than pass a lenient sentence on sin. It meets the strain of the situation by reducing the severity of the demand. It empties of meaning the wrath of God. And it reduces the holy law of His nature to a bye-law He can suspend, or a habit He can break.

And again:

> To lay the stress of Christ's revelation elsewhere than on the atoning Cross is to make Him no more than a martyr, whose testimony was not given by His death, but only sealed by it. His message must then be sought in His words; and His death only certifies the strength of conviction behind them. Or it may be sought in the spell of His character to which His death but gives the impressive close.

III

Dr. Forsyth was a caustic critic. He said of Dr. Reginald John Campbell's *New Theology* that it was a bad photograph, underdeveloped and overexposed. Of Dr. Joseph Parker, he said, "At one time I thought Dr. Parker was a good man touched with egotism; I have come to believe that he is an egotist touched with goodness." A student in Principal Forsyth's class in Hackney College once gave a curious exegesis of a text and quoted Dr. Campbell Morgan as his authority. Some of the other students smiled. Dr. Forsyth's reply was prompt. "I should be very proud," he said, "if the students of Hackney College knew *the* Bible as well as Dr. Morgan knows *his* Bible."

In his *The Best I Remember*, a book that fairly teams with preacher stories and anecdotes, the author, the late Arthur Porritt, of *The Christian World*, London, says:

> Sometimes Dr. Forsyth's verbal thrusts were not chivalrous, and he could be horribly bearish. . . . An allowance has to be made for the ill health from which Dr. Forsyth suffered all through his later life. Peculiarly sensitive to chills, he was in terror of draughts, and digestive trouble made him "pernickety" about what he ate and drank. He believed he had heart trouble, but in his last illness it was the soundness of his heart alone that kept him alive for months.[2]

On November 11, 1921, Peter Taylor Forsyth, at the age of seventy-three, finished his extraordinary course.

Note: In talking with scores of ministers about the Lyman Beecher Lectures, I found without exception that those whose opinions are most highly valued, rated Forsyth's series at Yale as unrivaled of their kind, and a "must" book for alert, studious preachers everywhere. This is superlative praise, for these distinguished preacher-scholars also rated highly the Lectures of Andrew M. Fairbairn, George Adam Smith, and Reinhold Niebuhr, in the same series.

[2] P. 128.

V. WILLIAM RALPH INGE

On May 9 we said good-bye to our kind hosts. We have enjoyed our visit immensely, and have been quite abashed by the kindness and generosity which have been shown us. Comparing this visit with our former visit twenty years ago, we think that the Americans are more assured of themselves and therefore less inclined to emphasise the vast size of their country and the smallness of ours. We were of course fortunate in meeting the most cultivated and intellectual society in the United States.

Our baggage was increased by a large crate of ginger ale, the gift of a man who had heard my little joke about prohibition and cold water. At the docks one of the officials came and patted me on the back and thanked me for all that I had said. We were photographed and a film taken of us both. "More than 23,000 photographs have been taken of the Dean during his stay here."

—WILLIAM RALPH INGE[1]

When it was announced that the famous Dean Inge of St. Paul's, London, was to lecture in the Yale Series the spring of 1925, expectations ran high, and as the event drew near the interest became intense. No wonder, for the Dean was about as often in the headlines as Bernard Shaw and fairly equaled him in racy, pungent epigrams. A philosopher, theologian, essayist, and provocative preacher of a Gospel which he considered too exacting for an effete generation to welcome, the Dean's advent in New Haven was awaited with an eagerness which was everywhere in evidence. One of England's most original thinkers was coming to the "States" to tell the clergy, both young and old, what it meant to preach the Word.

The somber appellation "the Gloomy Dean," first applied to this ecclesiastic by a clever newspaper man, is arresting but misleading; what there is of truth in it is due to his pessimistic com-

---

[1] *Diary of a Dean*, entry under date of May 9, 1925, p. 104.

ments on modern society.[2] Socially the Dean can be charming and witty when he chooses to be and is in a jovial mood which perhaps is often.

The Dean was sixty-five when he delivered his lectures at New Haven, and was at the peak of his mental prowess, a "peak" which lasted long, for under a date line of July 28, 1948, a special dispatch from London to *The New York Times* fairly sparkled with the Dean's wit. Thus:

Christian unity, dogma, the infallibility of the Bible and other ideals that many cherish were derided today by Dr. W. R. Inge, former dean of St. Paul's Cathedral, in an address read for him at the Conference of Modern Churchmen in Oxford.

Dean Inge, who is 88 years old and has been out of the hospital only a few weeks after two operations, showed that neither age nor infirmity had dimmed his wit or dulled his sharp pen.

"We must have churches," he wrote, "but a political or institutional church is a secular corporation in which the half-educated cater for the half-converted. It seems incredible that the presence of the spirit of truth has been canalized in one denomination. The claim suggests a not too creditable trick of trade.

"The baseless dream of corporate reunion with the unreformed churches is perhaps the worst enemy of church reform. It forecloses all debate on some urgent problems, such as birth control, ordination of women and marriage law. . . .

"We know now how formidable totalitarianism still is. Catholicism does 'deliver the goods.' It makes its votaries happy and, as Amiel says, there is no return from it any more than from the mutilation of virility."

Battell Chapel on the campus of Yale University was crowded to capacity when Dean Inge gave the first of his lectures from the general theme *The Social Teachings of the Church*. The president of the University presided and welcomed the distinguished guest in a brief address, gracious and replete with complimentary

---

[2] "Because of his forebodings based on the belief that the solar system would in time be engulfed by an icecap, the Very Reverend W. R. Inge, Dean of St. Paul's Cathedral, became identified in Britain's press as the Gloomy Dean."
—From a review of *Diary of a Dean* by G. Bernard Shaw, *Atlantic Monthly*, May, 1950.

phrases. Then Dean Charles Reynolds Brown introduced Dr. Inge in one of those felicitous speeches for which he was noted.

The great moment had come! The Dean of St. Paul's, London, in clerical attire correct to the smallest detail, "legs cased in hierarchical gaiters," arose, adjusted his spectacles, hitched his shoulders, and began to read, his voice inaudible to most of his hearers. The lecture was a dreadful disappointment. Of course it was stout thinking; the Dean was above commonplaces! But the address was not fresh and timely. Neither were the lectures which followed. Gradually it dawned on the audience and the faculty of Yale Divinity School that the celebrated scholar and renowned clergyman had made no special preparation for this high event but, instead, had brought over a collection of lectures given on various occasions across the years.

In a letter from a member of the Yale faculty to a correspondent occurs this paragraph:

The lectures were regarded by us and I think by him also as a failure. He had taken out of a rather deep barrel some old lectures of an historical nature which had very little to do with the work of preaching. His audience on the first day was large, but I should say fully one-third of them went out before he had finished; and there was a very sad falling off for the remainder of the course. . . . The Yale Press offered to publish his lectures but he declined. The Macmillans of New York sent a man to my home to ask him for his manuscript, that they might publish them, but he refused.[3]

It is difficult to account for this melancholy performance of a world figure who continued to preach brilliantly controversial sermons from his great and venerable pulpit. Not only so, but this

[3] In Dr. Inge's *Diary of a Dean*, p. 101, he writes under date of April 20, 1925, as follows: "To New Haven, Connecticut, a dull journey, through a densely populated district. New Haven has 150,000 inhabitants, nearly half of them Italians. Dean Brown met us, and drove us to his 'frame house' in a typical New England street, lined with an avenue of American elms, each house with its stoep and an unfenced grass-plot. Mrs. Brown is a gentle attractive woman. I gave my first lecture in the Congregational chapel. There are to be eight Lectures, on 'The Preaching of the Kingdom of God.' They do not satisfy me, and I do not mean to publish them. Yale University has been enriched by buildings in the English collegiate Gothic style, the gift of a Standard Oil magnate. Like most American buildings of this kind they are admirable architecturally."

unpredictable person continued to write books and deliver addresses in London and elsewhere which stimulated thought, captured the imagination of the intellectuals and literati. As recently as 1949 the Dean, then eighty-nine, was reported in an interview as comparing the clergy to "opticians trying to fit different sorts of glasses to people with different degrees and kinds of blindness. The main thing is to assist them to see." The Yale audience would have liked this. Still again, his Yale auditors would have relished this paragraph which was heard by his congregation on a certain Sunday at St. Paul's, London.

Science may speak doubtfully about the existence of a personal God. But it will not allow us to believe that, if there is a personal God, He is either a capricious Oriental Sultan, to be approached only through His privileged courtiers, or a magnificent Schoolmaster, or the Head of a clerical profession. Sir John Seeley said that the man of science has a nobler conception of God than the average churchgoer, and I think he was right.

In his delightful autobiography entitled *My Own Yesterdays*, Dr. Charles R. Brown quoted Dean Inge on an occasion other than at Yale as delivering himself of this choice observation:

There are three forms under which thought may be presented—solid, liquid, and gaseous. The first is for learned college professors writing dull, dry treatises for and at each other. The second is for books which were meant to be read. And the third is for an audience where the words of a man's mouth and the meditations of his mind "go on the air." In spite of all its competition the third still bids fair to hold its own.

Dean Inge's words at Yale did not "go on the air," which may have been fortunate for him and all concerned.

During the preparation of this chapter I turned up a copy of Dean Inge's *The Social Teaching of the Church*, six lectures delivered on the Beckly Foundation before the Wesleyan Methodist Conference in 1930, in Plymouth, England. The title is not the same as used at Yale in 1925, but it is reasonable to conclude that some of the material in this book was given at Yale. I found these lectures stimulating and, while brief, fully up to the author's reputation. Perhaps they read better than they sounded, since

William Ralph Inge

Joseph Fort Newton describes the Dean and his method of speech as "a sober dry-eyed, didactic personality, and an elocution atrocious in its angularity." Here is a characteristic passage:

> The church has to do with the motives and desires and passions which lead to disputes about the distribution of wealth. It condemns the irrational love of accumulation. But we have no right to say that one system of taxation is more Christian than another. The Good Samaritan in the Parables set the wounded man on his own beast and paid his hotel bill with his own money. The modern version of the Parables seems to make him run after the priest and Levite and take the horse of one and the purse of the other. But would not St. Paul have said: "Though I give all my neighbor's goods to feed the poor, and have not charity, I am nothing?"

If the Dean said this at Yale, he gave his hearers something to remember and to ponder.

I cherish the opinion that the Dean's lack of urbanity in public address and his indifference to popular appeal explain, at least in part, the unhappy incident with which I have reluctantly dealt. Nor can I believe that his words were altogether fruitless on that historic occasion, since it is reasonable to surmise that more than one iscouraged theologue who heard the lectures said to himself, if not to others, "If so great a man can fail in so important a Lectureship, there must be hope for me when I fall below my best," and so took fresh courage.

Here endeth a gloomy lesson![4]

[4] "There have been three Gloomy Deans in English history. One was Dr. Inge's far-off predecessor in the deanery of St. Paul's, the great and strange John Donne, poet, metaphysician, amorist, ascetic. The second was Dean Swift, bitterest of satirists, most exquisite of humorists. It was Harley, Earl of Oxford, who had the merit of promoting Dr. Swift to a deanery. It was Asquith, Earl of Oxford, who had the responsibility of elevating Dr. Inge. These three Gloomy Deans, by a singular coincidence, were the greatest wits of their respective epochs in the Church of England."—Ernest H. Jeffs.

Writing in his diary, May 3, 1925, and still referring to his visit to America, Dean Inge says, "This visit is the most extraordinary experience of our lives. I am boomed like a first-class celebrity. I am surrounded by reporters and photographers and I believe I have been filmed for the 'movies' more than once. The Americans say that perhaps Bernard Shaw or Rudyard Kipling would have as great a reception but nobody else. Very gratifying, but why don't they buy my books? They don't."

VI. REINHOLD NIEBUHR

Dr. Niebuhr is the most talked about and written about of all contemporary religious leaders. His picture in the newspapers and various journals of opinion is becoming as familiar to the public as was that of Henry Ward Beecher in his day. Wherever he speaks he is sure of a crowd. Whatever he writes is certain to be widely read and ardently discussed. Whether one wholly agrees with Niebuhr or not is a secondary matter, since he excites respect and admiration because of his erudition, brilliance, and courage.

If one is so fortunate as to be able to claim an acquaintance with a celebrity extending over many years, the temptation to dilate on the theme, "I knew him when," is quite irresistible. I do not pretend to try to resist that temptation, but surrender to it cheerfully. During the years 1920-1928, Dr. Niebuhr and I were contemporaries in Detroit and, for the larger part of that period, fellow members of the "Wranglers," locally famous free-lance preacher's club. I heard Dr. Niebuhr read his first paper before that group, and recall vividly the impression it made upon those who were present, including among others, Bishop Charles D. Williams, Dr. Joseph A. Vance, Dr. Gaius Glenn Atkins, Dr. Lynn Harold Hough, Dr. Chester B. Emerson, and Rabbi Leo M. Franklin. Niebuhr, unlike some theologians, is a clubbable man, friendly, companionable, and conversationally delightful. Still, he was a little shy in those days, not aloof exactly, but not inclined to put himself forward unless the circumstances seemed to require it. Something of this shyness still clings to him when he is out of the pulpit or off the platform.

In appearance Dr. Niebuhr has not changed much since those Detroit years. His figure is still imperially slender, the eaglelike countenance a little more matured, the high forehead more prominent because of thinning and receding hair. The old buoyancy of spirit persists, and his speaking style is, if anything, more flashing and fluently engaging. He would be superhuman if he were other than conscious of the recognition he has received, but fame has not spoiled him. He is too serious and troubled by the struggle of moral man with unmoral society to let arrogance have its willful way with him. The wonder is that he keeps his feet so firmly planted on the ground; but he does.

I

Not many notables, other than candidates for the Presidency of the United States of America, have their biographies written in their lifetime, but Dr. Niebuhr is an exception to the general custom. The Reverend D. R. Davies, Vicar of Holy Trinity, Brighton, the church where the eminent F. W. Robertson served from 1847 to 1853, came out in 1948 with a small and ably written book entitled *Reinhold Niebuhr, Prophet from America.* Mr. Davies is a close student of Dr. Niebuhr's writings and is in every way qualified to do justice to his subject without being lost in a flood of idolatry. Davies calls Niebuhr a "Christian Revolutionary," and just how much of a theological and social revolutionist this professor in Union Theological Seminary is, the book reveals, as the author expounds, analyzes, and evaluates the Niebuhrian theology and philosophy. Since the beginning of his Detroit ministry Dr. Niebuhr has switched from a liberal in theology to the right, and to the left in economics and politics. Mr. Davies gives a large place in the conversion of Niebuhr, both theologically and politically, to Henry Ford, and to a study of the organization which the Detroit motor magnate built from humble beginnings into a colossal mechanized industry, and himself into a multimillionaire. The Reverend Mr. Davies concludes his biography of Dr. Niebuhr with this paragraph:

Reinhold is a gift of God to a tortured and troubled world. He is, by any standard of judgment whatever, a leading, if not the leading theorist in the contemporary revolution in Christian thought. He has made orthodox theology relevant to our secular crisis. He has made it intellectually respectable. In our optimistic youth, many of us drifted into liberal Protestantism because we shared too easily the assumption that orthodoxy was intellectually discredited. It had ceased to be fashionable. It was out of date. Every bright young thing was modernist by definition. Niebuhr has powerfully helped to change all that. Nowadays, it is the old who are theological liberals. The young, who, as always, swim with the tide, are orthodox. Niebuhr has been one of the influences that has reversed the theological tide. But he has done more than that. By his prophetic insight and passion, he has made the Christian faith an inescapable social issue for a generation whose own secular faith has proved to be bankrupt. This achievement makes his place secure in the apostolic succession of Christian revolutionaries.

II

Dr. Niebuhr's *Faith and History* contains his lectures given at Yale, with considerable new material added. There are fourteen brief chapters quite closely integrated in thought. It is not easy to quote from this book in any satisfactory way. The author's style is not simple, and he needs to be quoted from *in extenso* if justice is to be done these lectures. He is a verbal artist who requires a "ten league canvas"; a lecturer whose field is the world. Perhaps to list some of his chapter headings will suggest his method and subject matter. Thus: "The Current Refutation of the Idea of Redemption Through Progress"; "The Extravagant Estimates of Freedom in the Progressive View of History"; "The Identification of Freedom and Virtue in Modern Views of History"; "The Foolishness of the Cross and Sense of History"; "The Validation of the Christian View of Life and History"; "Fulfillments in History and the Fulfillment of History"; "The Church and the End of History."

In Dr. Niebuhr's lecture on "The Extravagant Estimates of Freedom," are these grim and provocative passages:

There is a grim irony in the fact that mankind is at this moment in the toils of the terrible fate of a division between two great centers of power, one of which is informed by the communist and the other by the bourgeois liberal creed of world redemption. Both creeds imagine that man can become the master of historical destiny. The communists assume that the rationalization of particular interest will disappear with a revolutionary destruction of society which maintains special interests. The very fury of communist self-righteousness, particularly the identification of ideal ends with the tortuous policies of a particular nation and its despotic oligarchy, is rooted in the naive assumption that the rationalization of partial and particular interest, is merely the product of a particular form of social organization, and would be overcome by its destruction.

Meanwhile the liberal world dreams of the mastery of historical destiny by the gradual extension of the "scientific method," without recognizing that the objectivity and disinterestedness which it seeks by such simple terms represents the ultimate problem and despair of human existence. The two creeds are locked in seeming irreconcilable conflict. Whether the conflict eventuates in overt hostilities or not, it has already produced an historical situation which cannot be encompassed in the philosophy of history of either creed. An adequate frame of meaning to encompass it would have to contain the motif of the Tower of Babel myth of the Bible. In that myth God reduced the pride of men who wanted to build a tower into the heavens by confounding their languages, thereby reminding them that they were particular, finite, and conditioned men, who do not find it an easy matter to become simply "man."

Many of Dr. Niebuhr's flashing epigrams are readily quotable, for instance, "Humor is, in fact, a prelude to faith, and laughter is the beginning of prayer . . ." "The intimate relation between humor and faith is derived from the fact that both deal with the incongruities of existence . . ." "Laughter is . . . not only the vestibule of the temple of confession, but the no-man's land between cynicism and contrition." Not even Gilbert Chesterton was more the master of the paradox than Niebuhr. The latter's writings abound in statements that are, or seem to be, contradictory. The result is that the truth in each paradox is more intensely high-lighted. His preoccupation with sin inspired a now famous limerick, the authority for which has been attributed to the late Archbishop of Canterbury, Dr. William Temple:

> At Swanwick, when Niebuhr had quit it,
> Said a young man: "At last I have hit it,
> Since I cannot do right,
> I must find out tonight
> The best sin to commit—and commit it."[1]

A sermon preached by Dr. Niebuhr, any sermon, produces a strange effect upon the thoughtful hearer. It alternately depresses and exhilarates him. It is as different from the typical great and good sermon which soothes and comforts the hearer, as the patter

[1] Courtesy of *Time*. Copyright, Time, Inc., 1946.

of gentle raindrops on the roof differs from a storm, with the wind tearing at the cornices and the trees bending and breaking under the violent assault of all nature. On the one hand the hearer feels himself to be the object of God's goodness, and, on the other, he is not at all sure he has any claim on the love or goodness of God. Rather, he is moved to think of himself as a poor and miserable sinner. In the carefully chosen words of a contemporary: "Reinhold Niebuhr's new orthodoxy is the old-time religion put through the intellectual wringer. It is a re-examination of orthodoxy for an age dominated by such trends as rationalism, liberalism, Marxism, fascism, idealism and the idea of progress."[2]

Dr. Niebuhr's English biographer, the Reverend D. R. Davies, who has so much praise for this American theologian, finds one serious defect in his theology, namely, his failure as yet to deal significantly with the Church. Thus he writes:

> What is the significance and value of episcopacy in the economy of the Church? So far as I know, Niebuhr has nowhere raised or explored this question, which is vital to the existence of the Church, and therefore to the whole problem of the relation between Christianity and civilization. Whatever else may be charged against him, the one thing he cannot be accused of is indifference to the problem of the relation of Christianity to civilization.[3]

VII. HERBERT HENRY FARMER

Dr. Farmer argues for what he calls "radical personalism." Modern man is accustomed to think in terms of order, law, and "things." This is a laboratory point of view. So implicit is that attitude in our thought that we even attribute this point of view to God. From all we can deduct from the scriptures this is not the Divine point of view. In the Bible the Divine mind thinks of His universe in strictly personal terms. To Him the universe is a personal universe and His relationships with man are strictly personal.
—Rev. Clarence E. Lemmon, D.D.

[2] Courtesy of *Time*. Copyright, Time, Inc., 1946.
[3] *Reinhold Niebuhr, Prophet from America*, pp. 99-100.

Dr. Farmer, who has a superior mind, expresses himself clearly and with distinction. He is a thinker who can put profound ideas in simple yet decorous language, intelligible to laymen and his fellow theologians alike. He is still young, comparatively, being but fifty-eight, and was eminent in his field at thirty-five. He ranks high among contemporaries, and his books are widely read by persons of all shades of theological thought.

Professor Farmer was educated at Owen's School, Islington, London, and at Peterhouse, Cambridge, where he took his M.A. degree with honors. He then entered Westminister College, Cambridge, the theological seminary of the Presbyterian Church of England. (Dr. Skinner, the famous Old Testament scholar, was then principal.) He was Warrack Lecturer in the University of St. Andrews in 1940 and Lyman Beecher Lecturer at Yale University in 1946. He has worked steadily and fruitfully in the ecumenical movement, being at Oxford in 1937, Madras in 1938, and Amsterdam in 1948. From 1940 to 1949 he was on the staff of his old college as professor of systematic theology. He has been appointed to succeed Dr. C. H. Dodd as Norris Hulse Professor in the University of Cambridge. He will be the second Free Churchman to hold this office since the time of Cromwell. This is the only chair in divinity in the University of Cambridge to be held by a non-Anglican, and no such chair has ever been held by a non-Anglican in the University of Oxford since the Cromwellian period. This speaks volumes for the eminence of C. H. Dodd (Congregationalist) and H. H. Farmer (Presbyterian).

Principal William Robinson of Overdale College, Birmingham, England, writes:

I first met and heard H. H. Farmer at a S. C. M. Conference at Swanwick. He was addressing some 2,000 students from our Universities and Colleges. This was in the late "twenties." He impressed me immensely. He had the knack of getting over profound philosophical truth in a simple way. He simply captivated that audience in the great marquee. I marked him, not as *a* coming man, but as *the* coming man, someone who would take the place of P. T. Forsyth. Shortly after, he went to Hartford, and I was naturally disappointed that he was taken from my own country at a time when we sorely needed him. But, he was sure to be called back again, and the call came in 1937 from his old University. He stands easily as our most constructive theologian. His books, *Things Not Seen* (1927), *Experience of God* (1929), *The World and God* (1935), *The Healing Cross* (1938), *The Servant of the Word* (1941), and *Towards Belief in God* (1942), have made him known the world over amongst ministers and theological students. He owes much to his predecessor in Westminster, John Oman, and his emphasis on the *personal* relationship of God to man, but he has given this a deeper objective root in the Word of God. His best book is perhaps *The World and God*, which is a classic on the Doctrine of Providence. His doctrine of the Church and the sacraments is more profound than that of Oman and he is a much better preacher and lecturer than Oman was, as well as a better stylist, which makes his most profound books not too difficult to read.

He represents the same emphasis in theology which is common to thinkers like Barth, Brunner, Aulen, and Niebuhr, but he is a disciple of none of these, and has a deeper appreciation than any of them of the heritage of the classical culture, and of what we owe to the Liberal period in theology and what is owed to Christian experience. He is a scholar in the first place, but a scholar who is still human, a man of warm friendliness, and deep humility.

I

Dr. Farmer gave the Beecher Lectures in 1946, his subject being *God and Men*. The Contents of the chapters as listed in his book are of unusual fullness, and serve admirably as an epitome of the series:

I. THE WAY OF KNOWLEDGE
   Need for emphasizing unity, distinctiveness, and personalism of the Christian faith. The way of approach to Christian truth: (i) serious-mindedness, (ii) practical alertness, (iii) sincerity, (iv) adequate context, (v) spirit of adventure.
II. THE WORLD OF PERSONS
   Failure of modern thought (i) to consider the personal world, (ii) to see it as distinctly personal. (iii) "Claim"—the difference between laboratory and personal attitudes. (iv) The biopolarity of the world.

III. MAN THE SINNER
Personal view of man in contrast to (i) naturalistic, cultural, vitalist, and collectivist views. (ii) Entire truth found only in personal view. (iii) Sin—the failure to recognize claims of God and neighbor.
IV. GOD'S ACTION IN CHRIST
God's saving entry into world. Reasons for not accepting this fact: belief in (i) pantheism and laboratory science, (ii) the law of progress. (iii) Reasons for accepting the fact.
V. THE HOLINESS OF GOD
(i) God "wholly other" yet not "wholly other." These conceptions embodied in God as (ii) creator, (iii) omnipotent, omniscient, omnipresent, (iv) eternal, (v) infinite perfection.
VI. THE LOVE OF GOD
God's love inseparable from his holiness. (i) Purpose to make men good, (ii) working through freedom, (iii) independent of man's worth, (iv) for the community as well as the individual. (v) The final restoration.
VII. SKEPTICISM AND FAITH
God's love not apparent in nature and history. (i) Knowledge of it dependent on revelation. (ii) This love revealed in a Cross. (iii) God's purpose consummated beyond history. (iv) Entering the kingdom now.

Theological students are a critical audience to speak before. They can be and sometimes are hypercritical. A remark of an old minister as reported in Sir Robertson Nicoll's *Princes of the Church* is to the point: "I am not afraid to preach to probationers; I am not afraid to preach to ministers; but there is a thing called a divinity student. God preserve me from it."[1] Perhaps there were times when lecturers in this course agreed with this sentiment, but the students who listened to Dr. Farmer heard him gladly. He spoke on lofty themes, with a minimum of illustrative matter, yet held the attention of his hearers to the end. Something of this broad human spirit of the lecturer is communicated to the reader of *God and Men.*

In "Man the Sinner," Dr. Farmer's third lecture, he says, "I think we can perhaps most usefully make plain the Christian view of the essence of man by setting it in contrast with other views

[1] P. 105.

which in variant forms are current today." Next he lists four views more or less popular today which, while not without some truth, are unequal and inadequate to meet "the Christian view of the essential secret of human nature." These four views are (1) The *naturalistic*, which sees man as not *essentially* different from any other member of the animal kingdom. (2) The *cultural*, which distinguishes and isolates man from the rest of the world—even though in other ways he obviously is an animal—in that he is able to seek, and to be interested in, and to enjoy what are vaguely called higher, spiritual, or cultural values, and able to realize the progressive enthronement of these higher and nobler virtues. (3) The *vitalist* view, extremely vague but none the less real, the view that life is to be lived to the full here and now; let us *be* ourselves and express ourselves. (4) The *group* or *collectivist* view, which takes into account the *nationalistic* idea, the fact of race, or the *Volk*, the cult of one's own country "for which it is sweet to die." Admitting truth in all these views and citing the incompleteness of all, Dr. Farmer sets forth in the paragraph which follows what he believes to be the *Christian* view of life:

So then here at last is the Christian view of the essential secret of human nature, of the distinctive "humanity of the human." It is that he is a person standing all the time in personal relationship to God. It is that relationship which constitutes him—MAN. It is important from the Christian point of view to take this statement quite rigorously. That perhaps needs some effort of mind. It is so easy to think that a man can first be a man and then *afterward* enter into relationship with God, by becoming, for the first time, perhaps, consciously religious; or that he can cease to have relationship to God by ceasing to be consciously religious. We even speak of "godless" men. This, as I understand it, Christianity emphatically repudiates. It emphatically repudiates the idea that a man's relationship to God begins or ceases at the point where he begins or ceases to believe in God, or even to think about him. On the contrary, it says that man is distinctly man at all only because—whether he knows it or not—he stands, right down to the innermost core and essence of his being, in the profoundest possible relationship to God all the time in an order of persons. If, as is impossible, he could wrench himself out of that relationship, he would cease to be MAN. For when God creates a man, he creates that relationship by the same act—without the relationship there would be no man. Taken literally the phrase "a godless man" is a contradiction in terms.

One of the persistent and pathetic questions asked by those who cannot reconcile the love and justice of God with the facts of life is "Why?" Dr. Farmer has an answer, and not the answer that the questioner often hears, which commonly runs like this: "It is the will of God, bow humbly before him and he will heal your sorrow." Here is this preacher-theologian's answer:

It is important to insist, with ourselves and with those to whom we speak, that the Christian gospel has from the beginning claimed to rest on God's own active *disclosure* of himself in the midst of our world as holy love. The Christian gospel is not, strictly speaking, the simple statement that God is love; it is rather that God himself discloses, exhibits, commends, makes credible, his nature and purpose as love to us through Christ, and very especially through Christ's death on the cross. The Christian faith has certainly never claimed that the proposition that God is sovereign love is self-evident to the human mind. That would be absurd, for quite plainly it is *not* self-evident; judging, indeed, by the history of religions, the only statement about God which comes near to being self-evident to the human mind is that he is inscrutable power. Nor has it been claimed that God's love can be inferred or proved from, or read out of, the facts of nature or history; indeed, it fully admits that from the point of view of many of these facts the doctrine has very little credibility, if any at all. . . . Faith is that attitude of mind which, finding itself laid hold of by the truth concerning God's love as given through Christ, commits itself to that truth in adventurous trust and obedience, in spite of all the mystery and all the perplexity that remain. Discerning the love of God at work at that one point in historical time, the Christian is prepared to . . . trust it to be at work in all personal relationships whatsoever. Moreover, only in such adventurous trust and experimental obedience—particularly in the sphere of personal relationships—can the truth that God is love be authenticated to the soul and built up into a massive conviction, despite all the mystery and darkness.

And now for a majestic climax, with organ tones prevailing:

So the apostle Paul, after meditating on what he calls "the groaning and travailing together of the whole creation," is yet able to write what is surely the grandest expression of faith in all literature—an expression which is the more grand for burking none of the facts:

Who shall separate us from the love of Christ? shall tribulation, or distress, or persecution, or famine, or nakedness, or peril, or sword? . . . I am persuaded that neither death, nor life, nor angels, nor principalities, nor powers, nor things present, nor things to come (shall we say, no dimension of time, no long-drawn-out enigma of history?), nor height nor depth (shall we say, no dimension of space, no infinite immeasurability of the suns and the stars?), nor any other creature, shall be able to separate us from the love of God which is in (which meets us in, discloses itself to us through) Jesus Christ our Lord.

For the most part Herbert H. Farmer's Yale lectures, while not technically on preaching, were largely *preaching*, and great preaching it was, and is.

IV

PROPHETS OF SOCIAL
★ CHANGE ★

A wise observer of the social situation has lately said: "*When anyone brings in a complete solution of the Social Question, I move to adjourn.*"

—FRANCIS GREENWOOD PEABODY

1. WASHINGTON GLADDEN

The friendless poor get short shrift and summary vengeance; the rich rascal can secure delays and perversions of equity and often goes scot-free. The man who steals a ham from a freight car goes to jail; the man who steals the railroad goes to the United States Senate.

—DR. GLADDEN AT YALE IN 1887

Dr. Gladden belongs to that exclusive group, but four in number, who gave more than one full course in the Lyman Beecher Lectureship. He delivered the first, in January, 1887, on *Tools and the Man*, and the second, in March, 1902, on *Social Salvation*. These discourses were the first in the distinguished Series to invade the highly controversial field of industrial relations and social justice generally. The noted Congregationalist was the forerunner of Rauschenbusch, Bishops Williams, McConnell and Oxnam, Dr. Coffin, Dr. Tittle, and other churchmen who followed in the train of those Old Testament Preachers of Righteousness—Amos and Micah.

Much turbulent water has passed under the bridges of the world since Dr. Gladden pioneered at Yale and sought to save the pulpit and the pew from a purely individualistic acceptance of the Christian gospel. Since he spoke at Yale in 1887, the gains of organized labor have been so revolutionary and massive as to make it difficult to be sure which is the underdog, Capital or Labor. Then too, for nearly two decades we have had administrations at Washington which might be described as mild forms of labor government, although some would contend that they have been anything but "mild."

Many reforms which Dr. Gladden advocated at Yale, and elsewhere, such as stronger labor unions, government ownership of public utilities, and the aid of the state in behalf of the poor and the disinherited, have been achieved, at least in part, and the struggle still persists, and will continue. Dr. Gladden's "radicalism" in the realm of economic and social justice seems, on the surface at least, conservative today when compared with the views of some of our latter-day prophets of social change, Dr. Harry F. Ward, for example. But on closer scrutiny of the teaching of Dr. Gladden it will be found that he was much of the same mind as such bold churchmen as Francis J. McConnell, Charles D. Williams, or Reinhold Niebuhr, and what is more to the point, he took in his day a barrage of criticism which he bore humbly and with a certain knightly gallantry.

I

Take a look at the subjects of his first lectures: "Property in Land"; "Property in General"; "The Labor Question"; "The Collapse of Competition"; "The Reorganization of Industry"; Scientific Socialism"; and "Christian Socialism." He presented these subjects in clear, pungent, and powerful diction. But there was no bitterness, and on the whole the sanity of his handling of these moot questions was closely woven into the texture of his arguments. For illustration, this passage from his discourse on "The Logic of Christianity":

"Sirs, ye are brethren!" You cannot obliterate that fact. You cannot afford to ignore it. In all your strikes, lockouts, your black-listing and your boycotting, your combinations of capital to hold labor down and of labor to defy and coerce capital, remember that the law of your being is, not conflict, but co-operation, and that while you are fighting one another you are fighting against the stars in their courses, against the Ruler of the universe; that you are doing not only a wicked, but an absurd, an unnatural, a monstrous thing.

Dr. Gladden's second series, which was on *Social Salvation*, was less controversial than the first, less theoretical, and I judge more practical, but none the less forthright or spirited in content and style. He deals with such themes as "The Case of the Poor"; "The State and the Unemployed"; "Our Brethren in Bonds" (prison reform); "Social Vices"; "Public Education"; and "The Redemption of the City." This last subject, which treats of municipal problems, was dear to the Doctor's heart, because he knew it firsthand, having served in the Common Council of the City of Columbus. Likewise, he was a member of numerous committees and commissions dealing with various aspects of municipal policies and programs of city planning.

How Dr. Gladden felt about the relation of the ministry to the subjects he discussed is aptly summarized in the conclusion of his lecture on "Religion and the Social Question":

I trust, my brethren, that I have made plain to you my own deep conviction that the work of the ministry must be deeply concerned with social questions. I trust you will find in your own hearts a growing interest in these questions, and that you will be able to communicate that interest to the people to whom you are sent; to kindle in their hearts the enthusiasm of humanity, and to guide them in their thoughts and labors for their fellow men. And I trust that you can see that this social teaching and social service is not something outside of religion; that religion is and must be, the heart and soul of it all; that it means nothing but religion coming to reality in everyday life; the divine ideal descending upon human society and transforming it from glory to glory, even as by the spirit of the Lord.

II

During my ministry at Franklin Circle Church of Christ, Cleveland, Ohio, 1903-1906, I was privileged to hear Dr. Gladden when he spoke before the National Council of the Congregational Churches meeting in that city. Some impressions of the man and his address linger with me to this day. One was the honor and esteem in which he was held by his brethren and the ovation accorded him when he rose to speak. Another was his mastery of the manuscript which he manipulated dexterously. He spoke on some aspects of the Negro problem with the broad statesmanlike thoroughness for which he was noted.

In a noble address delivered by the Reverend McIlyar H. Lichliter, a successor of Dr. Gladden at the First Congregational Church, Columbus, and at the dedication of the new cathedral edifice, there occurs a passage which should be precious to all ministers of Jesus Christ, and especially so to the younger brethren:

Dr. Gladden never stopped growing. At eighty-two he was preaching in his old pulpit, exposing the fallacies of H. G. Wells with all his old-time vigor. Just a few months before he died, he sounded the prophetic message of the church in the midst of war: "If after the war," he said, "the church keeps on with the same old religion, there will be the same old hell on earth that religious leaders have been preparing for centuries, the full fruit of which we are gathering now. The church must cease to sanction those principles of militaristic and atheistic nationalism by which the rulers of the earth have so long kept the world at war. We must not wait till after the war, that may be too late. Is not now the accepted time?"

Dr. Gladden's surest immortality so far as his literary compositions can be assessed is enshrined in his lovely hymn which opens with a stanza, a prayer, best exemplified in the way the author lived out his full life:

> O Master, let me walk with Thee
> In lowly paths of service free;
> Tell me Thy secret; help me bear
> The strain of toil, the fret of care.

The closing paragraphs of Dr. Lichliter's dedicatory sermon fittingly conclude this sketch of one of the major prophets of his generation:

We dare not associate Washington Gladden with a building, or with a site, or with a city. He was too great to be cribbed, cabined, or confined. His spirit lives in the hearts that loved him. He lives in his books which are still read with interest and benefit. He lives in the hymn which is deathless. Who will dare to say that he is not hovering over us now—bidding us carry on in the spirit of the past to do the new things that challenge us today? Therefore, in loving memory of Washington Gladden—a saint after the Order of the

Pilgrim Fathers—we here dedicate this church to a continuing service to the community, to the free discussion of public problems, to the quest for a reasonable faith, and to the heartiest cooperation with every movement which means a better human life for all.[1]

Note: Dr. Gladden was the storm center of a number of controversial issues in which he was, as someone phrased it, "showered with verbal brickbats." He opposed with vigor the anti-Catholic movements as they emerged, and was accused by his enemies of being in the pay of the Catholic hierarchy—a ridiculous charge. Dr. Gladden made a national issue out of the acceptance on the part of the Foreign Missions Board of the Congregationalists of a gift of $100,000 by the president of the Standard Oil Company. Accordingly the phrase "tainted money" (which Dr. Gladden did not coin) became as familiar to the public as "He kept us out of war," the slogan of Wilson's second presidential campaign. Then when "Billy" Sunday and his party came to Columbus for an evangelistic crusade Dr. Gladden stood aloof from the project, and questioned the ethics of high-pressure evangelism, much to the chagrin of the local Ministerial Association. Yet in these and other controversies, when the storm had passed, the Happy Warrior's influence was, if anything, stronger than before.

II. HENRY SLOANE COFFIN

In Dr. Coffin's reply to the questionnaire which I sent to all the living lecturers in this Course, he added this P.S.: "Good Luck in a wearisome job." I appreciate the solicitude thus expressed and also his choice of certain words. "Job" is the right word to use in this connection, for a job it is. As for Lady Luck, she is coy, easy to woo, and hard to win. But no task that involves reading anything that Dr. Coffin wrote could possibly be "wearisome."

His lectures given at Yale in 1918, when we were in the throes of World War I, are as readable and opportune today as when they were delivered under the heading: *In a Day of Rebuilding*. What a singularly appropriate title for 1950, when so much of our broken world is still in wreck and ruin.

Dr. Coffin starts off with a prediction by "Robertson of Brighton" who, although he died in 1853, is one of the most quoted

[1] "The Heritage of Washington Gladden," dedicatory address of McIlyar H. Lichliter, successor to Dr. Gladden in the First Congregational Church, Columbus, Ohio, December 13, 1931.

preachers, rivaling in this respect Henry Ward Beecher and Phillips Brooks on this side, and Spurgeon and Chalmers in Great Britain. Dr. Coffin quotes this passage from a sermon by Robertson, preached the 11th of January, 1852: "We are told that that which chivalry and honor could not do, personal interest *will* do. Trade is to bind men together into one family. When they feel it is to their *interest* to be one, they will be brothers." Then he prophesied:

Brethren, that which is built on selfishness cannot stand. The system of personal interest must be shivered into atoms. Therefore, we, who have observed the ways of God in the past, are waiting in quiet but awful expectation until He shall confound this system as He has confounded those which have gone before. And it may be effected by convulsions more terrible and more bloody than the world has yet seen. While men are talking of peace and the great progress of civilization, there is heard in the distance the noise of armies gathering rank on rank; east and west, north and south are rolling toward us the crushing thunders of universal war.

On this, Coffin comments: "No Hebrew seer ever spoke words that have been more strikingly fulfilled," and *are still being strikingly fulfilled*, we of this day must add.

"A world shivered to atoms." This was spoken nearly a century ago by Frederick William Robertson, and repeated by H. S. Coffin in 1918, as a prophecy fulfilled. What, pray, is the suitable phrase to describe a world that has felt the horrible havoc wrought by the atom bomb? What would Dr. Coffin say on this subject today? Well, here is what he did say as he looked over his audience of clear-eyed, resolute seminary students:

The Church, like her Lord, possesses the authority of experience, the friendly power of the keys admitting to the household life of God. She is authorized to teach and to inspire, to declare and to urge, not to dictate and to enforce; and her authority must extend over the whole of human life. She has a message to nations and to individuals, a commission to conquer all the kingdoms of this world —art, science, industry, education, politics—for God and for His Christ.

The sorest need of a world in pieces is fellowship—the fellowship of nations, of races, of producers and distributors of the world's wealth. The Church of Christ whose distinctive note is fellowship, is the divinely created company for the world's reconstruction into a universal fellowship. Her programme for our day has been set forth by an ancient prophet: "They that shall be of thee shall build the old waste places; thou shalt raise up the foundations of many generations; and thou shalt be called the repairer of the breach, the restorer of paths to dwell in."

Does the stubborn, persistent, ugly fact that, on the surface at least, and doubtless deeper down, the prospect for *fellowship, understanding, friendship,* and *peace* seem more remote and desperately more difficult to attain today than they were when Dr. Coffin so spoke thirty years ago—does this indisputable fact controvert the truth of the passage quoted above?

What preacher of the Christian gospel with apostolic optimism would answer other than, "No, not in the slightest; rather, it accentuates and highlights such a calm, penetrating utterance and gives it a new and solemn urgency."

This latter-day preacher of righteousness, speaking before that group of ministerial students at Yale, had no illusions as to the long, hard, and rugged way before the Church and her ministry. Thus:

The sons of God are to answer the longing of the creation still in the pangs of birth. On the first pages of the Bible man is told to subdue the earth and have dominion over every living thing. In the Gospels the Son of Man assumes a subduer's position toward the creation. Whatever interpretation one may give to the narrative of the miracles, Jesus impressed His contemporaries as mastering deranged minds, diseased bodies, dangerous waves, deficient food supplies, and bringing sanity, vigor, calm seas, and enough and to spare for hungry people. We are to teach that as Sons of the Most High it is ours to refashion nature in man and stars, to find no comradeship with its strife, but satisfaction in its subjugation to the purpose of its Lord. "Instead of the thorn shall come up the fir-tree; and instead of the brier shall come up the myrtle tree." Man's ability to understand and rule is the faith which underlies all science and all art; but his knowledge and control may render his brethren fiends, and lower the lower creation. The brutalities of these unspeakable years, and the deadly use of nature's forces to achieve them, are only too evident. But human responsibility under God for the Cosmos is brought home to our consciences.

> Yea, the rough rock, the dull earth, the wild sea's furying waters,
> All with ineffable longing are waiting their invader,
> Still, when resisting and raging, in soft undervoice say unto him,
> Fear not, retire not, O Man; hope evermore and believe.

Heretofore in dealing with the various lectures I have made but slight use of the illustrative material in which some of the discourses abound. It is therefore a pleasure to include here one of Dr. Coffin's choice and telling anecdotes:

I once asked a group of Chinese pastors in an interior town what it was in Christ that most impressed them. None of them mentioned the account of any miracle. Chinese mythology could outdo the marvels recorded on Gospel pages. Various replies were given, when one elderly man said: "His washing His disciples' feet," and a sudden general consensus showed that this incident was peculiarly appealing to them. That a revered Teacher should overstep the lines of class and position and take a slave's place was an impressive moral miracle.

Here is something to think about, and the more one contemplates the incident the more meaningful it becomes.

The ministry of "Reconciliation," "Evangelism," "Worship," "Teaching," "Organization," "Friendship"—these are subjects to which Dr. Coffin devotes his lectures, and his closing address is on "Ministers for the Day." If the subjects seem conventional, the treatment is not. The style is smooth, warm; and the shepherd of the flock speaks to the hearts of his hearers, always. And how well qualified he is to speak to his fellow comrades of the Cross! The life story of this man is inspiring and deserves at least a summary here.

Dr. Coffin, like the prophet Isaiah, was born to the purple. He came of a fine old family in affluent circumstances. The allurement of business, political preferment, or a life of ease had no power to move this man. Instead, he chose the ministry, and following an exacting and thoroughgoing period of preparation, both at home and abroad, and a brief apprenticeship, Dr. Coffin entered on his long and fruitful ministry at the Madison Avenue Presbyterian

Church, New York City. His professorial years, the presidency of Union Theological Seminary, the moderatorship of the Presbyterian Assembly, U.S.A., and his numerous books have made him one of our best known and honored of religious leaders. In a modest way I lay claim to his friendship, and am thereby heavily in his debt for many of the best things of life.

Some evenings when the hour grows late and the house is very quiet, I am likely to turn to a certain shelf, take down a book bound in red cloth, with the title, *The Meaning of the Cross*, and read again, I know not for how many times, these words from the soul of Henry Sloane Coffin:

The cross of wood on which Jesus was nailed is the symbol of an eternal cross in God's heart and conscience. . . . The cross of Christ leaves suffering still a mystery, but he shows us what to do with it. . . . The cross is a family catastrophe in which the actors are our kinsmen, and the blood of the victim stains us as sharers in our brother's crime. . . . Men of awakened consciences, faced with Christ on the cross, feel themselves involved in that tragedy.

A man's soul is sometimes wont to bring him tidings more than seven watchmen that sit high on a watchtower.
So says the son of Sirach.

III. CHARLES DAVID WILLIAMS

In my ministry of twenty-six years in Detroit, home of a coterie of especially famous preachers for part of that period, I looked upon Bishop Charles D. Williams as the most prophetic of the group, and that opinion, I think, was shared by many of my fellow ministers. He stood out and above us all in his high office, proclaiming social justice and Christian ethics, quite indifferent to public or private criticism.

I can never forget his coming into a meeting of the Wranglers Club, which consorted that day in the study of the First Congregational Church, where Gaius Glenn Atkins was then minister. It was raining, and Bishop Williams appeared in a yellow slicker, an old felt hat pulled down over his noble head, and in between his lips a brier pipe dingy from much use. The Bishop had spent the previous summer in England, where he had made a study of the labor movement there. That was the subject of the address he gave us that day, which, delivered without notes, was a thorough and enlightening discussion of his theme.

In the preface to his published lectures given at Yale, the Bishop's candor about the high ecclesiastical office which he so ennobled is exhilarating. He writes,

> There is no motto more applicable to a modern Bishop than the text, "Gather up the fragments that nothing be lost." He is a man "scattered and peeled," troubled about many things, distracted with various and often mutually variant occupations. He must be a man of affairs and many affairs. He is expected to fulfill many functions. He is primarily a business man, an administrator and executive. Particularly he is the "trouble-man" of a large corporation. All the church quarrels gather about his devoted head. He has the responsibility for everything that goes wrong, often without the authority to set anything right. He serves as a lightning rod to carry off the accumulated wrath of the ecclesiastical heavens. He is constantly called on to act as judge and should have a judicial temperament. He is also a "travelly man," a kind of ecclesiastical "drummer," or salesman. He is even sometimes in demand as a social ornament, to say grace at banquets, make after-dinner speeches, adorn the stage at public meetings, and administer to the aesthetic needs of conventional society at fashionable weddings, baptisms, and funerals. In the midst of it all he is expected to find time and mind to be a preacher and teacher, a scholar and leader, and above all a man of prayer, and a man of God.

I

The Bishop entitled his series, *The Prophetic Ministry for Today*, and his treatment of the same is, as anyone who knew him would expect, forthright, powerful, penetrating, excitingly candid. In the first lecture, which is a key which fits the doors to those which follow, the Bishop does not minimize the priestly function of the ministry but he surely exalts the prophetic function, of which he himself was a superb example. One of his hearers in reporting this lecture wrote:

Charles David Williams

As in every such photograph, one saw when he had finished, dim traces of each type; but it was clear that the lecturer thought the prophetic faith and spirit ought to be supreme; the priest, the executive, and especially the rhetorician, ought to be subordinate, a point which he emphasized with some rather sharp words about flowery eloquence.

Bishop Williams was a controversial figure, as every man must be, who strikes hard and often at the evils of his day, no matter what or whom he hits. Following the delivery of his lectures at Yale, Bishop Williams preached a sermon in the Cathedral of St. John the Divine in New York City, which brought him a deluge both of criticism and of praise. Commenting on this sermon, *The Wall Street Journal* asked with some heat, "Was it the bolshevists or the businessmen who built and endowed the Cathedral of St. John the Divine?" The next Sunday the newly-elected Bishop of New York preached a sermon deprecating the preaching of politics, which deliverance also drew a barrage of brickbats and bouquets.

Those timid souls of the ministry, good men but cautious, and leaning strongly to the conservative side as to prophetical preaching, would do well to read these lectures several times a year. As for others who major in that type of preaching, a group always in the minority, one good, conscientious reading of the book will suffice. Bishop Williams' course in the Series stands alone in drastic, daring, but not embittered handling of the minister as a prophet of the Most High.

Bishop Williams at Yale delivering his lectures was the same preacher of righteousness he was in the pulpit, the House of Bishops, or meeting with the clergy of his diocese—courageous and kind; radical in social views, and tolerant; denunciatory of evil; and fatherly, always. His words could not be described as "winged"; rather they were solid, weighty and, sometimes, exciting. His sincerity was so deep and apparent that his hearers felt the power of it as one does the throb of a dynamo, yet this man was anything but a "wild-eyed" radical or iconoclast. Thus in speaking on "Prophet and Priest," the seventh lecture in his series, he said:

Prophet and Priest—they stand for radicalism and conservatism, the spirit of progress and the principles of edification, both absolutely necessary to a wholesome and strong society, church or individual ministry. A friend of mine aptly illustrated the comparative values and relations of these two elements after this fashion: "Radicalism is the growing power of the tree—conservatism is the bark. Given a tree all growing power with little bark and you have a cotton-wood, lush and lusty but spongy and porous, of no value as timber. Given a tree all bark and little growing power and you have the gnarled, knotty, spindling sapling of no use for any purpose. But given a mighty vitality with a tough, hard, close bark, and you have the mighty oak, the monarch of the forest."

II

The phrase "100 per cent Americanism" may have had a good birth, but something happened in adolescence, and it has steadily deteriorated. Bishop Williams gave his opinion of that kind of Americanism in a blistering paragraph:

My ancestry has been in America for two hundred years; my family has fought in all the wars of the republic. I am not a bolshevik, parlor or otherwise. I am not a socialist, pink or white. As far as I can tell I am a plain, downright American. But I cannot stand this stage brand of 100 percent Americanism that is up today. It is not Americanism. By the history of our nation, I call it Prussianism.

What did Detroit think of this fighting Bishop with the warm heart? While he lived they differed as to his ideas, political and theological, but those who really knew him respected him for his honesty and his courage. When he died, February 14, 1923, his age but sixty-three, the city mourned, and the powerful evening newspaper, *The Detroit News*, published on February 23, this editorial:

A TRULY RICH MAN

Charles David Williams, for several years a bishop, for four decades a minister of the gospel, leaves his widow, nine children and an estate of $5,000.

The public does not inquire too straitly into the resources of a prince of the church. There is a certain dignity of position, a sacerdotal elevation above the lay existence that discourages too close scrutiny and takes for granted a substantial reward and a freedom from material worries.

Yet here was a man who pursued the duties of his lofty office with tremendous energy and a broad charity. He leaves, at the close of his long and splendid labors, a sum equivalent to two-thirds of one year's salary. This represents the total of his private accumulation during forty years of devotion to the service of his fellowmen. It is not much.

Doubtless there is a special blessing in such modest means as this. For one thing that small estate serves only to heighten the grandeur of character of the man who exhausted himself and his income in the doing of duty. His wide repute was based not on worldly possessions and what they may purchase of position and influence, but on a godly character that elevated him. Pre-eminently, he was a leader of men, whose influence, even now that he has passed away, is incalculable.

It is an inspiring thing and a good thing for humanity that such men live to refute the cynics and to prove the eternal truth of the nobility of personal character and its ascendancy over every material value the world can offer. Bishop Williams, as true life is counted, died rich in great rewards of his own works, and in all of these he enriched others.

Greater tribute than this few prophets of the Church have received.

IV. FRANCIS JOHN McCONNELL

In the late autumn of 1936, in New York City, as president-elect of The Federal Council of Churches, I sat next to Bishop McConnell at a memorial dinner given in honor of the late Dr. S. Parkes Cadman. It was the first time I had seen Bishop McConnell at close range, so I studied him covertly and with eager interest. The Bishop sat quietly, talked but little, was of serious mien. There was a suggestion about him of hidden power, and I thought of him as a judge of some high court seated in austere dignity upon the bench. Actually, no ecclesiastic was ever less magisterial than Bishop McConnell, or more eager that justice be done though the heavens fell. That night he seemed preoccupied and buried in cogitation.

This "preoccupation" of the Bishop is a mood well known to his friends, and the subject of humorous comment. Bishop McConnell never could "loaf and invite his soul"; he is always busy thinking up something or carrying it out. On one occasion a friend saw him in a railroad station standing in a corner, with his back to the people, intently scribbling on a piece of paper. The friend stepped up behind him and peeping over his shoulder made a discovery. No, the Bishop wasn't working on a crossword puzzle; for a little diversion he was solving a problem in differential calculus.

I

So much for a human side of a prophet of righteousness, not without honor in his own country and also not without sharp and ranting critics. "Frank McConnell," as his crony, Bishop Edwin Holt Hughes, calls him, is not a "tired liberal." His critics, not so numerous now as of yore, have usually found him intellectually crisp and physically fit for anything. Despite the fact that one of the Bishop's wealthy parishioners called him, half in earnest and half in jest, an "old bolshevik," this noted churchman is far removed from the fanatical "leftist" or any other sort of an extremist. His feet, which suit his two-hundred-pound body, are planted squarely on good old mother earth, and his good-sized head is not at home in the clouds or in the rarefied air of speculative controversies.

In a series of autobiographical papers which ran in *The Christian Century*, Bishop McConnell tells, good-naturedly, of his conflicts with some of the well-to-do conservatives in the churches:

Thirty years ago, a rich layman in a fit of excitement told me, "You little fellows think you can run things." This had its humorous aspect, speaking literally and physically, for I was ten inches taller than he was and he had almost to stand on tiptoe to talk vigorously to me. Another churchman, a banker, told me shortly after I was elected bishop that he had for years been the adviser of the bishop in that part of the church and that his banker friends were watching closely to see if he was going to stand for me. He gave me to understand that if I would listen to him I could be made a wonderful force for good.

The Pittsburgh laymen were very kindly. One of them was asked if he was not going to leave the church rather than put up with me. "Oh, no!" he answered, "I'm not going to lose my religion because we have a fool for a bishop, and more than that I do like to hear the old bolshevik talk."

Another layman who was desperately reactionary asked that I be assigned to his home in Washington as a guest during a religious convention there. He greeted me with the information that he couldn't stand my social views, but he thought we could get on together for a few days. I think he had a good time, for he did just about all the talking. Some of these encounters remind me of a remark made to me by a most discerning woman years ago when the duty of personal evangelism was more insisted upon in the churches than today. She said the difficulty about such evangelism was that "some of the sinners were personally so fascinating." My Washington friend manifestly regarded me as an economic sinner and not at all fascinating, but he did the very best he could with me. He argued very well.

Not much is accomplished by these personal interviews of the kind of which I speak. Robert Smillie, one of England's greatest labor leaders, used to refuse to "accept invitations," by which he meant social invitations. Henry van Dyke once told a little circle, of which I was one, of his skill in converting a noted socialist to social sanity. Both Dr. van Dyke and the socialist were gentlemen, and their conversation had evidently consisted in mutual compliment. To say that Dr. van Dyke had converted the socialist was just as remarkable as to say that the socialist had converted Dr. van Dyke. The difference between them was too deep to be settled by mutual compliments.[1]

Having also served a term as president of the Federal Council of Churches, I can sympathize with the Bishop in what he had to endure, although my experiences of criticism, while not exactly mild, were not comparable with the fierce gantlets he so successfully ran.

Bishop McConnell has had about all the honors that a Bishop can tote without staggering under the burden: President of DePauw University, of the Religious Education Association, of the Federal Council of Churches, and of the American Social Security

[1] *The Christian Century*, January 18, 1950, p. 77. Used by permission.

Association; Lyman Beecher lecturer at Yale, Barrows lecturer in India; chairman City Affairs of New York City. Incidentally, he is the author of some seventeen books. Perhaps this immense amount of responsibility and labor helps to account for his "preoccupation" and laconic speech at the speaker's table of innumerable dinners.

II

It was probably ordained that Bishop McConnell's subject at Yale in 1930 should be *The Prophetic Ministry*. In print the result is a three-hundred-page volume, carefully written, serious but not ponderous, and as solid and substantial as the author himself. It does not yield as readily to quotations as do many of the volumes in the Beecher Foundation. Nor can it be read as quickly as some of the lighter lectures which abound in anecdote and illustration. The work shows much research and a wide knowledge of history, together with an insight into the environment of both the ancient and the modern prophets. Speaking on the same subject which Bishop Williams chose in 1921, a comparison between the two lecturers is of interest. The spirit and courage of the two Bishops are much alike, but McConnell's work is the more scholarly and comprehensive. Williams strikes body blows, McConnell leads for the head, and both land.

The third lecture, on "The Prophet and Mysticism," is a new approach to the subject in the Yale Series. The Bishop devotes thirty-six pages in his book to this topic, and some excerpts are in order. Here is one from this lecture which exhibits the Bishop's interest in mathematics:

There are still those among us who maintain that because prophecy began with induced ecstasy it has no value in religion. In many branches of study we have been able to rid ourselves of the fallacy that the history of an idea determines the worth of the idea, but not in all. In some realms the claim that truth is not truth because of the unseemliness of its origin is absurd at a glance. Take a table of logarithms. Here is one of the most potent time-saving devices ever contrived by the human mind. Suppose, now, some student turns away from the table of logarithms which has ten as a base and insists upon its worthlessness because it is the last step in a movement which started with man's counting on fingers and toes. To begin with, nobody would ever naturally suspect that the logarithm is descended from any such origin. It is too distinctly a creation on its own account. By the time we reach mantissa and characteristic we are far enough away from all reflections about the tens of fingers and toes. Here are the processes, useful in themselves. Even more pertinent here is the reminder that among the Greeks some mathematical studies were carried forward only after religious sacrifices. The gods were felt to be at work. We are told that the announcement that the proof that the sum of the angles of a triangle is equal to two right angles was attended by the slaughter of an ox. Ox or no ox, however, the proof stands by itself. We need not have the scantiest shred of information as to who first formulated the proof, or the circumstances under which it was formulated. These items may all be interesting to the point of picturesqueness, but they do not touch the validity of the geometrical proposition one way or the other. Of course it is easy to remark that mathematical propositions are in a class by themselves, altogether apart from religious considerations. This is not so certain, however. The appeal of mathematical propositions was so convincing that the Greeks regarded them as expressing divine truth. Pythagoras taught that the essence of being itself was number. Probably much of the attempt to connect religion with number in the days of the Greeks came, not from the desire to add to the regard for the mathematical discoveries, but just to recognize the greatness of these discoveries. I can easily imagine a society in which a thinker, reflecting upon the proposition that the square of the hypotenuse of a right-angled triangle is equal to the sum of the squares on the other two sides, might very naturally suppose that he was contemplating a divine truth. If there has ever been any proposition beautiful and convincing in itself, it is this. The after ages have not exhausted its fruitfulness, as readers of Einstein know. Today, when we are looking for signs of mind in nature, we still turn back to remarks like that of Plato to the effect that God, in creation, geometrizes. . . .

The prophet at his finest and best arrives at moral expertness. As I said at the outset, this expertness does not depend upon the possession of any special faculty, but upon the development of powers entirely human. The prophet reaches the stage where he is sure of his truth. He cannot tell just why, but he is certain as men become certain in any affairs having to do with mighty life concerns. God has spoken to him, because the message has that spiritual quality which can come from no source but God. Always the direct insight of the prophet appears to be the ground of his certainty. We have here the same mystery of expertness which we meet in any realm of extraordinary human attainment. The expert can seldom describe the secret of his own power. By long and absorbed practice he attains to the power just to do what seems to the untrained to be mysterious. In this sense there is no explaining "authority." The scientist comes to a discernment practically unerring, especially where skill is involved. With a surgeon, for example, the skill is wrought even into his fingertips. So with artistic insight. We do not wisely ask artists to tell why one picture, or sculpture, or cathedral is a masterpiece and another commonplace. Thus, finally, with moral seeing. The prophet arrived at the power to see—and he saw and spoke. In thus seeing and speaking he felt that he had seen the Lord and was speaking his truth. This moral insight, it seems to me, must be the touchstone of any mysticism claiming to be prophetic.

Mysticism is like radium—enormously powerful and incredibly beneficial for mankind, and excessively dangerous. The prophet with his keen awareness of moral values is the expert most capable of handling it.

Other titles in McConnell's treatment of *The Prophetic Ministry* are: "The Aim of the Prophets"; "The Prophetic Idea of God"; "Prophets and Priests"; "Prophets and Kings"; "Prophets and Progress"; "The Perils of Prophecy"; and "Jesus and Prophecy." It all accrues to a learned dissertation, exhaustive in treatment and of massive proportions. The style and processing are characteristic of the author. His is a heavy but a sure hand, and the power of it is felt as one reads the long paragraphs, in which the sentences are often also long but clear and penetrating.

What of Bishop McConnell's preaching? It too is powerful, but simpler in construction than his lectures. He speaks in a conversational tone, with pungent phrases and often a unique handling of familiar Scripture. A fellow Methodist who heard him on "The Prodigal Son" says that he spent most of his time on the prodigality of the father in the parable, the prodigality of his love, patience, sympathy, and forgiveness. "I went away from church that day" said this preacher-reporter, "wondering why that aspect of the parable hadn't occurred to me before."

Here, in truth, is an illustration of the effect of the *element of surprise* in preaching. Great preaching uses this element impressively, and Bishop Francis J. McConnell ranks with the mighty prophetic preachers of his day.

V. ERNEST FREMONT TITTLE

The death of Dr. Tittle in Evanston, Illinois, August 3, 1949, was followed by a wave of grief that swept not only over the churches of Methodism but likewise over much of America's Christendom. He was so widely known, so ardently admired, and so greatly beloved, that there were many who experienced a poignant sense of personal loss in his passing. Numerous editorials appeared in the religious press paying tribute to Dr. Tittle and, of these, one of the finest was from Dr. Paul Hutchinson, who wrote in *The Christian Century* under the caption "A Word About a Friend" these tender and glowing sentiments:

If there is such a thing as a Great Christian preacher, he was. . . . Most prominent ministers suggest the eminence they might have attained in other pursuits: "What a great jurist he would have made!" or "What a great corporation promoter!" or "What a great actor!" But it was never possible for me to think of Ernest Tittle as anything but a Christian preacher. . . .

For me, Ernest Tittle did more than any other to rescue the relevance of Christian preaching. He must have done the same thing for great numbers who came under the influence of his preaching during his thirty years in the Evanston Pulpit. And despite all that is said these days about the "foolishness of preaching" I should have much more confidence than I now have regarding the future impact of the church on the life of this land if I could believe that there are more preachers, many more preachers of his kind coming along.

Preaching is an art. But great Christian preaching requires more than art. It requires Christian personality which takes the art and makes it glow and throb with the wonder of the Christian gospel and the compelling nearness of salvation. Yes, and at times wakes the rumbling echoes of warning at the nearness of damnation.

Ernest Tittle's preaching was like that. The art was there in the simplicity of his approach, in the directness of his progress. From the point where he started he went by a straight line to the point where he wanted to come out. And he always came out somewhere. But that was not what counted most. He knew the God he was trying to preach—the God and Father of his Lord, who was Jesus Christ. In striving to make the nature of that God known, to show his will for men, to paint the promise of life implicit in doing the will of God, and its stern judgment on those who deny and reject that will, he found the materials for an inexhaustible preaching ministry.

Once in a while one heard it said that Dr. Tittle preached too much about war, or color discrimination, or slum clearance, or the social issues of our day. As a matter of fact, he didn't preach about them at all. The only thing he preached was theology—God, the Christian God as revealed in Jesus Christ. . . . He never tried to evade the problems which really torment men. But he wasn't preaching sociology or a disguised political reformism. He was preaching the Christian gospel. He began his sermon always with some aspect of the fact of God; he ended always with man at the moment of decision when confronted with the will of God.[1]

Dr. Tittle gave the Beecher lectures in 1932 under the title *Jesus After Nineteen Centuries,* and the Abingdon Press brought them out the same year, in a book bound in red and black, dedicated "To My Wife and Mother." The volume contains a preface in which the author says that the lectures "have been allowed to retain the style of spoken address, for they are an attempt to suggest a few ways in which the central ideas of Jesus may be used in modern preaching, whether from a pulpit, a soap box, or the men's end of a Pullman car."

From the first chapter on "Light for Men," to the last, on "A Creative Faith," the work is a serious treatment of the plight of our world nineteen centuries after Jesus came. There are no quips, no humorous sallies in these pages. Instead, the heartbreak of a preacher of righteousness is here, in spirit akin to the anguish of Jesus when he wept over "The city of the Great King," and exclaimed "O Jerusalem, Jerusalem, that killeth the prophets and stoneth them that are sent unto her! How often would I have gathered thy children together, even as a hen gathereth her chickens under her wings, and ye would not!"

This series, as has been true of most of the more recent ones, is concerned with the content of preaching rather than with the technique. Like Albert Schweitzer, Ernest Tittle fostered a rever-

---

[1] *The Christian Century,* August 17, 1949. Used by permission.

ence for all of life. His interest centered in people, no matter how lowly, no matter their color, race, or condition. Always this servant of the Lord heard "the still, sad music of humanity," and was thereby both gentled and disturbed. War!—how he hated it; jingoism!—how he fought it; racialism!—how he feared it! If it sometimes seemed that he fought on too many fronts at the same time, it was because he felt that wherever God's children were suffering because of the acts of wicked men, there he must be with them, and fighting their battles with tongue and pen.

Dr. Tittle is justly numbered with the prophets of social change among the Yale lecturers. He is ranged alongside Washington Gladden, Bishop Charles D. Williams, Charles R. Brown, and Henry Sloane Coffin, but his approach to the subject is different from theirs. Dr. Gladden, for example, was an expert in the industrial field, particularly that of capital and labor. How accurately he assessed the issues! What an array of figures and facts he marshaled, and so effectively! Dr. Tittle's lectures are short on statistics, and long on the human factor. He thought of the men, women, and little children involved in the agelong struggle in the terms of "blood, sweat, and tears," and there is good reason to believe he shortened his life for their sakes.

This series may not be as entertaining as are some others in this Lectureship. What of it? Neither is the Book of Jeremiah as entertaining as, say, the Book of Ruth. A "prophet of a broken heart," as Jeremiah has been called, is sorely needed now. As for urbane, witty "pulpiteers,"[2] they are always with us. Yet Dr. Tittle had his gay and lighter moods, and they too were precious. He was witty and sparkling when with congenial friends, but preaching was a serious responsibility which he took to heart.

Long shall I cherish a trip by bus which he and I took together in England in 1937. We were fellow delegates at the Oxford and Edinburgh Conferences. Between the two meetings the delegates were given a week for sightseeing, and a number of us went to Winchester to inspect the massive Cathedral there and, perchance, to stand by Jane Austen's grave. Dr. Tittle was a delightful companion on that holiday, and for me the experience was a remem-

---

[2] A distinguished American preacher, not now living, cordially disliked the word "pulpiteer"; he said it reminded him of another word—"muleteer."

berable one. This prophet was also a gracious gentleman, a widely read, and widely traveled man. But he was at his highest when he stood in a pulpit and proclaimed, not austerely, not magisterially, but soberly, seriously, and joyously, the unsearchable riches of Christ.

Dr. Tittle was essentially and constitutionally a preacher. He was never so great anywhere else as he was in the pulpit. An admirer of Dr. Tittle thus writes: "As a lecturer, while able and always prepared, he was much less himself than when he stood up to preach. Good as his Yale lectures were, and are, in book form, they suffer when compared with his sermons. In a lecture he did not (perhaps could not) let himself go as he did when he preached. In these lectures he was able; in his sermons he was majestically great." It is doubtful if some of Dr. Tittle's friends would wholly agree with this statement. A member of the faculty of Yale Divinity School has classed the lectures Dr. Tittle gave there as one of the four finest series he heard during his tenure as professor in the Seminary.

In 1940 Dr. Tittle was one of six lecturers who gave a symposium on *Preaching in These Times*. His subject was, "The Church and the Glory of God," and he spoke with prophetic power and insight, saying:

The glory man needs is the glory of God. No other glory can satisfy the hunger of his soul or keep him from vain pursuits that issue in disaster. The Church is bound by its own nature to give expression to the glory of God as revealed in Jesus Christ. Therefore, let the Church be the Church. It is now commonly supposed that the Church has lost the position it once occupied in the western world. Its steeple is no longer the highest point on the horizon. And there are those who believe that what has happened to its physical body has also happened to its influence; that its relative position in the world today is that of Trinity Church in Wall Street alongside of the skyscrapers that tower above it. And this, at least, is certain: The Church can gain nothing by aping the secular community— nothing save the contempt of men and the condemnation of God. If the Church seeks after what the secular community regards as glory, it is destined to lose whatever influence it now has. Only by repudiating the glory that is of men and seeking after the glory that is of God can the Church gain the confidence and respect of the world.

A copy of one of the last sermons Dr. Tittle preached in The First Methodist Church of Evanston came to my notice, and I read it eagerly. The sermon was delivered just ten days before this preacher "suddenly rose from the chair at his study desk and stepped into another world." The subject of the sermon is "Joy," and this paragraph caught my eye before I read the sermon as a whole:

Christianity makes for pain as well as joy, but it is first and foremost a religion of joy. The early Christians were mostly poor, and they were subjected to the most cruel persecution. Yet these poor and harried people were notably happy. In the third Christian century a Christian writer could say: "The church is the one thing in the world that always rejoices."

Ernest Fremont Tittle's ministry was not a bed of roses. What prophetic ministry ever is of that snug nature? He was misrepresented, bemeaned, and pilloried by certain ultraconservative newspapers and, also, by certain misinformed, patriotic organizations which looked upon him as a dangerous radical. None of these things moved him. He was loved and trusted by men of the business world in his church who did not fully agree with his social and economic views[3] together with a host of fellow comrades of the cross to whom he was mentor and very dear friend.

And now his joy hath been made full!

VI. GARFIELD BROMLEY OXNAM

This stockily-built, athletically-trained Methodist Bishop is noted for many admirable qualities, not the least being his meticu-

---

[3] "Ernest Tittle's great recreation was fishing. I don't think I have ever known a man who could gain more complete relaxation while fishing than he could. Unfortunately, the kind of fishing which meant most to him was fly casting in mountain streams for trout. After his severe heart attack in 1937, he could no longer go up into the Rockies where his favorite streams were. He tried it just once and had a very close call.

"I think that a few of the men in his congregation who were most likely to be antagonized by his social views were tied to him with hoops of steel because they had had the experience of going off with him on a fishing trip. He was a wonderful companion in the out-of-doors—as well as everywhere else."—Paul Hutchinson, in a letter to the author.

lous management of his mail. Alas! as much cannot be truthfully said of other famed ecclesiastics, and of some not so famed. It has been claimed for Bishop Oxnam that "there is never a paper on his desk, or a question left unanswered at a committee over which he presides." Reinhold Niebuhr has said of him: "He gets through a meeting faster and better than anyone I know." This is, I hold, superlative praise.

Now it happens that I have eloquent proof of the Bishop's punctilious handling of his correspondence. The questionnaire I sent to all living lecturers in this Course received, on the whole, prompt attention, with some exceptions, of course. A few of the recipients simply filled out the typed form and shortly returned it. But there were others, and among these several of the most widely known, who wrote delightful letters and at some length. Bishop Oxnam was one of the latter group, and his letter is so entertaining and revealing that I am pleased to present a part of it here:

. . . I shall try to set down some rather hastily dictated answers to your inquiry of July 20th. What a splendid task you have been assigned. We shall all anticipate the volume with great eagerness.

1. What were your emotions when you received the invitation to become a member of this glorious company?

The invitation came as a complete surprise. I noted the envelope, which was delivered to my home. At that time, Mrs. Oxnam was critically ill. I therefore opened the mail at home, and, to my amazement, found that I had received an invitation to give the Lyman Beecher Lectures. I am a little ashamed to say that my emotional reaction was one in which pride, fear, and joy were combined. I realized full well that I could not measure up to the demands of this great lectureship. On the other hand, I rejoiced at the recognition, and I resolved that I would give it the very best preparation possible.

2. How much time did you take for the immediate preparation?

I have before me a copy of my work schedule for 1944, and I note that the lectures were to be delivered April 11, 12, and 13, 1945. I assigned myself the task of having the manuscript ready by April 1st. There are six chapters, and the six chapter schedules were put down, as follows:

Chapter I   —February 27th,
Chapter II   —March 4th,
Chapter III —March 14th,

Chapter IV—March 18th,
Chapter V —March 25th,
Chapter VI—March 30th.

I read extensively from the time I received the invitation to give the lectures until I sat down to the actual task of writing. Of course, as you know, one draws from the years in such matters. First of all, I went down to New Haven, and spent a day with Dean Brown. He had copies of all the Yale Lectures. I leafed through these volumes, made notes of the books I wanted to read more carefully. I cannot therefore put down the amount of time that was spent, but I did take this seriously. I wish the lectures actually showed more of the time than they do. The writing schedule, as you see, was over a full month. I cannot estimate the time put in on reading and outlining.

3. Did you use manuscript, notes, or neither?

I read the lectures, because Dean Brown told me I must. This was a severe limitation to one who much prefers to speak without notes. I think I could have mastered the material so that the lectures could have been given almost as written. I am sure it would have meant greater freedom for me and far more influence upon the audience. However, in the light of the Dean's insistence, I did read them. Dean Weigle, however, advised me just before going in that it was quite up to me and that I could speak without notes, or read, or do whatever I pleased. It was then too late, of course, to make the change.

4. How do you evaluate this lectureship after your own experience in participating in it?

It is, of course, one of the great lectureships of the nation. The distinguished names that are read when the roll is called humble one when he realizes his name is to be included in the list. I felt when at Yale that the lectures were taken somewhat for granted. This is but natural. On many a University campus, great men in the realm of science, in history, literature, the drama, come to the campus, and because such riches are so plentiful, the campus may be somewhat surfeited. . . . To sum it all up, this is one of the great lectureships; and any man who stands in that extraordinary tradition counts himself honored far beyond his due.

This frank and disarming letter is important because it reveals how seriously the writer took his assignment, and also how he went about the preparation of the lectures. It is pleasant to speculate how many of the lecturers-elect journeyed to Yale in order to reconnoiter, so to speak.

I

Bishop Oxman chose as his theme: *Preaching in a Revolutionary Age*, an appropriate subject, for the year was 1945 and the mad war still raged. The Bishop spoke on: I. "The Revolutionary Era"; II. "A Common Faith and a Common Purpose"; III. "The One and the Many in a Revolutionary Age"; IV. "The Preacher in the Revolutionary Age"; V. "The Pastor in a Revolutionary Age"; and VI. "The Revolutionary Christ."

It may be strategic to confine this review to the fourth lecture, which dealt with the *preacher* in the revolutionary age—a theme of enormous interest to many a confused and perplexed minister.

The Oxnam style marches, has a swing to it, is graphic, abounding in pictorial material. If one thinks of Oxnam as a painter, the canvas is large, the strokes broad, the colors bright with here and there a splash of scarlet. He quotes freely, and usually, but not exclusively, from modern writers. The Bishop favors Shakespeare and opens the lecture under discussion with tragic lines from *Macbeth*. There is humor, too, some of it salty yet always in good taste. Wit? Yes, it is here too.

How does it feel to be a Bishop? Dr. Oxnam has a good time answering this question. He says:

From the college presidency to the episcopacy is in many ways a transition from ivory tower to circus tent. Of course, no college is an ivory tower; and the episcopacy is not entirely a circus. But being a bishop does involve lion taming. Bishops are called upon to face the shining teeth and awful roars of lionlike committees who insist that the new minister must have the ability of Harry Emerson Fosdick, must not be over twenty-eight, and should start at the substantial sum of $1200 and house. Then, of course, there is not a little of tight-rope walking. The balancing stick supplants the shepherd's crook. It would be wiser to come down upon one side or the other of an issue rather than to remain aloft, as the perfect symbol of balance. A bishop must have the ability to manage the occasional clown, check up on the jugglers and sleight-of-hand performers, and be certain that the side shows do not outshine the performance in the main tent. The episcopacy like the circus is an itinerant undertaking. There is much setting up of tents and moving from town to town. I must not forget the merry-go-round. To sounding brass and tinkling cymbals, a bishop clad in purple mounts his horse, all too often getting off at the spot where he mounted, sometimes clutching the gold ring heroically worn as the wooden horses rush by. But it is not the circus aspect of the episcopacy I would discuss. I would present a few prints from the candid camera of a new bishop.

There is a man who thinks he is a minister but he is really a high-pressure, boisterous, back-slapping, hand-shaking salesman. He is a politician gone religious. . . . There is the "professional." He is job-conscious, highly trained, professional, a master of religious ceremony, basically, though often a delightful fellow who looks out for his own interests in the job of serving the Lord. . . . There is another who might be called "The Gossip." Space does not permit a record of this print. The face is somewhat hidden behind a hand. The Gossip is whispering: "Yes he's a wonderful fellow, but he can't preach."

Dr. Oxnam has his hobbies; according to a newspaper reporter, the theater and art; and both interests appear in these lectures. His acquaintance with modern plays accounts for this passage:

No Time for Comedy is the title of a scintillating play marvelously done some years ago by Katharine Cornell and Francis Lederer. The laughter of joy is silenced in an atmosphere of pessimism. One of the characters is a playwright. His wife in criticizing one of his new plays, says: "I feel a revulsion from your play altogether because it is dominated by the idea of death."

"But," he breaks in, "we are living in an era of death. We are pervaded by death. Death is our hero, our protagonist—war and death —death and the fear of death. Death purrs over us, a giant bombing plane—its shadows over the green pastures, darkening the still water." The preacher dare not see the shadow over the green pastures, without remembering the table prepared in the presence of enemies, the still waters, but "the Lord is my shepherd."

II

Dr. Oxnam begins his sixth lecture on "The Revolutionary Christ" with a magnificent introduction. He describes his impressions as he stood before the murals in the Baker Library at Dartmouth College, painted by the artist, Orozco:

My first reaction was one of revulsion! The painter's brush had become party to blasphemy. Orozco had gone too far. Had he not made caricature of the Christ and brought contempt upon the Cross? Strangely enough, the painting possessed sufficient magnetic attraction to hold me fast; suddenly its meaning gripped me, and my mood became one of repentance. I speak again of the overpowering murals in the Baker Library at Dartmouth College and of the work of Orozco, the artist of revolutionary revelation.

It is the last panel, done in rich colors—the deep browns of the soil, the deeper reds of blood. A towering figure of Christ dominates all. He stands with feet apart, flesh torn, triumphant. At his side is an ax, the handle grasped tightly by his right hand. In the background are temples and tabernacles overturned in ruins amid the spoils of war, as though some terrible earthquake had made scorn of the religions of man. Rising above shattered stone and splintered timber is the Christ. Then one sees that the ax has been laid to the root of the tree. The cross itself has been cut down. It lies beside the stump from which it has been severed, and the Christ stands astride it.

Had the artist sought to ridicule the Cross? I thought. Was this sacred symbol of my faith to be made the sport of a revolutionist?

And then I knew that a dead figure hanging from a cross is not the sign of my faith. True, there could have been no Christian faith without the cross; but death upon the cross and that alone would not have summoned deserters, who had been disciples, to crusade and to crosses of their own. The cross, as well as death, was swallowed up in victory. Our Lord is not a poor broken figure hanging from the tree—hands imprisoned by cruel nails and feet held fast by spikes, eyes that do not see and ears that do not hear, a tongue that is stilled, a body with spirit gone—whose message is Miserere. No, he is Christ triumphant, living now and forever more, freed from the flesh, victor over men who vainly believe they can destroy the spirit by crucifying the body. He lives; and, lest the misguided with creedal crown and nails of fanaticism would make him prisoner to the cross, he lays the ax to the cross itself. It falls; and the sorry inscription, "This is the King of the Jews," is crushed beneath the cedar. He is King of kings and Lord of lords. He lives; his eyes do see, beholding in every man a brother and envisioning what man may become as a son of God; his ears do hear the cries of the oppressed, the low moan of the sorrowful, the glad shouts of children at play, and, like the sound of the sea, the swelling notes of joy chanted by the millions of men in that morrow when justice shall roll down as a mighty stream and righteousness shall cover the earth; his hands and feet are free, the hands of healing, the feet of the second mile; he speaks, and men learn of the way and the truth and hear that judgment will be rendered upon the simple rule, "Inasmuch as ye have done it unto one of the least of these my brethren, ye have done it unto me"—"Enter thou into the joy of thy lord."

Did the artist seek to speak as Paul spoke, to affirm that the last enemy, death, is destroyed, that all things are subdued to Christ? I do not know. Perhaps it was less a matter of theology than of social proclamation. Christ, alive and free from an imprisoning cross before which many bow to worship but from which too few hear the summons "Follow me"—how can he march, if he be nailed to a cross?— a living Christ, who, having been lifted up, does draw all men because of his gift of self but who leads all men because of his mastery of death—this is the revolutionary Christ, whose message will be Jubilate!

Bishop Oxnam is a controversialist, although that quality does not appear in his Yale lectures. This ecclesiastic is a Protestant of Protestants and unashamedly so. The day has not dawned as yet when Oxnam failed to find a reason for the hope that is in him, and to express it in unmistakable manner. The Methodist House of Bishops, like that of the Episcopalians, has within, both conservatives and liberals, which is well. It can be said that Oxnam sees things pretty much as does the noble Bishop McConnell, now retired. If the latter is the more profound, the former is vastly more colorful, and both are lion-hearted men.

Dr. Oxnam was not satisfied with his Yale lectures. He did not ordinarily use manuscript and felt handicapped by it. A minister who heard his series thus expressed himself: "One felt and was convinced by Bishop Oxnam's sincerity and his forthrightness. But those of us who have been thrilled by his speaking on other occasions where he used a free and spontaneous and somewhat extemporaneous delivery were greatly disappointed . . . whereas what he said was excellent, and had to do with preaching, yet it did not have the freshness and compulsion for which we had hoped."

In other words, the Bishop was *manuscript-bound!*

V

EDUCATORS AND
★ SCHOOLMEN ★

The schoolmaster is abroad, and I trust him with his primer, against the soldier with his sword.
—LORD BROUGHAM

1. JAMES STALKER

In our seminary days and first pastorates, ministers of my age will recall with what delight we welcomed certain books written by Dr. Stalker; for instance, his *Life of Christ*, *Life of St. Paul*, and especially, *Imago Christi*. The last-named book inspired many a sermon, revived lagging spirits, and made a host of young ministers, and older ones too, grateful debtors to one of Scotland's illustrious scholars and preachers.

That journalistic connoisseur of preachers and preaching, Arthur Porritt, has left this tribute to the pulpit genius of Dr. Stalker:

Of all preachers I ever heard, Dr. James Stalker is the one whose sermons fasten themselves most indelibly on my mind. I can remember quite distinctly the whole argument of the sermon he preached when I first heard him nearly thirty years ago. And when he has set out his divisions they are fixed in his hearers' minds. Take as an example his treatment of temptation. As regards temptation, all men, he says, are divisible into five groups, like Continental political parties. In the "center" are the tempted; on the "left center" the tempted who have fallen; on the "left" the tempted who have fallen and are tempting others; on the "right center" are the tempted who have resisted their temptation; on the "right" are the tempted who have resisted temptation and are helping others to resist their temptations. We are all of us in one of the categories. Which? A sermon like that is quite unforgettable.

I

Dr. Stalker's Yale lectures on *The Preacher and His Models* were delivered in 1891. Preceding him, in 1890, Dr. Adolphus J. F. Behrends spoke on *The Philosophy of Preaching*, and following him, Dr. Andrew M. Fairbairn, in 1892, lectured on *The Place of Christ in Modern Theology*. Not in the history of the Lectureship was there such a threesome of theologians, two being of the first magnitude.

Dr. Stalker's "Introductory" opened wide the door to the nature of the lectures which were to follow. This "Introductory" was also of the nature of a heart-to-heart talk with the divinity students, personal, warm, and friendly. Dr. Stalker was the second speaker imported from across the Atlantic, Dr. Dale having lectured at Yale in 1887. Of this fact Stalker took notice in a felicitous paragraph:

> I warmly reciprocate the sentiments which have led the Faculty to come across the Atlantic the second time for a lecturer, and the liberality of mind with which they are wont to overstep the boundaries of their own denomination and select their lecturers from all the evangelical Churches. It is the first time I have set foot on your continent, but I have long entertained a warm admiration for the American people and a firm faith in their destiny; and I welcome an opportunity which may serve, in any degree, to demonstrate the unity which underlies the variety of our evangelical communions, and to show how great are the things in which we agree in comparison with those on which we differ.

In reference to fellow students in his own seminary days, Dr. Stalker instanced two men who gave little promise of ability and later won distinction in their pastorates. "Both," he said, "had a spark of nature's fire, and this is the possession which outshines all others when college is over and practical life begins." A footnote on the same page contains two stanzas of a poem by Robert Burns from which the phrase "spark of nature's fire" occurs. The verses are so relevant to the subject it would be a pity to omit them:

> A set o' dull, conceited hashes
> Confuse their brains in college classes,
> They gang in stirks, and come out asses,
> > Plain truth to speak,
> An' syne they hope to speel Parnassus
> > By dint o' Greek.
>
> Gi'e me *a'e spark o' nature's fire*,
> That's a' the learnin' I desire,
> Then, though I trudge through dub an' mire,
> > At pleugh or cart,
> My muse, though homely in attire,
> > May touch the heart.

Speaking on "The Preacher as a Man of the Word," Dr. Stalker said:

In the pulpit not only must a man have something to say, but it must be a message from God. . . . He who receives the message of God now finds it in the Word of God. . . . Hence one of the primary qualifications of the ministry is an intimate familiarity with the Scriptures. . . . If I may give utterance to my own experience, I have never come to the end of a close study of a book of Scripture in the congregation, without having both a fresh respect for its literary character and a profounder impression of its Divine wisdom. The more the Bible is searched, the more will it be loved; and the stronger will the conviction grow, that its deep truths are the Divine answers to the deep wants of human nature.

In regard to the acquiring of a command of an excellent pulpit style, Stalker thus speaks:

To obtain command of language it is good to hear the best speakers and to read the best books. It has been my fortune to be acquainted with a good many celebrated preachers; and I have observed that, almost without exception, they have had a thorough acquaintance with the whole range of the higher English literature. To have the music of Shakespeare or Milton echoing in your memory, or to have lingering in your ear the cadence and sweep of the sentences of Thackeray and DeQuincy, will almost unawares give you a good style. In reading over an old sermon of my own, I can almost tell whether or not, in the week of its composition, I was reading good literature. In the former case the language is apt to be full **and** harmonious, and sprinkled over with gay flowers of maxim and illustration, whereas in the latter the style of the performance is apt to be bald and jerky.

Dr. Stalker took as models for preachers, Isaiah as the noblest of the Hebrew prophets, and St. Paul as the grandest of the Christian apostles, devoting four lectures to each. He stated that he chose Isaiah in spite of what Jeremiah and Ezekiel had to offer because "there is nothing in Holy Writ more unique than the call of Isaiah, and it is pregnant in every line with instruction." And of St. Paul he said: "It is my intention to speak of St. Paul, first as a man; secondly as a Christian; thirdly as an apostle; and fourthly as a thinker." Deliberately and with the logic so dear to a dialectician Dr. Stalker followed the plan he had prepared, and these two Biblical models received full and adequate treatment at the tongue of one who was "apt to teach." The lecturer interspersed his logic with memorable incidents, and as published, the footnotes are entertaining, being occasionally in a lighter vein.[1]

Under three heads Isaiah's call to his prophetic ministry is described in detail and graphically. Dr. Stalker concluded that section of the lecture with this comment:

Gentlemen, I have gone minutely into the details of this scene in the life of a representative preacher of the Old Testament, because every line of it speaks to the deep and subtle movements of our own experience. What is the inference to be drawn from it? Is it that at the commencement of a preacher's career there must be a call to the ministry distinct from the experience of personal salvation? This inference has often been drawn; but I prefer, in the meantime at least, to draw a wider, but, I believe, a sounder and more useful infer-

---

[1] "An esteemed friend, the Rev. John McMillan of Ullapool, some years ago repeated to me the following rhyme on the method of constructing a sermon, and, although I have never succeeded in coming up to its standard, yet it has often floated before me with advantage in the hours of composition
'Begin low;
Proceed slow;
Rise higher;
Take fire;
When most impressed
Be self-possessed;
To spirit wed form;
Sit down in a storm.'"

ence. It is this: that the outer must be preceded by the inner; public life for God must be preceded by private life with God; unless God has first spoken to a man, it is vain for a man to attempt to speak to God.

Lecture V, "The Preacher as a False Prophet," is especially valuable. The speaker gave enough space to the false prophets of Old Testament times to fix their place and evil influence in the minds of his auditors. Then he said:

The false prophets won and kept their popularity by pandering to the opinions and prejudices of the people. The times of Jeremiah were big with coming calamities, and he had to predict that these calamities were sure to come; for there were no signs of deep or genuine repentance, and, indeed, the time for repentance was past. The self-flattering, ease-loving people hated to hear these disagreeable facts. Their frivolous minds were engrossed with the gossip and excitement of the passing day, and it was too great an exertion to give their attention to the majestic views of the Divine justice and the far-reaching sweep of the Divine providence to which Jeremiah tried to direct their attention. They wished to enjoy the present and to believe that all would come right somehow. The false prophets flattered these wishes. They said that the calamities which Jeremiah was foretelling would not come to pass, or that at least they would be much less formidable than he represented. They were, as Jeremiah says, like an unconscientious physician, who is afraid to probe the wound to the bottom, though the life of the patient depends on it. Ezekiel accuses them of making nightcaps to draw over the eyes and ears of their countrymen, lest they should see and hear the truth, and of muffling with a glove the naked hand of God with which the sins of the people should have been smitten. The constant refrain of their prophecies was, "Peace, peace," though the storm-clouds of retribution were ready to burst. The people said to them, "Prophesy to us smooth things"; and the false prophets provided the supply according to the demand.

The final paragraph on the prophet Isaiah as a model preacher closed with certain weighty words. Since these words were spoken within the halls of a seminary, every word must have weighed a pound:

Allow me to say, in closing, that I believe the question, what is to be the type and tone of the ministry in any generation, is decided in the theological seminaries. What the students are there, the ministers of the country will be by-and-by. And, while the discipline of the authorities and the exhortations and examples of professors may do something, the tone of the college is determined by the students themselves. The state of feeling in a theological seminary ought to be such, that any man living a life inconsistent with his future profession should feel thoroughly uncomfortable, and have the conviction driven in upon his conscience every day, that the ministry is no place for him.

Having written a life of St. Paul, Dr. Stalker was *en rapport* with his theme for the next four lectures. He loved his subject, and handled it with ease and enthusiasm. In presenting "Paul the Man" he employs but three headings. For Dr. Stalker, this was unique. Usually he used twice as many.

1. St. Paul was a supremely ethical nature This perhaps was his fundamental peculiarity. Life could under no circumstances have seemed to him a trifle. The sense of responsibility was strong in him from the beginning. He was trained in a strict school. . . . His sense of honor was keen. When, in his subsequent life, he was accused of base things—lying, hypocrisy, avarice and darker sins—he felt intense pain, crying out like one wounded, and he hurled the accusations from him with the energy of a self-respecting nature.

2. St. Paul's intellectual gifts are so universally recognized that it is hardly worth while to refer to them. . . . We think of the intellect of the system-builder as cold. But there is never any coldness about St. Paul's mind. On the contrary, it is always full of life and all on fire. He can, indeed, reason closely and continuously; but, every now and then, his thought bursts up through the argument like a flaming geyser and falls in showers of sparks. Then the argument resumes its even tenor again; but these outbursts are the finest passages in St. Paul.

3. The intellectual superiority of St. Paul is universally acknowledged; and to those who only know him at a distance this is his outstanding peculiarity. But the close student of his life and character knows, that, great as he was in intellect, he was equally great in heart, perhaps even greater. One of the subtlest students of his life, the late Adolphe Monod, of the French Church, has fixed on this as the key to his character. He calls him the Man of Tears, and shows with great persuasiveness, that herein lay the secret of his power.

Dr. Stalker maintained that it is generally agreed that a certain modicum of natural gifts is necessary for those who think of entering the ministry. He quotes Luther's list of the qualifications of a minister and remarks that most of them are gifts of nature. Here they are: 1. He should be able to teach plainly and in order. 2. He should have a good head. 3. Good power of language. 4. A good voice. 5. A good memory. 6. He should know when to stop. 7. He should be sure of what he means to say. 8. And be ready to stake body and soul, goods and reputation, on its truth. 9. He should study diligently. 10. And suffer himself to be vexed and criticized by everyone.

Among several lively anecdotes which brighten the lectures, Dr. Stalker relates this one:

The polish given by education tells, no doubt; but the size of the primordial mass of manhood tells still more. In a quaint book of reminiscences recently published from the pen of a notable minister of the last generation in the Highlands of Scotland, Mr. Sage of Resolis, there is a criticism recorded, which was passed by a parishioner on three successive ministers of a certain parish: "Our first minister," said he, "was a man, but he was not a minister; our second was a minister, but he was not a man; and the one we have at present is neither a man nor a minister."

Expanding his ideas on "The Preacher as a Thinker" Stalker cites one of Yale's presidents as an illustration:

President Dwight preached in the Yale College Chapel straight through the doctrines of Christianity, taking them up one by one in systematic order; and his book was long a model to preachers both in this country and Great Britain. He was preaching to an academic audience, and there are probably few congregations for which such a course would be suitable now; although I know at least one able young minister in a country village who has been pursuing this method from the commencement of his ministry. Once a month he gives a sermon of the course; perhaps his people do not know that he is doing so; but he is giving his own mind the discipline of investigating the doctrines of Christianity in their order; and I am certain he himself is growing a strong man in the process and that his people, though unconsciously, are getting the benefit of it. In the Lutheran and Episcopal Churches the observance of the Christian festivals gives occasion for regularly bringing the circle of the grand Christian facts before the minds of the people. We have not this guidance; but a faithful minister is bound to make sure that he is preaching with sufficient frequency on the leading Christian facts and doctrines, and that he is not omitting any essential element of Christianity.

Dr. Stalker is not so sure that the advice to the minister to cultivate simplicity is well-grounded. His answer to that kind of suggestion is, we may believe, characteristic:

> Not unfrequently ministers are exhorted to cultivate extreme simplicity in their preaching. Everything ought, we are told, to be brought down to the comprehension of the most ignorant hearer, and even of children. Far be it from me to depreciate the place of the simplest in the congregation; it is one of the best features of the Church in the present day that it cares for the lambs. I dealt with this subject, not unsympathetically I hope, in a former lecture. But do not ask us to be always speaking to children or to beginners. Is the Bible always simple? Is Job simple, or Isaiah? Is the Epistle to the Romans simple, or Galatians? This cry for simplicity is three-fourths intellectual laziness; and that Church is doomed in which there is not supplied meat for men as well as milk for babes. We owe the Gospel not only to the barbarian but also to the Greek, not only to the unwise but also to the wise.

James Stalker was himself a model preacher of the scholarly, Biblical, and expository type. Whenever he was announced to preach crowds waited upon his deliverance and were not disappointed. He belongs to that small but powerful group of preacher-professors in Scotland who took great subjects and held their hearers for forty-five minutes or an hour, and sent them away instructed, elated, humbled, and their hearts overflowing with "wonder, love, and praise."

In the fullness of his years, honored, admired, and beloved, Dr. Stalker died February 5, 1927. His works survive him.

II. WILLIAM JEWETT TUCKER

This eminent clergyman-educator whose headship of Dartmouth College 1893-1909 won him national recognition, lived fully up to his reputation in the grand succession at Yale where he lectured in 1898. The pity is that his competent craftsmanship as demonstrated on that occasion is not better known. Talk with a group of present-day ministers, and where fifty speak in glowing terms of Beecher, Brooks, van Dyke, Watson, Scherer, Horne, and Fosdick, perhaps one will cite the excellence of Dr. Tucker's *The Making and Unmaking of the Preacher*, the title he chose for the lectures in published form.

One explanation of this sober fact is that Dr. Tucker's fame as an educator overshadowed his rare gifts as a preacher. He had but eight years in the pastorate, as against thirty in the professor's chair at Andover and as president of Dartmouth. Theological students and ministers naturally give their primacy of interest and admiration to men whose life-success has been won in pulpit and parish.

Dr. Tucker was often a guest preacher in prominent churches during his presidency of Dartmouth. In Boston Dr. Richard C. Cabot was so surprised by his sermons that he wrote telling him how much he had been helped spiritually and intellectually by his preaching. Now when a Boston Cabot goes to the pains to write at some length in praise of any man's preaching, that is something to treasure and, yes, to put in print if the opportunity comes, and this is just what Dr. Tucker did. The Cabot letter appears on pages 366-367 in Tucker's autobiography entitled *My Generation*.

I

In his lectures before the students, faculty, and friends of Yale Divinity School, Dr. Tucker limited his subject to the personality of the preacher. He thus set forth his purpose in an early paragraph. "I am intent," he said, "upon finding out and taking the measure of those forces which are steadily at work toward the making or the unmaking of the preacher, because they are actually determining at any given time the value of preaching. Some men are preaching better at forty or at sixty than when they began; others are not preaching as well. The unmaking process is going on side by side with the making process."

In some respects few other lecturers who have appeared in this Course are more quotable. The reason is that Dr. Tucker speaks much of the time in epigrams; short, pithy sentences of a proverbial character. For example:

Preaching is prayer turned around.

Nothing can be more fundamental to the preacher than his humanity.

Great truths announce their presence before they are formulated. They are tried, proven, and experienced, before they are ready for the confessional.

It has now become evident that there are but two valid positions for the church to take: to fall back upon authority and go to Rome, or to encourage a clear, straight, honest, reverent search after the truth.

The young preacher may want to express too much. The older preacher may not dare to express enough.

Fluency is the greatest foe of true extempore preaching. The fluent, easy, self-satisfied talker has none of the stuff in him of which extempore preachers are made.

II

What are the things that unmake the preacher? The chapter that answers this question is Number Three, and some who read the book will say: "This is the best lecture of the eight." This response is understandable, for the importance of the discourse is apparent on every page. However, there is not a weak lecture in the succession. All of them are of a high order, cogent, and relevant. The points, or divisions, are revealing and practical:

1.

The Foe Which Lies in Wait for the Preacher from Beginning to End Is Unreality.

2.

The Preacher's Danger from the Want of Direct and Wholesome Criticism.

3.

The Preacher Has Much to Fear from the Dissipation of Personal Energy.

4.
The Loss of Power to the Preacher from Frequent Changes.
5.
The Discouragement That Comes in One's Early Ministry Is Disappointment in Men.
6.
The Most Serious Danger to the Preacher Must of Course Come from Himself.

It is clear, or ought to be, from a study of this outline, why, to many a preacher who reads these lectures in book form, this particular chapter is for him the chapter of chapters. For if this process of making and unmaking goes on side by side, as the author says, then how imperative the duty that the preacher struggle valiantly to clear the obstacles from the path of making himself a workman who needeth not to be ashamed.

Ponder this choice and sapient comment as to the "short pastorate evil" which infests so many communions, and especially those of Congregational policy:

I see no need of frequent changes of pastorates in the interest of freshness, either to preacher or people, if the preacher will use all his opportunities to keep himself in close and quickening relations to truth and men. I cannot overestimate the power to the pulpit of men whose personality has begun to count for something before the public. Usually this power comes from men who are placed; they are institutions. What matters it just where the preacher is, if when he speaks he gets the wider hearing, if the book he prints is read, if the cause he advocates is forwarded, if the inspiration of his life and work goes out from heart to heart. I am not saying that a man should stay always where he begins, though I think he ought to stay long enough to pay the people for having taught him his apprenticeship; but I am protesting against the great restlessness which comes with so great frequency of change in the pastorate. Greater permanency would, I am sure, give us better churches and better preachers.

Dr. Tucker commends to the young ministers at Yale, this advice, which Charles Kingsley puts into the mouth of the wife of the country esquire of Harthover House:

So she made Sir John write to the "Times" to command the Chancellor of the Exchequer for the time being to put a tax on long words:

Francis Greenwood Peabody

a light tax on words over three syllables, which are necessary evils, like rats, but which like them must be kept down judiciously; a heavy tax on words of over four syllables, such as heterodoxy, spontaneity, spuriosity, and the like, and on words of over five syllables a totally prohibitory tax, and a similar prohibitory tax on words derived from three or four languages at the same time.

That is a precious quotation, though a trifle involved, and one the youthful minister might well have printed, framed, and hung on the walls of his study, in plain sight, for a "word fitly spoken is like apples of gold in pictures of silver." The right word spoken at the right time by the right person to another may work a miracle, in truth has done so many times. Still, it should profit us to remember what great Old Doctor Sam Johnson in the preface to his dictionary wrote:

I am not so lost in lexicography as to forget that *words are the daughters of earth, and that things are the sons of heaven.*

III. FRANCIS GREENWOOD PEABODY

Dr. Peabody was a Harvard man by tradition, training, and inspiring friendships. He was as much at home on her famous "Yard" as a bookman leafing through a rare edition or a gardener pruning his roses. He took degrees both in the College of Liberal Arts and in the Divinity School, was dean of the latter from 1881 to 1913, and a professor emeritus to the day of his death in 1936. Thus, "rich in experience which angels might covet," he was in the full-flowering of his intellectual and spiritual life when he became the thirty-fifth lecturer in the Lyman Beecher Course.

The elect coterie in which Francis Peabody moved was composed of those who, like him, were in the vigor of their mature powers and busy at their posts of duty. Dr. Gordon was at Old South Church; Dr. Eliot at the headship of Harvard; and Dr. Hadley ruled at Yale. Theodore Roosevelt, a Harvard man, was President of the United States; and Henry Adams, of that illustrious clan, and a one-time professor at Harvard, was working on his best-known book, *The Education of Henry Adams*. It was a great time for Harvard men to be alive when Dr. Peabody came to Yale to lecture in 1904 on *Jesus Christ and the Christian Character*.

I

A friend of Dr. Peabody, one who knew him intimately and loved him dearly, wrote:

Francis Greenwood Peabody was a winsome and gracious gentleman. He had a pretty sense of humor and let it play over the human scene. His long life was wholly bound up with Harvard and thus with Cambridge and Boston. He was related by marriage to Charles Eliot and thus was for many years near the academic throne. In 1886 the Harvard Corporation voted to give up compulsory chapel both on Sundays and week-days. They proposed, however, to continue both services on the voluntary basis. The administration of the chapel under the new conditions was handed over to a Board of Preachers created at that time. The Board is to be constituted of one Chairman who is to be a resident Professor in the University and five other members coming from outside the University representing the major Protestant denominations. The scheme is not unlike that of a Dean and Chapter of an English cathedral.

Professor Peabody was the first Chairman of this Board, and he left one of his most permanent marks on Harvard in the form of a Sunday service and an order for Daily Prayers which survive intact until this day.

Professor Peabody was one of the pioneers in interpreting the social gospel to American Protestantism. He shared this task with such men as Walter Rauschenbusch and Washington Gladden. His books in this field were widely read all over America and were translated into many other languages. He was one of the first Harvard Exchange Lecturers in Berlin and introduced the social gospel as we then conceived it to German academic life. The social gospel today has gone well beyond the outposts staked out 60 years ago by its early spokesmen. But their pioneer work opened up the whole field. They were men of courage, conviction, and genuine Christian charity.

Professor Peabody was equally well known for his little volumes "Mornings in the College Chapel." The books bearing this title were collections of his five-minute addresses at Daily Prayers in Harvard.

They are of their own kind unparalleled gems. No one has ever done this thing as well and, indeed, Professor Peabody did them so well that one can only imitate them from a distance or else abandon the effort altogether. Their literary skill is matchless.

Denominationally Professor Peabody was a Unitarian, but he always insisted, following early usage, that the word Unitarian was a synonym for non-denominational. He was a loyal churchman, but he moved freely among all denominations and was welcomed everywhere.

His gracious home in Cambridge was a center for friendships which in their intimacy and number increased as the years went on. He was fond of people and made them welcome to his hearth and his heart. His life was not without its share of trouble and sorrow. In particular, the death of his brilliant son, who was one of the most promising young men in the field of American medicine, was a heavy blow, but he bore it with quiet dignity and without complaint. His sermons and chapel talks as well as his longer books all betray the serenity of his soul and the strength of his character.

II

The subtitle of the Peabody lectures, "An Examination of the Teachings of Jesus in Its Relations to Some of the Moral Problems of Personal Life," is an admirable synopsis of the series as a whole. No other speaker in the Course dealt with a subject quite of this nature. It is true that Dr. Buttrick's *Jesus Came Preaching* and Dr. Tittle's *Jesus After Twenty Centuries*, given many years later, are on kindred themes, but their approach to the subject and the handling of the material differs decidedly from Dr. Peabody's method and treatment. In a striking manner, he did uniquely for the Christ, what Dr. Jefferson did for the Church and Dr. Fosdick for the Bible. The reader of the Peabody lectures is likely to be amazed at the erudition of the author in the realm of Christology. His footnotes, for instance, are far more abundant than those of any of his fellow lecturers in the Course. It would appear that he had read most of the numerous lives of Christ, including those of the French and German writers, and was as familiar with their critical positions, attitudes, and points of view, as American baseball fans are with the names and batting averages of famous players. Such a wealth of knowledge may excite no amazement in professorial circles, but it certainly has done so among laymen. This would also be true of ministers who are not accustomed to so much documentation in a work of this nature.

It is clear from the outset that the lecturer was troubled by the discrepancies between the preaching and the practice of Christianity, ceremony and character, doctrine and deed. He quotes in one of his footnotes a pertinent observation of Professor Fairbairn in his *Philosophy of the Christian Religion*, to wit: "Would it not have been to the infinite advantage of religion if these Councils had concerned themselves as much with the ethics as with the metaphysics of the person of Christ?"

Dr. Peabody spoke for a vast host who are likewise troubled by the discrepancy between ritual and righteousness. For example, the huge library of volumes and pamphlets written on Baptism, with insistence on the form, manner of administration, and doctrinal aspects, and so little said about the new life in Christ which that ordinance symbolizes, or implies. Dr. Peabody asserts:

> The criticism which the present age has to make on the ages of theology is not that they have gone too far, but that they have gone too fast. They have scaled the heights of heaven without providing themselves with the necessities of earth. "Give me the luxuries of existence," said a distinguished historian, when describing his personal tastes, "and I can dispense with the necessities." That is what one is tempted to say of a theology which substitutes a dramatic redemption for an ethical revival.

It is a multisided Christ as seen by painters, poets, essayists, theologians, and other interpreters of the Gospels: Prophet, Mystic, Poet, Master, Seer, Carpenter, Reformer, Redeemer, Savior, Messiah—and the end is not yet, nor can a "finis" ever be written to "The Greatest Story Ever Told." Peabody takes thirty-one pages of tight writing for his chapter on "The Character of Christ," and nearly three hundred pages to round out his eight lectures, conscious of the fact, no doubt, that his, too, was an "Unfinished Portrait," although competently and artistically done.

In his discussion of "The Personal Consequences of the Christian Character," the lecturer seeks an answer to the question, "What kind of a person represents the influence of Jesus Christ?" He finds three distinctive marks by which the Christian is recognized in moral bearing. The first of these, he says, is Poise. "The Christian character is neither excited nor temporizing; it is balanced and sound." Next he lists Simplicity. This means "not meagreness, but singleness; the simplifying, not of the content of life, but of the direction of life." And the third characteristic noted is Peace. "It is a freedom from inward conflict, the peace of single-mindedness and poise, the tranquillity of a character at one with itself. . . . Poise, simplicity, peace—all these mark the character which issues from the teaching of Jesus; but when his followers wished to sum up in a single phrase the most dominant aspect of this moral creation, and the special blessing which it received from him, they turned to one further word, which soon became the accepted form of benediction in his name. It was the word Grace."

What is this grace of Jesus Christ, which thus lingered like an aroma where he had been, and for which Christians in their worship still unite to pray? It is the issue of poise, simplicity, and peace, the total impression of a harmonious, unruffled, and disciplined character. Grace is not so much a virtue as an acquired instinct, not so much a duty done as a way of doing duty. External manners may be cultivated to become what is known as gracefulness; but graciousness is the unconstrained expression of the kindly, self-forgetting, and tranquil mind. Sometimes one sees a child blessed with this sweet reasonableness, this natural winsomeness. Such is—

> "The gracious boy, who did adorn
> The world whereinto he was born,
> And by his countenance repay
> The favor of the loving Day."

As the lecturer concluded this paragraph it is evident that he was thinking of his own "darling boy, so early snatched away," to whom he dedicates this volume in verses of exquisite tenderness. The father-heart supersedes the scholar's mind for the time, and the emotion, although restrained, is felt even in type. What must it have been as he spoke face to face with students and faculty in the Divinity School at Yale?

III

Dr. Peabody dwelt persuasively upon the spiritual solitude which distinguished the conduct of Jesus, a sphere of isolation and reserve in which he moved and had his being.

The reserve of Jesus is the background and the support of his sympathy. The throng that presses about him seems to drain his strength, and he seeks the solitude of the hills or of the lake to recover poise and peace. Here is the meaning of those passive virtues which appear to give the note of asceticism to the Gospels. Meekness, patience, forbearance, silence,—these are not the signs of mere self-mortification, they are the signs of power in reserve. They are the marks of one who can afford to wait, who expects to suffer, who need not contend; and all this, not because he is simply meek and lowly, but because he is also strong and calm.

To very many persons Judas is the enigma of the Gospel narratives. There is a mystery here which can never be cleared up by any writer or preacher no matter how competent. Yet often light has shined in this dark place, due to thoughtful observations by theologians of rare insight. It is therefore of vast interest to note how Peabody deals with Jesus and Judas Iscariot.

The truth appears to be that Jesus could not bring himself to surrender Judas, and hoped to the last that faith in him as a disciple might save him from the fate of a betrayer. The incidents of the last days when thus interpreted are unspeakably touching. Jesus is trying by force of confidence to hold the disciple from his shame. This faith is doomed to disappointment, yet the better nature in which the Master trusted overtakes the traitor when it is too late, and Judas hangs himself in self-reproach. It is startling to think how little was needed to reduce the character of Peter to that of Judas, or to lift the character of Judas to that of Peter. Both were traitors, yet in neither did Jesus find it possible to abandon hope. Both, he felt sure, still possessed the capacity for moral growth; both he trusted with a limitless patience and desire. One friend he saved, and history has almost forgotten the sin of Peter in the tradition of his leadership. The other friend Jesus seemed to lose, but even the story of the betrayal is illuminated by the inextinguishable faith of Jesus in potential repentance, and by the fact of that repentance when alas! it was too late.

William Herbert Perry Faunce

Here is a good example of this Christian scholar's manner of dealing with Biblical subjects that are confessedly hard. It does credit also to his generous nature as well as to his sensitivity to those inner conflicts which are part of our human lot, shared too, by Jesus, with poor strugling humanity. Dr. Peabody's interpretation of the case of Judas does not solve the mystery, but it helps our understanding of the betrayal and suffuses its harshness with a softer light. It leaves the reader no less dubious about Judas, yet all the more aware of the compassion of Jesus in his awful hour. A love that is reluctant to let us go passes our human understanding and vastly humbles us.

It is easier to make some men come to life in a book than others. The personalities of some rare characters are elusive and escape both the portrait painter and the biographer. There is a haunting quality about them like the scent of unseen roses. It is so, I think, with Professor Peabody, and the passages from his lectures quoted here, excellent as they are, little more than suggest the wide knowledge of the scholar and the spiritual glow of his character.

There have been times when I contemplated writing a book on "Certain Persons I Wish I Had Known." The project was not feasible and I abandoned it without regret. However, had I been able to write such a book, one of the men sure of a chapter would have been Professor Francis Greenwood Peabody, son of Harvard, and disciple of Jesus Christ.

IV. WILLIAM HERBERT PERRY FAUNCE

It is remarkable how many of the lecturers in this Course were Schoolmen: university, college and seminary presidents, professors, and principals. The number is fifteen, although only eight are listed in this book under the heading, "Educators and Schoolmen." Of the seven others, five, for good reasons, are placed in the company of "Theologians and Philosophers" and two are classified as "Modern Masters of Pulpit Discourse." This is a goodly proportion, nearly one-fifth of the total, and indicates the close relationship of minister and teacher, college and church.

On the whole these preacher-educators appear advantageously in this Course. Their thinking is clear and logical; their manner of speech fluent and effective. They lived full lives, knew both men and books, were independents theologically and politically, and often the spokesmen for unpopular minorities. At the same time these learned gentlemen kept their minds on an even keel and were not enmeshed in foolish controversies. Scholars they were, but not pedants. Fancy what an exciting event it must have been to listen to these men, since to read their spoken words is such an intellectual joy. They were sure-fire sharpshooters on the battle line of higher education.

I

Dr. Faunce was for fifteen years in the active ministry and the pastor of important churches. For thirty years he was president of Brown University—the successor of Wayland, Robinson, and Andrews. In 1908 he took the lecture platform at Yale to speak his mind on *The Educational Ideal in the Ministry*: I. The Place of the Minister in Modern Life; II. The Attitude of Religious Leaders Toward New Truth; III. Modern Use of Ancient Scripture; IV. The Demand for Ethical Leadership; V. The Service of Psychology; VI. The Direction of Religious Education; VII. The Relation of the Church and the College; VIII. The Education of the Minister by His Task.

A glance at these titles shows that Dr. Faunce anticipated Dr. Fosdick by sixteen years in the modern use of the Bible and Dr. Weatherhead by forty-one in the service of psychology in the pulpit. What Faunce did in single lectures, Fosdick and Weatherhead amplified in entire courses. Moreover, while some of Faunce's predecessors touched upon the teaching function in the ministry, he gave that subject major treatment, and the result was as timely as it was profitable to his student audience.

The speaker begins by a swift showing that both the medical and legal professions have become more important now than they were in past generations, and tells why and how this is true. Then he claims the same is true of the minister's vocation, frankly conceding that in popular opinion this is not the case. "Preaching out of date?" he queries. "There is more eagerness to hear a worthy appeal to the sense of duty today than ever before since Miles Standish stepped on Plymouth Rock." What a ringing sentence, and how it fairly tingles to be quoted.

Follow him in this fine paragraph:

In one respect the Puritan ministry of the American colonies was right,—it recovered and nobly maintained the idea of the ministry as involving fundamentally the teaching function. Those wearisome discourses with their innumerable subdivisions were at least addressed to intelligence, not to mere sentiment or passion. The doctrinal sermons, long since relegated to dust and oblivion, had at least this dignity,—they conceived the congregation as a thoughtful assembly, demanding and deserving serious instruction, and the preacher addressed himself year after year to the task of indoctrinating a whole community in truth. Dogmatic as the method was, formal and remote from life as the discourses now seem, we must at least acknowledge that such sermons were a species of deliberate and continuous public education, furnishing an intellectual basis for the great religious awakenings and the patriotic uprisings of a later time.

Dr. Faunce is sure that while the magisterial conception of the ministry seems alien to our modern world, the belief that the minister should be an orator does not fit into the basic idea of preaching. Not only is this true, but that while the small number of real pulpit orators, such as Beecher, Finney, Storrs, and Bellows "became the mouthpieces of democracy," the age of the superorator in both pulpit and politics has gone. "The master of assemblies has his place in this age as in every other," he says, "but our generation could not listen today with patience to Edward Everett or Charles Sumner."

Moreover, the preacher's output must be a continuous weekly production. Can any living man produce forty or fifty orations each year? Not even Daniel Webster could have evolved a reply to Hayne once a week. The essential condition of the great oration is a great occasion, an unusual contingency, the stir and zest of some rare and momentous event. He who is to address the same assembly twice a week for ten years must adopt a different aim, or he will in the very nature of things disappoint himself and all who hear him.

What then, since great orators are rare, is the preacher's method of bringing his sermon to the needs of the people? Dr. Faunce's answer is the teaching ministry, the unfolding of the doctrines, ideals, and standards of Christianity, in as able an arrangement of sermonic excellence as the minister can produce. Aptness to teach is a necessary qualification for preaching the Word. Not the sermon as a work of art, but as a means of instruction in the tenets of our faith, carefully worked out, simply and impressively presented so as to convict, convert, and transform those who come to church to worship and to pray.

What is the minister to preach?

For example, how shall men conceive God? Shall they think of Him as the Jehovah of the Old Testament who cried, "I, the Lord thy God, am a jealous God," or with the apostle John as "light in whom is no darkness at all"? . . . How shall they think of Christianity—as a "form of rent paid to God," as insurance against the perils of another world, as a series of logically defensible propositions, or as simply an attitude toward God and man? How shall they think of the moral law—as an arbitrary enactment enforced by Sinaitic thunders, or as a revelation of what God is and man may become? How shall they think of life—as probation, or education, or both? . . . Who is greatest in the kingdoms of earth,—the warrior, the captain of industry, the missionary, the monk, or the poet? What is the Christian view of competition in trade, the Christian view of the duties of citizenship? . . . To sum up these questions in one: What sort of ideal has the greatest moral value, and what kind of life is most worth while? . . . The answer to such far-reaching questions is not to be given by dogmatic deliverance from a pulpit "just three feet above contradiction." . . . The creation and maintenance of Christian ideals is the preacher's function.

II

In Lecture V, which is on "The Service of Psychology," Faunce holds that modern science has helped the modern preacher in eight ways, namely: 1. It has demonstrated beyond question or cavil the reality of religious experience. 2. Psychology has with equal clearness shown us the unreality of many conventional sins and traditional virtues. 3. Another gain from the newer psychology is a knowledge of the mutual interrelation and interdependence of mind and body. 4. Such a conviction of the unity of personality will necessarily shape a preacher's method in arousing and holding the attention of his congregation. 5. In the same line is the emphasis of psychology on the emotions and the will as the center of personality. 6. Educational psychology is also among the prophets in its emphasis on the value of action in the development of character. 7. One of the greatest services that psychology has rendered to our time is its far-reaching study of the meaning of adolescence. 8. But perhaps the chief value of the study of human growth and development is in the re-enforcement which comes to the central truths of Christianity when they are interpreted in terms of life.

The religious leader is above all other men in danger of acquiring merely personal standards of judgment. The chemist, or physicist, or biologist is dealing daily with a mass of objective fact, where personal likes and dislikes must be ignored, where subjective moods must not be allowed to affect conclusion or action. But the man who, like the poet, or preacher, or teacher, or statesman, lives mainly in the world of personality, and must contend with human fickleness, prejudice, and misconstruction, is in danger of estimating all men and movements solely according to their relation to himself. The man that agrees with him must be right; the man who ignores his appeal must be depraved; those who suggest another method must be malicious; those who prefer to follow another leader must be schismatics and troublers in Israel. But whoever assumes that attitude finds life full of thorns and stings. He becomes tender and touchy, and his work capricious and fitful. He is the sport of the varying winds of popular favor. A rainy Sunday or a slender congregation depresses such a preacher utterly; a large and responsive assembly fills him with short-lived enthusiasm. The apathy of good men nettles him; the opposition of evil men calls out his anathemas; and the whole world seems roseate with dawn, or black with woe, according as it does or does not indorse his petty personal policy.

But the man who is able to take the objective standpoint of psychology can see things in their larger and more permanent relations. He has acquired a practical knowledge of human nature,—the material in which he has to work,—just as the physician has mastered his anatomy and physiology.

III

It has been my privilege to read the addresses given at the memorial service for Dr. Faunce, on February 22, 1930, in Sayles

Hall, Brown University, shortly after his death. The speakers were: The Honorable Norman S. Case, Governor of Rhode Island, The Reverend Frederick Lynch, director of the New York Peace Society, Fred T. Field, Justice of the Supreme Court of Massachusetts, Thomas B. Appleget, vice-president of the Rockefeller Foundation, Dr. Harry L. Koopman, librarian of Brown University. Also included is the radio tribute by Dr. Clarence A. Barbour, Dr. Faunce's successor at Brown. These addresses, brief, eloquent, tender, reveal the character of President Faunce as not even his own finest productions could do. In the words spoken by his intimates, the versatility and charm of the man came to the front, touched here and there by incidents of his humor and hobbies.

Dr. Appleget:

Few men whom I knew loved life more or found more beauty in its every aspect. One can only speak of a few instances. His taste in poetry was catholic; his understanding and appreciation vivid and discriminating. His enthusiasm, when aroused, was always gregarious. It was his custom to make copies of verses which interested him particularly and to send them to his friends. To receive those little packets of beauty—sometimes several complete sonnets, sometimes only a single stanza—was to feel a fresh breath of spring. The last came to me only a few weeks ago. I quote it simply because it reflected his serenity in his retirement.

> When quacks with pills political would dope us,
>   When politics absorb the livelong day,
> I like to think about the star Canopus
>   So far, so far away.
>
> When Temporary Chairmen utter speeches,
>   And frenzied henchmen howl their battle hymns,
> My thoughts float out across the cosmic reaches
>   To where Canopus swims.
>
> For after one has had about a week of
>   The arguments of friends as well as foes,
> A star that has no parallax to speak of
>   Conduces to repose.[1]

[1] Bert Leston Taylor (B.L.T.).

President Barbour:

He loved books, but he loved people as well. His students were objects of intense personal interest to him. Many a time words which fell from his lips were sparks which kindled into leaping flame the dry tinder of intellectual and spiritual aspirations which had been accumulating on the altar of a young man's heart.

He was creative in his contact with young life, creative not particularly by deliberate design, but by the inevitable contagion of his spirit. Scores of his boys, as he loved to call them, can testify to this. As lately as three days ago I had a letter from Mrs. Dallas Lore Sharp, wife of the brilliant and suggestive preacher and essayist who has but recently gone from us, in which she spoke of her husband's appreciation of Dr. Faunce as his inspiration in adventurous thinking and courageous living.

And the contagion communicated itself not only through his personal contacts but through his letters. He was a wonderful letter writer. His heart was warm, his thought was clear, his diction was very beautiful. He wrote many letters. A multitude of his old students, his business and professional friends, his fellow citizens near and far, were the recipients of letters which they cherish among their priceless possessions. Many a one has been strengthened for high and courageous endeavor by his word of cheer. Many a one has been enabled to carry on because of the realization that with such a friend he must not fail. With many a one his counsel has been a decisive factor in clearing up a baffling situation.

So passed this preacher-scholar for whom there was "no moaning at the bar" when he "put out to sea."

V. WILLIAM DeWITT HYDE

As the expert interpreter of the Gospel of Good Will: as the leader in the fight against all meanness and cruelty: as the restorer of the penitent: as the infuser of spiritual meaning into secular life: as the champion of costly sacrifice: as the challenger of social injustice and the non-partisan herald of social reform: as the officer of a church that derives its sanctity and unity from the efficiency with which it serves all forms of personal and social welfare,—the Christian minister has a mission beneficent beyond all others.

—WILLIAM DeWITT HYDE

Professor George Herbert Palmer, in the introduction to Charles T. Burnett's *Hyde of Bowdoin*,[1] "A Biography of William DeWitt Hyde," says that Dr. Hyde "was called a Republican, and that name served as well as any. But he was an aristocrat and a radical. . . . In my time I find three presidents, and only three, who were as truly presidents of all other colleges as of their own. . . . W. D. Hyde, W. G. Tucker, and Mark Hopkins." Of these three, the first and second appeared in the Yale Series, a pleasing fact to note here.

Ordained to the Congregational ministry in 1883, Dr. Hyde held a three-year pastorate in Paterson, New Jersey, before he became president of Bowdoin. He was a prolific author, with a score of books and hundreds of magazine articles to his credit. The list of his religious, educational and political writings fill a long column in the index to his biography. His most widely read and best selling volume was titled: *From Epicurus to Christ* (Five Great Philosophers of Life), a strong, solid book, which is still highly rated and approved reading for students majoring in philosophy.

I

In 1916 Dr. Hyde gave a unique series in the Yale Course. Through eight lectures he brought together, as illustrating his general theme, which was *The Gospel of Good Will*, two popular religious plays: *The Passing of the Third Floor Back*, by Jerome K. Jerome, and *The Servant in the House*, by Charles Rann Kennedy; a poem, *The Widow in the Bye Street*, by John Masefield; *Within Prison Walls*, by Thomas Mott Osborne; *An American Citizen*, the biography of William H. Baldwin, Jr., by John Graham Brooks; *How Belgium Saved Europe*, by Charles Sarolea; *The Making of an American*, the autobiography of Jacob A. Riis; and the sensational novel about church people, *The Inside of the Cup*, by the American Winston Churchill.

[1] P. 16.

William DeWitt Hyde

Nothing quite like this pattern of presentation had been followed before, or has been since, in the Beecher Lectures. The method deserves more than a casual comment, not only because of its effectiveness, but also for the possibilities it suggests in homiletical variety and artistry. Speaking on *The Gospel of Good Will: Christ's Expectation of Men*, Dr. Hyde began his course at New Haven by saying:

Our lesson for to-day is from "The Passing of the Third Floor Back"; the text is the remark of a Jew converted from cunning trickery to frank honesty. This play is the drama of conversion by expectation; regeneration by appreciation. It portrays the influence of THE STRANGER, who is Christ, on as unpromising a lot of persons as ever gathered together in a boarding house. The Prologue shows us a satyr, a coward, a bully, a shrew, a hussy, a rogue, a cad, a cat, a snob, a slut, a cheat, and a passer-by, THE STRANGER,—Christ. In the Epilogue we meet these same individuals again, yet with all their objectionable characteristics gone: we meet them as a generous old bachelor; two pure lovers; a devoted husband and wife; an honorable Jew; an entertaining party; a self-respecting maiden lady; a generous rich aunt; an important person; the refined lady of the house, and THE STRANGER who now is the friend of them all.

How has THE STRANGER-FRIEND, the Christ, wrought this wonderful transformation? By seeing and revealing to each one of them his or her ideal. In the grasping lodging-house keeper he sees and reveals the generous lady she really is; unwilling to charge him as much as he is able and willing to pay. In a powdered, painted, giggling, gushing, silly simpleton he sees and reveals a "clever, witty, beautiful, graceful, comely woman, perhaps a little pale—there are white roses and red—with delicate features on which the sculptor Thought has chiselled his fine lines, giving to them character, distinction; her still-bright eyes unspoilt; with her fit crown of soft brown hair that time has touched with no unkindly hand."

There follow then, three cases in which the Stranger meets and finds the better nature of, 1. Harry Larkcom, "a low, ill-mannered, mercenary fellow who has just been trying to make an assignation with the servant girl in return for a gift of imitation emeralds . . ."; 2. "a rich, broken-down, smutty, shady old book-maker, who is trying to get a beautiful girl who loathes his very touch to marry him as a means of supporting her indigent and quarrelsome parents . . ."; 3. "a tricky Jew who is trying to sell the stock of a non-existent silver mine." The result is the miracle of one man, in this case, the man, Christ Jesus, transforming these tortured and twisted personalities into new creatures, even as He had transformed Mary Magdalene and Zacchaeus, the publican, nineteen centuries ago.

In the sixth lecture a similar use of *The Servant in the House* is made as demonstrating "By-Products of Good Will: The Christian Virtues." This play, which held the boards so long and so successfully in America and abroad, yields readily to such vivid treatment. From the play the lecturer turns quickly to the moral and spiritual teaching it contains, saying:

> That is a Gospel every right-minded man in the world accepts as soon as he clearly sees it. Of course it is hard to give a twenty-minute sermon the clearness and force of a well-acted two-and-a-half-hours' play. But if we take the same theme; show the greatness and glory of Good Will however humbly done; we shall get something of that response which this great play wherever presented has evoked. Good Will, whether in a play or sermon, is the only thing big enough to make a thoughtful man give all his little self possesses in happy wholehearted exchange. All the Christian virtues flow out of this love for God and all one's brothers: this devotion to their real good regardless of the honors and emoluments one's service to them may involve.
>
> Christian character, and all its constituent virtues, are by-products of living in Good Will. To aim at character directly; to cultivate the Christian virtues like Benjamin Franklin, giving one day to patience, another to chastity, another to generosity, is to miss altogether the Christian point of view, and become a conceited prig. If we trust and serve Good Will, all these graces will come trooping after us. But if sought directly they fly beyond our reach.

Quite purposefully, in these topics, it would appear, Dr. Hyde popularized a pattern for a style of sermon which flourished following the publication of these lectures, and is still in use, namely, the book or drama sermon. By this term just used, the reference is not to the reviews of books and plays, given perhaps too often from the pulpit, but to *sermons* based on books and plays of a religious character which have caught and held the public interest. Some of us can recall the numerous sermons preached on *The*

Inside of the Cup, following the publication of that book and the newspaper controversies that ensued. In my old pulpit at Bloomington, Illinois, I spoke on this subject to a well-filled church, on a Sunday night when a cold rain poured down and the streets were flooded. Afterwards I gave the same sermon to a capacity audience in the adjacent city of Normal, seat of Normal University.

Now this kind of preaching is not of the highest and most enduring pattern, but it can be and often is effective. To employ it as a substitute for a sermon which exacts close study and careful preparation is a mistake which may prove costly. Actually, this sort of preaching requires hard work and ingenuity to do it well. At their best, sermons which are built on biographies, plays, and works of popular fiction should be regarded as "occasional" and "special." Dr. Hyde's use of such material was exceptionally well-managed; likewise it was wisely balanced, a fact which could easily escape the notice of any preacher eager for dramatic pulpit effects and sensational topics.

Dr. Hyde's standard for pulpit and parish was high and exacting. He had nothing but contempt for shoddy work in classroom or pulpit. Among the epigrams of a sparkling speech he made in Boston, here is one to remember:

No wonder that there is a deadline of fifty in the ministry. For the man who is dead at fifty is simply the man who was not intellectually alive at twenty-five.

VI. LAWRENCE PEARSALL JACKS

Along in the late nineteen-twenties, Dr. L. P. Jacks made a brief visit to Detroit, and Dr. Lynn Harold Hough gave a luncheon in his honor. I was one of the invited guests and enjoyed the affair hugely. Dr. Jacks at that time was riding the crest of his editorial headship of *The Hibbert Journal,* having attracted to it a galaxy of brilliant writers. He spoke informally, sprinkling his speech liberally with lively anecdotes. As I recall him, he was slight of build, quiet of demeanor, and gave the impression of an intellectual who had companied with many of the great of the British Isles, on the Continent, and in America.

In 1942 Dr. Jack's *Confession of an Octogenarian* came off the Macmillan press. Besides giving the story of his early struggles, the book brought to life a delightful company of literary, educational, and ministerial celebrities whom he had known, many of them intimately. His marriage to a daughter of the Reverend Stopford Brooke, a renowned Unitarian minister and the biographer of Frederick W. Robertson, was a big event in Dr. Jacks' life. Later he became assistant to his father-in-law and, after the latter's death, his biographer. As an author, Jacks wrote a dozen or more volumes, some of them enjoying a wide reading. On this side, his little book *The Lost Radiance of the Christian Religion* had a popular reception among church people, and justly so, for it struck a needed note.

Dr. Jacks was principal of Manchester College, Oxford, for thirteen years, and held pastorates in Liverpool and Birmingham. But we do not think of this English intellectual chiefly as preacher, but rather as author, editor, and critic, whose liberating influence in educational and religious circles was strong and helpful. It would seem too that his most significant achievement, other than winning the hand of the lovely Miss Brooke in marriage, was his conspicuous success as editor of *The Hibbert Journal*.

I

Dr. Jacks was the oldest lecturer to appear in the Yale Course, being seventy-three at the time. His subject was *Elemental Religion*. The published volume contains but 143 pages, and includes three sermons in addition to the six lectures. For brevity, no other lecturer approached this record, except Bishop Sherrill, in 1948; his book contained 159 pages. If Dr. Jacks delivered his discourses in their published form, the hour allowed the speaker must have been but partly consumed. Perhaps the left-over time was pleasantly spent by the students quizzing the Doctor, a thing he probably welcomed and enjoyed, but which to Dr. Jowett was an ordeal.

Dr. Jacks' lectures as printed are so slight in length and so much of the essay type that it would be easy to discount them at a hasty reading. But on closer scrutiny they stand up fairly well, although they fall below the excellence of the Course as a whole. They reveal native ability and a well-trained mind, but they are not especially exciting, nor are they warm and enthusiastic. Moreover, a strain of mild pessimism runs through this treatise on *Elemental Religion*; not bitter or iconoclastic; rather, is it plaintive, subdued, and subduing. Now and then the lecturer flings this mood aside as one would a hampering garment, and it is good to follow him in this excerpt:

Was there ever a time when the burden of the Lord was not too heavy for the man who had to bear it? It is of the very nature of the Lord's burden that it should be so. The shoulders of Atlas are unable to carry it. The hands of Moses that dropped in weariness, the cry of Elijah "I, even I only am left," the Figure that collapsed in the Garden of Gethsemane, these are the hands, that is the cry, that is the figure of every man who has ever dared to take upon himself the burden of the Lord. Be assured that if your burden affects you otherwise, if there never comes a time when it seems utterly beyond you and absolutely crushing, then it is not the Lord's burden that you carry. But just because the burden is the Lord's it is not you alone that carry it. The Lord carries it with you. Take the Lord's burden upon you and you shall find that the strength of the whole universe is in you to help you bear it. Yes, we do get help. If it were not for that we should all break down.

This is a noble utterance and expressed with a disarming simplicity.

Or, take this fine paragraph:

I cannot help thinking that there is an element of pulpit scare in the current talk about the present crisis in religion. A living faith is always on trial; we call it faith for that reason. When, therefore, I read in some alarmist book that the Christian faith is now on trial, or "at the crossroads," my impulse is to answer, Why not? Does anybody know of a time when the Christian faith was *not* on its trial, or when the Christian life was a simple walkover, with neither principalities nor powers to dispute its advance? Was there ever a pilgrim on that road but came sooner or later to a point of crisis where Apollyon barred the passage "straddling quite over the whole breadth of the way, and swearing by his infernal Den: thou shalt go no farther; here will I spill thy soul?" Is not the freedom of the soul a thing "to be won afresh every day," and in the teeth of opposition? Did an age ever dawn for a Church or a nation but a challenge went forth in the morning of it, "See, I have set before thee this day life and death, good and evil; therefore choose life, that both thou and thy seed may live?" . . . The trial before it is the very cause for which it came into the world. "Then did Christian draw, for he saw 'twas time to bestir him."

II

On Sunday, April 16, 1933, Dr. Jacks preached a remarkably fine sermon in Yale University Chapel, on "Death," a subject not often selected for such an occasion. Strange to relate, he was less gloomy in preaching on this solemn subject than he was when lecturing to the seminary students. The question "What Shall We Do with Our Lives?" was the motif of the sermon, and the preacher answered in a noble and climactic passage, which it is a pleasure to quote:

What shall we do with our lives? *Give them away*. Make a generous gift of them to mankind. Find the thing that is worth dying for as well as worth living for. Die for it daily, not in a spectacular way, but in a silent way. Keep it, if you will, a secret between you and God. Spread your dying out over the weeks, the months, and the years. Let your life be consumed in service. Consume yourself valiantly, cheerfully, creatively, skillfully. Put all your intelligence into your self-consumption; put all your skill into it; put all your courage into it. Waste no thought on asking whether you are as happy as you have a right to be. Ask for no guaranties.

Believe me it will be a great relief. It will be an immense liberation. You will not be miserable. Not a gleam of radiance the less shall fall on your life, but a hundred times more. Your eye shall be brighter, your step firmer, your hand more dextrous, your brain more alert, your heart more enkindled with heavenly fire. Your life shall be anchored on the rock of Immortality. You shall become a "Son of God *with power*"; you shall share in the triumph of the death-conqueror, whose life no man took away from him, but who laid it down of himself, who *gave it away*. O death, where is thy sting? O grave, where is thy victory?

Note: The following letter from a noted clergyman and university professor who knew Dr. Jacks helps to explain the failure of the latter's lectures at Yale to reach a high level of excellence:

"I used to know L. P. Jacks rather intimately, but of late years have not been in touch with him.

"He never was a preacher, in the formal sense of that word. He was an essayist. I agree that the Yale lectures were thin. He was old and I don't think he took much interest in them. I was a good deal disappointed in the Octogenarian book. It adds nothing to his stature.

"Jacks is essentially a poet. He was at his best and most characteristic in books like *Mad Shepherds* or *The Legend of Smokeover* in which he threw the reins over his very great capacity for whimsical and most suggestive invention.

"One of his early essays, of this sort, was called *Devil's Island*, in which he pitched into the habit of professional philosophers of negating and vacating every idea they met. Devil's Island was a kind of honeycombed place full of holes into which you fell if you took a step. He once told me that this essay, which had a bit of acid on the tip of its argument cost him his reputation in Oxford as a serious thinker. The man has always had an untrammelled mind as far as the conventions are concerned, and his great service to our time has been in the utter freedom of its pages given to contributors to the *Hibbert Journal.*

"On his last long trip to America, which carried him from coast to coast, he told me that he was talking more or less constantly about the futility of too much talk. He fully appreciated the amusing irony of the situation!"

VII. J. EDGAR PARK

Born in Belfast, Ireland, Dr. Park was graduated from Royal University, Dublin, and took his theological course at Princeton Seminary, New Jersey. He began as a Presbyterian and became a Congregationalist. Whether this transition is a fair demonstration of the doctrine of the perseverance of the saints is not for me to say. However, since the procedure is often the other way around, the transfer should not be regarded as "an abrupt variation from type," but accepted as a marker on the road to the reunion of the divided House of God.

"Delightful," "Sparkling," are words that partly describe the style and character of Dr. Park's *The Miracle of Preaching.* Some of the lectures in this noted Series—fortunately not many—require both grit and grace to read them through from start to finish, but no such disciplinary exaction is present in the case of this treatise on the fine art of preaching. Sitting down to read J. Edgar Park's lectures in book form is much like having a conversation with a cultured host in the living room of his hospitable home, but with this difference—you rejoice in the fact that he does all the talking while you listen attentively, not wanting to miss a sentence or lose a word. For, be it known: these lectures are attuned to the conversational, not the oratorical pitch, wherein is one secret of their charm.

I cherish a theory that a blend of Scottish and Irish strains in one's lineage is likely to presage a sunny disposition, facile speech, wit, and stalwart religious convictions. These qualities are present in Dr. Park's nature, and impart piquancy to his lectures on *The Miracle of Preaching*.

I

Certain volumes in the long list of the Yale Series might have been shortened to their advantage. This is one that could have been lengthened, to the pleasure of the reader. There are no arid pages in the book, and there is a welcome absence of hackneyed phrases. In truth, Dr. Park warns against this tendency in public speakers. Among the list of expressions to avoid, he says, are these: "Had few equals and no superiors"; "More sinned against than sinning"; "Not wisely but too well"; "The irony of fate"; "Leave severely alone"; "Which would be laughable if it were not tragic"; "The psychological moment." Such writing and speaking, he holds, "are uninteresting; they make an impression like that of a large basket of tumbled clothes for the wash."

A reference has hitherto been made to the questionnaire which was mailed to all the living lecturers in the Course. A few correspondents simply filled in the space under the questions asked and returned the sheet, but by far the majority of those so queried replied at length—letters I shall treasure all my days. One of these, which I reproduce here in its entirety, came from J. Edgar Park:

J. Edgar Park

Dear Dr. Jones:

Yours is a very fertile field! A study of these lectures would tell much about the world, the church, and the devil, as well as something about our growing opinions, not to say knowledge, about God. It would be interesting to know how many copies of the various series were sold, what the geographical location of the various lecturers was, what the life of the average volume was, if any received a hostile press, the ages of the lecturers, how many were or immediately became professors and how many were and remained pastors of churches. I was one of the few, if there were any others, who was neither a pastor nor connected with a theological school at the time of my appointment. My preaching work for some years had been entirely in schools and colleges (only one layman, wasn't there, among them?). It would be interesting to get a man like Luccock who has heard so many of them to give his remembrance of their reception by the audience at the time.

As your questions go: (1) My letter of acceptance stated that I got quite a shock at the invitation, remembering the giants of the past, to think that such a one as I, was thought of in this day to give the lectures. My father, grandfather, and great grandfather were all Presbyterian ministers, two of them professors of theology, my son was also a Presbyterian minister; they all seemed to have more assurance in their calling than I had, as, except when I was actually delivering a sermon, I felt deeply before delivery, that I had a great idea, but had not quite sounded its depths; and after delivery that I might now be in a position to write a really good sermon in that topic. But I did feel astonishingly pleased at the thought that someone must have listened and appreciated the truth I did try to convey to my audience. (2) I spent the free time of a whole year in preparation, working early in the morning all through the "long vacation," in a small shed in the woods on the Cape. (3) I used manuscript, most of which had been re-written twice or three times before delivery. (4) I have had many indications that the Yale volumes are both read and studied, and that groups of ministers use them for discussion material years after their publication, that they are quoted both in sermons and books, that they are used as study material in theological schools very widely, that they have a good circulation outside of the USA, that they are to a certain extent read by laymen as well as by the clergy.

While the series varies much in value, due sometimes to the time given to the task by the lecturer, I am of the opinion that they have as a whole a much more wholesome effect on the ministry than published books of sermons, as not tending so much to straight stealing of illustrations and slavish imitation.

I hope these random remarks may be of some use.

Cordial regards,
J. Edgar Park

Dr. Park is a man of letters, with above a dozen books to his credit. One of these bears the startling title, *Bad Results of Good Habits,* and another, *Disadvantages of Being Good.* The titles suggest H. L. Mencken's iconoclastic pattern, but here the resemblance abruptly stops. As an essayist Dr. Park has something in common with the late Dr. Samuel McChord Crothers. Both use impeccable English and alike indulge in whimsy and a choice brand of humor. Dr. Park's third lecture on "The Churchgoing Traditions in English Literature" is a fusion of mellowness of style and factual material supported by a wealth of literary references bearing on the theme. To some readers it will rate as first in literary appeal, but it is also disillusioning, as we shall see.

How does the preacher and preaching fare at the hands of novelists, essayists, and poets? The answer is not altogether favorable to the clergy, although several notable exceptions serve to salve our wounded vanity and prepare us for this observation: "It is an awful thought for English-speaking preachers that in the whole of the encyclopedic-minded Shakespeare, whose works are a mine of reference to every interest of human life, there is not a single legitimate reference to a sermon, to preaching, or to preachers."

II

Dr. Park has a pertinent comment on the confessional trend which, when he gave his lectures, was just beginning to engage the mind of many a hard-pressed pastor. I do not think he objects to counseling as an adjunct to good preaching and patient shepherding, but foresaw the extent to which this confessional ministry might go. Strange too that other far-sighted ministers do not sense an incipient danger in this innovation. Thus in his second lecture Dr. Park has this to say:

The last few years have seen a great revival in the belief in the confessional as opposed to public worship and preaching. It is said to be ridiculous to administer the same remedy to a crowd of people each of whom needs special treatment, as well might a doctor dose his patients en masse out of the same bottle, irrespective of their complaints. Each human being, it is said, should consult an expert who will analyze him psychically and show him exactly what is the matter with him. It is a useful method, and has been proved so by generations of use in the Roman Catholic Church, but its weak point is that the number of people who have such abundant sources of inner inspiration as to be normally balanced themselves at all times and in all respects, is so few, that it sometimes seems as if it might be necessary to produce a group of super-experts to analyze these experts continually, and keep their lives magnificently wise and profoundly human, so that they may continually live at the heights necessary for their difficult work. The method is not enough unless it is in the hands of great artists in the art of living.

There is more of this, equally good. Dr. Park feels strongly that the main business of the preacher is to preach as ably as he can and to shepherd his flock competently. This is a superhuman task unless the preacher is conscious of spiritual empowerment as he goes into the pulpit or mingles with his parishioners.

He says:

The minister must respect his congregation, remembering Dr. Johnson's penetrating words of charity when Boswell told him that Dr. John Campbell drank fourteen bottles of port at a sitting, and Johnson said: "However, I loved Campbell; he was a solid orthodox man; he had a reverence for religion. Though defective in practice he was religious in principle." It is clear that scolding is out of place in the pulpit. Under a rain of denunciation most modern hearers put up their umbrellas and let the drips run on to their neighbor's shoulders. It is better to lead the congregation along, starting with certain general principles to which they gladly give consent, and then applying these to unexpected special instances, and modestly inferring how it is possible to escape the obvious applications. It is not a question of cowardice or of courage, it is a question of method.

Still, Dr. Park had no hesitancy in telling the ministerial students this unpleasant truth:

There is a curious connection between orthodoxy and meanness; evangelical rapture and financial untrustworthiness; liberalism and bigotry; temperance and gluttony; the expansiveness of the pulpit and the constriction of personal generosity. An expert is "an ordinary man far enough away from home," and a saint's reputation too often depends upon the silence of the family.

The theological students who heard J. Edgar Park deliver these lectures were a lucky lot, and the preachers who are so fortunate as to read the chapters in print will go into their pulpits with a new light in their eyes and a new song in their hearts.

VIII. WILLARD LEAROYD SPERRY

In the preface to the lectures he gave in the Yale Series in 1938, *We Prophesy in Part*, Dr. Sperry relates this incident:

Some months ago I went into the study of my former colleague, the late Professor Francis Greenwood Peabody, to ask him to share my pleasure at the honor which Yale had done me in inviting me to give the Lyman Beecher Lectures for the coming year. He congratulated me warmly, and then said with a touch of genial malice, "But what are you going to say? There isn't anything left to say. Phillips Brooks said all that can be said about preaching, and all that needs to be said, in his lectures long ago." Professor Peabody need not have labored the point. I was already painfully aware of my dilemma.

All of the men who participated in this Lectureship, since say 1900, were also painfully aware of this dilemma, with the possible exception of Dean Inge who, like some mountain climbers unawed by mist-shrouded peaks, seemed indifferent to the illustrious men who had preceded him. Dean Sperry knew his lectures would be compared with those of Washington Gladden and Bishops Charles D. Williams and Francis J. McConnell, who spoke on the same topic, and what is more, were fighting prophets on the line of battle. However, this Harvard scholar quite held his own with his predecessors whose battles for social change made headlines in their embattled days. His advance to the subject is from a point of view which differs from that of Dr. Gladden and the militant bishops; is fresh, vigorous, and courageous. Especially important is the ecumenical note which the Dean sounds often in clear and ringing tones. In this respect he ranks next in the Series to Dr. Morrison in a majestic plea for Christian unity.

I

"The Austerity of Prophecy" is the theme of Lecture I, and no better could have been selected to open the course. "Austerity" is scarcely a popular word today. Yet austerity has its rightful place in religion and in the Christian pulpit. Flippancy and slapstick humor go far to vulgarize the pulpit and the preacher who indulges in them. It is probably true that no prophet worthy of that high mission was without a strain of austerity in his character and manner of speech. Two fine paragraphs from Dean Sperry's first lecture cry for inclusion in this chapter. Thus:

In our attempt to reincarnate the prophetic pattern we are liable to fall into the error of scaling down our demands upon ourselves rather than scaling them up. We can see that the gods of the market place are not sufficient seats of authority, and the lawless animal which survives in each one of us enjoys playing the iconoclast. Cromwell's soldiers irreparably destroyed a wealth of Christian art in the churches of England and, whatever our theological view, we find it hard to forgive them; but they must have had a thoroughly good time smashing things. Any man can have equally good sport today smashing the formal conventions of religion. He may even hallow his natural enjoyment by persuading himself that he thereby does God a prophet's service. He gets, temporarily at least, a feeling of emancipation and a sense of an enlargement of his nature and its powers.

The danger is, however, that initial irreverence toward lesser authorities may unconsciously crystallize in a man's character, so that he becomes incapable of reverence toward a higher authority. The pathway of deliberate irreverence is one which, on occasion, may be necessary. It seems sometimes the only plain way out of a moral and spiritual impasse. But conscious irreverence does not provide permanent direction for the prophetic life. A prophet should be a man who is more reverent than his conventional fellow-religionists. He asks more of himself, because he is accountable to a more exacting tribunal.

In our reflective moments we all realize that the appeal from ecclesiasticism to prophecy must be an appeal from a lower to a higher court. If, therefore, we intend to make the appeal we must be prepared to take the consequences. We need no longer fear what man can do to us, precisely because we have the fear of God in our hearts.

What subjects yield to prophetic handling? Some of us can recall a time when the disciples of Henry George were most numerous and articulate. Not infrequently they said to ministers who had read *Progress and Poverty* and were deeply stirred by it, "Why don't you preach Single Tax from the pulpit? It's Christian and it's gospel." Dean Sperry's reply to such appeals for this economic theory or that political issue as pulpit theme, is strictly to the point and preachers generally may well take it to heart:

So likewise when the preacher attempts to make relative pronouncements about money, as though they were prophetic utterances, he confuses the issue. A prophet cannot determine at what economic level the income tax shall begin to operate and how rapidly the surtax shall rise. The fairer distribution of the wealth of the world is a consummation devoutly to be desired. It is a perfectly proper theme for a sermon. But a sermon dealing with this subject in detail cannot be a prophetic utterance, and any attempt to make it so is instantly felt to be unwarranted. That, I think, is why the pews often have a real case against the pulpit. The pews are wrong in saying that we ministers ought not to talk about such subjects. But the pulpit is wrong in assuming that, because the man who stands there is theoretically vindicating the liberty of prophesying, his ideas about the redistribution of wealth have an authority and sanctity which do not attach to similar pronouncements in the columns of a newspaper or in any other frankly secular medium.

Who of us long-time preachers of the Word have not preached on the "Social Gospel," or perhaps have failed to give a series on "Social Christianity"? Not many I imagine. Suppose we listen to Sperry as he too reminisces:

Ever since I can remember, I have been hearing sermons on the social gospel. Important as the subject is, sermons on this theme are no easier to remember than sermons on more abstruse matters; and, alas, most of those once-heard sermons on the social gospel have gone down the wind of forgetfulness. But there was one such sermon that I have never forgotten, and whenever I remember it I can always recover its imperious power. It was not a sermon preached in church at all. It was not a long sermon; it was in fact very short, a matter of seven words used to underwrite a picture that appeared on the title page of a number of "The Survey" many years ago. It was preached during a bitterly cold winter, when unemployment was general and suffering correspondingly widespread. A newspaper photographer wandering around the East Side of New York in the earliest and darkest hours of a February morning happened upon three or four little children, clad in the thinnest rags, lying asleep on a sidewalk grating where they might catch what little heat escaped from the windows of an underground bake-shop. They were covered with a threadbare, tattered horse-blanket which they must have filched from some dump heap. And so he photographed them. The picture was printed on the front page of "The Survey" and under it these words only, "For so he giveth his beloved sleep." That is prophecy.

II

Dean Sperry belongs to a noble company along with Bishop Brent, Peter Ainslie, and E. Stanley Jones, pleaders for a reunion of a splintered Christendom.

There is abroad today, as there has not been for the last four hundred years, a desire to close up the Christian ranks. The task of church union is not at the moment one which is to be prosecuted in the interests of financial economies or administrative efficiency. We need church unity for the sake of a common Christian mind. In our field nothing is more necessary than this. We ought to have a single Christian faith to profess, and substantial agreement on Christian ethics to oppose to the clean-cut dogmas of anti-Christ with which we are faced. A guerilla warfare conducted by brave and solitary individuals will not save the cause of Christianity, in the face of its consolidated modern enemies. The need is the greater because the more aggressive forces of the time have themselves the quality of a debased religion. You cannot dispose of a bad religion by attacking it as such; you can overcome it only by confronting it with a good religion. It must be answered in kind. But at the moment the members of the widely scattered Christian Churches are hopelessly out of touch with one another and at variance regarding the meaning of their creed when it seeks ethical expression in the terms of race, sex, money, industry and the state.

Of all these able lectures, so ably phrased and illustrated too, my own favorite is the Fifth on, "The Cult of Unconventionality." It is packed with shrewd comments on preaching, subtle thrusts sometimes sharpened by satire and whetted with wit, and never without relevance. Sperry cannot endure artificiality in the pulpit any more than he can put up with insincerity. With some hesitancy I quote here a paragraph which mentions but not by name a famous preacher of recent years, who lectured in the Yale Course and naturally has a chapter in this book. I knew of the incident Dr. Sperry relates in the quotation that follows, but refrained from using it for reasons which were sound. To reproduce it here without the name of the famous preacher and on the authority of Dr. Sperry's mother is quite another matter.

My mother once described to me hearing in New York the same sermon preached in three different churches by one of the reputedly great preachers of the last century. His name is known to you all, but since the rule *de mortuis nil nisi bonum* is binding, I withhold the name. At a given point in the sermon, as first heard, he hesitated for a word, and said, "What is the word I want?" The congregation leaned forward with eager sympathy to shout the word he could not find, and settled back with a sigh of relief when he got it for himself. He did precisely the same thing at the same moment in the sermon on a second occasion, and again on a third, with like effect in each of the latter cases. With like effect save upon one woman, who realized that the transaction was not honest, and who therefore lost moral confidence in a man for whom she had previously had the greatest respect. Once a congregation suspects and then slowly realizes that the unconventionality of your preaching is studied and not spontaneous, you have done yourself mortal hurt as their helper. Preaching can survive countless honest errors; it cannot stand insincerity.[1]

Dean Sperry in addition to directing the Harvard Divinity

---

[1] This stricture on the preaching of a renowned pulpit genius and a noble character, may seem hypercritical to ministerial readers generally. It is severe and possibly too sweeping. But it highlights an insidious temptation to which public speakers are constantly exposed, and none more subtly than the man in the pulpit. Moreover it was a mother in our Israel who said it.

School, is frequently the preacher at Harvard's Chapel services and at other universities. He served nine years in the pastorate after five years as an assistant minister in Fall River, Massachusetts. He has written many books on religious subjects and among others these: *Reality in Worship, The Paradox of Religion, The Divine Reticence, Religion in America,* and *Those of the Way. Atlantic Monthly* readers are familiar with his choice essays, written in chaste English, of which he is a master.

In replying to my inquiry as to his evaluation of the Lyman Beecher Lectures, he wrote:

The lectureship itself is one of the most historic and important in our American religious and academic life. Any lecturer at this late date is confronted with the difficult option of choosing between, (a) a classroom treatment of the technical aspects of sermon making, or (b) an "inspirational" interpretation of some contemporary aspect of preaching. The former has been pretty well worked out; the latter offers probably the best field for a lecturer.

VI

EDITORS AND
★ PUBLICISTS ★

A Fourth Estate, of able Editors, springs up; increases and multiplies; irrepressible, incalculable.
—Thomas Carlyle

I. HENRY CLAY TRUMBULL

H. C. Trumbull was a New Englander by birth and rearing, with something of Yankee shrewdness and thrift clinging to him to the end of his days. Always of simple tastes, of sincere and unostentatious piety, Trumbull never belied his Puritan legacy, confident that the Puritan way of life is the Lord's way. With scarcely any academic training, he successfully educated himself, read widely, and learned much from the eminent men of his acquaintance. His indebtedness to Horace Bushnell was vast—a debt he never tired of acknowledging in generous tribute. By constant practice and an inherent good taste this editor came to wield the pen of a clear and ready writer, shunning prolixity and rhetorical embellishments.

He served effectively as chaplain of the Tenth Regiment of the Connecticut Volunteers in the Civil War, and on the advent of peace returned to the work of the Sunday school, in which he had made an effective beginning. Dr. Bushnell repeatedly urged the young chaplain to enter the ministry, but unavailingly. Trumbull was confident that God had called him to the Sunday school field.

There are still some of us around who were subscribers to *The Sunday School Times* during Trumbull's twenty-eight years of successful editorial headship. He made that weekly the leading journal of its kind in this country and won a constituency abroad. Conservative in theology, primly and sedately printed, the "Leader," as they call it in England, was written by Trumbull each

Henry Clay Trumbull

week, while the illustrative, poetical, and expository material, as well as other articles, were done by capable staff members or honored contributors who were reverent Bible scholars of conservative views. The format of *The Sunday School Times* in those days was as familiar to ministers and Sunday school workers and as readily recognized as are copies of *The Christian Century* and *Harper's Magazine* today. The circulation must have been, for that period, large and gratifying. Practically every wide-awake Sunday school superintendent and teacher treasured *The Times* along with the Bible, to the reliability of which the journal was reverently and loyally committed.

I

Since Trumbull gave his Yale lectures, on *The Sunday School,* the progress in religious education has been hailed as phenomenal and the changes certainly revolutionary. Nevertheless, the editor's lectures stand up surprisingly well, and leaders in Christian pedagogy should find them wholesome, helpful, and *tantalizing.* Yes, that is the right word. He opens with a chapter on the Sunday school's Jewish origin. Fifty-one years later Charles Clayton Morrison was to lecture in the same Series, one of his subjects being "The Church before Christ," pushing Trumbull's position still further and making bold to tie Jewish and Christian institutions in a close embrace.

Quoting the Great Commission, Trumbull comments:

As the Jews would have understood that charge, and as we have every reason to suppose that our Lord meant it, the direction therein is, to organize Bible-schools everywhere as the very basis, the initial form of the Christian Church, grouping scholars—the child and the childlike—in classes, under skilled teachers, for the study of the Word of God by means of an interlocutory co-work between teachers and scholars; that is the starting-point of Christ's Church, as he founded it. Whatever else is added, these features must not be lacking.

A long, and for Editor Trumbull, a lumbering sentence, yet clear in meaning.

Trumbull's treatment of the development of the Sunday school is full and detailed. He omits nothing that he thinks important.

He integrates closely the schools with the churches, so that there is no sense of competition but an awareness of complete unity of purpose and operation. He links the home with the school; the school with the pastor. He quotes Horace Bushnell often with reference to the Christian nurture of the child. He exalts the minister's opportunity and duty of preaching to children. In fine, Mr. Trumbull believes that when Jesus put the child in the midst of his disciples, the act was symbolic, and for all times the child was set in the midst of the church for instruction and Christian culture, so that like his Master he may grow in stature, in wisdom, and in favor with God and man. To Trumbull the Sunday school is the Church training its children, and not secondary but primary and fundamental. The school he holds is not intended to be a puny, anemic body but a powerful institution and fraught through and through with evangelistic zeal.

As one reads these able lectures delivered sixty-one years ago at Yale, in spots their freshness and pertinency are startling. Here one finds sanity, sympathy, sound and seasoned judgment directed at the heart of the matter, and a first-class mind is perceived at work wrestling with big ideas in the field of Christian education. Editor Trumbull is fully alerted on the subject. Are we?

A patient study of these able lectures is a disturbing experience when the reader pauses to take a searching look at the plight of the Sunday school in modern Protestantism as it exists today. During the last quarter of the nineteenth century and the first quarter of the twentieth, the Sunday schools throughout the land were flourishing, the interest in teacher-training was contagious; the huge numbers of children and adults in attendance and the eager hosts of high-minded leaders of both sexes which thronged conventions both national and state, not forgetting the county gatherings—all was good to see. By way of contrast, the apathy and indifference to the Sunday school today, with a few notable exceptions, is pathetic and ominous.

Certain questions rise that will not down. Have modern educational methods succeeded in proportion to the investment in revolutionary theories and methods of pedagogy? Has the emphasis placed upon the new child psychology been as effective for good as we had hoped? In short, has our modern Sunday school equaled the older school in nourishing a wistful devotion to the Christian way of life and a loyalty to the same? An honest answer to this question must be "No."

How many pastors today regard the Sunday school with anything like the serious responsibility of their predecessors of fifty years ago? Why are so few capable laymen identified with the Sunday school movement today? A review of Trumbull's Yale lectures provokes these and other questions that ought to trouble the sleep of the preachers of this generation, and I take my medicine with the rest.

II

Trumbull's book is anything but dull reading. He enlivens its pages with incident, anecdote, and pleasing stories involving eminent leaders of his day. For example, in his chapter on "The Pastor and the Sunday-School," he describes a meeting of the Annual Convention of Sunday school teachers of New York State and an evening session held in Plymouth Church, Brooklyn, in the autumn of 1858. The speakers were three "bright, particular stars" of the pulpit, the Reverend Henry Ward Beecher, the Reverend Dr. Stephen H. Tyng, and the Reverend Dr. Richard S. Storrs. The house was packed to capacity. Dr. Tyng was delayed in reaching the church, so that Mr. Beecher was well into his address before Dr. Tyng took a seat behind him. Mr. Beecher said that the kind of preaching that he valued most was the face-to-face and eye-to-eye kind with "thou art the man!"; and it was the opportunity of such preaching as this that gave the Sunday school teacher a peculiar power, which he as a pulpit preacher often envied. Then Mr. Beecher went on to say that he was compelled to leave this face-to-face work with children to other persons in the field of his church and congregation. All of this was said by Mr. Beecher before Dr. Tyng arrived.

At the opening of his address, which followed immediately, Dr. Tyng referred to the genius and eloquence of the speaker who had preceded him, and who, as he had expressed it, had, in his remarks, not only touched the entire circumference of the theme but filled the whole disk within. Then he launched out upon the subject for himself. "It seems to me," said Dr. Tyng, "that the Devil would never ask anything more of a minister than to have him feel that his mission was chiefly to the grown-up members of his congregation while someone else was to look after the children." The aptness of this thrust, at the admission made by Mr. Beecher before Dr. Tyng's arrival, was plain to the audience, and it was greeted with ripples of laughter. Pointing down to the main entrance door before him, of the Plymouth Church auditorium, he exclaimed dramatically: "I can see the Devil looking in at the door, and saying to the minister on this platform, 'Now you just stand there and fire away at the old folks, and I'll go around and steal away the little ones—as the Indians steal ducks, swimming under them, catching them by the legs, and pulling them under.'"

Mr. Beecher felt that the laugh was fairly on him, in his own church, and was equal to the situation. He came forward at the close of Dr. Tyng's address, admitting that the hit was a fair one: "I wondered," he said, "what Dr. Tyng was up to, when he covered me all over with 'soft soap' to begin with, but I found out before he was through. He was only doing as the anaconda does, when it licks its victim all over, from head to foot, in order to swallow the poor creature down at a single gulp." The congregation hugely enjoyed the sparkle of the repartee. Can anyone imagine today a meeting of such magnitude called to consider the Sunday school, and participated in by clergymen of like position and ability as principal speakers? How these embarrassing questions bob up to disquiet some of us who recall the days when the Sunday school was a glowing and going institution! Is this merely a nostalgic sentiment? I wonder!

Did those who heard H. Clay Trumbull rate his lectures highly? The answer is found in the official letter which was written by the faculty shortly after the series closed. It is a pleasure to reproduce it here:

Yale Divinity School, Feb. 29th, 1888

Rev. Henry Clay Trumbull, D.D.,
  Dear Sir,
    The Faculty of the Seminary desire to offer to you their cordial thanks for the course of Lectures on the Lyman Beecher Foundation, which you have recently given in this Institution. We beg leave to

express the hope that these instructive and interesting discourses may soon be given to the public.

     Timothy Dwight
     George E. Day
     Samuel Harris
     George P. Fisher
     Lewis O. Brastow
     John E. Russell
     George B. Stevens

II. LYMAN ABBOTT

The Christian Ministry is the title of the lectures given by Lyman Abbott at Yale in 1903, and before the Pacific Theological Seminary at Berkeley, California, in 1904. The book which emerged from these engagements reflects the qualities of mind which made Dr. Abbott the intellectual and moral force he was in the nation for more than half a century. The work is distinguished by a knowledge which had become wisdom, a pellucid literary style, and a remarkable insight into the responsibilities and opportunities of the ministerial calling.

I

In 1921, at the age of eighty-six, Dr. Abbott published his *Silhouettes of My Contemporaries*, a book of delightful reminiscences, with vignettes of nineteen Americans and one Englishman. Two of these were fellow lecturers in the Lyman Beecher Course, namely, Henry Ward Beecher, beloved friend whom he succeeded at Plymouth Church, and Phillips Brooks, whom he met but twice and both times auspiciously. Of Beecher he wrote: "His life was more eloquent than his speech. He was most eloquent when he failed to say what he wished to say. He was not logical; no seer ever is." Of Brooks he said: "He believed in this life because he possessed it; and it so abounded in him as to overflow, as water out of a great fountain; so irradiated him as to shine out, giving light and life always and everywhere."

Abbott lived long and fruitfully. He came from one of New England's best families, where religion was a primary interest and books revered. He was trained for the law and practiced for several years. Ordained to the Congregational ministry in 1877, his success, marked from the first, won him esteem and admiration, though his advocacy of a liberal interpretation of Christ's teaching naturally brought forth some criticism. His succession to Beecher came as a surprise to many, and inspired his remark that the pulpit committee began by trying to find a successor who resembled Henry Ward Beecher and ended by selecting the man most unlike him. This was a witty saying but not wholly true. In appearance, versatility, and in oratorical gifts the two preachers were totally unlike; but in qualities of mind they had much in common.

Dr. Abbott was editor of *The Outlook* for twenty-nine years and made that weekly journal of opinion, as well as his own name, known to millions of his fellow Americans. When the League to Enforce Peace convened at Philadelphia as World War I neared the end, and such celebrities as Lord Reading, Sir George Adam Smith, William Howard Taft, Senator John Sharp Williams, and other notables spoke, Dr. Abbott delivered a short address. I heard him on that occasion and recall vividly how vigorously he indicted official Germany for the holocaust of 1914-1918. He averred that when Jesus prayed on the cross "Father forgive them for they know not what they do," Christ did not include in that prayer Caiaphas, Annas, Pilate, and Judas, for, said he, "they knew what they did." I was surprised at his fire and fury, for he spoke with unusual vehemence, with anything but the philosophical calm that usually was his. He was both an Elijah and a John the Baptist on that occasion.

Dr. Abbott says in the preface to his *The Christian Ministry*, that he spoke extemporaneously both at Yale and Berkeley. Not many of the men in this Lectureship took that risk, although there are perhaps a dozen who did so. I have heard it said by one who ought to know that the authorities at Yale Divinity School prefer that the lectures be read, which is understandable. Not many ministers, educators, or publicists are sufficiently endowed by nature or adequately trained to deliver so important a course without manuscript. Dr. Abbott succeeded without the text of his lectures at hand, and twelve years later Dean Inge "failed" with a manuscript. How capricious this thing of public speech is, with or without manuscript!

II

So much has been reported in this survey pertaining to the preacher as a preacher, so much bearing on the sermon—artistry, content, and technique—that it seems best in considering Dr. Abbott's volume to devote some space to his chapter on "The Minister as Priest." That there is a tendency to exalt the prophetic functions of the ministry at the price of disparaging the priestly, is, I think, observable in much of the literature of Protestantism. One difference between Catholicism and Protestantism is just here; the former exalts the priest and assigns preaching to a secondary place; the latter reverses the process. Actually, the relation of the two functions of the ministry is like that between faith and works. Each is not fully orbed without the other. Dr. Abbott identifies the priestly function of the ministry largely with public worship, and what he has to say on this vital subject is precious:

If the Roman Catholics and the Episcopalians have made relatively too much of the service and too little of the sermon, the Puritans and their descendants have made too much of the sermon and too little of the service. In my boyhood days this used to be called "preliminary exercises," and still is sometimes so called, as though it were a kind of grace before meat—short grace, long meat; for we come to the table, not for grace but for food. . . .

. . . The old sacrificial system has gone. There is no more in our temples the lowing of cattle, the bleating of lambs, no more the drawn knife, the rivers of blood, no more sacrificial altars. . . . It is true that the whole Roman Catholic Church, and a few even in the Protestant Church, believe that the sacrifice is a perpetual sacrifice and must be offered Sabbath after Sabbath. I do not need to discuss the question here. I shall assume that there is no longer need of a sacrifice to be offered or a priest to offer it. But both the priestly office and the prophetic office remain. What are they? I call a priest one whose function it is to interpret man to God; I call a prophet one whose function it is to interpret God to man: these two functions constitute the function of the Christian ministry, and they are needed today as much as ever they were needed.

The lecturer considers public worship, which includes music, singing, prayer, and the celebration of the Lord's Supper, with the penetrating logic for which he was noted. He makes a convincing plea for the advantages of extemporaneous prayer, while not forgetting to praise the use of a noble liturgy. He says:

If all public prayer had been limited to those furnished by the church we should have no such book of devotions as the Prayers of the Ages; we should not have the prayer of Paul for his friends and companions given in the third chapter of Ephesians, nor the intercessory prayer of Jesus Christ, given in the seventeenth chapter of John, nor indeed, the prayers in the Book of Common Prayer; for these, like all true liturgies, grew out of original acts of free, spontaneous devotion.

In this connection, and bearing on the preacher in the role of priest as he takes his people before God in public prayer, Dr. Abbott lifts from one of Henry Ward Beecher's lectures on "Preaching" this compassionate passage:

I can bear witness, that never in the study, in the most absorbed moments; never on the street, in those chance inspirations that everybody is subject to, when I am lifted up highest; never in any company, where friends are the sweetest and dearest,—never in any circumstances in life is there anything that is to me so touching as when I stand, in ordinary good health, before my great congregation to pray for them. Hundreds and hundreds of times, as I rose to pray and glanced at the congregation, I could not keep back the tears. There came to my mind such a sense of their wants, there were so many hidden sorrows, there were so many weights and burdens, there were so many doubts, there were so many states of weakness, there were so many dangers, so many perils, there were such histories,—not world histories, but eternal world histories,—I had such a sense of compassion for them, my soul so longed for them, that it seemed to me as if I could scarcely open my mouth to speak for them. And when I take my people and carry them before God to plead for them, I never plead for myself as I do for them,—I never could. Indeed, I sometimes, as I have said, hardly feel as if I had anything to ask; but oh, when I know what is going on in the heart of my people, and I am permitted to stand to lead them, to inspire their thoughts and feelings, and go into the presence of God, there is no time that Jesus is so crowned with glory as then! There is no time that I ever get so far into heaven. I can see my mother there; I see again my little children; I walk again, arm in arm, with those who have been my companions and co-workers. I forget the body, I live in the spirit; and it seems as if God permitted me to lay my hand on the very Tree of Life, and to shake down from it both leaves and fruit for the healing of my people.[1]

When a minister can speak about prayer on so exalted a plane, his prayers are likely to be more powerful than his preaching, however powerful that preaching may be. It is probable that Beecher had in his congregation every Sunday those who were more eager to hear him pray than to hear him preach.

III

Dr. Abbott, in his handling of his theme, seems to find no place for the personal, priestly function of the minister with the individual, although one of his lectures is on "The Individual Message of the Ministry." By this he means the message to individuals in his congregation through preaching. Dr. Fosdick's *The Need of a Protestant Confessional* was not to appear in a leading monthly for two decades, and "counseling" as a Christian art was yet to have its day in the Court of the Lyman Beecher Lectureship. Forty-six years later Dr. Weatherhead was to devote an entire series to the counseling and healing ministry, in the conduct of which he is a specialist.

Dr. Abbott was proud of America, and closed the preface to his *Silhouettes of My Contemporaries* with this tribute to his fellow countrymen:

If he is the greatest who serves his fellowmen the best, then I do not believe that any other country has produced in a century and a half as many great men as America has produced. Depressed and discouraged as we are apt to be by the flood of filth and falsehood, of corruption and crime, which the daily paper offers us for our daily food, it is well sometimes to stop, take a quieter and less partial view, and realize the right we have as Americans for pride in our past and for hope in our future.[2]

Lyman Abbott said this twenty-eight years ago, and it still holds good.

[1] Henry Ward Beecher, *Lectures on Preaching*, ii, pp. 46-47.
[2] P. vii.

III. CHARLES CLAYTON MORRISON

In Dr. Morrison I come to a long-time and intimate friend. To deal with him objectively is an assignment not as easy as it might seem, since in a large way he has been not only friend but mentor as well. When I first knew Dr. Morrison he was denying himself many conveniences and doing it cheerfully, in order to keep *The Christian Century* from going on the rocks. It was a bitter struggle, demanding sacrifice and courage of a high order. He won the battle by his own efforts plus the generosity of two or three interested laymen, and made *The Christian Century* the leading journal of liberal opinion in America, with numerous readers abroad.

As an editor Dr. Morrison was resourceful, daring, and sharply controversial. A "born *protest*ant," as a competent contemporary called him, he loved a fight and still does, provided he deems the cause a worthy one. The author of a half dozen volumes, he transferred his fighting spirit to his books, embellishing the pages with fresh and original treatments of theological and political subjects. Having achieved early a reputation as a liberal, he is rounding out his useful life as "a high churchman" in one of the most democratic of communions, the Disciples of Christ.

Dr. Morrison is primarily a preacher whether as publicist, editor, debater, or standing in a pulpit. Preaching blood is in his veins; son of a manse and trained in a school of the faith of the Founding Fathers. His preaching is forthright, tinged with the controversial spirit, confessedly dogmatic, and oratorically exciting. He begins in a low voice, is hesitant, seems to have difficulty in finding the right word, gathers power, increases the volume of his voice, and before he concludes, often reaches torrential heights of real eloquence.

Dr. Morrison manages a manuscript skillfully. In his hands sheets of paper present no obstacle to a freedom which is sometimes amazing. In public speech when he is aroused his face flushes, his eyes flash, and his tones take on a thunderous quality. It is not easy for Dr. Morrison to make an effective short speech; he needs plenty of time, and a sermon of his under forty-five minutes is exceptional; he is best when he has a full hour.

I

When Dr. Morrison was asked to give the Yale Lectures his first reply was that he could not qualify as an expert in homiletics. He was assured that the content of preaching was as important as the technique in the mind of the faculty of the Divinity School. His acceptance followed, and shortly he went to work on what turned out to be the most controversial contribution to the entire Lectureship, and bearing the title, *What Is Christianity?*

The product in book form is a sturdy, closely-written volume of eleven chapters and more than three hundred pages. In a foreword he explains that "several of the lectures have been expanded beyond their original length in the interest of a more complete statement than could be made in the one hour allowed for their delivery."

Now Dr. Morrison is a skillful polemicist, and his usual method in a dispute or argument runs something like this: He states the position of his opponent fairly enough and then proceeds to demolish it completely, and upon the stark ruins he sets up his own proposition which he straightway buttresses fully and defends with fiery eloquence couched in stately diction. This is precisely the plan he followed in his Yale lectures, and the result was the most sensational set of discourses in the entire history of the Lectureship.

As one reviewer put it, "a host of familiar definitions of Christianity he rejects, classifying them as doctrinal, institutional, experiential, in the subjective sense, and those which define Christianity as a way of life. Over against all such definitions he places the Christian community: This living community whose center and head is Jesus himself—this is Christianity. Its ideology is not Christianity—itself is Christianity." Another and severer critic says that Dr. Morrison in his lectures "appears as the would-be herald of a new, latter-day counterreformation against almost all that has been most characteristic of evangelical Protestantism." But there are others who believe that the lecturer was clearing away a lot of rubbish which had accumulated through the centuries and that the Chicago editor was making straight the way of the Lord. A third reviewer calls Dr. Morrison's book "a landmark in the interpretation of Christianity." Not being theologically minded myself I simply pose the assertion that the "returns are not all in" yet on Dr. Morrison's Yale lectures. Perchance twenty-five years from now more will be heard of his discussion of *What Is Christianity?* than we now hear.

II

It was Dr. Morrison's eighth lecture on "The Heresy of Protestantism" that caused an unprecedented thing to happen in the delivery of the Yale lectures—he was interrupted! It came about in this way: He was in the midst of a discussion of evangelism and the experience of conversion. He was pointing out that the New Testament does not concern itself with the psychological or subjective aspect of conversion as modern Protestant evangelism does. Our evangelism, he said, overlooked the function of the church in mediating salvation and conceives conversion as an event which takes place in the deep privacy of individual experience. It is an unmediated transaction between man and God in the solitariness of the soul. After conversion, the individual may join the church, but the joining of the church is no part of his salvation. This, said Dr. Morrison, is contrary to the New Testament treatment of conversion.

At that point a strong voice broke the stillness of the audience with the question, "What about Paul?" Unaware at the moment who the questioner was, Dr. Morrison replied that he intended to examine Paul's conversion in the next lecture, but would say now that Paul's experience was a perfect illustration of the view he was expounding. Paul's conversion took place in the medium of the church, said Dr. Morrison. The Voice on the Damascus road, which he heard, did not come from the distant heavens. It came from the midst of the community which Paul was persecuting. "Saul, Saul, why persecutest thou *me?*" It was the voice of Christ speaking through his harried church. There had been a mounting conflict in his soul between Israel which he loved and served in all good conscience and this so-called "new Israel" which he hated and persecuted. The conflict was resolved by his encounter with the Risen Christ in the body of Christians whom he was persecuting. The persecutor was not saved by his private experience of hearing the voice. He languished in remorse and confusion until the Christian community, in the person of Ananias, stretched forth its hand of fellowship saying, "*Brother* Saul," and received him into itself by baptism.

After the lecture it appeared that the question, "What about Paul?" had created a sensation among the students because the questioner was none other than Dr. Charles R. Brown, dean emeritus of the Divinity School. On the last day of the series, as Dr. Morrison came into the common room with Dean Weigle, he found the students grouped around the piano rehearsing a new song which they asked him to hear. The song was entitled, "What About Paul?" and its words, composed by the students, ran as follows:

> Doc. Morrison came from "The Century"
> To lecture to New Haven gentry;
>   Thundered he: "Take the Church—
>   It's been left in the lurch,
> And the fight's become purely defensory!"
>
> Chorus: "What about Paul?
>   What about Paul?
>   Alone on the road to Damascus."
> Joined the Church,
> That is all.
> Good question—I'm glad that you asked us.
>
> The Protestant life ideational
> (Not the least tiny bit inspirational)
>   Seem the poor little sect
>   By its doctrines hen-pecked,
> (And the pecktest of these Congregational).
>
> Chorus: "What about Paul?" etc.

> What we need is ecumenicity,
> To return to our basic catholicity,
> Purge the clergy with hyssop
> Then veto the bishop,
> And thus we may dwell in felicity.
>
> Chorus: "What about Paul?" etc.

This, too, I think, was something new in the annals of the Lyman Beecher Lectureship and it supplied an antidote of humor to a rather heated discussion.

Be it said just here and with elation, that Dr. Morrison's lectures at New Haven were ecumenical to the core. The closing lecture on "Restoring the Body of Christ" is a noble plea for "the reunion of the divided House of God," to borrow a phrase from the late and beloved Peter Ainslie. And on so high and so hopeful a note Charles Clayton Morrison brought his Yale lectures to a close.

The late President Eliot of Harvard in referring to Woodrow Wilson, whom he admired, said that there is a fierce side to reformers and that this was true of Mr. Wilson. It is also true of Dr. Morrison, who is likewise a reformer. There is a grim and fierce side to him when he is on the firing line. Yet on the social side he is one of the most companionable and delightful of men. As for his *What Is Christianity?* which provoked so much controversy at the time of its delivery, I venture the prediction that time will vindicate some of his brilliant contentions, particularly his emphasis on what he calls the "Christian community," the corporate life of the church over against the individualistic interpretation of Christianity so prevalent in American Protestantism.

VII

MODERN MASTERS OF
★ PULPIT DISCOURSE ★

I do not believe that any man ever made a great sermon who set out to do that thing. Sermons that are truly great come of themselves. They spring from sources deeper than vanity or ambition.
—Henry Ward Beecher

I. CHARLES REYNOLDS BROWN

Dr. Brown, whose name is almost a synonym for the Yale Lectures on Preaching, gave two of the Series, both of them significant. In 1906, while minister of the First Congregational Church, Oakland, California, he delivered the first lectures, taking for his subject *The Social Message of the Modern Pulpit*. It is a plausible speculation that this engagement at Yale, coupled, of course, with Dr. Brown's personable qualities, had much to do with his appointment as dean of the Divinity School. In 1923, in the twelfth year of his deanship, he gave the second series on *The Art of Preaching*.

Dr. Brown's lectures on *The Social Message of the Modern Pulpit* were enthusiastically received at Yale, and when published, enjoyed a wide reading. His use of the deliverance of the Israelites from Egyptian serfdom by Moses, was unique. Of the Book of Exodus he said: "This book might not inappropriately be called, *The Story of an Ancient Labor Movement*." Of Moses he asserted: "It is interesting, and I believe significant also, to notice that he was not a ready talker.... It would almost seem as if the divine Author of this ancient social effort, in making choice of a suitable leader, foresaw the fact that in labor movements of the future the glib talkers would frequently come unduly to the front, to the serious detriment of the movements they espoused."

The six lectures were entitled: "The Need of Moral Leadership in Social Effort"; "The Scriptural Basis for a Social Message"; "The Oppression of a People"; "The Call of an Industrial Leader"; "Radical Change in the Social Environment"; "The Training in Industrial Freedom"; "The New Social Order"; and "The Best Line of Approach."

Those familiar with Dr. Brown's piquant style of later years must have missed in these discourses the humorous touches which give sparkle to his second series, and also to many of his other books. The nature of his subject goes far to explain this omission. There is too much sorrow and suffering in the drama of industrial slavery and social injustice to warrant the subtle play of the author's delightful humor. It is a prudent preacher who suits his style to his subject.

In his autobiography, *My Own Yesterdays*, published in 1931, Dr. Brown writes:

> When Yale Divinity School came to celebrate the one hundredth anniversary of its founding, in the year 1922, my colleagues on the Faculty invited me to give a second series of the Lyman Beecher Lectures. For thirty years we had had no set of lectures on that Foundation dealing directly with the technique of preaching. It seemed fitting therefore, that as a teacher of homiletics and as one whose main office had been that of preaching, I should take up in a more intimate way the making of a sermon. This course of lectures was published under the title *The Art of Preaching*. I believe now with all my heart, as I believed forty-two years ago when I was first ordained, that to preach the gospel of the Lord Jesus Christ is the highest office and the most alluring interest to which any human being can be called. The true sermon, in order to achieve the high purpose for which it is designed, should therefore, in the best sense of that abused phrase, be "a work of art."

My copy of *The Art of Preaching* bears this inscription: "To my good friend Edgar Dewitt Jones with high regards and warm affection. Charles R. Brown, Detroit, January, 1935." He was in the study of Central Woodward Christian Church when he wrote this and we had been standing before the section in my library that held the Yale Lecture volumes. A little later he stood in the pulpit of our beloved church and preached with a refreshing gusto, as he was accustomed to do.

The earlier Yale lecturers managed the technique of preaching after the manner of the old masters that they were. On reading Beecher and Brooks on the homiletical art, it would appear that they had said everything that needed to be said, and in truth all that could be said, on the subject. But it is given to no man to say all that can be said on any subject. If it were otherwise the zest for life and labor would be at an end. To read Beecher on preaching is like gazing awestruck on the Falls of Niagara and feeling proud to be near enough to have the spray wet one's cheek. To read Brooks on the same theme is like nothing so much as to try to glimpse the top of a giant redwood, all the while humbled by its sheer grandeur. To read Brown on the art of preaching is like listening to Lincoln discuss the solemn issues of the hour, and after the speech chuckling with him over some homely phrase or bit of drollery.

"The poor sermon is everywhere spoken against. 'Dull as a sermon!' 'Prosy as a preacher!' 'He has the homiletic habit.' 'Whatever you do don't preach!' 'His book is lifeless as a sermon.'" In such a tone the Dean began his first lecture. He goes on to say:

In these familiar phrases, caught up at random from the swiftly flowing currents of popular speech, we find the common appraisal set upon the sermon. It is a dull day when some light-hearted newspaperman does not make merry over the unpopularity and the futility of the unhappy sermon. In many a quarter the conventional sermon has fallen so low that none shall count himself so poor as to do it reverence.

Yet in the very teeth of this easy and widespread detraction of that form of address, I am here to maintain against all comers that the sermon is by right, and may well be in fact, the most august expression of mind, heart, and will to be heard anywhere in human society. I would agree most heartily with the estimate placed upon it by one who was himself possessed of fine literary skill, by one whose little books are read from the rising of the sun to the going down of the same. It was Ian Maclaren, the author of *The Bonnie Brier Bush*, who said, "The most critical and influential event in the religious week is the sermon."

"Sing hallelujah forth!" Shout "Bravo!" For here is a preacher who not only loved his vocation with a very great love, but took no cheap fling at preaching, lying down. There may be some ministers, not many it is to be hoped, but some, who give the impression of being apologetic about their calling and not above belittling it themselves. After reading this proud and militant defense of preaching and the high calling in general, any man of the ministerial ranks who has been otherwise minded, should repent himself in sackcloth and ashes; but since this ancient form of expressing godly sorrow is outmoded, he should at least sink to his knees in contrition, and pour forth a humble prayer for God's forgiveness.

How long should a man preach? The Dean has ideas on the question:

. . . The clock has nothing to do with the length of a sermon. Nothing whatever. Clocks know nothing about the matter; clocks are in no wise competent to pass upon the proportions of a sermon. A long sermon is a sermon that seems long. It may have lasted an hour or it may have lasted but fifteen minutes. If it seems long it is long—too long. And the short sermon ends while people are wishing for more. It may have lasted twenty minutes or it may have lasted an hour and a half. If it leaves the people wishing for more, they do not care what the clock said about the length of it.

Is humor permissible in the sermon? Dean Brown thought so and used it, not immoderately but in nice proportion. Hear him on this point:

It is not well for a minister to go out of his way even six inches to make a joke. But when some unexpected turn comes naturally in his treatment of some great truth, he is unwise to turn aside in order to avoid it. Let him study the great masters of delicate humor in the literature of the race! Let him use if he will those lighter statements which bring a sense of surprise. Let him employ "the finest of the wheat" in this matter of humor, just in passing, with a touch and go, never waiting for a laugh, and he will find that by this method he has added greatly to his power of spiritual appeal. The people whose minds are quickened and refreshed may not laugh with their mouths—they will laugh with their eyes and they will be all the more ready to recognize and to accept the full value of the solid truth which is thus proclaimed.

Having quoted Dr. Brown's opening paragraph of his first lecture, it is appropriate to quote the closing passage of his last:

John Robert Paterson Sclater

Come now let us reason together, saith the Lord, come now let us build together a new heaven and a new earth wherein dwelleth righteousness! Come now let us make men after the likeness and image of the Eternal! This is the word of God which is nigh thee, even in thy mouth and in thy heart. And in this vast work of creative evolution, under the Great Taskmaster's eye and in open alliance with His full strength, the mind, the heart and the will of man in that high exercise known as preaching are to bear an honorable and an indispensable part.

In November, 1950, just before this book went to press, word came of the death of Dr. Charles Reynolds Brown at his home in New Haven, Connecticut. He lingered in a soft, misty twilight, not suffering greatly but unable to move about, or to speak with his one-time ease and sparkling eloquence. In the eventide of his life he was surrounded by the thoughts of a host of his beloved students and loyal friends in the ministry he so honored and so adorned.

Note: Dr. Brown dedicated his volume on *The Art of Preaching*

"To

George A. Gordon

Whose Preaching Kindled My Own Heart with Fresh Impulse During My Three Years in the Seminary; Who Has Nobly Maintained the Intellectual Dignity of the Ministry in Times of Stress; Who for Well-nigh Forty Years Has Made the Pulpit of the Old South Church, Boston, a Place of Power and of Spiritual Impartation, I Dedicate This Book in Grateful Appreciation."

II. JOHN ROBERT PATERSON SCLATER

It was for me an eventful day when I sat in the book-lined study of Dr. Sclater in his pleasant Toronto residence. He talked about books, and preachers, and his lectures at Yale. He got his sturdy pipe going good and settled back in a pensive mood.

"I don't remember my feelings on receiving the invitation to give the lectures, except a vague impression of pleasure and surprise—particularly surprise. I had previously held the Warrack Lectureship in Scotland, but I had never imagined holding the Yale one.

I think my main curiosity was as to whence the suggestion of my name had come—a thing I have never found out. But I have no doubt that I was 'surprisedly gratified'—together with a good deal of perturbation as to what I could say that would be of any use.

"How long did I take to prepare? I don't know. I had some material to start from in the Warracks. I remember working regularly up at my summer cottage for a couple of months—but only for a short time each day; but I forget if I was ready when I came back to Toronto in September. It is twenty years ago, and I am good at forgetting.

"I wrote full notes and photographed headings on my mind, then spoke without notes—in the same way that I preach. I remember that this surprised some of the professors. I wrote the book afterwards, which was a mistake, for by that time I had lost zest. The lectures were (I humbly hope) much better than the book, because they were spontaneous and because I was keen on what I was doing. The writing of the book was a "chore." There is a point here, I think, for lecturers to face. Which is more important, the lectures or the book? If the latter, they had better write them and read them; if the former, they had better realize that the subsequent writing will be dreary, if they 'deliver' the lectures.

"You ask what is the value of the Lectureship? My own feeling is that good preaching *can't* be taught. Teaching is a kind of preventive medicine against really bad preaching. But, apparently, a great many do not agree with me. Certainly, the Lectureship has given us some 'permanent' books and has kept alive the sense of the importance and dignity of the preaching office—a vital contribution to the well-being of the Churches of the Reformation, where the 'spoken word' occupies the central place. I hope that the Lectureship may increasingly be taken to cover worship as well as preaching. There is great room (and need) for teaching in that region, in nonliturgical churches."

Dr. Sclater filled his pipe and lit it with the skill and deliberation acquired only by the seasoned smoker. I asked him about Kelman, Jowett, Alexander Whyte, and others, and he related many anecdotes of these and other pulpit celebrities. It was the kind of preacher talk I love and I was reluctant to leave. But at last this

John Robert Paterson Sclater

preacher-scholar saw me across the street and put me on my bus. Thus ended a perfect hour.

Dr. Sclater's Yale lectures on *The Public Worship of God* are the work of a man of artistic temperament and acquainted with the best in literature. Moreover, he is a preacher in the great traditions, thoroughly grounded in theology and church history, with a genius for the details and embellishments of public worship. While many of the lecturers at Yale devote single chapters to the art of public worship, Sclater has four, captioned thus: "The Order of Worship"; "Public Prayer"; "The Sacrament"; and "The Celebration." I do not know of another treatment of the Communion of the Lord's Supper and its celebration so complete and satisfying as that of this wise and reverent Presbyterian minister. Every young preacher should find it helpful, and those long in the service will find it useful.

The section which sets forth the meaning of the Sacrament is particularly fine and rewarding. Dr. Sclater finds the "weight of its different elements" under eight headings, in each instance impressively developed: 1. *The Sacrament Is a Memorial Feast*; 2. *A Method of Teaching Truth by Symbol*; 3. *A Sacrificial Feast*; 4. *A Sign of a Fixed Agreement*; 5. *The Chief Thanksgiving Occasion of the Church*; 6. *The Family Meal of the Church*; 7. *A Badge of Christian Discipleship*; and 8. *A Prophecy of the Perfected Kingdom*. Here are the pegs on which to hang a sermon, and indeed the Doctor may have preached a sermon from this outline. To read this chapter on "The Sacrament" and the one that follows on "The Celebration" is to realize anew the sacredness of the ordinance and the spiritual possibilities of a reverent and beautiful observance of the ancient institution.

Hearken to this:

The common cup, however, should always be on the Communion Table, and the minister should use it when reading the Scripture warrant. Seeing that the whole Sacrament is a symbolism, he should be very careful about all the symbolic acts. An unbroken slice of bread should be ready to his hand, which he will break in the sight of the people; he should lift the Cup high when he utters the words "this cup is the new covenant in my blood." These little things add so much. Nothing is too slight or too immaterial to be negligible.

Every arrangement, every detail should be given all the reverent care at our command; for the Supper may be the simplest meal in the world, but it is a Supper with the King.

For one I would feign keep the divine appointment at Old St. Andrew's, Toronto, with Pastor Sclater presiding at the Lord's Table.

Dr. Sclater has told us he makes careful sermon outlines or notes, photographs them on his memory, and preaches freely out of a fulness of brooding preparation. In his chapter on "Preparation of a Sermon" he gives an outline of a discourse he preached from his pulpit in Toronto on the text in John 20:29, "Blessed are they who have not seen and yet have believed." He informs us that the sermon did not prepare smoothly and that he had to recast it twice. Also he says that "with notes of this kind" he can "recapture a sermon even after many years." Now such notes as he made will interest, yes fascinate preachers generally. Lo! here they are:

Introd.
  i. We must all feel sympathy with doubting Thomas, because—
      a. He was so much in accord, intellectually, with our time, and because
      b. He was the possessor of an unfortunate temperament—pessimistic and melancholic: for which he was no more to blame than for a tendency to rheumatism or tuberculosis.
  ii. Moreover, he was a very fine fellow—loyal in spite of melancholia, hopeful in spite of dread. There will be a lot like him in heaven.
  iii. In this story, we see his sort symbolised as satisfied at last. The "sorrowful spirit" transmuted into joy in the perfected kingdom.
  iv. The incident is specially significant for the generalism to which it gives rise.
      The risen Christ is looking forward to the Church that is to be and foreseeing its difficulties.
      No literal proof: no seeing of wounds. Nothing but His spiritual presence and power.
      And of them He says—"Blessed are they . . ."
      Blessed are they who may not walk by sight, but succeed in walking by faith.

John Robert Paterson Sclater

I. *Religious faith is ultimately trust in a particular Person: for Christian faith that Person is Christ.*
   i. It involves
      a. Intellectual assent to His teaching.
      b. Practical obedience to His commands.
   ii. It implies the possibility of mistake.
      It would not be trust if there were not reasonable grounds for thinking that conceivably, in so trusting, we are wrong. There is an element of *risk* in faith.

II. *The Regions of Risk in Faith.*
   i. We have to choose, often, between different goods.
      a. The denial of either means the denial of a full life.
      b. And we *may* be "martyrs by mistake."
         e.g. the clash between duty and happiness. The denial of the latter means the denial of elasticity and buoyancy. In the perfect life, God shall wipe away *these* tears, at any rate.
   ii. Or, to take the same point from another angle, there is a clash between our duty to ourselves and to our neighbours. "Thou shalt love thy neighbour *as* thyself."
      It is that "as" that creates all the trouble.
   iii. Further, there is the clash between our ideal of duty and our own power.
      On the one hand "I know I ought."
      On the other "I am sure I can't."
      Is a clash like that God's will; or are we mistaken about the "ought"?
   iv. And, finally, there is the perplexity due to the fact that the harsher demands of right are often caused by
      a. Other people's sin, or
      b. Their *inevitable* imperfection.
      The former has nothing to do with God: the latter seems to make Him an imperfect worker.
      e.g.
      under (a) a daughter with an unreasonable, selfish parent.
      under (b) a wife, or a husband, with a mate that was born a "mollusc."
      What *is* the right thing to do in these circumstances? At any rate, there is plenty of room for walking by faith.

III. *The call of Christ to take the risk.*
   This is explicit, unhesitating, clarion-like.

    i. It contains
        a. "Seek ye *first* . . ."
        b. The path of search is the path of the Cross.
        c. "Follow *Me*."
      There is no question about the Christ-demand: either in precept or example. When in doubt, listen to the inner voice that calls to self-denial.
   ii. Wherefore, our duty is
        a. Cultivate the ear that is sensitive to the "long, low note of sacrifice."
        b. If we would satisfy our minds, let us "universalise our conduct."
        c. When things are bad, turn sharp into His society. "Straight to His presence get me and reveal it . . ."
  iii. If we do that last, certain results follow.
        a. A feeling that we must not let Him down, and of utter shame, when we remember that we have done so.
        b. A compelling thought that His loveliness must be right.
        c. A remembrance of the results that followed on His own loyalty to the inner voice.
      After all, He does not ask us to go where He feared to lead. Our worst is but a shadow of His pain.
Concl. Thus, at least, the heart grows warm again; we feel the gallantry of "Stand thou on that side . . ." and then, in assenting, there touches us, "with a ripple and a radiance," the promise of His renewal—when at last pain shall yield to peace for those who, having been faithful, are blessed in their Heavenly Father's realm. Amen.

Whew! There's an example of preparation that bowls over the lazy and careless preacher and fairly startles the moderately alert and industrious minister of the Word!

And "finally" this gem from Sclater's last lecture in his series on the "Guidance of the Wise":

If our people act unworthily, we shall try to pity them as a doctor pities a sick child. And if they act meanly to us, let us keep in our hearts this wisdom from William Blake, "Friendship cannot exist without the forgiveness of sins continually." Moreover, we must rejoice greatly in their affection for us and keep it as a treasure and a prize, not forgetting that one of the most charming of writers has said that, "The world has a million roosts for a man, but only one nest."

Dr. Sclater died in 1949 in his beloved Scotland, just after completing an exposition of a section of the Psalms for *The Interpreter's Bible*. *Requiescat in pace*, O thou preacher scholar!

III. GEORGE ARTHUR BUTTRICK

"New York is the graveyard of preachers." Who of us has not been regaled with this silly saying? Not many. This hackneyed saw is neither clever nor wholly true. Failures, ministerial and otherwise, depend not so much on places as on combinations of circumstances, and these may emerge in county-seat towns and hamlets as well as big cities. If some preachers have found metaphorical graves in New York City, others have found pulpit thrones, as has Dr. Buttrick. Coming from Buffalo, where his ministry drew a large hearing, he inherited the mantle of Dr. Henry Sloane Coffin, his noted predecessor at Madison Avenue Presbyterian Church.

Dr. Buttrick's preaching follows closely the approved English criterion, by which I mean it is scholarly, often brilliant, and largely Biblical in the best sense of an abused term. While there is little in common in theological concepts or method of Scriptural interpretation between Dr. Buttrick and the late Dr. G. Campbell Morgan, I think there is some similarity of delivery, and this is meant to be complimentary to Dr. Buttrick, since Dr. Morgan was dramatic, versatile, and fascinating in his pulpit utterance.

I have heard Dr. Buttrick at least half a dozen times and he never failed to impress and inspire me. I listened to him address several hundred ministers, at which time he took for his text Hebrews 11:13: "These all died in faith, not having received the promises, but having seen and greeted them from afar, and having confessed that they were strangers and pilgrims on the earth." The effect of this sermon upon that preacher audience I have tried to describe elsewhere, and reproduce it here because of its relevance to the subject:

I looked about me. Across the table sat the minister of a county-seat town, where the going was hard, the task grinding. His eyes were shining. By my side sat the able minister of a strong city church; his face was aglow. A little farther away was a country preacher whose parish covered a section of the wind-beaten plains of Nebraska. He sat enraptured. I glanced toward an old preacher to my left, wrinkled of face, hair white, cheeks sunken, no longer much in demand, serving as supply as opportunity came. His eyes were brimming; his cheeks wet. I looked—but the sermon was going on, my wandering gaze returned to the preacher. He spoke with quiet force, noble dignity, now and then increasing the vigor of his voice.[1]

I

Dr. Buttrick's series at Yale Divinity School in 1932 was up to his high standard; some thought he outdid himself on that occasion. To begin with, the subject, *Jesus Came Preaching*, is alluring. Ministers of maturity as well as theological students find such a theme of absorbing interest. Then too, literarily, the workmanship of this series is of superior quality. Buttrick knows books, poetry, pictures, and music sufficiently to make use of these enchanting subjects, and all this in addition to his expository, exegetical, and homiletical gifts, which are rare.

The titles of the lectures, like that of the general theme, are carefully chosen, and keep well within the range of the treatise as a whole:

1. *Is There Room for the Preacher Today?* This preacher thinks so. He answers, and with severity at times, such criticisms as these: "The pulpit is not democratic, and has no place in a democracy." "The preacher doesn't do anything." "The pulpit has lost its authority." To which he replies:

Preaching is grounded in the awareness of Another. Isaiah's impassioned plea for righteousness sprang from his sense of eternal rectitude: his only hope of success was that his hearers had that same sense, though beclouded, while his was bright. Preaching is rooted in a sense of Another. Christian preaching is rooted in the persuasive faith and piercing conviction that in Christ that Other has made known His love and will for mankind.

2. *Is Christ Still the Preacher's Authority?* His final answer to this query is given in a paragraph of just four sentences. Thus:

[1] Edgar DeWitt Jones, *American Preachers of Today*, p. 273.

Christian preaching in our day has that one Word from which all other words derive their life. The cults of our day have in their nights a thousand stars: our gospel has but one Sun. All *our* arguments are clinched, and all our commands are sealed in Him. We test all worlds by the spectrum-colors of His soul, who is the one white Light.

3. *Preaching Christ to the Mind of Today.* Dr. Buttrick avers that the mind of today is a worthy mind, a mind in revolt, a scientific mind, a sceptical mind, and he asks:

Was Jesus free from the inrush of doubt threatening to overwhelm faith? Not if He genuinely shared our nature! Did He never fear that God might prove at the last an immense nothing dwelling in nowhere? Was not that paralyzing fear a dread ingredient of the "cup" which He prayed might "pass"? Surely He hath borne our doubts and carried our misgivings! Preaching will win the heart of the doubter (though it may not at once clarify his mind) if it shall say: "I know the force of that onset, I also have prayed: Lord I believe; help Thou mine unbelief.[2] Jesus knows it too. Look at Him and you will see."

4. *Preaching Christ to the Social Order.* Here is a long, tense lecture, and the last paragraph sums up clearly what was said at length in the body of the discourse:

Let the preacher preach the social gospel. If he shirk that task, he may escape discomfort, but he will not escape himself or Christ. Let him preach a truer nationalism. Let him preach a fairer industry— whose smoke becomes the pattern of His Face against the sky. Let him cleanse the Temple. Let him overturn by his zeal the tables of the money changers. But let him keep that preaching ever in the constraint of Christ's love; lest, wandering into propagandist realms it is slain. Let him so preach that in all things "He may be exalted."

5. *Preaching to the Individual Today.* Among many strong sections of this lecture this one is picked because of its pertinency:

Ask an honest man in the pew what he requires of his preacher, and he will admit ere long that he has scant respect for a pulpit that does not make the pews uncomfortable. People are driven from the church not so much by stern truth that makes them uneasy as by weak nothings that make them contemptuous. If we fail to preach sin and its redemption, the novelists and dramatists will become

[2] Mark 9:24.

worthier ambassadors in our stead. Some Shakespeare will paint the darkness of remorse:

> "Canst thou not minister to a mind diseased,
> Pluck from the memory a rooted sorrow?"[3]

6. *The Craftsmanship of the Preacher.* A master craftsman himself, Dr. Buttrick's first paragraph in this lecture says much and says it well:

> There is the story of a king who required of a famous artist an example of his genius, and expected to receive some glowing canvas. The artist, however, drew a perfect circle with one sweep of his brush and sent that as answer. A circle seems very simple—all too poor a demonstration of his gift; yet to draw a perfect circle had levied the tax of a lifetime's labor. A great sermon is likewise simple. Hearing it we say, "That is just what I have often felt." Its ideas are transparent, its words are shining-clear. Anybody could preach it. But, no! Preaching is both an art and a craft. It may be learned, granted some initial gift, but "not without dust and heat."

7. *The Personality of the Preacher.* What is one passage among so many? That is a fair question. It depends on *the* one. Ponder this one:

> There is, in strict fact, nothing commonplace in God's world. The replicas, the drab samenesses have come from man's hand by mass production. God does not manufacture: He creates. "One star differeth from another in glory."[4] Every leaf of a tree is variant and distinct. Likewise every man is another man. He has his own finger print, his own ectoplasm (if you will!), his own accent of voice and soul. One possession we do not hold in common—our personality. That is our best capital. That also is the medium of the preacher's best service.

8. *The Preaching of the Cross.* There are seven divisions to this poignant last lecture. If somehow a single paragraph must tell the story, I imagine Dr. Buttrick would choose this one:

> *Preach the cross as salvation from sin and unto life eternal.* We shall not waste time to argue that we need forgiveness. If we do not sense that need, no argument will help us. Indeed, we are most of us

---

[3] *Macbeth.*
[4] I Cor. 15:41.

too conscious of our own sins to dream that we have much right to talk to other people about theirs. Shallow minds may say that sin is nothing—a trifle, an immaturity, a besetment we cannot avoid. But the saints have not so described it: their pages are blotted with tears and twisted with anguish. Nor have the great dramatists or the great novelists so described it. Macbeth in Shakespeare's drama, with blood of murder on his conscience, asks a doctor to
"Raze out the written troubles of the brain."

II

Dr. Buttrick returned to Yale in 1940 to give one of the six lectures contributed by as many speakers. The title of his lecture was "Preaching the Whole Gospel." The heart of the lecture is in the last paragraph where he said:

A small statuette of Thorwaldsen's *Christ* stands on a bookcase top in our living room. Slowly it drove away from that shelf the pictures and the clock, because no picture can compare with him, and because he has no parley with time. An elder took issue with us about that scattering. He said Christ would gather round him, not drive away; he would redeem, not banish. My friend, the elder, was right. Now the surrounding treasures have returned—an unpublished Lincoln letter, the clock, a favorite etching, a vase modeled after the Greek—for was he not "found in fashion as a man"?[5] On most Sundays, when sermons have been preached, there is no shining in those eyes. The only good sermon a man ever preaches is on his way home from church—or on his knees. Often, the sermon becomes badly entangled with the preacher. But sometimes the eyes seem to smile, as if he were saying, "I do believe that one day, a million years from now, you may learn. Feed my sheep." Then the room is like that high tower above an ageless sea where a man saw the Holy Grail, "blood-red with beatings in it." The whole Gospel requires that we so speak and pray and live that Christ rules the room of this world; and calls us, when this adventure is ended, to an Upper Room beyond our eyes and time.

Personally, Dr. Buttrick is one of the most genial of friends, yet withal a cultured gentleman who has something of that aloofness which one detects in other masters of pulpit discourse. The same

[5] Phil. 2:8.

trait was observable in Dr. Charles E. Jefferson, and to a much greater extent than it exists in Dr. Buttrick. Dr. Fosdick, while friendly and gracious, sometimes gives the impression that he has important work to do and no time for dillydallying. And this is not a fault. Men who win distinction in anything must toil terribly. Great preachers must be toilers and are seldom "clubbable" men. Out of harness these same men are usually royal fellows and the best of companions.

I fancy Dr. Buttrick was going fishing the day he replied to my questionnaire sent to all the living lecturers in this Course, for he neglected to sign the letter, which was written from Charlevoix where he spends his summers. This, of course, is not a serious matter. I heard of a man who never signed a letter he wrote or dictated, saying he never put his signature to any paper except legal ones. Why? Because he feared he'd get into trouble. But he was not a minister; and was confessedly queer.

Dr. Buttrick writes books, and of a quality that gives them priority over the numerous volumes on religious subjects which pour from the presses annually. In 1942 was published his imposing work on *Prayer*, which ranks among the comparatively few volumes of enduring value on that important subject. How did he find the time to write it? Largely, but not altogether, because he husbands his time, and keeps his study hours unprofaned.

IV. A SEXTETTE OF LECTURERS

Under the title *Preaching in These Times* the Lyman Beecher Lectures for 1940 were published the same year. Dean Luther A. Weigle of the Divinity School wrote a brief foreword of an explanatory nature, to wit:

Only once before, in 1880-81, have the Lyman Beecher Lectures on Preaching been delivered by more than one man. That this was done in 1940 is due to the conviction of the Faculty of the Divinity School that the purposes of the Lyman Beecher Foundation might best be met, in these troublous times, by a series such as is presented in this volume. That conviction was amply sustained by the lectures, which afford not merely specifications for preaching in these times, but wisdom for preaching in all times.

Two of the sextette who gave the 1940 lectures, George A. Buttrick and Ernest F. Tittle, had already appeared in the Course, and an assessment is made of their contribution in this Series in the chapters bearing their names. Four of the speakers were new to the Foundation, namely: Arthur H. Bradford, Rhode Island; Elmore M. McKee, New York; Edwin McNeill Poteat, Ohio; and W. Aiken Smart, Georgia.

One of the first things to note and admire about these discourses is the captivating titles they bear. Observe: "Preaching the Whole Gospel"; "The Dilemma of Civilization"; "Preachers Must Listen"; "Leadership Uncensored"; "Old Wine in New Bottles"; and "The Church and the Glory of God." Naming the sermon is next in importance to naming the baby. The preacher who gives careful consideration to the titles of his sermons, other things being equal, is likely to achieve pulpit distinction.

These are serious lectures, overcast with the dark shadows of the war into which we were then drifting. The note sounded by all the speakers was sober and burdened with apprehension. These eminent preachers of righteousness were palpably conscious of the weakness of the church when it ought to have been strong; sensitive to the truth that it was not Christianity that had failed but instead its adherents and even its exponents who also had lamentably failed. The specter of the troublous times haunted their minds and they had no time nor wish for the lighter side of pulpit speech.

Dr. Poteat

Dr. Poteat, born in New England, educated in the South, missionary to China and professor in Shanghai University, won recognition also in the Baptist ministry. Highly cultured, a lover of books and poetry, he is an interesting personality in the pulpit or on the platform. He began his discourse on "The Dilemma of Civilization" with a scene from Dostoevski's *The Brothers Karamazov*, a bleak, stark, and bitter passage, commenting on the dialogue between Ivan Karamazov and his brother Alyosha. Dr. Poteat said:

It is the eternal problem of the relation of suffering to the harmony of life; Ivan feeling both the suffering of the world and his powerlessness either to relieve or explain it, revolts against its palpable injustice. . . . He will have nothing to do with a God who permits it, and against his angry rebellion Alyosha can speak no word of dissent or censure.

Deep calleth unto deep in this lecture, and the preacher gropes his way through gloom to light, and indicts his generation baldly. Thus:

The aim of modern civilization is: Harmony by the banishment of pain; or, to put it in the language of religion: Redemption by the elimination of suffering of all sorts. Civilization is less a matter of civility, piety, or intelligence, than of comfort. The assumption is that if people can be comfortable, life will be one grand and endless harmony; and the extent to which man can acquire gentility and decency is due to the measure of his physical and spiritual contentment. Therefore our trust is in the engineers who can create comfort, and not in the philosophers who can explain evil, or the preachers who preach a social gospel. The very idea that pain or suffering of any sort can produce good of any sort is abandoned with the similarly discredited nonsense that dust breeds lice, or that granaries create rats *ex nihilo*. We have revised Jesus' estimate of the source of harmony or beatitude, along with Aristotle's judgments on the source of pests; and the price we will pay for harmony is as much comfort as the traffic will bear. We have entered, says Berdyaev, the kingdom of bourgeois commonplace smugness. Even our idea of the good is becoming unendurably stale and commonplace because it is no longer creative; and men are led to evil as a remedy against boredom.

A little later in the lecture, Poteat, with a sensitivity that is poignant, reflects on the paradoxes of what Wordsworth calls "the heavy and weary weight of all this unintelligible world," and on this wise:

It is easy to moralize about this; and that's what makes moralizing repugnant. If our moralizings were the result of spiritual anguish— well, perhaps we'd have less to say because we had more to do. I heard a man protest indignantly the other day at a Lenten sermon

Arthur H. Bradford

by a preacher who lives in luxurious bachelor apartments. "Endure hardness as a good soldier of Christ" was his text, and the commentator was fairly itching to give the dominie a taste of hardness to test his endurance. But what good is moralizing? It is hard to explain the mystery of suffering to pious sufferers, and it is impertinent to try to explain it to impious victims. The result is that preachers who are the beneficiaries of the comfort engineers very easily forget their complicity in the sins of the social order that protects them, and under such circumstances, their moralizing about suffering may be as odious as it is futile. Carl Sandburg expressed it thus: "I don't want a lot of gab from a bunkshooter in my religion. I won't take my religion from any man who never works except with his mouth and never cherishes any memory except the face of the woman on the American silver dollar."[1]

A brief single paragraph and an impressive quatrain bring the thoughtful, pensive lecture to its close:

Some time ago I heard a fragment of a play that had been going on over the radio before I entered the room. I left the room almost instantly, but not before hearing the voice of Gertrude Lawrence say: "Don't be niggardly with life, and make friends of pain." Strange exhortation, you say? Perhaps. And yet,
>He cannot heal who has not suffered much,
>For only sorrow sorrow understands:
>They will not come for healing at our touch
>Who have not seen the scars upon our hands.

Dr. Bradford

"Preachers Must Listen" was Dr. Bradford's unique subject, which in content and arrangement is very good indeed. There is humility in his utterance and courage too. It is an address prepared especially for and preached to his fellow ministers in process of training, and it "clicks." He holds that preachers must be better listeners if they would be better preachers, and cites a letter from a layman who had been to church and wrote: "I went to church this morning and I wish I had not gone. This war is not good for orators."

This pastor of Central Church, Providence, Rhode Island,

[1] *To A Contemporary Bunkshooter.*

advises his fellow ministers to sit in a pew of his own church and think through the sermon he is to preach the following Sunday morning, bearing in mind the while the congregation to which he will speak and their individual needs. On this suggestion he muses:

It is a moving and rewarding experience for a pastor to sit in his own church, alone, listening with all his heart and soul and mind. It may be that he can do as did John Woolman, the Quaker, who said of his busy life among many kinds of people: "We were taught by renewed experience to labour for an inward stillness; at no time to seek for words, but to live in the spirit of truth and utter that to the people which truth opened in us."[2] If we can do this we may hear the voice of the Eternal speaking not just to us but to our people. We may, if we care enough about our people, hear, as it were, their very heartbeats, telling us of their needs, as we sit where they sit to listen to us. Looking up at the pulpit where it is our privilege to stand on Sunday, we shall feel an overwhelming sense of humility, as we realize what our people need and what we may have to give. We shall find ourselves praying. In our prayer we may experience something of what Laurence Housman felt when he wrote to Dick Sheppard on September 27, 1928: "I've never been troubled about God since I left off thinking of Him as an Outsider; and therefore the question of His listening to my prayers hardly arises, for if I do pray, He is Himself my prayer—supposing it to be a good one. What concerns me more is whether He is able, through me, to listen to the prayers of others. Am I a good wireless?"[3]

Dr. Bradford is a thoughtful preacher, with a disciplined mind and a great heart overflowing with tenderness for all mankind. He rounds out his discourse in a wistful mood and on a high note of Christian fortitude. Thus:

There are many questions we cannot answer. As Donald Hankey wrote in his diary,—"Christianity is a way, and not an explanation of life."[4] We see through a glass darkly, but we do see through. We know and we affirm that there is a way to be found and followed; a way in which a living Christ ever goes on before; a way in which we find a Cross as Christ found his; a way wherein God is found, here and now, all powerful and all loving too,—God, whose nature

---

[2] *The Journal of John Woolman*, p. 83.
[3] *What Can We Believe?* Edited by Laurence Housman, p. 136.
[4] *A Student in Arms*, p. 186.

Elmore M. McKee

is to turn the darkness of the Crucifixion into the glory of the Resurrection; God, who can be trusted for time and for eternity.

So the Will heaves through Space, and moulds the times,
With mortals for Its fingers![5]

The world passeth away and the passions thereof, but he that doeth the will of God abideth forever.

Dr. McKee

At the time of the delivery of the 1940 lectures Dr. McKee was a clergyman in the Episcopal Church, and rector of famous St. George's Church, New York City. He had earlier served as chaplain at Yale University, and his eloquent voice has been heard on many platforms of an ecumenical character. A prophetic strain runs through his preaching and a forthrightness that is arresting. He was very much at home with his theme at Yale in 1940, which was, "Leadership Uncensored." One gets the impression from this sermon that anybody who attempted to censor McKee would not enjoy the experience. Here is a quotable section of his discourse, which is not without a humorous slant:

Were some of us intrigued into belief in easy answers back in 1933? Do we recall how in the autumn of that year the government asked the churches to take the NRA to the people? As I motored from the White Mountains where the official request had followed me, to Buffalo, I pondered on how best to do it on an early autumn Sunday. I got it in somehow, I don't know how. But the NRA sat snugly somewhere at the heart of my sermon. After all, didn't the welfare of the nation depend on me? No, it didn't, and I was one fool among a multitude of foolish parsons who, through our belief in certain humanitarian trends, justified a bit of educational work for a particular experiment.

We are really not so important as all that, and if government plans are so weak that they need advertising from the churches, then the plans themselves must be rather ill-founded. And of course once we get into the habit of talking whenever the government tells us to talk, they might get to counting on us too much,—and that would never do.

It is altogether probable that there are forces in our beloved

[5] Thomas Hardy, *The Dynasts*, Pt. II, ii, p. 3.

Republic which would cheerfully and sincerely wish to "censor" Dr. McKee for this and kindred passages in this sermon.

Now it would be difficult to preach to these times without making it quite clear that a redeeming God means to redeem us from economic injustice. We have tarried too long and that is one cause of our anarchy. If we constantly seek to bring ourselves back to comradeship with God we shall want to bring everyone else too. In fact, we are learning that we can only go back fully *together*. So let Christian preaching constantly sensitize men's souls to the spiritual significance of social democracy which can come only as, by the grace of God, we learn to care mightily for the security and happiness of our fellows. We shall not vanquish totalitarianism until we generate a religious passion for economic justice within a democracy. The real war is not against Hitler but against the general decadence that produced Hitler. The war behind the war is the real war, and that is the war against injustice everywhere.

Rector Elmore McKee is one of the prophetic men in the Protestant pulpit of America and has reached the summit of his preaching power.

Professor Smart

Dr. Smart is an able Methodist minister, who is now a professor in Emory University at Atlanta, Georgia. He is an author, theologian, and an authority in the field of the New Testament. Incidentally, he is a South Carolinian, and a most companionable gentleman, as I have reason to know. His subject, "Old Wine in New Bottles," promises much and fulfills that promise. Early in his discourse he announces: "My subject will be doctrinal preaching, or the necessity of reinterpreting our basic beliefs in terms intelligible to our age." That sounds good, and good it was. For example:

In addition to the timidity resulting from intellectual confusion, we have suffered also from an excessive desire to be liberal, another fortunate attitude which may be carried to unfortunate lengths. One naturally rejoices in the passing of the old dogmatisms and religious controversies, but liberalism tends to measure itself by its tolerance, and thus moves toward loss of virile convictions. One boasts of the things on which he no longer insists until he is in danger of seeking a kind of salvation by subtraction. A visitor, invited to lead a devotional service in a Christian Association in the Near East, was asked not to read from the Bible because it might give offense to some Mohammedans whose friendship they were trying to cultivate. One wonders why they did not also delete the word "Christian" from their name. President King, of Oberlin College, is quoted as having said that one of the moral dangers of a liberal education was in the fact that it enabled a man to argue with equal effectiveness on either side of almost any question. It is a truism that if the Christian religion is to save the world it must have a very definite gospel which it can preach with confidence both as to its truth and as to its relevancy, but too often our liberal attitude has made us uncertain as to just what that gospel is. A liberalism which reduces the messages of our pulpits to the least common denominator will also reduce it to the least possible effectiveness. If these times teach us anything at all, they should teach us that men are looking for something in which they can believe enthusiastically.

Baffled by the limitation of space, out of many quotable paragraphs in this choice discourse there is room for only one more excerpt, and that the closing section, which is a summary of the whole:

Those who preach in these times must preach to the people who live in these times. Some day Christian ideals will put an end to wars as they have put an end to other social sins, but the people who listen must live and die in a war-cursed world, and they look to the Church for a message of comfort and strength and hope. Christianity opposes a business system organized primarily for profits, but this generation will not see the end of the profit system, and the victims of the system, both rich and poor, have a right to some sure word about God and their relation to Him. Christianity is opposed to class barriers, and is slowly beating them down, but men and women must live within them, and they need a spiritual power which will enable them to transcend such limitations.

When the Roman Empire was crumbling, Augustine wrote his *City of God*, as God's answer to man's failure, to show what was permanent in the midst of ruin. Many think that we are on the verge of chaos again, and certainly multitudes of individual lives face frustration and bitterness. The religious man, doing all that he can to make a better earth for his children, still wants to lift his eyes to the Eternal, and to say with the saints of all ages, "This is the victory that overcometh the world, even our faith."

Preaching in These Times is an important and valuable part of this Lectureship, for here we have six full-length discourses which, if they were not delivered by these gifted scholars not only in their own but from other pulpits as well, I am a poor prophet and without honor at home or anywhere else.

V. RALPH WASHINGTON SOCKMAN

The invitation to deliver the Lyman Beecher Lectures at Yale University is a signal honor which mingles apprehension with appreciation. The question at once rises in the mind of the recipient: Is there anything significant to be said in a lectureship which for seventy years has explored the subject of preaching by its leading exponents?
—R. W. SOCKMAN

Now that Dr. Fosdick and Dr. Scherer have gone off the air and Dr. Walter A. Maier has finished his remarkable course, the best known preacher on the radio is Dr. Ralph W. Sockman, Dr. Fosdick's successor in that capacity.[1] But long before Dr. Sockman took to the air he was a celebrity, due to his writings, lectures, and his brilliant ministry at Christ Church, New York City, his only pastorate, and dating to 1917.

Dr. Sockman is a personable gentleman, of engaging presence, with a sympathetic voice of cultured accents and pleasing flexibility. On the air he is more urbane than was Dr. Fosdick, less the poet than Dr. Scherer, and much quieter than the late Dr. Maier. He has duplicate services on Sunday mornings, the first going on the air at ten o'clock. His radio congregation is huge and the correspondence which follows this coast-to-coast broadcast is also huge.

On receiving the invitation to give the Yale Lectures on Preaching, Dr. Sockman took a survey of the Lectureship before deciding on his theme. After the manner of a cautious military commander,

[1] The regular Sunday audience to the "National Radio Pulpit" is about 1,250,000.

Ralph Washington Sockman

he reconnoitered before he took to the field. His choice was a series in which he used as background and setting the ministry of John the Baptist, forerunner of Jesus Christ. Employing both artistry of arrangement and homiletical skill, he gave an arresting series at the Divinity School. Moreover, the lectures, which were published in 1942, added to his pulpit and literary reputation.

The ministry of John the Baptist as recorded in the four Gospel narratives is brief, dramatic, and of tragic intensity. The reader of the New Testament first glimpses him as the preacher in a revival which swept through the wilderness of Judea like a mighty storm, sweeping everything before it. The preacher himself was a dramatic figure, stern, uncompromising, heroic, and human in his hour of weakness and doubt. To such a theme Dr. Sockman brought his highly-trained and well-stocked mind, which, coupled with his wide and varied experiences, made him singularly at home with his theme and also effective in delivery.

The arrangement of the Contents is so full and revealing that it is reproduced below as it appears in the volume entitled *The Highway of God*:

I. A VOICE IN THE WILDERNESS
   1. From Confidence to Confusion
   2. Bewildered Youth
   3. The Wilderness of Work
   4. The Encompassing World Chaos
   5. The Perplexed Pulpit
   6. The Road Map.
   7. Lights for the Journey

II. A REED IN THE WIND
   1. Mortgaging the Minister's Soul
   2. Caught in the System
   3. Some Guiding Principles
   4. Love Amid the Relativities
   5. The Timely and the Eternal

III. A PROPHET
   1. A Voice Not Our Own
   2. How God Speaks
   3. Where God Speaks
   4. The Listener Speaks

IV. MORE THAN A PROPHET
  1. The Primacy of Personality
  2. Forerunner As Well As Follower
  3. Preaching to Life Situations
  4. Creative Compassion
  5. The Cure of Souls
  6. The Peril of the Partly Cured
  7. Custodians of the Crises
  8. Preparing the Way of the People

V. THE LEAST IN THE KINGDOM
  1. The Kingdom of Heaven Is at Hand—But Where?
  2. The Kingdom That Is Here
  3. The Kingdom That Is Coming Here
  4. The Grace of God
  5. The Force We Forget
  6. The Charmed Circle

VI. THE CHILDREN OF WISDOM VS. THE CHILDREN OF THE MARKET PLACE
  1. The Pipers
  2. The Mourners
  3. Judgment and Mercy
  4. Realism and Hope

I

Dr. Cadman once began a sermon based on I Corinthians 14:10, "There are, it may be, so many kinds of voices in the world, and no kind is without signification," by saying: "Ours is a voiceful era." Dr. Sockman gets but a little way into his first lecture, which is on St. Luke 3:4, "The voice of one crying in the wilderness, Prepare ye the way of the Lord, make his paths straight," when he declares:

Moreover, ours is a listening wilderness. Not only are bewildered men listening for voices, but many are in the state of near-hysteria wherein they are hearing voices. . . . Cults capitalize on the uncertainty of the pulpit, and the more dogmatically they announce their bizarre beliefs, the stronger their appeal. The books of Daniel and Revelation are becoming the favorite scriptures of many and their visions are fantastically treated to fit our times. Premillennial and messianic voices multiply as the present social order seems settling into twilight. And while, as has been said, faith in specific social reforms is weakened among the thoughtful, all sorts of panaceas take quick though flimsy rootage in wayside minds. Many proposed remedies are more trivial than those suggested in the following conversation:

"Self-determination," one of them insisted.
"Arbitration," cried another.
"Cooperation," suggested the mildest of the party.
"Confiscation," answered an uncompromising female.
I, too, became intoxicated with the sound of these vocables, and were they not the cure for all our ills?
"Inoculation," I chimed in. "Transubstantiation," "alliteration," "inundation," "flagellation," and "afforestation."[1]

Verily the voices now crying in the wilderness constitute a "conversation at midnight."

In Lecture III, subject "A Prophet," Sockman speaks to the point and instances a criticism of Protestantism which although not pleasant to hear, is good for us to know:

A distinguished Roman Catholic spokesman charges that Protestants have squandered their spiritual patrimony in prodigal fashion. In the sixteenth century, he says, they gave up belief in the authority of the church; in the seventeenth century they ceased to believe in the authority of Scripture; in the eighteenth they gave up faith in the divinity of Christ; in the nineteenth they relinquished the belief in God as Judge; and in the twentieth they surrendered belief in the necessity of religion and obligation to God. Again, let us not allow the irritating inaccuracy of such a charge to lessen our determination to recover whatever valid bases of authority may have been lost. But the point to be kept in mind is that these bases must be relevant to all rational living. The only valid religious authority for us is one that is acceptable to free and enlightened minds. . . .

Some years ago the New York *World* ceased publication. It was credited at the time with having probably the best staff of editors in the metropolis. One explanation of its financial failure is worth pondering. The critic said that the *World* failed to hold its readers because it emphasized its editorial page to the neglect of its news columns; and the public, he went on to say, wants to know what is

---

[1] Logan Pearsall Smith, *More Trivia*, p. 41.

going on in the world but it does not wish to be told what it should think about it. The current vogue of the press columnists and radio news interpreters may seem to belie the statement that the public does not wish to be told what it should think. While we are so bewildered by contemporary chaotic events that we crave guidance, nevertheless we soon weary of those who are too pontifical or dogmatic in their interpretations. Reverence for personality includes respect for mental freedom. Such is the attitude of God in his gift of self-revelation; such must be the spirit of the prophets who interpret that revelation.

Dr. Sockman's fourth lecture has for its laconic title a phrase of Jesus', "More than a Prophet." St. Paul matches this with another, also laconic, "more than conquerors." Is it ever enough to be just a successful preacher, lawyer, poet, President, or just a successful anything? No. There have been many conquerors but how few *more* than conquerors. Try to think of one. Eisenhower? Yes. And Robert E. Lee, in defeat. We have had thirty-two presidents of the United States. How many of the number were *more* than president? Washington? Assuredly. Abraham Lincoln? Yes. And perhaps a dozen others.

Preachers are always eager to know how celebrated men of the pulpit go about their work, and never tire of the "shop talk" about ministers who occupy conspicuous pulpits. In this lecture on "More than a Prophet," Dr. Sockman, in an elaborate footnote takes his readers into his confidence, as indeed he took his ministerial hearers at Yale, and let them have a peep into his study:

My personal policy is to preach very few special sermons devoted solely to public issues, such as peace, neutrality, salacious literature, corrupt politics, share-croppers, and the like. Rather, it is my aim to take basic principles and try to swing their searchlights so that they fall upon the various phases of our social, economic, and political environment. Thus there are very few sermons which do not make a thrust at war and other current issues. Some of our most distinguished clergy devote an entire sermon to a single political or national or economic issue, thresh it through in a thorough-going fashion and thereby deliver a really significant pronouncement. Perhaps if my parish were a settled one wherein the same persons were present Sunday after Sunday and could follow through a constructive course of instruction, I too should deal with special issues in a more detached and definitive fashion. But in a church at the heart of a great city, with a large proportion of transient listeners, I deem it advisable to center the sermon on some life principle or life situation and then let the radiations reflect on the current problems. In this way I try to preserve the personal element in each sermon and also bring the public problems to the attention more frequently. Furthermore I find that by repeated pricks some persons are aroused to action who take a major operation unmoved because under the anaesthetic of disagreement!

For many years now I have been writing about preachers, reviewing their books and occasionally doing an introduction or foreword to their publications. Now and then I hear from one of these busy men, and I treasure what they write, because I know from experience how easy it is to overlook these amenities which add so much to life. When this volume of Yale lectures came off the press, I reviewed it in a well-known quarterly, and shortly after the review appeared received this note:

May I thank you for your very generous and felicitous review of my book.
I have just read it in "Religion and Life." While I think your critical judgment was perhaps colored by personal friendship, I nevertheless appreciate it.
Thanking you again, I am
Very sincerely yours,
Ralph W. Sockman

II

Dr. Sockman is a much-quoted man in the press of his city. What he gives to the newspapers, whether as an interview or as sermonic material, is carefully prepared and not watered down or the sterner passages deleted. There follows an excerpt of a recent sermon preached in Christ Church as it appeared in The New York Times:

The American people were characterized yesterday in a sermon by the Rev. Dr. Ralph W. Sockman, pastor of Christ Church, Methodist, 520 Park Avenue, as "such go-getters that we struggle feverishly to get ahead of others instead of striving to surpass ourselves."
Describing the nineteenth century as "sentimentally foolish in its

optimism about human progress" and the "bloody twentieth century" as "cynically foolish in its pessimism about man's possibilities," Dr. Sockman added:

"Still under the shadow of two global conflicts, many have surrendered to the idea that man is by nature a fighting animal and hence wars are inevitable. They yield assent to the doleful doctrine that human nature cannot be changed any more than the leopard can change its spots. Therefore they think security lies only in strengthening the cages to contain man's increasing power of bestiality.

"We must lift our standards of comparison. We of America are complacent in conscience because our methods are better than those of the Soviet Union. But if we are to save our souls and have a better world, we must measure our ways by Christ rather than the Kremlin.

"If we as individuals and as nations gave ourselves to developing what we have where we are, we would lessen the mad race which spoils our peace of mind and destroys the peace of the world. We must learn that true progress comes by development and not by displacement."

In a group of ministers attending a church convention of national scope the conversation turned to a survey of the New York pulpit. "Who is the leading preacher of New York since Dr. Fosdick retired from Riverside Church and Dr. Scherer from the Evangelical Lutheran Church of the Holy Trinity?" That was the question, and it was warmly debated. The choices for this distinction finally narrowed to four, then to three, and ended with but two. One of the two was Ralph Washington Sockman!

VI. MORGAN PHELPS NOYES

It is a bad sign when too many people in a congregation think exactly as their minister does on all subjects. It was said of Dr. Jowett of Balliol College, Oxford, "That he sent out more pupils who were unlike himself than any Oxford teacher of his time." Dr. George Herbert Palmer once wrote, "Every teacher knows how easy it is to send out cheap editions of himself, and in his weaker moments he inclines to issue them. But it is ignoble business." It is no more noble when it is done by a pastor.

—Morgan P. Noyes

Morgan Phelps Noyes

Dr. Noyes is a Pennsylvanian by birth, and since 1932 minister of the Central Presbyterian Church, Montclair, New Jersey, a city which has enjoyed the ministrations of an amazing number of eminent preachers. He has been lecturer on public worship in the Practical Theology Department of Union Theological Seminary, New York City. Dr. Noyes has also served his communion on many commissions and committees, and also in like capacity on ecumenical and kindred movements. His reply to my questionnaire is a model of courtesy, modesty, and conciseness. Moreover, his letter reveals, more than some letters do, the mind and disposition of the writer. It is a privilege to include it here in entirety:

My Dear Dr. Jones:

Please pardon my delay in replying to your letter, which came to me when I was on my summer vacation; and I am afraid all correspondence was sadly neglected.

I do not know that I have anything of value to contribute to your study of the Lyman Beecher Lectureship, but here are some brief answers to your questions.

1. My emotions, when I received the invitation, were incredulity, a feeling that someone on the Yale Divinity School Faculty had become unbalanced, and a sense that I had nothing to contribute which any other working pastor could not give the students at Yale.

2. It is hard for me to say how much time went into the immediate preparation of the lectures. I worked an hour a day on them most of the winter prior to their delivery. I had put in quite a solid block of time on them during the summer preceding their delivery also.

3. The lectures were written out in full, and I read them from the manuscript.

4. My own participation in the series certainly brought down the average in so far as the distinction attached to the Lectureship is concerned. Over the years, it has certainly been the outstanding series of interpretations of the work of the ministry.

The problem now is, of course, that of saying something new in a series in which so much has already been said about the preaching pastorate. The prevailing tendency seems now to be to use the Lectureship as an opportunity for discussion of some theme vital to preaching, without holding too closely to the terms on which the Lectureship was originally founded.

As for myself, I am not a scholar nor a specialist, but merely a minister who loves the pastorate; and I attempted to address not the general public, but the students of the Divinity School and to bring them one man's impressions of some aspects of his calling.

With best wishes to you in your study, I am

Cordially yours,
MORGAN P. NOYES

Dr. Noyes' scholarly attainments are too much in evidence in his preaching and writings to be overlooked or minimized, but his disclaimer here does him credit, nevertheless. However, if the Yale Divinity School in selecting lecturers had been restricted only to scholars and specialists, it is unlikely the Seriate would have persisted so long and so worthily. A successful minister quietly and effectively doing the day's work in his parish and doing it significantly, is as highly qualified to appear in this Lectureship as are also the distinguished scholars and specialists who have won fame in fields akin to the Christian ministry.

I

Dr. Noyes' theme at Yale in 1942 was Preaching the Word of God, and the addresses bore the following titles: I. The Word and the Preacher; II. The Word and the Church; III. The Word and the World; IV. The Word of God for Every Man; V. The Word and the Pastor; VI. The Word and Worship. It is a meaty series, well-balanced and eminently practical. Dr. Henry Sloane Coffin, than whom there is no better judge of good preaching and of lectures on that subject, thus wrote of the Noyes lectures: "If one wishes a book to put into the hands of some young man who wants to know what a minister has to try to do today, here is the volume to give him. If a seasoned minister needs—(and all of us do need reminders of what our work is at least once a year)—a book which sets forth what the ministry at its best may be, here is the book for us."

I took up my copy of these lectures as soon as the postman left the volume on my desk. Not being harassed for time at the moment, I read the book through before I got out of the chair. Later I read it more slowly, stopping now and then to mark a phrase or paragraph which I especially liked. There is an appeal in these lectures which goes to the very heart of the minister who reads

Noyes' pages. It seems to have been written for me, and I can believe almost every minister who reads the book feels as did I about it. Some books are good in spots; this one is good from "A to Izzard," to use Lincoln's homely term. Open the book anywhere and some sparkling sentence or wise observation is sure to attract the eyes and hold them. This cannot be said of every volume in the Yale Course. Some of them, but not many, provide pages that make good skipping. The quotation which ensues is selected because it contrasts two schools of theology and does it in such a manner that the truth in both is assessed without disparaging the weakness of either. The fairness of Dr. Noyes must be apparent to those of us who know the strife which partisans can so readily incite. It is a long excerpt but warranted:

In the expansive days at the turn of the century, it was the fashion in theology to think of God as Immanent in the evolutionary process, present in man's thoughts and aspirations and best efforts, the urge to a higher life of which no man could be totally unaware. It is unfair to the prevailing liberalism of that day to say that it represented a belief in automatic and inevitable progress. A study of the preaching in outstanding liberal pulpits will show that they were in constant protest against the escalator view of life. But when overemphasized the doctrine of the Immanence of God did sometimes lead to so close an identification of divine activity with the highest expressions of human genius as to make God hardly distinguishable from the sum total of human virtues. The Bible became in the hands of some interpreters hardly more than a sociological document recording some interesting phases of man's development. Since cataclysmic events have rudely shattered the optimistic outlook of the Victorian era, it has become the fashion in some theological circles to go to the other extreme and to concentrate attention exclusively upon the Transcendence of God. God is the Wholly Other, we are told, who cannot be known in any wise in the achievements of this world, but who breaks through into this world in special revelations of the Reality in which He exists beyond this world. What He reveals is not a power to make this world better, it is said, but a Heart which forgives those who are caught in the meshes of a sinful world from which they can be extricated only by a grace which makes them, at the same time that they are caught in the toils of sin, dwellers in another world which is outside history and unrelated to space and time. The Bible, say some of those who concentrate on the Transcendence of God, is valuable not for its literature, or for its history, or for its moral teaching, or for its religion, but because "in the Bible, the strange new world of God has broken into this world of space and time." These theologians do not say that the Bible is the Word of God, or even that the Bible contains the Word of God, but that it bears witness to the Word which was spoken with absolute, not relative, authority to men whose capacity to receive and record was not absolute but relative. The Word which comes to us through the Bible, they say, is an eschatological Word, promising not development or intensification of this present life, but an utterly new life of forgiveness and redemption, forgiveness being interpreted as a new status, with faint if any emphasis upon moral renewal as a concomitant of forgiveness. Fortunately most adherents of this theology are better than their creeds. While they preach the helplessness of man they prove themselves anything but helpless in combating wrongs and working for righteousness. If carried out rigorously to its logical conclusions, however, this view of the Bible does tend to remove it from a position of influence on contemporary life.

In *Beside the Bonnie Brier Bush*, it will be recalled, that "lad o' pairts" who was entering so proudly on his first ministry was admonished by his dying kinswoman to "say a good word for Jesus Christ," an admonition on which "the statute of limitations" never expires. It is also important to say a good word for Christ's Church, and in his second lecture on "The Word and the Church," Dr. Noyes says that good word, several hundred of them, in behalf of "the ground and pillar of truth." And he does it with discrimination. The late Dr. Burris A. Jenkins of Kansas City had a chapter in one of his books which bore the title, "The Church: A Necessary Nuisance." His treatment of the subject was not quite as iconoclastic as the title. Dr. Noyes speaks of the church as a problem and a necessity, and here is the beginning of part two in this valuable chapter:

This is not to say that the church is not a problem as well as a necessity. Sometimes at great church gatherings when he hears the church spoken of in exalted terms as the universal spiritual fellowship of Christ's followers of all generations, a man's mind wanders off to some particular church that he knows, and he has qualms when he tries to believe that God has ordained the church to be His messenger to men. He may believe, with liberal theologians, that

Jesus was the Founder of the Church, not because he actually set it up as an organization, but because it arose inevitably out of his message of the Kingdom of God; or he may hold with Continental Europeans that along with the family and the state, the church is one of the orders through which God by fiat has decreed that human life should be governed; or he may accept the view of certain church bodies that Christ commanded the organization of the church in the particular forms which they believe have been followed ever since in their communions. And yet, as he looks at some particular church with its apparent lethargy of spirit, its absorption in the elementary business of making ends meet, its zeal for new members not as souls to be saved, but as potential contributors to the budget, its slavery to old ways and reluctance to receive new ideas or to follow new paths, its placidity as the custodians of a gospel meant to turn the world upside down—he wonders. Of course that is not a true picture of any church, however complacent it may look on the surface. "How do you stand being the minister of these smug people?" a young collegian asked a ministerial acquaintance. The minister thought of those people, not as the collegian saw them when he was home for the holidays, ranged in rows in the pews of the church on a Sunday morning. He thought of them as he knew them at close range, human beings with their share of faults, but men and women who had seen a light that they followed, who were, many of them, carrying sorrows with a quiet heroism, who were in unostentatious ways doing constructive things to make their community a better place, who were giving money with a generosity which in proportion to their means was astonishing, who were the first people to be called on when some need arose and who were the last people to demand public recognition for the community service which they rendered, who went home from church on Sundays to homes where there was a quality of idealism quite distinct from the shoddy advertising of many other families, and who went on Monday mornings to places of business and professional life which they knew were far from the kingdom of God but where they were making an honest attempt to introduce and work out the spirit of Christ. The minister said to himself that these so-called smug people were better Christians than he was, and that he was proud to be their minister. He remembered that he had read that a church "is not a society of select persons, but the home and school both of saints and sinners,"[1] and he was glad that the church he served was of that kind. And yet he, like all thoughtful churchmen, knew that the church is a problem as well as a necessity.

[1] F. R. Barry, *The Relevance of the Church*, p. 67.

II

Naturally this lecturer would make some reference to the dreadful war into which we had been catapulted less than six months previously. The incident involving President Lincoln in those faraway war years is of abiding significance:

The most tragic aspect of international war is that it is a disruption of the family of mankind, during which the ordinary expressions of a fraternal relationship are cut off. It is the privilege of the Christian church to keep stressing that family bond until such time as we can renew the normal relationships of the children of God. During the American Civil War, Dr. Horace Furness, who later edited the Variorum Shakespeare, served with those who tended the wounded at Fredericksburg. He was in the railroad station one day when President Lincoln entrained there after a visit to the Union Army. Opposite the station was a factory, which was in use as a hospital, and, as the President boarded his train, the windows of the factory were crowded with wounded men watching him. He went immediately to the rear platform to address them. Said Dr. Furness in a letter, they were anxious for a stirring address, but Mr. Lincoln merely reminded them that their enemies were their "brothers in error" and that after the war had ended their children and grandchildren would have to live together with those from the South for many generations. The crowd was very much disappointed. But is not that authentic Christianity? When this war is over, the children of men must go on living on a very small planet, and while we can make no peace with oppression, we must keep alive the conviction that we are all one family under God.

Dr. Noyes asks the minister to remember that he is a minister and not a psychiatrist or a social worker. He thinks a pastor ought to know enough about mental hygiene to be familiar with the more common mental illnesses. He ought, too, to be informed about social work to know what the resources of his community are for people who have problems, and how to relate people in need with the provisions which the community has made for just such situations. But these, important as they are, should not be the main concern of the minister. They are more than incidental perhaps, but never the pastor's chief concern. And again, "however valuable office or study consultation may be, it can never take the place of the more casual contacts between pastor and people which have been traditional in the Christian ministry."

In this connection Dr. Noyes quoted a poem which he found in the Book Section of *The New York Times* of July 7, 1940. The poem is so unusual that I am moved to let it stand, with Dr. Noyes' comment on the line at the close of the chapter on this gifted minister of Jesus Christ and his instructive and inspiring lectures at Yale Divinity School in the war-troubled spring of 1942.

And now, the poem, written by one Jeanne D'Orge, and entitled, "The Interpreter":

I wish there were some one
Who would hear confession.
Not a priest—I do not want to be told of my sins;
Not a mother—I do not want to give sorrow;
Not a friend—she would not know enough;
Not a lover—he would be too partial;
Not God—He is far away;
But some one who would be friend, lover, mother, priest, God,
  all in one,
And a stranger besides—who would not condemn or interfere;
Who, when everything is said from beginning to end,
Would show the reason of it all
And tell you to go ahead
And work it out your own way.

Perhaps something like that is what the pastor at his best can be, except that he is not a stranger but a friend in whose presence one can be sincere, and that his greatest service is to help his friends to have confidence that God is not far away but nearer than they have ever known, with spiritual resources available for them which are more than adequate for any difficulty with which life may confront them.

VII. PAUL EHRMAN SCHERER

Paul Scherer's preaching has a prophetic quality which springs from the depths of the man. The great tradition of the Christian faith is genuinely real to him, and his persuasive power to transmit his convictions to his hearers and to share his experiences with them is extraordinary. His preaching is an engineering operation, by which a bridge is built from God's resources to man's need, and spiritual goods are actually transported from one side to the other.

—Harry Emerson Fosdick

To many of us in the ministry there is no more delightful place to drop in at lunch time than the pleasant refectory of Union Theological Seminary. Oil portraits of famous scholars of other years look down from the walls, and almost any day of the school year living celebrities may be seen sitting at the tables chatting with students and fellow professors.

In this spacious and friendly room I sat at lunch with Dr. Paul Scherer on an autumn day in 1947—a day to which I had looked forward with no small eagerness, for I had heard this eminent preacher lecture in my home town, Detroit, and had read his writings with delight and profit. We talked about books and preachers, a congenial theme to both of us. By-and-by we got around to the Beecher Foundation and the series which he gave at Yale Divinity School in the spring of 1943. "Dr. Scherer," I inquired, "tell me what your emotions were when you received the invitation to speak in this historic Course, and please don't stop there; I want to know how long it took you to prepare for the great occasion, and also your evaluation of the Lectureship." After a meditative pause he replied:

"My emotions when I received the invitation were a strange complex of delight and utter, abysmal fear. To the delight I became gradually accustomed; the fear waxed mightily as the time approached. At midnight on the evening before my first lecture, after being delightfully entertained by Drs. Kraehling, Calhoun, Schroeder, and Luccock, I insisted that my wife listen once more to what I was going to say the next day. Bless heaven for our patient wives! English is a strange language. I have only one wife, but she is a compound of many!

"As to preparation, I had worked over all my material during a period of enforced silence. My larynx was out of commission and in the quiet I wrote. The material over a period of several years was reworked again and again. When the invitation came,

I still had about eighteen months, as I remember, for addition and subtraction.

"The lectures were delivered from manuscript, though somewhat freely . . .

"And now about evaluating the Lectureship. From your acquaintance with the whole Series you are in a far better position than I am to reach some considered judgment. It would seem to me that whenever the lecturers took seriously the terms of the Foundation, the Series has made an unique contribution, both theologically and homiletically, to the literature of the pulpit. I remember with never-ending gratitude, for instance, Forsyth, whose book needs constant rereading in our own day. The others that have had a profound influence in my own life are too many for me to mention. The amazing thing to me is that within a rather narrowly defined area such bewildering variety has been possible."

I

Dr. Scherer is not only a superb preacher, he is also a man of letters. The arrangement of his material in his Yale lectures of 1943 is original and done with artistry. The style is not what is popularly known as rhetorical, although among his other gifts he enjoys that of the rhetorician. The seeming artlessness of these lectures is misleading and may well be a case of art concealing art. The choice English which so adorns Scherer's pages one fancies might have been the conversational pattern of Samuel T. Coleridge and Charles Lamb during a long, leisurely evening when those two worthies folded their legs and talked it out. Such a style of writing seems easy to acquire; actually, it is a result of constant study, the reading of great books, and laborious composition. The "enforced silence" to which Dr. Scherer alludes helps to account for the literary excellence of this volume.

Readers of the book *For We Have This Treasure* do well not to overlook the preface. In it the author relates how the lectures took form and gives a brief analysis of the chapters which follow. "What is said in these pages," he writes, "as will be evident at a glance, is intended frankly and primarily for ministers. And yet I am not wholly without the desire, secretly cherished, that there may be others here and there who in leafing through them will find some help and encouragement as they set about their own stewardship of 'God's varied grace.'"

Dr. Scherer takes his Scripture references, with a few exceptions, from Dr. James Moffatt's new translation, and thus enlivens his pages with striking rephrasings of familiar texts. Moreover, the use he makes of the texts as paragraph headings is unique. Observe the manner in which he opens his first lecture:

> Our story, then, begins with what the apostle calls
> My Divine Commission[1]
> *as a priest of Christ . . . in the service of God's gospel.* It was this sense of high appointment that undergirded him all his way along. It sent him back to the stones at Lystra. It filled him with a passion that turned as at a signal now into some desperate entreaty, now into a hymn of gratitude. Here is some quick severity, there an eager tenderness. Over and over again are sentences that pay no attention to grammar, with the words tripping on one another's heels, piling up into a kind of chaos, with the light of God on it, the gallant sunshine of the soul. If I could only clear these windows of mine to let it through! *Wherever I go,* he writes after the trouble he had had with the Church at Corinth, *God makes my life*
> A Constant Pageant[2]
> The whole procession of the days—peril, shipwreck, hunger, thirst—moves along some Via Sacra, brilliant and full of color. Nothing drab about any of it!
> Perhaps, with such an end in view, we should at the very start clear out of the road all the nonsense we have picked up if any in the matter of the call to the Christian ministry. There is such a call; and when it comes, it comes straight from God. I believe with all my heart that a man must hear it and feel its imperious constraint before he can ever give himself with any whole-hearted devotion and abiding wonder to this stewardship of the gospel. But I believe, too, that more than one minister has been confused by many of the things he has been taught about it and by a great deal that he has read. As a result, there are times when he begins to suspect the validity of whatever call he once felt himself to have had. He wonders if, after all, he too is not one of those prophets who ran, though not sent,

[1] Rom. 15:15, 16.
[2] II Cor. 2:14.

who prophesied though the Lord had not spoken (*Jeremiah* 23:21); and that plays utter havoc with his work. He cannot go on with any peace or with any power if he questions long the very fact of his own vocation. He comes upon such a passage as this:

"I would affirm my conviction that, in all genuine callings to the ministry, there is a sense of the divine initiative, a solemn communication of the divine will, a mysterious feeling of commission, which leaves a man no alternative but sets him in the road . . . a servant and instrument of the eternal God."[3]

And my hypothetical minister wonders pretty much what it is all about. His experience has been far less rotund and far less intangible. If this is what it means to be called, then—God knows—maybe it's all to do again.

It must take a lot of courage for a friendly fellow craftsman of the High Calling, and a sound exegete too, to spoil a sermon title which some of us have fairly hugged to our hearts. Dr. Scherer does this disillusive thing in Lecture III, and does it so quietly, yet devastatingly, that we who have erred in this respect are left speechless, and grateful too, realizing as we do that Scherer is another Daniel come to judgment. Here is the spirited paragraph:

. . . We have come, I suppose quite inevitably, to use the phrase "preaching for a verdict." It is not, I dare suggest, the happiest phrase we could use. There is about it far too much of the argumentative, the evidential, the forensic, to express the full, true genius of the Christian pulpit. Verdicts are too often won by mere brilliance, even by trickery. Nor are they always rendered in accordance with the facts. And having been rendered, they have to be executed by somebody else. I sometimes think we should do better perhaps to borrow not from the courts but from courtship. There is a knocking at the door that wants an answer. A quiet talk. A question is asked. And mind and heart and will together are shut up not alone to a true decision but to a life, *till Christ be formed within you* (*Galatians* 4:19).

II

The six lectures in the Scherer series reach and sustain a high level of excellence. There is no "let down," no deviation from loftiness of thought, beauty of diction, or pertinency of illustrative

---
[3] J. H. Jowett, *The Preacher, His Life and Work*, pp. 13-19.

matter. My own favorite of the six lectures is the fifth, which is entitled "A Sound Workman." It is replete with wise counsel and vivid phrasings. It is opulent in homiletic hints; half-forgotten texts leap to light, while more familiar scriptures take on a new and urgent meaning. There are echoes in this lecture of Dr. Scherer's own wonderful preaching, his masterful use of texts and Biblical incidents. As one reader put it, "The lecture on 'A Sound Workman' does something to me. After reading it I can scarcely wait till Sunday comes to be about my preaching business." This is the kind of praise that more than repays an author for the hard work which makes an able production possible.

There follows better than a page from Lecture III on "The Weapons of My Warfare":

This it was that happened at Calvary. Not in Bethlehem, not in Nazareth, but on Golgotha. The cross is not a symbol; it is an act. It is God's conquering presence in the world that he made. If we should conspire against it and refuse to mention it any more for a century or so, life would still come back to it, sure that something was missing, rediscover it, and sit down in its shadow again oddly at home.

I wonder if you have ever noticed how all the "great, sad literature of the soul" does just that. In Shakespeare, for instance, how straight and unerring the movement is! When he began to write,[4] he wrote comedy, facile, tender comedy, drawing men with such sympathy that you cannot help adoring them, even that fat, swashbuckling liar, Falstaff, set on his huge legs so kindly to carry his stomach about! But then something happened. Shakespeare threw Falstaff away, had to be rid of him. If such a fellow could conquer the world, the world was not worth conquering. There were bare, rude heights of human life, mysterious, dark caverns that had to be explored; and it was painful business. It is for all of us. For a while the great poet's sympathy seems to have turned sour, his gentleness into a passion of contempt. He acts as if he wants to lash out at humanity and wither it. If I were God,—did not Luther say so once of the world?—I should kick it to pieces! Shakespeare writes as if he were nauseated by it, trying to fling it from him like filth, putting his heel on it as you do on an insect that drags its slime over God's green earth. Then little by little it dawns on him: the way to supreme happiness is by

[4] See Carlton, *Shakespearian Comedy*.

love, and that love moves forward inevitably to awe-inspiring tragedy. There is no scorn in Macbeth, no sneer, nothing so cheap or shallow as disdain. You stand in the thane's shoes, live poignant hours with him, feel the fierce fires kindling so weirdly in his soul; until, except for the fires that still rage, it turns black, and the flame leaps and sears its horrible red will, and life comes crackling and tumbling down in appalling ruin, as if on your own head. But there is something like the pity of God in it, and in Hamlet, and in Othello, and in Lear: something very like the shadow of a cross.

And from Lecture V, "A Sound Workman," which I especially favor, this:

Watch Yourself and Watch Your Teaching[5]

Frequently, and I judge that I am to set down here my own experience, I leaf back through my latest manuscript book of sermons, for instance, to see in a kind of perspective what I have preached about over the period of the last six months; or it may even be a year. And as I think of the lives of my people, and of the great, stirring trends becoming so obvious in the life of mankind, out of my very omissions and silences springs now and then the consciousness of needs that I have not even tried to meet, of truths clamoring for their share of recognition. However elaborate our creed, says James Reid, the things we live by are very few. I dare say offhand there are no more than fifty, if that many, pivotal truths in the whole sweep of the Gospel. Set them down some time for yourself: The Nature of Man, The Greatness of God, The Meaning of Life, The Fact of Sin, The Mysteries of the Cross, The Power of the Spirit, The Destiny of the Human Soul, and so on. List them; and if you are ever at a loss for a subject, go back and see which of them you have been side-stepping. Then make your choice, not so much of something you want to do perhaps, as of something you ought to do.

However, for our purpose here, we shall not let that work either. Then I suggest that you leaf through some other man's sermons for an hour: Gossip's, Hutton's, Buttrick's, Fosdick's, Sockman's, Farmer's, Stewart's, Reid's. Give them a chance to make your kettle boil. I do wish that Burnet's were available. You do not need to be captivated by them and led off nose first to say what they said. You can be kindled by them. Hough has done that for me, besides these others that I have mentioned, and Stanley Jones, and Leslie Weatherhead,

[5] I Tim. 4:16.

and Reinhold Niebuhr, not to mention the preacher's perennial help, Halford Luccock! I am not talking now of plagiarism; I am talking of ideas, born of other ideas, and giving birth to your own in turn. They will belong finally to him who provides them with the best expression.

III

Scherer is within the great traditions of preaching. He never stoops to conquer. If there is a strain of mysticism in some of his finest utterances, he is never foggy or obscure. The excerpt that follows is from a sermon on "Facts that Undergird Life":

But there is that strange man on a cross and he won't allow it now! Just a handful of people saw him die. Their dreams died with him. Then on a queer day, with what seemed like the sound of a rushing, mighty wind, the dreams were alive again! It wasn't simply that hope springs eternal in the human breast. Peter at least was confident that much more was going on than that. "This it is," said he, "which was spoken by the prophet Joel; and it shall come to pass in the last days, saith God, I will pour out of my Spirit upon all flesh; and your sons and your daughters shall prophesy, and your young men"—no longer living, as young men do in the present—"shall see visions, and your old men"—no longer living, as old men do, in the past—"shall dream dreams."

I do not believe that since then humanity could have stood alone and held on to its dreams if God had left it to itself. You couldn't have stood alone if God had left you! There have been too many disappointments, too many wretched disillusionments along the road, for anybody to suppose now without God that there is anything in dreams. I heard of one disillusionment not long ago, put with all the bitter irony of life. Dick Sheppard was here,—some of you will remember his book, "The Impatience of a Parson," and his great ministry at St. Martin's-in-the-Fields, there on Trafalgar Square in London; he was here in America and told of a lad who was shot through the neck in the great war and died in his arms. The last words the poor chap spoke were about the child his wife was soon to bear him. "If it's a boy," he whispered, "I'm glad he won't have to go through this. This is a war—to end war—isn't it?" And Dick Sheppard comforted him, saying—because he believed it too—"Yes, Yes,—a war to end war!" Today the child that was born is just twenty years old, dressed in a soldier's uniform, drilling somewhere in

England! In God's Name, isn't that enough to kill a dream? And the answer—here is the marvel of all marvels—the answer is "No!" It's not enough to kill a dream—not while the Spirit of God is abroad in the earth! We're building yet on this—this off-chance of God that we are not all going down in foolish ruin. If some of us do—why then with sweat and tears, the others will build again! For you see, it isn't the ideal that lives: it's God, and the dream in his great heart, his dream of the world and of you![6]

I have not quoted from the rewarding contents of Lectures II, "Like a Man of God," IV, "God Appealing By Me," or VI, "The Way You Handle the Word of Truth." They are reserved to profit those who, stimulated by what has been quoted here from Scherer's *For We Have This Treasure*, will hurry straightway to a bookshop to buy for themselves a copy of the work, for a *Work* it is.

Paul Scherer is a personable man, and an imposing figure in the pulpit or on the lecture platform. His noble head is crowned with graying hair, and there is a majesty in his mien.

VIII. HAROLD COOKE PHILLIPS

On the Sunday of the week Dr. Weatherhead lectured at Yale, which was in 1949, I attended services at Battell Chapel, where Harold Cooke Phillips was the preacher of the day. I had not heard him preach for several years, and welcomed the opportunity to do so. The spacious chapel was well-filled, and the proportion of young people large. Dr. Phillips looked slightly older than when I last saw him; a few silver threads had crept into his auburn hair, but not many. He read his scripture lesson carefully and at length. He was unhurried without being too deliberate; was at ease in the pulpit.

He spoke from the text John 17:15, "I pray not that thou shouldest take them out of the world, but that thou shouldest keep them from the evil." It was a strong sermon, austere in places, exegesis sound, diction clean-cut, and pleasing to hear—a sermon

[6] *Facts that Undergird Life*, pp. 34-35.

in the traditions of great preaching. I have heard other sermons from this text preached by men of no small reputation. I rank his sermon with the best, and came away from the service much the better in mind and spirit for having worshiped in Battell Chapel that day.

One of Dr. Phillips' closest friends, a loyal admirer, himself a preacher and author, thus described the minister of First Baptist Church, Cleveland, Ohio:

"The greatest enemy of the Prince of Darkness," said Thomas Carlyle, "is a thinking man." Harold Cooke Phillips is a "thinking man" who *thinks straight*. This ability to cut through the maze of complex and often confused patterns of thought and get at the meat of the matter is characteristic not only of his mental habits but also of his social and personal habits as well. His keen, alert, discriminating mind makes him the enemy of crackpot or half-baked ideas and also the foe of complacency which takes too many things for granted.

This makes for intense living on his part which is sometimes construed as aloofness. He has a profound love for his fellow man and a tender heart for all who suffer. To those of us who have enjoyed his intimate friendship we know him not only as one of the great living preachers, but as a warm human being who loves humor, art, music, travel, antiques and the beauty of the universe. His favorite animal is a cow and he has a fine dairy herd on his farm in Jamaica. His collection of prints, Windsor chairs and other antiques is outstanding. As his fellow-traveler, in a tour of several European countries, I found he was interested in everything, but most of all in human beings. He has deep human sympathies and strong abiding convictions of truth and justice. I have felt his keen enjoyment and appreciation of the great painting in the Vatican library and I have seen him blaze in anger at the social inequities, spiritual poverty and economic injustices of the Italian people.

Harold Cooke Phillips is a man of strict integrity of character who has disciplined himself to hard work and patient toil. He cannot be content with second rate standards for himself nor is he satisfied to see them held by others. Yet he is no iconoclast. He carries mirth, and joy and good cheer, and radiates a feeling of kindliness wherever he goes. He is a royal preacher and a royal liver. By this I do not mean he is without a flaw. For after all he is a human being but I think an extraordinarily fine one. The impeccable man who never finds it difficult to make an important decision, or who never makes a wrong one, is no kinsman of mine.

Sometimes he holds too close a rein upon his galloping mind and his prophetic fire. He is more like Hosea than Amos, more akin in tenderness of spirit to his Master than to John the Baptist. As a preacher he is more like Robertson of Brighton than Rauschenbusch of Rochester.

I

Dr. Phillips gave his lectures at Yale in 1947, on the theme *Bearing Witness to the Truth*. I am indebted to his publishers for this list of his topics and a brief synopsis of each:

THE LECTURES

WHAT IS TRUTH? Truth is "the correspondence between our thoughts and reality": it is objectively real and hence indispensable; it is one and hence universal; it is indestructible, imperishable.

TRUTH AS MORAL REALITY. "Morality is the basic ingredient of all truth," and man's "inner moral sense" has its source in God.

WAYS OF KNOWING THE TRUTH. The author cites authority, reason, intuition, experiment, and especially revelation, because it "is the uniquely religious way of knowing the truth."

THE SERMON AND THE TRUTH. The author describes how he prepares sermons, and discusses the literary and spiritual qualities of a good sermon.

THE PREACHER AND THE TRUTH. The preacher who is a worthy witness to the truth must have industry, integrity, interest in people, independence, and a firsthand knowledge of God.

CHRIST THE TRUTH. "In Christ we confront truth in a life, truth in personality"—the essential heart of all truth about human life.

The lecturer tackled a big subject when he set out to answer "What Is Truth?" Before Pontius Pilate asked that question, and since, the thinkers of the world have sought to find an answer. Dr. Phillips marshals an echelon of illustrious and weighty names in this first lecture, to wit: Bacon, Kant, Nietzsche, Gautama, Copernicus, John Knox, Carlyle, John Hus, Balthasar Hübmaier,

Einstein, Archbishop Temple, William James, Mark Twain, Robertson of Brighton, Dean Inge, Reinhold Niebuhr, John Dewey, Tagore, Bergson, Keats, Wordsworth, Tennyson, Browning, Klausner, William E. Hocking, Edgar Sheffield Brightman, John Bennett, Spurgeon, Herbert Agar, Beethoven, Elgar, Sibelius, Grieg, MacDowell, Chopin, Tchaikovsky, Paderewski, not to mention names in the footnotes, which are twenty-five in number minus a few names included in the roster above. No other lecture in the Series is so bejeweled with shining names as is this one. Why do I list these names? For just one reason, namely, to exhibit the painstaking research and study Phillips put on this one chapter alone. There is a down-to-earth quality in this lecture too, as for example:

> Not all the moral idiots, however, are across the seas. When Mussolini was riding high, thousands of American tourists came back from Italy singing his praises because he made the Italian trains run on time and provided hotels with American plumbing. These "innocents abroad," morally speaking, were wholly unconcerned about the moral incongruities of fascism. They did not realize that a system based upon tyranny, oppression, and expediency was doomed sooner or later to destruction. They did not understand that to gain an immediate advantage by betraying an ultimate truth was to strike a poor bargain. Our country is full of such citizens—men and women who do not seem to understand that "one's own truth" has to reckon with the objective realities of a moral universe which we shall have to learn to get along with, if we are going to get along at all, since truth is its indispensable ingredient. The morally obtuse are the greatest enemies of society, especially when they occupy places of power, as unfortunately for the world they so frequently do.

Dr. Phillips' faith in the triumph of truth, though embattled, is unfaltering. Thus he avers as he nears the end of this lecture:

> As we think therefore of the brave men who have died for truth we feel sure that they were not fighting for a lost cause. The dawn for which they looked has not broken but it will break. Light is stronger than darkness, for "God is light." God is on the side of light. The good they envisioned has not come but it will. Good will conquer evil, for "the Lord is good." God is on the side of good. The truth they cherished is not yet on the throne, but it will be. Truth is

stronger than error. God is "the God of truth." He is on the side of truth. Does this mean that we may fold our hands and naïvely assume that everything will come out all right? Not so. This faith of ours presupposes that God will continue to find men who will love truth, labor and sacrifice for it; yea, and if need be, die for it. "These all died in faith, not having received the promises, but having seen them afar off, . . . that they without us should not be made perfect." (Heb. 11:13, 40.) "They without us"—it cannot be accomplished *without us*.

Phillips is invariably interesting when he talks on preaching, as numerous attendants at ministerial institutes, "retreats," and church conventions can testify. In lecturing on "The Sermon and the Truth," Phillips cites the sermon preached by Father Mapple in Herman Melville's classic, *Moby Dick*, and has a grand time with that sermon which it will be recalled was on the Book of Jonah and its chief character. It is all so good that it seems a shame to cut the several pages devoted to Father Mapple's, shall I say—"effort"? No, that's not the word, for the sermon was effortless, as we shall see:

Not only was Father Mapple's sermon biblical but it was relevant, timely, and timeliness is an unfailing mark of truth. Truth is never irrelevant. This preacher, Father Mapple, was talking to real people about real issues. His audience was a group of seafaring folk, whalers. It is perhaps more than a coincidence that his text was "The Lord had prepared a great fish to swallow up Jonah" (Jonah 1:17). We cannot always find texts that fit situations as well, nor do we need to. We do not need to be quite as literal as the famous divine who, in preaching to the girls at Wellesley College, is reported to have chosen for his text: "Follow me, and I will make you fishers of men" (Matt. 4:19). Yet our preaching must be relevant. Father Mapple's was. He was talking about Jonah, a man who lived a long time ago, yet he does not speak of Jonah as though he were a mummy, a relic of some dead age. Jonah is alive. He sits right there in the pew beside those whalers.

Let us look again at Father Mapple's sermon. Not only was it biblical and relevant; it was also direct. Note how it begins: "Shipmates, this book containing only four chapters—four yarns—is one of the smallest strands in the mighty cable of the Scriptures. Yet what depths of the soul does Jonah's deep sealine sound!"[1] And he is off.

---

[1] *Moby Dick*, p. 54.

Perhaps we preachers need not get going quite so suddenly, but I am sure that in preaching we often take too long to get started. When I sit down to write a sermon I am usually plagued by the fear that I shall not have enough to say. The result is that not infrequently after I get into the sermon, and eventually finish it, I have to go back and throw the first three or four pages into the wastebasket, that good friend of every congregation. Incidentally, I never miss them! Henry Ward Beecher used to say that a text is like a gate into an open field, and that the preacher should waste no time swinging on the gate. Too often preaching is like the speech of the proverbial Irishman who started his address by saying: "My friends, before I begin to speak I want to say . . ." We often say too much before we begin to preach!

II

Lecture V, "The Preacher and the Truth," reveals Phillips in his most captivating mood. You imagine him in his study surrounded by a group of clerical intimates while he talks shop. Hear him as he discusses four characteristic marks of "a workman that needeth not to be ashamed," ministerial, of course:

The first mark is industry. The workman who needs not be ashamed will be an industrious workman. The cause of truth will not be helped by sluggards. David Christie, in his little classic *The Service of Christ,* says that there are three great temptations every minister faces:

> The temptation to recline.
> The temptation to shine.
> The temptation to whine[2]

It is the first of these that now concerns us—the temptation to recline. The ministry is the last place on earth for a lazy man. There is no substitute in the Christian ministry for downright hard work and lots of it. The man who wants an easy berth had better flee the ministry as though it were a plague. "I would have laziness held to be the one unpardonable sin in all our students and in all our ministers," said Alexander Whyte.[3] The minister must be industrious.

A part of this industry will be intellectual—study. The intellectual demands on a modern minister are far greater than those his fathers

[2] P. 66.
[3] G. F. Barbour, *Life of Alexander Whyte,* p. 282.

faced. George Matheson once came to the defense of preachers who were called "high" and "low" by declaring there was one worse than either, namely, the preacher who was "thin."[4] The story has it that a minister once recognized as the most regular attendant at the worship service a hard-working washerwoman who Sunday after Sunday was observed in her pew. He wanted to find the reason for such fidelity and so asked: "Is it that you enjoy the beautiful music?"

"Na, it's no' that."

"Perhaps you enjoy my sermons?"

"Na, it's no' that."

"Then what brings you here every week?"

"Weel, it's like this. I work hard a' week, and it's no' often I get sic a comfortable sate wi sae little tae think aboot."

And the "high," "low" and "thin" preachers suggests another story. It was told me in London by a Church of England clergyman. He said that there came over from America a bishop and his wife, who were entertained in one of London's great houses. One morning when the Bishop's wife was having a late breakfast alone, and being waited upon by the butler, she asked him: "Can you tell me just what is the difference between the 'low church' and the 'high church' "? "That I can, my Lady," he replied, "the low church they eats the most and the high church they drinks the most."

Traveling at home or abroad Dr. Phillips keeps his eyes open. The passage which follows is a good example of his habit of observation:

Outside the town of Winchester, England, is the quaint old priory of St. Cross. In the church is a lectern, an eagle with spreading wings, carved out of oak. As I once examined the lovely carving I observed this strange fact, that while the bird was an eagle all right, with mighty wings, his beak was not the beak of an eagle but the bill of a parrot. It seemed such an undignified modification to put on this otherwise majestic bird—a squawking and chattering parrot's bill. I observed further that on the head of the eagle there was carved a heart. I pointed out these strange facts to the old verger and asked what they meant. He said that a parrot's bill had been substituted for the eagle's beak and a heart placed on the eagle's head so that when

[4] D. MacMillan. *Life of George Matheson*, p. 246.

the minister goes to the lectern to read the Scripture he will remember that he is not to read it like a parrot but from the heart.

From the above incident, which in less skillful hands might "gang aft agley," Phillips deduces the need of heart power for the preacher's myriad tasks. Perhaps no other need has been so urged upon us as the primacy of the affections in Christian living. And wisely so. St. Paul made this teaching the subject of his immortal chapter on love. Horace Bushnell held that unless a man lives in his affections he doesn't really live at all, and long ago the Scottish bard sang lustily:

> The *heart* ay's the part ay,
> That makes us right or wrang.

IX. LESLIE D. WEATHERHEAD

The Lyman Beecher lecturer for 1949 was the Reverend Leslie D. Weatherhead, D.D., M.A., of City Temple, London, England. The choice was a popular one. Dr. Weatherhead was a noted man before he became minister at City Temple in the illustrious succession of Joseph Parker, Reginald John Campbell, Joseph Fort Newton, and Frederick Norwood. He served in World War I as Lieutenant (Staff Lieutenant in the Mesopotamian campaign) and after the Armistice was chaplain in Mesopotamia and Persia. In 1919 he became minister of the English Methodist Church in Madras. From 1922-25 he was minister in Manchester and from 1925-36 minister of Brunswick Methodist Church, Leeds. He had a special flair for psychology and lectured for the Workers' Educational Association on the subject. He was for a time an examiner in the subject for Methodist ordinands. This led him to develop a great deal of clinical work during his ministry at Leeds, where he became famous.

His books, which are popular, are numerous and among the best sellers. They include such works as *After Death*; *The Afterworld Poets*; *Psychology in the Service of the Soul*; *Psychology and Life*; *The Mastery of Sex*; *The Transforming Friendship*; *Jesus and Our-*

selves; His Life and Ours; Discipleship; How Can I Find God?; Why Do Men Suffer?; It Happened in Palestine; A Shepherd Remembers; The Eternal Voice; Thinking Aloud in Wartime; This is the Victory; Personalities of the Passion; In Quest of a Kingdom; The Will of God; The Plain Man Looks at the Cross; The Significance of Silence; When the Lamp Flickers. He is a frequent writer for religious journals and in the press, and commands a wide public.

The Convocation opened on the afternoon of Tuesday, the 26th of April, 1949, in Marquand Chapel atop the quadrangle, which is a lovely replica of Thomas Jefferson's grand design at the University of Virginia. The audience, which came early and was composed of graduates, students, professors, ministers and their wives, with here and there a celebrity from a distance, was delightfully informal. It resembled nothing quite so much as a family reunion, buzzing with conversation, replete with greetings, and never unmindful that the best was yet to come. The audience fell silent as President Charles Seymore of Yale University gave a brief address of welcome and Dean Luther Weigle of Yale Divinity School presented the lecturer.

Dr. Weatherhead belied his fifty-six years when he stood up to speak. He looked wonderfully youthful, and having spent much time on the sun deck coming over, his face bore a becoming tan. He wore a blue double-breasted business suit, a blue shirt, and a blue tie. He spoke freely without manuscript and consulted his brief notes infrequently. The Weatherhead style is pleasing. He speaks fluently and with a freedom that suggests the extemporaneous method, but one surmises out of much writing, careful preparation, and continuous practice. His hands, which are those of an artist, play what appears to be an unconscious part in his delivery.

Listening to Dr. Weatherhead lecture or preach (I heard him in his City Temple pulpit in 1937) it is not difficult to account for his popularity. His voice is finely modulated, and simplicity the hallmark of his diction. He is an excellent example of conversational oratory, freely employing humor and wit. The thing, however, that sets him apart and gives him his large following, is his message of hope and redemption to confused, frustrated, and disconsolate individuals. Then too, he is a daring exegete of the

Scriptures, and is possibly aware of the notion that a little heresy now and then is relished by the best of men. Yet when I say this I hasten to add that his is a constructive ministry both by word and pen, and he speaks with the authority of much study and experience in the field of psychology. Nor has he, I venture to say, reached the peak of his usefulness as a surgeon of the soul.

"In Conducting Worship"

Not even St. Paul's introduction to his defense before King Agrippa was more felicitous than Dr. Weatherhead's remarks as he began his series at Yale. He won his hearers completely. He created an atmosphere of friendly expectancy. So, on happy terms with his audience, he said:

I am rather proud of the fact that at the City Temple we have the order of service printed so that one does not even have to give out the hymns, because the way in which some people give out a hymn will get right in the way of a would-be worshipper. "Let us now sing to the glory of God that beautiful hymn which begins," and so on. From first to last let us remember to get ourselves out of the way so that those who come to worship may get nearer to God. Would to God that some organists believed that was also important;
      "Then with swelling chords that rent the air,
      The organist proclaimed that *he* was there."

Do not stand in the middle of the pulpit, especially if it is in the center of the church, waving the hymn book about, and do not sing too lustily. That intrusive "I" that always gets in the way. We have a story in England, you know, that comes from America, a newspaper report of a service in which the reporter said, "The preacher then offered the finest prayer that was ever offered to a Boston audience."

Be relevant, be simple, and then I would say be loving. I think the most beautiful thing I ever heard said about a preacher was this. Somebody said: "Why is it that he has such power over people, and why do they come so far to hear him?" and the answer was this: "He puts his arms around the whole congregation and no one feels left out." . . . The great preachers have been great lovers. The great preachers have been the people who made simple, homely folk, such as you and me, feel that they were loved.

This London preacher has a way of taking familiar incidents of Scripture and putting them in a new light. That, I think, is one of the reasons why so many love to hear him preach and why so many read his books. In this first lecture there are two instances of this fresh exegesis. Referring to the storm on Galilee, the fright of the disciples, and the words of Jesus, "Peace, be still," he stated that he believed most intensely that the words were spoken not to the waves but to the disciples. "It seems to me," he said, "senseless to talk to the waves. It seems to me most important that we should discourage men from the emotion of fear. I agree that probably Peter thought and dictated to Mark the idea that Jesus was muzzling the demons, but we are not bound to the interpretation of the first century." The other instance of a new and novel interpretation of a famous text was this, in reference to Jesus' words, "Where two or three are gathered together in my name, I will be there too." Dr. Weatherhead said,

That two or three is not a reference to a very small congregation. It might include that kind of a reference, but whenever I preach at City Temple, I know that I shall have a good time if the two or three that I know about are there, because I know they will have prayed before they came; and I know they will bring their spirituality into the congregation so that however badly I preach, the atmosphere will be charged with their power and men will find God.

"Private Counseling"

The lecturer began by reminding his preacher-hearers that the ministry becomes an impossible job if the minister pays attention to all that people think he ought to do. There would always be criticism, and

If you lie awake worrying about what you think people think about you, you won't sleep at all after the first six months. Regardless of what the preacher does or doesn't do, he'll have his critics. One of the rights which he'll have to claim is how to use his time to the best advantage. Make up your mind that the only person you are responsible to is Christ, and if you can look Him in the eye, and say: "You know my capabilities, give me the grace of sincerity," then you can go on.

Dr. Weatherhead was sure that the private interview with persons seeking advice from the minister is the last thing the minister should give up when pressed for time. He thought the private interview in the church was more important than calling on people in their homes unless it was in response to an emergency. He also questioned the wisdom of interviewing persons in the minister's home. In this connection he said:

> The shy person doesn't want to meet a maid servant or members of the family. See them in the room at the church and do not keep them waiting. [The furnishings of that room where the interview is held are important.] Do not have a light blazing upon their face. I have my patients sitting in the Light of the World. Just behind the chair where the patient sits, which is there so that he need not look right at me or I at him—just behind him on the wall I have a picture of Holman Hunt's "The Light of the World," showing "Jesus knocking at the door." It is a very small thing but it helps me very much because if I am tired, and these interviews are very exhausting, then I get my perspective right by remembering that I am talking to that person so that he may hear Christ seeking to come in and I may be able to help him to open the door. I don't know whether that appeals to you. It saves me from a great deal of impatience and ill-temper and the sort of feeling which is communicated to the patient that you are really very busy and longing to get on with something else. The interview exists so that our Lord may open the door into that patient's heart.

The speaker spent a revealing period on the qualifications of the counselor; the most important he held to be that "as ministers we should never be caught up when our own relationships with God are distant; in other words, the finest qualification for doing this kind of work is that we should ourselves be living close to God. I may say that out of many failures, if my prayer life has not been maintained, if it has become artificial, and if my work has become professional, God teaches me a severe lesson by sending me a person whom I am quite unable to help." Other qualifications which the minister needs for counseling are "the sympathetic outlook," "the readiness to listen without interrupting," and "never show that you are shocked," closing with the admonition, "let us remember that these people with personality, with something that is God, entrust us with the task of the Good Shepherd, leading them back, not because we are wonderful, but because we, too, have often been lost, but by His grace at last have found the path again, bringing back the sheep again to the path that leads them home, and let us not fail them in the hour of their need."

"PUBLIC INTERCESSION"

Prayer is one of the few subjects that are permanently interesting, and any man who can speak out of this "supreme use of silence" with power and understanding is sure of a hearing. Dr. Weatherhead is such a man. He looked out upon an audience that was wistfully awaiting his interpretation of intercessory prayer, and said:

We are going to deal with the long prayer. This is what is probably the hardest part of our conducting public worship, the matter of public intercession. Probably all preachers agree that what used to be called the "long prayer" in Free Church worship is really the hardest part of the service to conduct with any sense of reality, and I think it would be very humiliating if the people who listen to the "long prayer" turned out their minds at the closing. If they could turn out their minds like a rag bag, what a rag bag it would be! I think they probably listen and try to pray for the first thirty seconds and then probably their minds wander off thinking of other things altogether, the nature of which would surprise us, perhaps shock us. Therefore, the aim of this talk is to see whether a sense of reality could be brought into public intercession by trying to understand it. For instance, does it really make any difference? Do you think that in the minds of our listeners, and even perhaps in our own mind, there is a sense that it really doesn't make much difference? The public intercession worded in the familiar phrases, perhaps has no real effect. If so, that is a paralyzing feeling, and in order to make the matter focus down to a definite point, I would like to think of intercession this morning as intercession for John Smith who is ill, you see, and then ask you to think over if you care to do so the fact that *mutatis mutandis* what we think about John Smith can be applied to other themes of public intercession as well. Supposing then that we imagine that we are leading the public intercession of the congregation and asking them to pray for the sick. There again I think that there is so much unreality unless we ask the congregation to pray for sick *persons*. That is why I am taking the illustration this morning of this imaginary person, John Smith. Now, I am sure that the thought arises in many people's minds "Why should we pray at all for him, for John Smith? Presumably God knows that he is ill, and presumably God cannot be told something about his case that He doesn't already know, and presumably God loves John Smith more than we do, and presumably God wants his well-being with a greater intensity than we want it." The first thing that we want to do is to dispel the illusion that public intercession is persuading a reluctant God to intervene.

Dr. Weatherhead told his hearers that he had less faith in prayer for causes than in prayer for persons, and stated, smilingly, that he didn't know what the result is in heaven when people make a list of things like: the United Nations, the England-China Mission, and forty other organizations, and put "God bless" at the beginning and "Amen" at the end. He went on to say:

I don't know what they do with that kind of prayer. Perhaps it has a result in the unseen which I am not capable of assessing, but it seems unreal to me and therefore I cannot pray that kind of prayer with confidence; but if you pray for a person, if I can make a little picture of a missionary in China, and tell my people the problems he is up against and let them see in imagination that situation, then I can lead them in prayer for the person. I don't think in the New Testament there is any evidence of our Lord praying for a cause, unless you say the Kingdom of God, which He delegated very definitely to the persons who were near Him. However, let that go. Here is an actual case which I would like to quote to you. We had at the City Temple a young nurse of twenty who was lying in St. Bartholomew's Hospital very dangerously ill, unconscious, unable to take nourishment. We say to the congregation, if we have the permission of the relatives, "Now here is Nurse X. She is in such-and-such a ward. She is lying there ill. Will you pray for her in this way: Imagine that our Lord is moving up the ward. Now imagine that He is standing by her bedside. Now imagine that He is laying His hands upon her. Don't let your mind wander. Our Lord is now laying His hands upon her. Believe that at this moment her mind, her deep unconscious mind, is responding to Him; believe that your love and caring are making an atmosphere, a psychic atmosphere around Nurse X which gives the healing power of God a better chance. Now believe that at this moment she is beginning to recover. Don't let your mind wander. (You have to say that to people or else in a few minutes their mind is off on something else.) Believe that you are doing imaginatively and by faith what you would do if our Lord were here in the flesh. You would take her into His presence. Now hold her there for a moment. Christ is there, she is there. We are providing the atmosphere in which He can work. Without that faith He could do no mighty work."

"IN OFFERING DIVINE FORGIVENESS"

One surmises that Dr. Weatherhead's subject helped to account for the eager faces turned toward the pulpit as he entered it, for he dealt with a fundamental of fundamentals.

He began:

I suppose that at our clinic at the City Temple we have more cases of neuroses due to repressed guilt than to any other cause. Whether you look up to the heights to which we have to climb spiritually, or whether you look to the depths in which men wallow in unhappiness and misery, you find the importance of the idea of forgiveness. In the end, God's plan for everybody is to make him one with himself. If that is so, then we more and more need forgiveness. If there is any hope of people like you and me ever attaining to union with God in any sense of those words, then we realize how greatly we need forgiveness. In fact it is a very interesting and remarkable thing that the greater the saint the more conscious he is of his need for forgiveness. A man like St. Paul, climbing to the heights, thinks of his sins, fears that he might instead of having preached to others be cast away, calls himself the chief of sinners. So with John Wesley. On his deathbed as they leant over the dying saint seeking to hear his last message, it was in terms of a plea for forgiveness, and an assertion of his sinfulness. "God be merciful to me a sinner." And in marked contrast, we find our Lord on the heights, looking still into the face of God and saying, "I and my Father are one."

The lecturer took his hearers with him all the way when he averred:

. . . We ministers here have something in our hands which the psychotherapist has not. If it is true, as I allege, that a great mass of people are in all kinds of physical trouble because of repressed guilt, the attitude of the psychotherapist is to analyze back to the repressed guilt until he lifts the incident, the traumatic incident, and the relevant emotions up to the level of consciousness. He says to the patient, "Well, there you are, there is where you went wrong." He as a psychologist, as a psychotherapist, has no authority to say "Your sins are forgiven you." In my experience, unless the psychologist is a Christian psychologist, he generally doesn't do that. He tells the people what they have done and he tells them they will get over it in time, and leaves them to find their way. Now in the idea of forgiveness you have in your hands the most powerful therapeutic factor there is in the world. I think I could write a book on the psychotherapeutic value of the idea of forgiveness. It isn't any good if it can only be gotten over to the patient as an idea, because although the mind receives it, the heart does not appreciate it. Until forgiveness is emotionally realised as well as intellectually understood, it won't "work." . . . You see if a man gets to the point at which he realises that his trouble is tied up with his sins and you say to him, "But God will forgive you," he says, "I know He will forgive me," but he doesn't know. He knows here (mind) but not here (heart). If I said to you "Bereavement is a sad thing, isn't it?" you might say, "Yes, bereavement is a very sad thing." But if this morning you had a cable to tell you that one of those dearest to you was dead and I said to you, "Bereavement is a very sad thing, isn't it?" you would say "Yes, I know," with a completely different connotation of the word "know."

On prayer and forgiveness Dr. Weatherhead explained:

You are not to regard prayer for the sick as in the category of a treatment. Thank God it often does get sick people well, but I am not attracted to the sort of people who say: "Well, I have tried ovaltine, and I have tried vegetarianism, and I have tried the wonderful light rays; what about a spot of prayer?" I use that phrase incisively because that is a phrase that was actually used by a brother in England —what about a spot of prayer? The idea behind prayer is communion with God, not getting better. Prayer is not to be rubbed in because ointments fail. . . . The idea behind prayer is communion with God in order that we and those for whom we pray may become one with God, and inasmuch as a great deal of illness is due to the fact that people are *not* one with God, it may often be that as a by-product of prayer people get better. . . . It is a dreadful thing to fall into the hands of the living God. There is only one thing that I can conceive of that would be worse and that is to fall out of His hands, but you can't do that.

"On Offering Divine Love"

To many this was Dr. Weatherhead's finest lecture. They were all good, but to some of us this was Weatherhead the preacher rather than the psychologist, although he used his knowledge of that science as he preached, and used it helpfully. There were times when he seemed to be back in his London pulpit, preaching to thousands instead of hundreds and to clerks, secretaries, businessmen, nurses, and sin-scourged wreckage that had drifted in from the streets, instead of to university professors, theological students, ministers and their wives, a highly respectable audience, but nevertheless, like all other human beings so needy, so tempest-tossed, so sure now that Marquand Chapel had become a narthex to heaven.

The minister of City Temple, London, began by commending to his hearers books by Dr. J. A. Hadfield, a one-time Congregationalist minister who is now a highly respected psychiatrist, the foremost in Great Britain, and retains the spiritual point of view along with the scientific. Dr. Weatherhead admitted:

> I know him very well, and, alas, he knows me very well. I have been analyzed by Hadfield and have two hundred separate hours of psychoanalysis. If he doesn't know you after that there isn't anything to know. . . . He claims—and this is where I want to kick off—he claims that ninety percent of neuroses are caused by a sense of deprivation of love on the part of the patient. In fact I think if he were pressed, he would put the percentage higher than that, that nervous breakdown—that is not a phrase that I like but it is more widely understood—neurosis or nervous breakdown is in ninety percent or more cases caused by a sense of deprivation of love at some point in the emotional development of the patient. I said in "a sense" of deprivation of love, because often a person imagines that love is withheld when it is not intentionally withheld and may not be actually withheld, but if the patient thinks it is, it has the same effect on the personality. By love in these sentences I don't mean *philos* and I don't mean *eros*; I mean *agape*. I hope that sounds as impressive to you as it does to me! And I would define that as endless good will and appreciation. Now a little child coming into this world should ideally be surrounded by love in that sense; appreciation and good will, the attitude that makes his own self-respect blossom, the attitude that is said to spoil him, though when in doubt—this to all parents—when in doubt, spoil. The world is so hard to people—don't add to the hardness of the world, so when in doubt, spoil.

In the same vein and keeping this idea of offering divine love to love-starved people Dr. Weatherhead resumed:

You see if you are looking for love and are deprived of it, you seek a love substitute. Well, fame is one, ability in this or that direction is another, the applause of the multitude is another, but it is wine, very heady wine, but it is not food. It is intoxicating but it does not build up personality; so you have your famous singer who thrills thousands in great music halls, and concert halls, and has got there because he is always trying to be loved and admired, but the plaudits of 2000 people do not make up for the lack of the love of one woman. Now you think that out. And again, if you look into the private history of some of the most famous people who ever lived, you will find that their home life was unhappy. Now then, see what a happy marriage is going to do for you—deprive the world of your fame! But I am quite sure that that is the first reaction of those who are deprived of real personality—building love.

A woman wants to be loved and she finds somebody who will love her body and give her an hour or two of something that is simulated love, so she gives herself in that way. She isn't any worse than you and me, but we have been loved. I am not a bit surprised at our Lord's love for people who fell sexually, His kind, interested understanding of them. He said the harlots will go into the kingdom of heaven before you Pharisees. At least they knew how to love. Indeed it was love that brought their downfall. The woman taken in adultery —this has startled the masters of ethics but it doesn't startle the masters of psychology—this woman who was a sinner—He said she was a sinner but she loved much. Now then, let us understand that this deprivation of love is of the utmost importance, fundamental importance, and the key which opens up to our understanding and sympathy the lives of so many whom we tend to condemn.

The close of this lecture was in the form of a touching incident, simply told, the whole giving the effect of a sunset of lambent beauty which promises a clear tomorrow:

I remember going in earlier days to visit a home where death had been busy, where a young husband died. I can see the picture so clearly now. There was the fire with just a low flickering flame as if the very fire felt that it dare not burn brightly in such a house of sorrow, and near the fire in a chair was seated an old woman with white hair. I see her hair now, lighted by the firelight. And sitting on the hearthrug, right on the floor at her knee was the young wife of the man who had died, and I can see too, in imagination, the gold of her hair illuminated by the fire, and the older woman's arm was round the younger woman's shoulder, and the younger was very, very bitter and very resentful and very hostile to God, and she looked up at me standing behind them both and she said: "You talk about the love of God. I don't believe it. You talk about the everlasting arms. I don't believe it. Where is God to let this thing happen to my husband? We were so in love with one another and now he has been taken away." Well, there is a lot of bad theology in that, but you can't explain things in such an hour of sorrow; but I could say this and I did say this to her: "My dear girl, the love of God is within a foot of you, in your Mother. And the everlasting arms you don't believe in—why, they are round you at this moment. Whose do you think is the arm across your shoulder now? As Browning said in a beautiful line, 'Hush, I pray you, what if that friend happen to be God?'"

You know, I envy some young ministers going out. This is the finest job in the world. You will mediate to hungry spirits and distorted lives the love of God, the greatest thing in the world!

"In Healing Certain Types of Diseases"

An audience that packed Marquand Chapel, overflowed into the chancel, with standing room at a premium, greeted Dr. Weatherhead at his closing lecture.

He told us that in 1937 he had the honor of making three propositions to the Methodist Conference in England, and that they passed the following three resolutions: (1) Forthwith and subsequently, the training of theological students should contain enough teaching in psychology to enable them to understand when a patient should be referred to a Christian psychologist. (2) That experimental clinics should be set up in which doctors and ministers begin to work together, and consult so that in consultation they could do the best for patients suffering in certain ways. (3) That in the future our churches should emphasize intercession for the sick. In commenting on these resolutions Dr. Weatherhead surmised that something might be done about them in twenty-five years or so. He was of the mind that ecclesiastical assemblies are much the same everywhere, a comment which tickled the audience.

Perhaps one of the Doctor's most telling statements occurred along toward the close of the lecture when he said:

> I am quite sure in my own mind that the Church has lost something. I am quite sure that when Jesus said heal the sick, He didn't mean become clever psychologists. I think that all that is of God and all that we can do in that field the better, the more we co-operate with doctors and psychiatrists the better, but I believe that one day the Church will wake up to this fact, that there is available an energy that would override these laborious long psychoanalyses—mine took nine years—that would override these headaches and things. When you try to pigeonhole the healing miracles of Jesus into the pigeon holes of the psychotherapeutic practice you are doing a dangerous thing. You can if you like—and I have tried to write about this—you can if you like take every healing miracle and study it and indicate the psychological mechanisms which are at work in each one, but nobody has ever cured a skin disease like that and nobody else has ever cured paralysis as quickly as that and nobody else has been able to have a man walking after years of inactivity and disability by forgiving sins. There is available on our level an energy of the spirit which we are not using and we have got to do some pioneer work in finding out what it is, and how it may be released, and how it may sweep through us and how we may use it to get sick people well.

And he closed with this passage:

> Do you sometimes feel when you read, for instance, the story of somebody who gets better through Christian Science, or the story of somebody who gets better through Spiritualism, do you feel as though these people are just dabbling in it but that just beyond the borders of sense there is an enormous field of energy and we are just not using it? I feel as I think an engineer would feel who stands on the beach and sees the mighty breakers come in, the great sea and all its power, who says if only I knew how to harness that energy I could do the work of the world. When I read the story of our Lord's healing miracles and when I think of Pentecost and when I think of Him saying, "Greater things than these ye shall do," I feel like a silly child standing on the beach and seeing this immense energy and then not knowing what to do about it and how to harness that power to human needs. Let us go forward in a healing ministry with prayer, with experimental work, with co-operation, trying to understand how much physical trouble is caused by spiritual disability, but don't let

us forget that the saints may be able to teach us more than the psychologists, and open up to us the kingdom of heaven.

So great was the interest in the services that in response to many requests Dr. Weatherhead agreed to devote an hour to a conference with students and others who wished to ask him questions. Immediately after the last lecture there was an adjournment to the Common Room, where every seat was occupied, some chairs held more than one person, students sat on the floor while others were obliged to stand and did not mind it in the least. Perhaps 60 per cent of the questions asked had to do with sex problems; others with the healing of sick and unhappy souls. Dr. Weatherhead handled the questions with the skill that comes from long experience at that sort of thing. But the hour was all too short, and when the conference broke up he was at once surrounded by groups still plying him with questions. This was to be expected for his lectures dealt with themes of universal and unending interest, and Dr. Weatherhead's explorations were in a realm novel yet shrouded by a purple mist to millions, and often as he spoke his words seemed to be a commentary on the truth in Whittier's lovely lines:

> But warm, sweet, tender, even yet,
> A present help is he;
> And faith has still its Olivet,
> And love its Galilee.
>
> The healing of his seamless dress
> Is by our beds of pain;
> We touch him in life's throng and press,
> And we are whole again.

How did Dr. Weatherhead's hearers respond to his lectures? Already it has been stated that he spoke to capacity audiences which gave every indication of intense interest. Here follows part of a letter from one of the most brilliant young preachers in New England in which he gives his impressions, not only of the lectures, but of Dr. Weatherhead himself:

And how shall I describe the effect of Weatherhead! It was almost impossible for me to get to bed at night or to get through my meals in the daytime because of the group of eager fellows who were glowing with enthusiasm for, and bursting with a desire to talk about the Weatherhead lectures. They seemed to have helped for some such reasons as these: (1) the obvious humility and sincerity of the man; (2) the delicious sense of humor with which he spoke, and the refreshing freedom he displayed in the presence of a great tradition which hampers and smothers some lecturers. He was not afraid to display genuine emotion, nor to depart from the manuscript if by doing so he could better make his point. He did not appear to be tied down or shackled by the knowledge of all the great men who had acted as the Lyman Beecher lecturers before him across the decades; (3) the fact perhaps that he did not actually use a manuscript, but spoke freely and vigorously from an outline only. This ties in with, and forms a part of number 2; (4) his liberal and effective use of vivid, apt and telling illustrative material; (5) his ability not merely to talk about great and effective preaching in an interesting and compelling fashion, but more importantly his ability to *demonstrate* it. It was quite common, for example, for me to hear many of the fellows say, not "Boy, is he a great lecturer!" but "That is great preaching!"; (6) his ability to cut across the stereotyped method of developing ideas, or of indicating the progression in the development of a theme. One of the transitional phrases that he often used, for example, was one which went something like this and which many of the fellows said they were going to adopt: "I wonder if you will agree with me in this?" or "Is this, do you think, an overstatement of the matter?" or "Will you follow me now in this further consideration of the matter?"

Such praise, so candidly and so generously expressed, more than compensates for the painstaking preparation and endless toil involved in such a series of lectures.

Note: The fact that this is the only one of the Series which I heard in its entirety, seems to justify the fuller treatment I have given to Dr. Weatherhead. I had a delightful visit with him at New Haven and a most informative interview.

VIII

A PAGEANTRY OF
★ PREACHERS ★

You are come ... to the general assembly and church of the firstborn who are enrolled in heaven ... and to the spirits of just men made perfect.

—HEBREWS 12:22, 23

1. WILLIAM MACKERGO TAYLOR

The Scottish Pulpit

Ten years after his first appearance in the Yale Lectures Dr. William M. Taylor returned to give a second series, and this time on *The Scottish Pulpit*, a field in which he was very much at home. This course, delivered by Dr. Taylor in 1886, marked a departure from the general trend of subject matter, which hitherto had been almost wholly devoted to the technique of preaching, sermonic content, and the various aspects of pastoral responsibilities.

"*The Scottish Pulpit*"! How hearts beat high and eyes sparkle on the part of the preaching fraternity at the thought, for preaching in the land of the heather is justly renowned. Memories of John Knox, Chalmers, Guthrie, Candlish, Norman McLeod—they are all in the verbal portraits which Taylor does with consummate art. What drama, poetry, and fierce controversy too, are in the annals of Scottish church life, fictionized so unforgettably by George Macdonald and Ian Maclaren! It is a tough assignment, and Taylor is equal to it.

His first lecture is historical. In the compass of thirty-four pages this preacher, himself a Scotsman, sketches in a background which spans more than two centuries; the result is all that could be asked, and more. In the closing paragraph of this lecture the author refers to the struggle against heavy odds which so many of the ministerial brethren endured and says:

> Indeed, most of the Scottish clergy might adopt the words of Edmund Burke with but a single change and say, "I was not swaddled, and rocked, and dawdled into a minister. *Nitor in adversum* is the motto for a man like me." But they have not been the worse for that; nay, they have been all the better for that, since knowing what struggle is, they have been so much abler to speak "words in season" to those who are struggling, and that has been one element in their power.

It certainly has, and for that matter how very few of the great preachers of any age or clime were coddled in luxury. Name ten. Think hard!

The mighty figures with whom Taylor companies in this series, and whose life and labors he so skillfully delineates, must necessarily be inadequately reported here. Little more than silhouettes do they appear.

John Knox. Of his sermons only one complete specimen, printed under his own supervision, remains. He was a diligent student. In one letter he describes himself as "sitting at his books." He did not become a preacher until he had reached the age of forty-two. From the latter part of 1539 till his death in 1572 he continued to labor for Scotland. In style he was plain, direct, homely, sometimes humorous, and always courageous.

The description of Knox in his last days is graphic:

> In the opening up of his text he was moderate for the space of half an hour, but when he entered on application he made me so to shiver (*Scottice* "grue") and tremble that I could not hold my pen to write. He was very weak. I saw him every day of his teaching go slowly and warily, with a fur of martens about his neck, a staff in the one hand, and good, godly Richard Ballantyne, his servant, holding up the other armpit (*Scottice* "oxter"), from the abbey to the parish kirk, and by the said Richard and another servant lifted up to the pulpit, where he behooved to lean at his first entrance, but before he had done with his sermon he was so active and vigorous that it seemed as if he would knock the pulpit in pieces (*Scottice* "ding the pulpit in blads") and flie out of it.[1]

[1] From a letter by James Melville, a student at St. Andrew's.

William Mackergo Taylor

John Knox, of whom it was said that he "never feared the face of man"—nor for that matter, the beautiful face of a queen!

Samuel Rutherfurd is not even a name to many in this century, but he left a heritage of courage, and his letters are esteemed by scholars in the same class as those of *The Confessions of Augustine* and *The Imitation* of Thomas à Kempis. Even among his admirers, Rutherfurd was a controversial character. "There were two men in him, and the two were so distinct that you could hardly call him 'a strange mixture,' for they did not mix," says Taylor. He was a scholar, educated at Edinburgh, and held the office of Regent and instructor in Latin in that institution for two years. Men said of Rutherfurd, "He seemed to be always praying, always preaching, always visiting the sick, always catechising, always writing and studying." As for the style of his preaching—an English merchant during the Protectorate, describing some of his experiences in what was probably a business tour through Scotland, said: "I went to St. Andrew's, where I heard a sweet, majestic-looking man (Blair), and he showed me the majesty of God; after him I heard a little fair man (Rutherfurd), and he showed me the loveliness of Christ; I then went to Irvine, where I heard a well-formed, proper old man, with a long beard (Dickson), and that man showed me all my own heart." One feels like paraphrasing a familiar text, "And now abideth Blair, Rutherfurd, and Dickson and the greatest of these was"—well, Taylor did not say. Anyhow, all three abide in the annals of Scottish church history.

Thomas Chalmers. Dr. Taylor calls Chalmers the greatest of Scottish preachers, and few will dispute his claim. He strides the period of his public life like a colossus. He dominates his day by the sheer force of his powerful personality and an ardor for the poor and the undone which quite transfigures him in the end. What of his appearance? Here is Taylor's description:

> In person he was stout and almost stocky. His countenance when in repose was mild, his eye watery, almost dull, with a far-off look in it, as if he were gazing on things invisible to others, but when he became excited it lighted up as with celestial fire, and shone with the lustre of genius. His speech betrayed him everywhere. It was not merely Scottish, but it was roughly provincial, and withal he read his discourses closely. Yet over all these disadvantages the force of the orator triumphed so

that even the cool, critical Jeffrey said of his eloquence that "it reminded him more of what one reads of as the effect of the eloquence of Demosthenes than anything he ever saw"; and again, that "he could not believe more had ever been done by the oratory of Demosthenes, Cicero, Burke, or Sheridan."

To do justice to the unreportable pulpit eloquence by including here a brief extract seems as futile and unsatisfactory as to attempt to do justice to a Raphael by exhibiting a segment of one of his masterpieces. But there is a passage credited to John Brown, M.D., author of *Rab and His Friends*, one of the world's famous short stories, which Taylor includes in his chapter on Chalmers, and of which I quote but a part:

We remember well our first hearing Dr. Chalmers. We were in a moorland district in Tweeddale, rejoicing in the country, after nine months of the High School. . . . As we entered the kirk we saw a notorious character, a drover, who had much of the brutal look of what he worked in, with the knowing eye of a man of the city, a sort of big Peter Bell—

"He had a hardness in his eye,
He had a hardness in his cheek."

. . . The kirk was as full as it could hold. . . . The minister comes in, homely in his dress and gait, but having a great look about him, like a mountain among hills. . . . We shall never forget his smile! its general benignity; . . . He read a few verses quietly; then prayed briefly, solemnly, with his eyes wide open all the time, but not seeing. Then he gave out his text; we forget it, but its subject was "Death Reigns." He stated slowly, calmly, the simple meaning of the words; what death was, and how and why it reigned; then suddenly he started, and looked like a man who had seen some great sight, and was breathless to declare it; he told us how death reigned—everywhere, at all times, in all places; how we all knew it, how we would yet know more of it. The drover, who had sat down in the table-seat (square pew) opposite, was gazing up in a state of stupid excitement. . . . The tide set in—everything added to its power, deep called to deep, imagery and illustration poured in; and every now and then the theme,—the simple, terrible statement, was repeated in some lucid interval . . . and after shrieking, as if in despair, these words, "Death is a tremendous necessity,"—he suddenly looked beyond us as if into some distant region, and cried out, "Behold a mightier!—who is this? He cometh from

Edom, with dyed garments from Bozrah, glorious in his apparel, speaking in righteousness, travelling in the greatness of his strength, mighty to save."

It is a pity to stop in the midst of this vivid description, but it must suffice until the day the reader himself opens Dr. Taylor's volume and turns to pages 225-229. There was room in Scotland for but one Chalmers, as in America one Niagara Falls suffices.

Robert Smith Candlish. Dr. Candlish is a great name in Scottish Church circles of a century that is past. He was one of the noted debaters in the Disruption controversy and a preacher of curious yet unmistakable power. Talk about mannerisms in the pulpit! Candlish was apparently to mannerisms born. Dr. Taylor thinks no one seeing him for the first time could suppress a smile.

His body was diminutive, but what it lacked appeared to have been given to the head, which for size would not have sat amiss upon the shoulders of a giant. His hair hung all around it in tangled luxuriance, sometimes almost like a mop. His mouth was large, with the under jaw slightly protuberant. His eyes were restless and flashing, and his forehead full. He went up the pulpit stair with a hurried step, and running his fingers through his hair, he gave out the psalm in a defiant tone, as if he meant to let some one know that he would not be put down. When he came to the sermon, he indulged unconsciously in all manner of convulsive movements, twisting and writhing like one in agony. He clutched at his gown, he took hold of the Bible as if he would lift it and throw it at his audience, he grasped the pulpit like one who feared he was about to fall. But all this while he had been opening up his text in a manner so clear, so comprehensive, so suggestive, that, as he proceeded, you forgot his eccentricities of manner, and felt only the power of his words.

The thing to remember is that *he could preach!*

Thomas Guthrie. This eloquent Scottish preacher was called by Dr. McCosh, one-time president of Princeton, "the pictorial preacher of his age." America has produced no first-class preacher like him, although Bishop William A. Quayle in elocution and imaginative imagery most resembled him. Guthrie bore a striking likeness to Henry Clay, the celebrated orator-statesman. After hearing Guthrie Mrs. Theodore Cuyler wrote her husband, "I've heard Guthrie and he's spoiled me for everybody else." Celebrities like Dr. James Y. Simpson, the discoverer of chloroform, the eccentric Professor John Stuart Blackie, and Sir William Hamilton, were frequently in Guthrie's audiences. Dr. Taylor thinks Guthrie's sermons were "too pictorial," and questions the solid results of his ministry, but concedes his extraordinary pulpit gifts, saying that "to hear Guthrie was an experience long to cherish."

Dr. Taylor's list of Scottish preachers is long and luminous: Archbishop Leighton, Norman McLeod, Robert Rainy, Ralph Wardlaw, Alexander Henderson, John Ker, W. L. Alexander—these and many others are in the huge roll of honor. Of Dr. Alexander, whom he ranks high, Taylor relates an incident which may appropriately bring this chapter to an amusing close. Dr. Alexander was seldom troubled with a drowsy audience, but he could not tolerate a deliberate employment of the pew as a sleeping place. One day just as he was giving out his text he saw a man in the front seat of the side gallery, almost within reach of him, carefully fold his arms upon the book board and lay his head upon them as if settling himself for a snooze. He could not let such an act pass unnoticed, and the way in which he reproved it was characteristic. He stood still and silent for what seemed quite awhile, until the culprit, wondering what the matter was, raised his head a few inches and looked up. This was all the doctor was waiting for, and gracefully bowing to the offender he said, "Good night."

Dr. Taylor comments, "Needless to say there was no sleep for him throughout the service."

II. JOHN BROWN

Puritan Preaching in England

Dr. Brown, long-time minister at Bunyan's Meeting House, Bedford, England, and author of what many say is the best biography of John Bunyan, did at Yale for the English Puritan preachers what W. M. Taylor did for the Scottish pulpit, and both made their preacher heroes live. Taylor and Brown possessed alike two basic qualities without which they could not have succeeded in the task assigned them, namely, familiarity with the history of the period about which they wrote, and a devotion to the ministerial calling.

Both men wrote in an easy, fluent style and were especially effective in descriptive qualities. Nor was the salt of humor lacking in either, though it is more apparent in Taylor's volume. Brown's introductory lecture is on "The Preaching of the Friars," both Dominican and Franciscan. Nowadays preachers, unless they specialize in church history, are apt to minimize the high service these wandering brethren did for the church at a time when the pulpit was deemed secondary to ritual and the ceremonial. Dr. Brown gives these pioneering Friars their just due. "Taking their best days," he says, "that is, the first twenty-five years of their history, we can see how they form a link between modern and mediaeval times."

The thirteenth century was the century of the great schoolmen of the continent, Albertus Magnus, Bonaventura, and Thomas Aquinas; and in England, Alexander of Hales, John Duns Scotus, and Roger Bacon. Thus it was "a noteworthy fact for all time and for every generation of preachers that in the case of the Friars we have the most effective popular preaching of the thirteenth century associated with the best learning to which the human mind had attained in that century." So avers Dr. Brown, and in this connection it may be profitable to recall that of the fifty-five men who gave us the Constitution of the United States twenty-two were university or college graduates.

Of John Colet and other preachers of the Reformation, theme of Dr. Brown's second lecture, it will suffice to say here, that Colet was an expository preacher of merit; Hugh Latimer, both martyr and prophet; John Bradford "was of a most sweet, humble and melting spirit"; Bishop Jewell and others are of an elect company, brave, persistent, counting no sacrifice too great for Jesus' sake.

Among other makers of Puritanism were the Cambridge men, such as William Perkins, Thomas Goodwin, and the Cambridge Platonists. Dr. Brown devotes two lectures to these, and an amazing amount of history of that period is epitomized skillfully. In reading these chapters, the debt we owe to reverent scholarship, in the long story of where the church's caravan has rested from time to time, is ever to the front and given factual emphasis. Thomas Goodwin, a pale figure to most of us, takes on flesh and blood. We wish we had been in the audience when he preached on "The Heart of Christ in Heaven to Sinners on Earth." Had we been there as skeptics, the likelihood is we would have given our hearts to the Lord. Richard Baxter, "the Kidderminster pastor," is a name one meets often in homiletics. Taylor has a reference to him in *The Scottish Pulpit*, citing an opinion of his on Rutherfurd's letters. (It is odd that Dr. Broadus does not mention him in his monumental *On the Preparation and Delivery of Sermons*.) Brown cites "a competent witness in our time" who expressed the opinion that of all the English preachers of the past, probably those who have been most strongly marked by the peculiarities of the true genius for public speaking were Hugh Latimer, Robert South, and Richard Baxter.

When Baxter came to Kidderminster it was a tough town of between three and four thousand, mainly carpet weavers, a place sunk in immorality, and this Puritan preacher made the town over again into a place of decency, neighborliness, and sobriety. It was a capacious church building to which Baxter went; he filled it to overflowing, and "gallery after gallery had to be added to the interior." Some seventy-five years ago a statue was erected in the town where his fruitful work was done, and Dean Stanley said on the occasion of the unveiling: "There have been three or four parishes in England which have been raised by their pastors to a national, almost a world-wide fame. Of these the most conspicuous is Kidderminster, for Baxter without Kidderminster would have been but half himself, and Kidderminster without Baxter would have been nothing but its carpets."

Due to Dr. Brown's biography of John Bunyan, an authoritative work and widely acclaimed, together with his long and fruitful ministry at Bunyan Meeting House, Bedford, his lecture on "John Bunyan as a Life Study for Preachers" deserves more than passing notice. Bunyan has gone out of fashion save as a name and few preachers have a copy of *The Pilgrim's Progress* on their shelves. What they know about the "immortal tinker" is pretty much hearsay. This lecture, which is number five and consumes but thirty-one pages, is a fascinating chapter. The heart of John Bunyan is in it, and if the reading of it does not send the preacher to Bunyan's writings to drink at the fountainhead, he will at least have quaffed at the brimming cup Dr. Brown supplies. The characters troop by: "Evangelist," "Watchful," "Mr. Greatheart," "Sincere," "Pliable," "Valiant," "Mr. Facing-Both-Ways," "Madam Bubble," "Mr. Fearing," "Stand-Fast," "Feeble-Mind," "Faithful" —these and others. He quotes Bunyan: "I have counted as if I had goodly buildings and lordships in those places where my children were born; my heart hath been so wrapped up in the glory of this excellent work that I counted myself more blessed and honored of God by this than if He had made me the Emperor of the Christian world, or the Lord of all the glory of the earth without it."

Perhaps I may appropriately refer just here to my supplying the pulpit at Bunyan's Meeting House twice on a Sunday in August, 1937. I spent two days in Bedford, and having asked to be directed to the best authority in the city on John Bunyan, I found my man. The better part of a day, with my guide, I visited all the places connected with Bunyan and his famous book, some of which are now shrines. I stood before the statue of the great Puritan in the heart of Bedford, and mused with my companion at a hallowed spot where once stood the "wicket-gate." Before I returned to London, I procured a copy of John Brown's *John Bunyan*, which occupies an honored place in my library. To this day Bunyan's Meeting House perpetuates the practices Bunyan initiated, and among others, the choice of the mode of baptism, although Bunyan himself was an immersionist.

Dr. Brown's seventh, eighth, and ninth lectures are devoted to a study of Thomas Binney and Charles H. Spurgeon, Robert W. Dale of Birmingham, and Alexander Maclaren of Manchester, holding all four to be truly representative of modern Puritanism. Binney from the first was recognized by the men of his own time as a lineal descendant of men of the Puritan days, preaching with a beauty and freshness all his own. Of the marvelous success of Spurgeon's preaching, voice, manner, substance, Dr. Brown thinks Spurgeon's popularity was largely due to his "perfectly natural" style of speech. No pulpit twang had he: pathos, humor, and an unshaken faith that God has spoken to us in the Holy Scriptures. "A born preacher" Brown calls him. Dr. Dale he puts upon a pedestal, and of Dr. Maclaren his praise is ardent and lofty. He thinks that English nonconformity gained new laurels and found new friends among the intellectual leaders and a new respect from the Established Church. That may well have been. Yet these superb minds served the middle estate and some of the working class.

As for Dale and Maclaren, to whom Brown devoted a lecture each, the contrast is striking, and this is true despite the fact that they were alike in industry and sermonic genius of a high order. Dale was theological and philosophical; Maclaren, Biblical and expository; and both made painstaking preparation. Dale wrote much, Maclaren but little apart from his expositions and sermonic volumes, and these masterfully. Dale appeared on many platforms at home and abroad; Maclaren was reluctant to leave his own pulpit, and the few times he was induced to accept invitations out of Manchester, it was necessary to bring pressure to bear upon him from every quarter. He was at his best in his own pulpit. Neither of these princes of the pulpit was what is known as a "popular preacher," although, as has been noted, persons of all walks of life heard them joyfully.

Binney, Spurgeon, Dale, Maclaren—representative preachers of modern Puritanism! What a quartet! A revival of interest in these extraordinary personages on the part of the modern minister could only be for his moral and spiritual gain. These four superb preachers are legendary to most of us of the High Calling. Dr. John Brown wrought a miracle at Yale when, it seemed, he raised these noble dead and made them live again, and not only for his hearers in New Haven, but for us also who read his book, *Puritan Preaching in England!*

Note: Dr. John Brown's massive biography, *John Bunyan, His Life, Times and Work*, as published in 1885, with new editions in 1886, 1887 and "Reprinted 1888, 1889, and 1900," is a volume which all lovers of the immortal allegory *The Pilgrim's Progress* should have on their shelves. The edition which I have is the Tercentenary Edition, revised by Frank Mott Harrison, with marginal notes, addenda, appendices, and an index of 21 pages. This volume was presented to me in Bedford in 1937, when I supplied the pulpit of Bunyan Meeting House in August of that year. This edition is profusely illustrated, and if there is such a thing as a "definitive biography," this is one.

In an appreciation of the late Reverend John Brown, by the Reverend J. D. Jones of Bournemouth, occurs this pertinent paragraph: "His work as minister and author bore his name and fame far beyond the bounds of Bedford. Yale University conferred the D.D. upon him in 1887. In 1899 the same great University invited him to deliver the Lyman Beecher Lectures on Preaching. Nor was he without honor in his own country. He had become a national figure, so far as Congregationalism was concerned, and in 1891 his brethren recognized his outstanding position by electing him Chairman of the Congregational Union of England and Wales."

III. CHARLES SILVESTER HORNE

The Romance of Preaching

In the spring of 1914, with World War I but three months away, a singularly winsome Englishman stood up to speak in the Yale Divinity School, the thirty-ninth lecturer in the widely acclaimed Course. Of years he was but forty-nine, and in love with life, humanity, and his high calling. The slender, magnetic speaker, so it fell out, was to give his "last full measure of devotion" to a series of addresses unsurpassed in the great succession, for eloquence, evangelistic fervor, and in the enduring impression left upon those who heard him.

The speaker was the Reverend Silvester Horne, minister of Whitfield's Tabernacle in the heart of London, member of Parliament, a brilliant and beloved leader of the Free Churches of England. Throughout a memorable week this welcome visitor to Yale delivered eight lectures under the arresting title, *The Romance of Preaching*. When these addresses appeared in a book bearing the same title, Dr. Charles Reynolds Brown, then dean of the Divinity School, wrote the introduction, in which he said:

Few lecturers have ever so gripped the divinity students, the larger audience of pastors in active service, and the thoughtful people of New Haven as did Silvester Horne when he spoke to us on *The Romance of Preaching*. . . . The intellectual distinction which marked his utterances, the fine literary form in which they were phrased, the moral passion which gave to their delivery that energy which belongs to words which are "spirit and life," together with the rare spiritual insight displayed, all combined to make notable the service rendered by Mr. Horne to Yale University. It seemed tragic that just three days after he had finished this course of lectures, he should suddenly be caught away like the prophet of old, from the deck of a steamer as he neared the city of Toronto, where he was to preach the next day at the University. Here, indeed, are his last words, spoken in an upper room to his brother ministers, younger and older, upon whom he had breathed his own spirit of intense devotion to the high task of proclaiming the Gospel of Christ!

The reception given this volume when it came off the press was exceptional for a work of its kind. Ministers of all denominations and of various theological views bought the book and read it with undisguised emotion. Nor was this surprising. The book came to us "wrapped in the solemn mystery of death," as Sir W. Robertson Nicoll once said of another book written by a minister cut down in his prime.

Ordinarily the Contents of a book, that age-old device for listing the chapter headings, while useful is seldom exciting. It is otherwise with Silvester Horne's *The Romance of Preaching*. The Contents of this book seem to be designed to whet the interest of every member of "the majestic Fraternity," a phrase coined by Horne and one worthy to live. Here are the subjects, appealing as an opulent menu to a hungry diner-out: I. The Servant of the Spirit; II. The First of the Apostles; III. The Apostolic Age; IV. The Royalty of the Pulpit: Athanasius, and Chrysostom; V. The Rulers of Peoples: Savonarola, Calvin, and John Knox; VI. The Founders of Freedom: John Robinson and the Pilgrim Fathers; VII. The Passion of Evangelism: Wesley and Whitefield; VIII. The Romance of Modern Preaching.

I

Some years ago John Spargo, a prominent Socialist, wrote a much-discussed article on "The Futility of the Pulpit," a ghastly title which describes the emotions of many a preacher when low in spirit on an especially "blue Monday." He has looked for results, failed to find them, and is haunted by the thought that he made a mistake when he chose the ministry as a life work. When such periods come, as they do to all of us of the preaching tribe, Silvester Horne has a word for discouraged ministers that is a veritable balm of Gilead, an elixir of new life. It is in the closing paragraph to his first lecture on "The Servant of the Spirit":

> Some trades and professions, it is clear, will die out as the kingdom of God comes to its own. But for every voice that carries inspiration to its fellows; for every soul that has some authentic word from the Eternal wherewith to guide and bless mankind there will always be a welcome. No changes of the future can cancel the commission of the preacher. . . . Let every village preacher who climbs into a rude rostrum, to give out a text and preach a sermon to a meagre handful of somewhat stolid hearers, remember to what majestic Fraternity he belongs and what romantic tradition he inherits.

When one reads this glorious passage, the enthusiasm which the delivery of these lectures inspired is more readily understood. To this concert pitch the entire series is attuned. There are no humorous sallies, no witty "asides," no anecdotes to speak of. The man is deadly in earnest. The time is short, oh, so much shorter than he thought; and he speaks, as the preachers of an older generation used to say, "as a dying man to dying men." This is one reason why the trumpet tones of the speaker rang in the memory of those who heard him those golden days at Yale—for days and months after the voice that gave the notes verity was hushed in the Great Silence.

> I feel as if this is the one thing to pray for [he cries]—That God will raise up a new race of genuine orators of the Evangel, who without any unworthy artifices will shake men's souls and thrill their hearts. . . . Let every preacher resolve he will be churchman and evangelist in one. The call of the church and the call of the wild are both to be heard, I think, in the soul of every true ambassador of Christ. We may not love Jerusalem less; but the song of the pioneer must be ever in our hearts and on our lips, "They shall build the old wastes—the ancient wilds,—they shall repair the waste cities,—the civilizations run to waste—the desolations of many generations."

In this pageant of great preachers passing by I select one not as well known to us as the others, Pastor John Robinson, a Pilgrim Father of majestic mien, and a wisdom not of this world.

Silvester Horne studied this half-forgotten scholar, preacher, and shepherd of the flock, and said of him as Tennyson said of another, that he "wore his weight of learning lightly as a flower." This is the man who inspired "the voyaging Mayflower" to brave the dangerous Atlantic, bidding that sturdy little ship and its valiant passengers adieu with a prayer that must have lingered in the memory of that heroic company forever. Horne speaks of John Robinson's "forceful writings," and cites this passage as a specimen for preachers to ponder:

As a woman, over-curiously trimmed, is to be suspected, so is a speech. And indeed he that goes about by eloquence, without firm ground of reason to persuade, goes about to deceive. As some are large in speech out of abundance of matter and upon due consideration, so the most multiply words either from weakness or vanity. Some excuse their tediousness, saying that they can not speak shorter, which is all one as if they said that they have unbridled tongues and inordinate passions setting them a-work. I have been many times drawn so dry, that I could not well speak any longer for want of matter; but I could ever speak as short as I would.

Commenting on this Horne says:

I ask you could the thing be better put? Could there be a better comparison than this of a highly-rhetorical speech or sermon to "a woman over-curiously trimmed"? Have we not had to listen to many discourses where you could not see the dress for the trimmings? It may be impossible to lay down any canons of good taste in this matter, but I shall venture to submit to you, that the Puritan frugality of illustration and adornment is far more effective than the prodigality and profligacy of quotation and ornament which is sometimes popular among us today, and which may dazzle, but does not really subdue and persuade an audience.

Mr. Horne instances the sermon that Robinson preached to the Pilgrims for the last time before they set sail. He found his text in the Book of Ezra, "I proclaimed a fast there at the river Ahava that we might afflict ourselves before God, to seek of Him a right way for us, and for our little ones, and for all our substance." Could any other text have been so appropriate? Horne speaks:

Often when I study the preaching of our fathers, "I am impressed by the fact that they knew their Bibles better than we do. They had less of the light of criticism, but they had, I think, a more exact knowledge of Holy Writ. To this day this great territory of Scripture is like a modern continent, extreme and unhealthy at certain well-known centres, and vast tracts of country uncultivated and unknown. How many of those listening to me have been led against the "Philistines at Keilah," or have heard "a fast proclaimed at the river Ahava"?

Not many we fear.

II

Sir William Robertson Nicoll, so long the able editor of *The British Weekly*, and a bookman of parts, knew the great preachers of his generation, knew Joseph Parker and Charles H. Spurgeon, knew Alexander Maclaren and Robert W. Dale, knew John Watson and Canon Liddon, and he knew, admired, and loved Charles Silvester Horne. In Sir William's *Princes of the Church*, a book that every wide-awake dominie should have on the shelves of his library and within easy reach, this editor-preacher says of Horne:

His great and supreme gift, however, was the gift of speech. He was what is called a born speaker, and the man was behind the speech. Preaching was his delight. His Yale lectures dealt, we believe, with the romance of preaching, and told the story of great Gospel victories in the past. His own beliefs were deeply evangelical. He was broad and sympathetic; he welcomed thought and study; he was never tied to forms. . . . Those who imagined that Mr. Horne habitually preached on the political controversies of his day did not know the man. In the pulpit he dealt chiefly with the high and solemn mysteries of faith. . . . He could rise on occasions to almost matchless eloquence. Victory beamed from his brow. He believed in God, man, and woman. Through the worst squalor he saw the transfiguration.

From these vivid sentences one can fashion a fairly accurate likeness of this gifted preacher who perished in his prime. Sir Robertson Nicoll wrote that Horne never knew how to husband the taper. Alas, there are many like him, and their light goes out too soon, and leaves us to sorrow. Some men accomplish more in fifty years than others in seventy, but the advice of the editor of

The British Weekly that the taper of life should be husbanded with humble faith and pious care is good.

I recall a conversation I had with a brother-minister who heard Silvester Horne at Yale on this high business for the Lord. "I can never forget Horne," said this friend. "He left an indelible mark for good on my soul. He was so earnest, so eloquent, so much in love with his work, and he won our hearts. I went back to my own difficult field, humbled, yes, and eager to go into the work again. I bought his book and have read it so often and marked it so plentifully that it looks a little shabby perhaps, but money couldn't buy it, even if a new copy were available."

When Silvester Horne was installed in his ministry at Kensington in 1889, the great Dr. Dale of Birmingham preached the sermon to the congregation, in the course of which he said:

> Pray for him that his courage may be high; that his faith may have the fortitude of granite rocks; that the fires of his love for God may burn higher and higher, and with a clearer flame as the months and years pass by; that his zeal for your righteousness and your full realization of the Christian redemption may grow in intensity; that his joy in the vision of God may become fuller and fuller.

Shall we not say with joy and thanksgiving that the prayers of Dr. Dale and the church at Kensington were answered?

> A death like thine hath called a truce,
> Heard about thee many a mile,
> And men forgot their daily use
> To stand beside thy grave awhile.

IX

SHEPHERDS OF THE
★ FLOCK ★

I am the good shepherd, and know my sheep, and am known of mine. As the Father knoweth me, even so know I the Father: and I lay down my life for the sheep.

—John 10:14, 15

1. WILLIAM FRASER McDOWELL

Of all the volumes of lectures in this Series, Bishop McDowell's is the one that I have resorted to most often and have marked the margins of the pages most liberally. It has been in my hands so often that the binding is a trifle loose, and this despite the fact that I am a careful man in handling books. How account for this favoritism in a Series I revere as a whole and which contains among its seventy volumes at least a dozen that I have reread several times? This is not the most scholarly of the lot, neither is it the most brilliant. Literally I should suppose it does not rank with a score of other volumes I might mention. Why then am I so fond of *Good Ministers of Jesus Christ,* the discourses given by Bishop McDowell at Yale in 1917?

I think it is because of both the subject matter and the beneficent spirit of the author, which imparts a month-of-June-and-roses atmosphere to the book. I also think my affection for the volume is due, in part at least, to this impression: When I read it I seem to see the stately form of the Bishop as I once saw him in a pulpit, benignant and courtly, preaching his famous sermon from the text in John 6:9, "There is a lad here who has five barley loaves and two fishes, but what are these among so many?" He took the first clause, "There is a lad here." Yes, the lad with his luncheon! What a sermon it was, and how it gripped the large congregation which heard it in good old Bloomington, Illinois.

Still again, I am drawn to *Good Ministers of Jesus Christ* because of the pertinency of its themes, which go to the very heart of our faith, to wit:

I. *The Ministry of Revelation*
"Show us the Father."
II. *The Ministry of Redemption*
"He shall save his people from their sins."
III. *The Ministry of Incarnation*
"The Word was made flesh, and dwelt among us."
IV. *The Ministry of Reconciliation*
"We are ambassadors for Christ."
V. *The Ministry of Rescue*
"The Son of man is come to seek and to save that which was lost."
VI. *The Ministry of Conservation*
"It is not the will of your Father which is in heaven, that one of these . . . should perish."
VII. *The Ministry of Cooperation*
"We are workers together . . . and members one of another."
VIII. *The Ministry of Inspiration*
"The Spirit of the Lord is upon me."

I

Bishop McDowell was adept in the use of illustrations in public address, and these lectures are notable in this respect. Whoever it was that called illustrations the "windows of a sermon" had an inspiration. He might have gone further, however, and said that some discourses are sermon "glass houses" and he would have told the truth. Artistry, temperateness, and a nice sense of propriety are involved in this aspect of homiletics. While the Bishop led all the others in the use of incident and anecdote, he refrained from excess and showed discrimination in his selections. Long illustrations in a sermon are hard to manage, consume too much time, and may get out of hand. Yet, when employed by a powerful speaker, a lengthy illustration can be tremendously effective. Take, for example, an incident related by McDowell in his discussion of "The Ministry of Incarnation," and observe he gave credit to the source:

William Fraser McDowell

There was an English missionary in India who always had trouble with his accounts and finances. He was not at all a capable business man. He spent all his money for missionary work, but not according to the plans. He got his accounts mixed and could not balance his books. And, of course, that could not be endured. Unless a missionary or a minister is capable of double-entry bookkeeping he has no capacity at all except for mischief. So many seem to think. Many congregations would apparently rather have a business man's administration than to have a true prophet in their pulpit. This poor missionary was dismissed as being unfit for missionary work, whereas he was only unfit for bookkeeping. He went off alone to a section where he would not be bothered by accounts. "Several years later a woman was visiting a distant village in the jungle. She tried to make the simple village folk understand what manner of person Jesus of Nazareth was. She told them how he was the poor man's friend, how he used to eat with them and visit their homes, how he used to go about healing wherever there was sickness, how the children used to run after him in the street and clamber about his knees. Her description seemed to meet with an unusually intelligent response; and as she finished some one exclaimed, 'Miss Sahib, we know him well; he has been living here for years!' Amazed, the woman discovered that this missionary had settled there on his own account. It was he who fetched the old men and women their water and their food. Where anyone was sick it was he who would sit outside the door until evening and then come in to watch through the night. When plague and cholera visited the village he was the intrepid nurse. In the old man who could not keep books the people of that village had seen and recognized Jesus Christ." (Robinson: The Interpretation of the Character of Christ, pages 21, 22)

In speaking on "The Ministry of Reconciliation," the Bishop draws on his personal experience:

Many years ago I was riding across a part of Ohio with a well-known judge of a superior court, a devout man and wise. We talked of many things in earth and heaven and under the earth. I was still young enough to be able to ask large questions, which ability belongs to the unspoiled wisdom of youth. Finally I put this large question to that famous man: "What is the most important and the most difficult thing in the world?" We both smiled. After a moment the judge turned to me and answered: "The question is large and staggering, but proper. I think the most important and the most difficult thing in the world is to get the spirit and principles of Jesus to prevail in the lives and relations of men." And the train rolled on as though no epiphany had come, but to that young minister the bushes we passed seemed burning bushes out of which the voice of God had come again as in the olden time. "To get the spirit and principles of Jesus to prevail in the lives and relations of men!" That would seem to be the task of the ministry of reconciliation all the time, and doing it would seem to glorify that task.

The evangelistic note in these lectures is paramount and at times it rises to a passion. It is especially strong and vibrant in Lecture V, "The Ministry of Rescue." In one fair-sized paragraph the lecturer employs two incidents to enforce his appeal for *expectancy* as an antecedent to winning souls:

A minister was complaining to Mr. Spurgeon about the small number of conversions in his ministry. Mr. Spurgeon said, with an apparent seriousness, which was only apparent and not real: "You surely do not expect conversions as the result of every sermon, do you?" "O, certainly not," was the quick reply of one who did not want to seem to have unreasonable expectations. Then the great preacher cut clear through the case by the quiet words: "Of course if you do not expect them, you will not have them." Only those who look for them see them, only those who must have them will have them. I think many men have the desire, but not the expectation. They have adopted a low standard of expectation. They are quite willing to attempt great things for God, to engage in large programs, superb enterprises. But they do not expect great things from God. The blight of small expectation is as fatal as the blight of small motive. Many a ministry is dead, and many a congregation ready to be buried, because they no longer expect any mighty thing to happen before their eyes. Think of that story that is told of President Finney. He laid down before the Lord a long list of people for whose conversion he earnestly prayed. He had upon him the passion of desire that they should be saved. He poured out his very soul in eager asking that God would give him the longing of his heart. And he wound up his prayer with this stroke that fairly takes the breath of conventional men: "And thou knowest, O Lord, that in these matters I am not accustomed to be denied." No wonder great things happened to him. God does not disappoint men who have such expectancy of faith and have it all the time. For the vice of occasionalism in expectation is as deadly as the vice of smallness.

II

The shepherd heart glorifies this series, and the pastoral ministry is highly exalted. Bishop McDowell quotes Matthew Simpson, "The church by its neglect of childhood loses more people to the Kingdom of God than all our revivals are able to bring back." Then he adds to this strong statement his own, which is even stronger. Thus:

Our churches are organized as adult bodies, with incidental reference to children. "The great blunder of our churches is the blunder of 'adultism.' " Our church services and creedal statements are made for adults, people of maturity. Our sermons are for "grown-ups," with occasional "little sermons" to children. The average sermon to children, preached by a man who does not like to do it and thinks he must, may be described in the language of the honest Scotchwoman's verdict on her own photograph: "It's a sad sight." Men are afraid to get the reputation of being children's preachers. They are even careful not to seem to be getting or keeping children in large numbers in the church. They would rather have their churches known as the church of the automobiles than the church of the baby carriages. They will report their accessions after a revival or a retreat or at the end of the year, adding with evident pride the words, "Mostly adults." Adults are already somebody. They belong in Nicodemus's class. He and they have to be born again, made all over from above before they could even see the kingdom of God. That is the kind of somebodies they are. Of course they may add considerably to the social standing or the financial strength of the church, and that is very important. Children enrolled are in a different class. They are not yet somebody.

Strong friendships between strong men are strangely beautiful. Bishop Edwin Holt Hughes and Bishop William Fraser McDowell were lifelong friends. They loved to be together and were unhappy when circumstances separated them for but a few months. They had similar tastes in books, pictures, poetry, music, and a fondness for God's great out-of-doors. How fitting then that a Jonathan should pay tribute to his David. The paragraph which follows is taken from Dr. Hughes' autobiography, *I Was Made a Minister:*

William Fraser McDowell continued to live in Washington as a retired bishop, so that our long-time intimacy helped to dovetail the two administrations into unity. He gave solicited counsel, but never interference. He was a magnificent predecessor. Between us there existed that wordless affection which often marks the relations of two men. At his funeral services I pointed out that the historic friendships had been between men—David and Jonathan, and Damon and Pythias. I have elsewhere written that as he grew older he walked the path of sanctity that lies between two worlds. Yet I never detected in him the slightest self-consciousness of superiority. The surrender of the years was made complete. Life was given over wholly to God, as his deeds of kindness and his will and testament proved. The shadows lengthened for us both, but they fell far toward the eastern horizons: they never dropped between us. He moved out of this life while asking an anxious question about my sick wife—and stepped quickly into another Land to be greeted by Clotilda Lyon McDowell, his own faithful and brilliant helpmate.[1]

To which should be added, and with a singular appropriateness, the last sentence of Bishop Hughes' own life story:

And I will meet you in the morning.

II. WILLIAM PIERSON MERRILL

On a pleasant day in 1947 I sat in Dr. Merrill's apartment at Number One Lexington Avenue, New York City. It was there that I subjected him to a barrage of questions about the lectures he gave at Yale in 1922. He had received me with what we used to call "Old World courtesy," a phrase which, I fear, has lost something of its one-time luster. I suggested he write down his answers to my queries, and he replied: "I am sorry I can't do what you suggest, for I haven't a secretary. Being 'emeritus,' I have to do my own work. By the way, have you heard the definition given, I believe, by a prominent wit, from two Latin words, 'e' meaning 'out,' and 'meritus' meaning 'he deserved it'? I told that to my congregation when they gave me the title."

I followed his merry quip with the story of a famous university professor who, at the close of a brilliant career, was made an

---
[1] P. 128.

emeritus, and a dinner given in honor of the event. Among those present was a friend of the professor who was not familiar with the meaning of "emeritus," and at the close of the dinner, congratulated him warmly, saying, "I am sure this is a deserved distinction, but I can't see why it wasn't given you long before your retirement." Being a gentleman, Dr. Merrill laughed heartily, but I had a faint misgiving it was not new to him.

"How long did it take you to prepare for the Yale engagement?" I inquired.

"I can't measure the time taken for the preparation, for it ran over a considerable period. I hit upon my subject almost immediately, influenced in that probably by the tremendous struggle then going on between the Fundamentalists and the Liberals."

"Did you use manuscript?"

"Yes, it is my method of speaking on such an occasion, but I spoke freely and was not fettered by the manuscript," Dr. Merrill rejoined. In using this method of speaking he had plenty of company, for I estimate that more than two-thirds of the lecturers in this Course read their discourses. That there were remarkable exceptions to this rule, is true, and these have been noted in the proper place.

Merrill was picked by Henry van Dyke to be his successor at the famous Brick Church, New York City. Dr. Merrill did not tell me this; I read it in Tertius van Dyke's biography of his father. On page 297 of that book occurs this statement:

> Meanwhile in the Sixth Presbyterian Church of Chicago, where he had quietly sat in the rear pew, during a service, Henry van Dyke had found Dr. William P. Merrill. Matters went swiftly forward and on October 8th (the year was 1911), Dr. Merrill was installed pastor of the Brick Church. Henry van Dyke took part in the installation of his third successor . . . and thus concluded the official side of an extraordinary relationship between a church and pastor.

Dr. Merrill served this historic church for twenty-seven fruitful years, becoming emeritus for life at the close of his pastorate.

Dr. Merrill chose as his subject at Yale, *The Freedom of the Preacher*, an engaging title. Likewise, he chose to follow, and rather closely too, the pattern of a dozen or so who preceded him in the Course and several who followed him. Now when so many in the same Course discuss the minister as "Pastor," "Preacher," "Priest," and "Administrator," it requires a genius, or a humorist, or both, to bring a fresh and original treatment of such lecture-worn themes. To be sure, the fact that each lecturer addresses a new student audience relieves the situation not a little, but what about the faculty, many of whom have served the Divinity School for years? Aye, there's the rub! It needs to be said here that Job had nothing over these lecture-scarred professors in the virtue of patience, nor Barnabas in the quality of good will. Then, too, it should be remembered that the charm of personality in a speaker and the nobility of his character, like love, can cover a multitude of repetitious sins.

Dr. Merrill had both the ingenuity and the sense of humor necessary to traverse these familiar paths as if he were blazing trails and enjoying it immensely. He stepped nimbly where angels could use their wings, and out of his rich mine of experiences drew forth much fine gold. More practical than poetical, he said some of the best things on preaching, pastoral ministry and public worship that have been said in the entire Lecture Course, thereby proving himself to be a wise and helpful counselor.

It is probably true in many instances, as Dr. Merrill asserted in the beginning of his first lecture, that "the prophet is the preacher's ideal" and, equally true, that "few attain that ideal." Vision and fearlessness are basic in the prophet's equipment, and there are many good men in the ministry who do not possess either in distinctive measure. Not only is this true, but given these superior qualities, the conditions under which the twentieth century preacher works make the prophetic ministry difficult to achieve. Once in a Wranglers Club meeting in Detroit, a distinguished young clergyman read an able paper on "The Preacher as a Prophet." In the discussion that followed, an Episcopal rector, whose mind had a razor edge and who was noted for his wit, heaved a great sigh and with the solemnity of an actor declaiming, "To be, or not to be," erupted: "Sirs, when I graduated from the seminary I dreamed of being a prophet, and when I went to my first parish I still cherished that dream, but, Sirs, by the Lord Harry, I have deteriorated into an ecclesiastical chambermaid!"

Uproarious laughter followed this candid eruption, but reviewing the episode here one wonders if Shelley did not express the feeling of some of us when he wrote: "Our sincerest laughter with some pain is fraught."

Dr. Merrill was himself prophetic when he uttered these burning words:

> Every preacher should go into his pulpit every Sunday full of faith in the absolute and unquestionable pre-eminence of the spiritual; fearful lest the divine flame of the prophetic gift should be quenched in some child or youth there present; in a very agony of dread lest, through dullness or insensitiveness on his own part, he thicken rather than keep plastic the cooling and hardening surface of the souls before him. "Thirty minutes to raise the dead," is Ruskin's definition of a sermon.

These passionate words stir my memory of a preacher of singular power in my own communion to whom I owe much, Dr. George Hamilton Combs, of Kansas City, now an emeritus, but still preaching with fire, if not fury. I heard him say once that "preaching, real preaching, is blood-letting; it pulls at the very heart of the preacher and for the time depletes him utterly, and his virtue goes out of him." That was certainly true of Dr. Combs. I have observed him following the delivery of a sermon that struck fire, a shrunken figure, a weary and spent eagle.

Returning now to Dr. Merrill, still speaking on the prophet in the pulpit:

> It would be sufficient to justify the existence of the American Church, the time and strength and resources spent in its maintenance, if somewhere in this land, sometime within the next decade, the divine flame in the soul of a single youth were, through the influence of the church, kept from dying, fanned and fed until it became a fire in the bones, and an Isaiah, an Amos, or a Jeremiah appeared in our national life. One such prophetic figure would be worth infinitely more than the cost of the church. And part of the glory of preaching is that one never knows whether the ministry of his own pulpit may not be the humble but effectual means of saving a true man of God from death of the spirit, and leading him into the exercise of the prophetic function.

The sentiment so well expressed in the paragraph quoted, an ennobling one, is a favorite theme of the older poets, and nowhere is it given more beautiful yet mournful expression than in Thomas Gray's "Elegy Written in a Country Church-yard." It is part of the high mission of the preacher to see to it that there are no forgotten "village Hampdens" or "mute, inglorious Miltons" in the congregation who listen to him Sunday after Sunday. Preaching which fails to inspire usually fails to enlighten. More's the pity.

It was good for the students at Yale to hear such sage observations as these: "The preacher must make his way toward freedom in the pulpit clearly and surely in three acts:—the art of gathering material, the art of clear and ordered thinking, and the art of effective delivery"; and likewise, this: "There are too many men in the pulpit who know a good deal, and think well enough, but have never gained the mastery of effective and simple language, through much companionship with the best writers, through deliberate and painstaking cultivation of a homely, forceful use of words. A preacher without skill in words is like a knight with no knowledge of sword play."

It would be a pity to bring this chapter to an end without a passage from the last lecture which bears the title: "In Christ."

Freedom from self; that is the preacher's first, and last, and deepest need. Given that he is free indeed. The dark shade that hovers over his best work is his own shadow. He never finds himself until he has lost himself. He is never free until that Old Man of the Sea is off his back. And how he clings! How he finds his way back, and springs on one's shoulders, and holds tight, just when one thinks he is free forever from the incubus.

A strange tale is that little story from the Norseland of a man who was uneasily, though dimly aware of someone ever following him. He could not be sure that he heard steps; he could see no one; but the consciousness of a malicious sprite or troll dogging his steps grew ever clearer. He wandered far to escape the pursuer, even to the lonely, frozen North; but the steps sounded ever louder. At last he turned suddenly,—and was face to face with himself.

Two men, according to Dr. Merrill, were passing in a railroad car through one of the gigantic industrial districts which lie on the outskirts of our great cities. One of them pulled down the shade. "Why do you do that?" asked the other. "Because I hate to see that dehumanizing place" was the answer. "I know it is wrong, but there is nothing I can seem to do to help it." "There is one thing you can do," came the answer. "What is that?" "Stop pulling down the shade."

William Pierson Merrill was never guilty of pulling down the shade to shut out the ugly facts of life, nor has he abused the freedom in which his ministerial life so rejoiced.

III. RAYMOND CALKINS

On rereading *The Eloquence of Christian Experience*, which is the felicitous title to Dr. Calkins' Yale lectures given in 1926, the impressions gained by the first reading were confirmed and greatened. I felt I had been to church and in the hush of the sanctuary knelt at the altar rail and partook of the Holy Communion. It is a strong treatise on the subject and although both theological and philosophical, it is human, warm, and friendly. There is nothing in this volume on how and what to preach in the technical sense; there is in it just about everything that goes into great preaching: the note of certainty, Biblical language, and illustrations drawn from both Old and New Testaments.

The title of these lectures is singularly attractive. No other name that Dr. Calkins could have selected would look so good or sound so mellifluous. It is a choice subject for a sermon and doubtless has been so used by many who read the volume. To church people generally there is little appeal in such a title as *Lectures on Preaching*; but as for *The Eloquence of Christian Experience*, here is a title of wide appeal.

There is a letter in the introduction to these lectures which is too important for any reader to overlook. It was written a hundred years ago by the author's grandfather in reply to one received from his son, then at Yale College, asking for advice about entering the ministry. Only the last paragraph is included here, but it is sufficient to indicate the kind of a family heritage Dr. Calkins cherishes and also the seriousness with which a "call" to the ministry was regarded in New England a century ago.

... To be a minister, comfortably settled over a comfortable people, with a nice comfortable church, a comfortable salary, with no ideas of what mankind is doing save what comes through some comfortably conservative religious newspaper, that is not only behind the age but behind all ages; with no charities save those doled out through a few comfortably safe societies that once a month take their "collections by appointment," with no thought save to get through the world with ease, without rapping the knuckles of anybody who happens to be rich or "respectable,"—rather than see you such a minister, I would have you a hewer of wood or a drawer of water.

This letter in its entirety deserves a place in one of the anthologies of "The World's Great Letters," but the chances for its inclusion are slim, alas! Moreover, any minister who reads this letter and does not feel *uncomfortable* has missed his calling.

On Religious Experience

Dr. Calkins defines his use of the term "religious experience," as meaning the contact of "our whole human personality with God." "It is," he affirms, "no mere preoccupation with inner states and moods and feelings. It is an immediate apprehension of the reality which lies beyond and behind and within all the framework of the invisible universe." . . . "By religious experience in the deepest sense, we mean that we are immediately aware of a spiritual world made known to us in, and through the actions of the soul, no less truly than the physical world is made known to us through the organic motions which these sensations originate."

Experience thus understood, and thus defined, he holds, is the final basis for certainty in religion. It is in this sense that one may affirm that experience is the solid foundation of a truly Christian apologetic and the best basis for a philosophy of the Christian religion. The soul's experience of God is thus the ultimate ground of religious certainty. The possibility of this experience is conceded by both philosophy and science. Modern psychological method does not and cannot explain it away. It lies within the grasp of every earnest man, and once he has grasped this, no further proof, in the strict sense of the existence of God, is needed or demanded.

Calkins holds that all great preachers are distinguished by a simplicity of style. He reminds us that the Old Testament prophets were great preachers, and that their language is as direct and simple as their message is clear and easy to understand. Bible preaching is always positive because it is the utterance of a firsthand experience of God. Martineau used to go to hear Spurgeon preach. A friend asked him why he did: "You do not believe a word that he says." "No," replied Martineau, "but he does."

The high note of Christian certainty is in major throughout these lectures. No "grand perhaps" can satisfy Dr. Calkins; he is magnificently sure that Christianity has the answers to the questions that all the world is asking. He seeks to recover for the modern pulpit the certainty of St. Paul and his co-workers; the certainty of Peter and John before their captors, when under pain of death they cried, "We cannot but speak the things which we have seen and heard." "We need the recovery," he holds, "in our vocabulary of the familiar symbols of the Christian experience, the well-worn and loved battle flags under which generations of Christians have fought a good fight and won their victory."

The Christian experience of God alone answers the quest of the human soul for certainty. It alone is the unshakable ground of Christian faith and of Christian knowledge. It alone gives us the key to a truly Christian theology. The possession of the Christian experience of God is the source from which all Christian preaching flows. It alone provides the temper and the equipment of a true Christian pastor. Calkins defines Christian theology as the effort to describe in intelligible terms the report of the Christian experience. There would be no theology if there were no experience. Experience comes first. If one be a Christian he will always want, in a way, to be a theologian. Because religion comes first, it does not follow that theology does not come at all.

The Bible fares bountifully in these lectures. Only one equipped with both secular knowledge and spiritual discernment born of Christian experience will be able to comprehend and interpret the messages of the Bible, for the Bible is more than a record of man's experience of God. It is the record also of a unique, an authoritative, and a final revelation of the moral character of God to man. If a Christian preacher does not believe this, then he lacks the basic belief on which for two thousand years Christian theology has rested. It has rested on the idea, to use Maurice's magnificent phrase, "that in the Bible we do not have men's thoughts about God, but we do have God's thoughts about men."

On Preaching

I cannot get away from the idea that, if a man is going to speak for God, God has got to choose him for the work. I am sorry for a good many people today. But on the whole the man I am the sorriest for is the man who stands before a Christian congregation without feeling that God has put him there.

There is no satisfaction like the satisfaction of a human being who stands before a company, large or small, and declares to them the oracle of God which it has been put in his mouth to speak. . . . The humblest preacher in the land if he be that kind of a preacher, can know a joy which no one else can know. And from my soul I envy the man who is going to taste it for the first time and know it for what it is.

It is the Bible preacher, always finding in it inexhaustible spiritual treasure, who keeps himself fresh year after year and never fails to satisfy the human hunger and thirst for God.

Calkins quotes with enthusiasm this from Bishop Quayle: "Preaching is the art of making a sermon and delivering it? Why, no, that is not preaching. Preaching is the art of making a preacher and delivering *that*."[1]

There is a direct connection between great themes and great ministries. If you will render account of the preachers who have long and fruitful ministries you will find that almost invariably their preaching is on high subjects, far removed from the trivial, never degenerating into superficial comments on current events.

The pulpit is the grandest, freest rostrum on earth. A parish minister might seem to be the hired chaplain of the people who pay him. As a matter of fact he never thinks of it; and what is more they never think of it. . . . A congregation except in the rarest instances, does not dismiss its minister because of what he preaches, but because of what he does not preach.

[1] Dr. Harold Cooke Phillips also quotes this definition of preaching by Bishop Quayle.

Raymond Calkins

In Cambridge there resides a young preacher whose rare privilege it is to know Dr. Calkins intimately and to receive from time to time his patriarchal blessing. He thus writes of his distinguished neighbor:

Dr. Calkins has the rare gift of taking a simple incident in everyday life and telling it in such an interesting fashion as to hold the attention of all. He has the gift also of great humor, and a flawless English style which would grace the pages of *The Atlantic Monthly*. I have often urged him to collect these little stories and have them published. For example, our talk on one occasion had to do with the purchase of a pair of new rubbers in a Boston store. He described how disreputable his old ones were and his purchase of the new. He then described his sense of guilt in determining to leave behind his old rubbers! He left them in the store, on the subway and in the home of a friend, all of whom conspired to return them to him. Like the famous cat, those rubbers always came back. This simple outline seems quite bare, but as told by him it was priceless.

I first met Dr. Calkins when as a student at Yale Divinity School I heard him deliver the Lyman Beecher Lectures on *The Eloquence of Christian Experience*. He based his whole lectures around the words of St. Paul to Timothy: "O Timothy, keep that which is committed to thy trust." He returned again and again to that point, and after these many years it still impresses me.

Dr. Calkins is a careful and accurate student of the Bible and is always able to fit into any schedule of subjects. . . . He never "hums or haws" in his speech, but every word that proceeds out of his mouth seems well thought out, aptly phrased and seasoned with salt. . . . He reads many books, with discrimination and insight. He is President of The Directors of the General Theological Library in Boston, which lends theological books to clergymen and church workers. I count it one of the blessings of my life that for the past four years I have had the blessing of his presence, the inspiration of his preaching, and the kindly encouragement of so eloquent a preacher of Christ Jesus.

Dr. Calkins published, in 1944, a book entitled *The Romance of the Ministry*, one of the choicest volumes on the subject to be found anywhere. Place it alongside Charles Silvester Horne's *The Romance of Preaching*, and here are two books worth a prominent and permanent place in the library of every preacher, young or old. Dr. Calkins closes his book on *The Romance of the Ministry* with a personal reflection which goes to the heart of the subject:

LOOKING BACK UPON IT ALL . . . I WOULD LIKE TO LIVE IT ALL OVER AGAIN, FOR MY LIFE HAS BEEN PURE POETRY, REAL ROMANCE FROM FIRST TO LAST. THERE IS NO MORE ROMANTIC CAREER THAN THAT OF A MINISTER OF JESUS CHRIST.

Note: As this is written, Dr. Calkins is eighty years old, having had fifty-three years of preaching, twenty-eight of which were spent with the First Church (Congregational) of Cambridge, Massachusetts. He has written many books, addressed many meetings; and in this time of Sunset and Evening Star is still active and with the exception of deafness, enjoying, for his years, excellent health. A sermon by this strong man of God is still an event, and people throng the church to hear him.

IV. ALBERT EDWARD DAY

Mt. Vernon Place Methodist Church, Baltimore, is imposing and well located, with a record of brilliant ministers. Dr. Day is in his second pastorate with this church and enjoying it to the fullest. I want to share a goodly part of the letter he wrote me in answer to the questionnaire I sent to all living lecturers in the Lyman Beecher course. It is characteristic of the man:

DEAR DR. JONES:

I have just returned from vacation and, at the first opportunity, am answering your generous letter of July 20th.

When the invitation to deliver the Lyman Beecher Lectures came, I was sick in bed with influenza. It was an awesome and humbling yet exciting and exalting experience. Such an opportunity had never even crossed the landscape of my dreams. Remembering the distinguished men who had occupied the lectureship, I felt that I was not worthy to unloose the latchet of their homiletic shoes. But with the unexpected summons, there came a comforting sense of mission and a confidence that He who had opened such a door would help me to enter it and fulfil the responsibility which lay beyond the threshold.

It was almost exactly a year from the date of the summons to the date of the lectures. . . . While the entire year was a time of research, meditation, prayer, the immediate preparation required about four months. It was during this intensive period of creative labor that the lectures as given finally took shape.

I used neither manuscript nor notes. That seemed like a foolhardy adventure to some; others said it could not be done. But I had been preaching in such fashion from the beginning. I knew the increased power it gave to the spoken word. I thought it might encourage the divinity students to try such a method of delivery in their own ministry.

Events put me to a severe test in the matter. Only two weeks before the date, my elbow was shattered in a fall, and I went to Yale with my arm in a sling and suffering a ceaseless pain that made sleep almost impossible. But the unforgettable kindness of the Luccocks, who dressed and undressed me, put me to bed at night with tender solicitude and guarded my days, and the grace of God who seemed to find in my weakness His opportunity, enabled me to fulfil my intention and to give the eight lectures without manuscript or notes.

I have occupied a number of other lectureships at colleges and universities and am humbly grateful for their gracious hospitality, but none equalled the Lyman Beecher Lectures in the emotions awakened, the vistas opened, the awesome sense of destiny that accompanied them. When I sat on the platform that first day and Dean Weigle read the names of those who had preceded me in that office, involuntarily I said to myself, "Albert Day, what are *you* doing here?" I still wonder at the providence that brought me there but will be eternally grateful for the high privilege which, by the mercy of God, was mine.

Cordially yours,
Albert E. Day

I

Dr. Day was the first of the Lyman Beecher lecturers to devote an entire course to psychology and its relation to preaching and the preacher, on the general subject, *Jesus and Human Personality*. Fifteen years later Dr. Leslie D. Weatherhead, who had become an authority in this field, chose the same subject, though he gave it a different title, and developed the theme more intimately and experimentally than did Dr. Day. The American speaks here primarily as a minister. The Englishman spoke as both preacher and psychologist on something like a fifty-fifty basis. Dr. Day was a kind of John the Baptist preparing the way for Dr. Weatherhead, who is regarded among ministers here and abroad as a specialist in the realm of psychotherapy.

Both Dr. Day and Dr. Weatherhead are daring exegetes of the Scriptures. They give the impression of trying hard to get back to the real person of Jesus Christ and his essential gospel. The exegetical freedom they enjoy gives to their writings a zestful interest to many readers, and also subjects them to a cross-fire of criticism from conservative theologians. In Lecture IV, "The Ideal Person," Dr. Day, speaking of the personality of Jesus, says:

We, ourselves, have come to the conclusion that some things written about him are not true, and we are glad that they are not. And yet we let our people continue to think that they are true and we wonder why they are not enthusiastic about him. We have found great help for the discipleship of his mind and heart in reading the records with a disciplined liberty which can say: "That does not sound like Jesus; he never said it. That does not look like Jesus; he never did it. Ah! that is like the man of Calvary and I take it to my heart." But we pass the Gospels on to our laymen with an all-or-nothing gesture which has refused them the right of discrimination or has not given them any clue to a method of discrimination. And the result has been often a reaction which said, "If it is all or nothing, then it must be nothing, for I cannot take it all."

And again:

Knowing the kind of a Man he was, we can be rather sure that he did not destroy the herd of Gadarene swine nor rebuff the Syrophoenician woman who came to him for help, nor curse a fig tree because it offered no fruit to his hunger, nor send a disciple down to the lake to find a fish with enough money lodged in its throat to pay the temple tax, nor espouse the doctrines of the apocalyptics with their notions of a militaristic God. It is by this process of discovery of a central reality and the enthronement of that Reality in the seat of history that the person of Jesus has at last revealed itself before one preacher's mind. He knows the peril involved in such a process. He can appreciate the scorn with which a laborious student like Goguel speaks of the "host of literary men and philosophers" who are "advancing in good order to take possession of the territory abandoned by historians in their retreat." Imagination and devotion cannot take the place of technique in the writing of history. But even Goguel confesses, "In order to understand the thought of Jesus we must have or must acquire the spirit of a Christian. Erudition is indispensable, but where there is nothing else an essential element is lacking. The Jesus whom it will paint will not be the real Jesus. . . . In order to understand Jesus the historian ought to have in himself something that is like Jesus."

Such subjects as "Personality and Society," "The Secret of Personality," "Personality and Success," "Personality and Self-Respect," "Personality and Comradeship," and "Personality and Moral Failure" are of absorbing interest to hosts of people, and this lecturer handles his excellent material skillfully and in a warm, friendly spirit. When it is remembered that Dr. Day stood up at Yale and spoke without manuscript or notes, the effect upon his hearers must have been one of rapt attention and a satisfaction that was not simulated.

Speaking on "The Realization of Jesus" Day has this critical comment on much of modern preaching:

Abstraction, generalization, verbalization, are the besetting sins of the ministry. People are urged to "come to Jesus," to "accept Jesus as Saviour," to "believe on Jesus," to "profess Jesus," but are not given any specific directions which will make those exhortations something more than mere evangelistic verbiage or provide for those who hear them a technique for the appropriation of those rich values for personality which are found in him. The result is that many who sing most easily "Jesus saves" are not saved from the ills which mar life. They believe with much assurance but are not blessed with any noticeable deliverance from crippling tendencies in human nature. They accept Christ but are not any more acceptable than some who are said to reject him. They "come to Jesus" but do not seem to be as near to his moral and spiritual beauty as many who apparently stay away.

II

The first chapter in these lectures, published in 1934, Dr. Day tells us was not part of the course as delivered at Yale. The subject is "Preaching and Personality," and one of the most valuable in the book. Preachers should love it. For instance, this fine dissertation on an experience which every preacher must know somewhere along the ministerial way:

> Every preacher knows too the pang of facing a congregation with something which an hour before was to his own heart a living, fascinating characterization of reality, and then of having that creation disintegrate under influences emanating from his congregation, leaving him with halting mind and horrified heart, aware that what he is and believes and has felt are neither understood nor appreciated. The most brilliant do not escape such frustrations. There are five preachers in America whom every competent judge would rank among our dozen best. Of one of them an enthusiastic but discriminating hearer said, "His preaching is awfully thin sometimes." Another preached before a university audience a sermon which made them wish ere the sermon was done that some good angel might descend and leave something for them to carry home. They were receiving no gift from the man who stood in the pulpit. Another appeared at a church celebration preceded by great anticipations. He is one of the most uniformly successful preachers in his denomination. His perfection has long been the envy of many who still groan and travail in pain, waiting for their homiletic redemption. But on that great occasion Apollos floundered heavily in the mire for a half hour and then stuck. Not all the king's horses nor all the king's men could have saved him or his sermon that day. The fourth is as true a prophet of God as the American pulpit boasts. He came to a gathering of preachers with what he hoped would be a masterpiece. But as the hour proceeded he knew and all the spectators knew that his sermonic brush had merely daubed another canvas. Failure was not the result of lack of toil nor of sturdy Christian manhood but of those imponderables which distinguish an art from a science. . . . There is something almost eerie about the work of preaching. A man may come to his hour with thorough preparation and the confidence of discovered and wrought-out truth and yet fail. He may be summoned in an emergency to speak with little or no preparation and achieve a triumph.

Yes, the "imponderables"! What a part they play in the preaching of a sermon. A minister is not very long in the harness before he realizes that there come occasions when he simply cannot pull the sermonic load. It is a humbling experience and the cases instanced here by Dr. Day make it clear that no minister, however able, is exempt from occasional failure in the pulpit. The line, "The harder you fall the higher you bounce," does not seem to apply to situations where the sermon fails to come off as expected. There is not much "bounce" left in a preacher after the "imponderables" have got him down.

V. WALTER RUSSELL BOWIE

I first met Dr. Bowie on a ship voyaging from England to New York. It was on the *President Harding* in 1932. Walter Russell Bowie was at that time rector of Grace Episcopal Church, New York City. We saw each other every day, discussed current events, preachers, and a new book just out by one of the Oxford Groupers entitled *For Sinners Only*. Three days out from Southampton gloom settled over the passengers when it became known that the bride of an attractive honeymooning couple had died at sea. We had seen the couple come aboard at Greenock, on the Clyde, and they were so gay and happy, that following her death we found it difficult to talk of anything else without coming back to this saddest of honeymoons. I recall a day when Dr. Bowie told me he was trying to see the husband to comfort him if he could get through to him. Whether he succeeded in this I cannot now be sure, but the concern he felt for the grief-smitten husband showed in his face and registered in his voice. Good ministers of Jesus Christ are always so disposed when human need is present.

I

Dr. Bowie's Yale lectures were given in 1935, and as soon as they appeared in print I purchased a copy. His subject was *The Renewing Gospel*, with seven lectures, expanded somewhat in the printed form, so he tells us. This clergyman is no novice in writing books. He has published above a dozen volumes, and one of these, *The Story of the Bible*, first issued in 1934, is still in print and in demand.

Anyone familiar with the seventy published volumes of the

Yale Lectures must marvel as he notes the contrasts in style, diversity of material, and difference in approach to the subject, which is, of course, the Christian ministry, with preaching "the paramount issue," as William Jennings Bryan used to say. Musically, it is the same tune with many variations. It is like a cameraman photographing a person from every possible angle, and now and then taking a "close-up."

Dr. Bowie was preceded by Dr. Albert E. Day, who spoke on *Jesus and Human Personality*, and was followed by Dr. J. Edgar Park, who spoke on *The Miracle of Preaching*. Dr. Day dealt with the technique of preaching in so far as it bore on his subject and, also, with the use of psychology on the part of the minister. Dr. Park, on the other hand, was concerned with the art of preaching, and employed both humor and wit, not too much, but with a nice balance. Dr. Park was also critical of the preacher meddling in the field of psychotherapy, and said so unequivocally. Dr. Bowie, sandwiched in between these two able lecturers, turned neither to the right of Day nor to the left of Park, but pursued the even tenor of the middle path, eschewing humor, and succeeded in imparting to his series a distinctly pastoral flavor. He was less discursive than Dr. Day, less literary than Dr. Park, and as earnest as both. But let him explain for himself the path he sought to take, and why:

> Now a book on preaching is obviously designed first, for the interest of those who are to preach; but as we have already observed, the very fact of a preacher implies those he preaches to. Therefore all that we shall go on to think and to say should concern not only the man in the pulpit but equally the man in the pew. Certainly the congregation has a stake in what the preacher thinks about his work and in what he wants to make his mesage. So it is to no limited and professional class that our consideration will be directed. We shall be thinking of truths which one man may voice, but which a whole congregation of people must share if they are to be deeply real.

Most of the books of lectures in this historic Course are designed primarily for ministers, either in the making, or for those who are willing to be made over. Occasionally it happened that a series was given, quite suitable for either minister or layman, and that is true of *The Renewing Gospel*. It is an unpretentious work, simply and beautifully written, with much therein to ponder and to try to practice. Devotional in nature, the serenity of the 23rd Psalm, the spirit of the Sermon on the Mount, and something of the intimacy of the fourth Gospel are here.

The subject of the third lecture is "The Christ That Was and Is," a haunting title that promises much and does not disappoint. I note a phrase which I penciled at the top of a page in my copy of this book. It reads, "Goodness Passing By," which, at the time I wrote it there, seemed to describe that particular section fairly well. And is it not true that goodness may be better than "*greatness* passing by," as John Drinkwater wrote it? That depends, perhaps, on how one defines greatness. Dr. Bowie has a knack of making goodness attractive, because the kind of goodness he writes about is not a "goody-goody" goodness, but a goodness with the accent on good thoughts and good deeds. He loves to exalt the common virtues and press them home.

Dr. Bowie spends some time on the character of Jesus, probing for the secret of his strength and his serenity. Consider these passages:

Human life to him was like an estuary opening to the ocean and feeling forever the mighty tides that set in from the sea.

He looked to God for his own strength. He drew from long vigils of prayer the illumination of his purpose.

Students of the Gospels have not yet been able to answer surely what the apocalyptic conviction of Jesus was—and doubtless never will. It is impossible to say with precision how he felt himself to be the Messiah, and what he believed he was destined to achieve; nor to say fully what he thought as he went up to Jerusalem to be crucified, and why he chose to die, and what he expected in and through his dying.

But one thing is unmistakable. He believed himself to be in the hands of eternal power and eternal love. He lifted up his eyes to the mountains, and found there his sufficient help. Overshadowing all the foreground of every day's contingencies was the background of his certainty of God.

Walter Russell Bowie[1] took his ministerial training in the Theological Seminary of Virginia, at Alexandria, that State. This is

[1] Dr. Bowie was for years professor of homiletics at Union Theological Seminary, and is now teaching at the Theological Seminary at Alexandria, Virginia.

Phillips Brooks' old school and, like the scent of unseen roses, the spirit of this noble preacher permeates the pages of Bowie's book. That school at Alexandria, had I been an Episcopalian, would have surely lured me to its hallowed walls and sacred rooms where not only Phillips Brooks but a long and illustrious company of Episcopal leaders were trained in the Christian ministry. One of the tenderest incidents related by Dr. Bowie at Yale had for its setting this revered institution in Old Virginia. It has to do with a much loved professor who once taught there, by name, Wilbur Cosby Bell. But Dr. Bowie is the one to tell the story:

Stricken with abrupt unexpectedness, by a heart attack, and told by the doctors that he had only a few more hours on this earth, he took that news with a glow of new expectancy. For several hours, oblivious to pain, he talked with his wife of their life together, and of the life he believed was opening ahead. And then he dictated to her this message to the men he taught: "Tell the boys that I've grown surer of God every year of my life and I've never been so sure as I am right now. . . . I'm so glad to find I haven't the least shadow of shrinking or uncertainty. . . . I've always thought so and now that I'm right up against it, I know." Again he went on: "Life owes me nothing. I've had work I loved, and I've lived in a beautiful place among congenial friends. I've had love in its highest form and I've got it forever. . . . I can see now that death is just the smallest thing—just an accident—that it means nothing. There is no real break—God is there—and life—and all that really counts in life—goes on."

This is a good place to "wind to the close," as a circuit rider used to say as he neared the end of the sermon, so let the beauty of the words of that dying teacher of ministerial students have their way with us, for we need them sorely. Thus, spending and being spent so early in life, he rested his case in the spirit of that prophet of Israel who also wrote of the renewing Gospel,

But they who wait upon the Lord shall renew their strength; they shall rise up with wings as eagles; they shall run, and not be weary; and they shall walk, and not faint.

X
CHURCHMEN AND
★ ECCLESIASTICS ★

> *The Church is not a society of parsons. A clerical Church is a contradiction in terms. If God is the Creator of the world, and if through Christ He wills to redeem it, reconciling it with His own will at the cost of the Passion and Crucifixion, we cannot suppose that He is mainly interested in the preoccupations of ecclesiastics.*
> —Canon F. W. Barry

1. DAVID HUMMELL GREER

The Protestant Episcopal Church in this country, despite its prestige and strength, has produced only one preacher of Olympian stature, which, as almost everybody knows, was Phillips Brooks. But not everybody knows that from the Episcopal communion have come a score or more of clergymen of exceptional pulpit ability—men who preached with persuasive power and brilliance.

One of these preachers of distinction was David Hummell Greer, Rector of St. Bartholomew's, New York, 1888-1904, and Bishop of New York for eleven years. In this high office which he so adorned death came to him in 1919.

I

Bishop Greer gave the Yale Lectures in 1895 on the subject *The Preacher and His Place*, publication occurring the same year. Coming late to this volume I read it with avidity, wondering as I read why I had not heard more about the Greer lectures from those who specialize in the Yale Series. For the mind of the author as mirrored in the work is that of a scholar, a wise administrator, and a preacher of depth and compassion. Of such stuff are the best of preachers made.

Alas! it has sometimes happened that high ecclesiastical honors have dwarfed the human, and frozen "the genial currents of the soul" of some who wore the Bishop's ring. But not this Bishop, who moved among his fellow churchmen as simply and unostentatiously as some obscure curate, often discarding his canonical clothes for business suits of brown or gray. Usually the greatest are the humblest and in his rich and powerful diocese Bishop Greer knew no man after the flesh.

It adds to our interest in this clergyman to learn that he studied law and had experience in the business world before he took orders. In his early years he spent a year abroad, traveled in Europe—the kind of prolonged and gorgeous holiday which many of the ministry dream about but never know in reality. Such experiences prepared young Greer for the busy, fruitful years he was to know in the church he loved.

The Bishop began his Yale lectures with the confession that the theme was too big. He declared:

It is an all-out-of-doors theme, like "The World and Its Contents," or the universe and its contents. For the work of the ministry touches and includes within its compass all sorts and conditions of things, in the heavens above, and the earth beneath, and the waters under the earth, and in the soul of man. It deals with things human; it deals with things divine; things physical, things metaphysical; things natural, things supernatural; mental, moral and spiritual. In at least the form of the speech, if not the speech itself, which Ruth addressed to Naomi, it says to all of these things: "Where you go I go; where you lodge I lodge; your interests are my interests; your work is my work; your truth is my truth, and your God is my God."

Musing on this spacious statement one wonders how many young men decide for the ministry with such a conception of its appalling largeness as the Bishop sets forth in the opening of the first of his lectures. Naturally not many, since that which is first is natural, and then that which is spiritual. But it may be best to hear this comprehensive view of the ministry stated so impressively by one who made of his calling so great a success, and not merely in preferments but in the splendor of his spiritual life and helpful ministrations to a needy generation.

Looking, then, at society today in its relation to the preacher, what do we find? We find, in the first place, that it does not care about preaching as much as society yesterday did, or society the day before; and that while it may need it just as much, it does not just as much think that it needs it. Preaching has been hitherto a very effective and much-appreciated factor in the development of the social life, and has helped very much to make it what at present it is. "It was by a sermon," says an English reviewer, "that the movement was inaugurated which has since grown into Christendom, and which is now by more silent though not less potent agencies visibly overspreading the earth. Men went forth preaching 'Jesus and the Resurrection'; and from their generation we date, not our years only, but a new movement of human society which is filling the world with its pressures and its progresses still." That was true of preaching once. Is it true of preaching now? Is preaching equally valuable and important now? Does it still have in the world an important work to do, or has it become today an anachronistic thing, a something out of date, a venerable institution which has survived in form, but in form only, like a rudiment which has lost its function, and which in the vast and varied, and more highly developed economy of the modern social life has no proper place?

Now this is a paragraph to weigh and to ponder. The speaker continues: "This latter view of preaching is the view of many. They do not care about it, or do not care very much about it. Eloquent preaching they care for, but chiefly because it is eloquent, and not because it is preaching." So candid a reflection may not please the theological student, but he needs to hear it. Once there was an aspiring young preacher, just called from an obscure field to an important city church. Suffused with pride and not yet sufficiently humbled by the responsibilities he was soon to assume, he remarked to an older minister with whom he was consulting, "Everything I have will go into my preaching." The older man looked at his young friend earnestly and replied, "If you think you will succeed in that church just by preaching good sermons, you will be disappointed; a preacher's life counts as much and often more than his best sermons." The young man never forgot that observation of the older minister, although at the time it dampened his ardor and subdued his pride.

II

Bishop Greer knew he was saying hard things to his student audience, preachers in the embryonic stage, so he throws in this explanatory word:

Now, I am not saying these things to discourage you, young gentlemen, I am saying them rather to encourage you by telling you about them beforehand, so that you may not be discouraged when hereafter you meet and experience them. The physician is not discouraged—when he knows what that sickness is which he is expected to treat and cure. Why, that is half the battle; and he cannot cure it unless he does know. Neither can you; and my purpose in this lecture has been to try to show you what that sickness is which you are to try to cure.

Could anything, in the way of considerate advice, be more practical or so kindly spoken?

If the lectures of Bishop Greer be set alongside those of Sylvester Horne, given nineteen years later, the contrast is impressive. Greer sets forth the difficulties, the obstacles, the apathies the preacher must face; Horne presents the victories, the grandeur, the romance of which the preacher may know and partake. Both presentations are true, and both are needed.

St. Paul wrote of being all things to all men in order that he might save some, and Bishop Greer would have the minister mingle freely with men. "Let the minister," he says, "be a man among men; not careless, not lax, not indifferent, but at the same time not afraid of what they say or think, and not anxious about it. Let him go and be among them, not thinking much or at all of the impression he makes upon them, but only of what is right, and careful only for that,—honest, fearless, straightforward, and scorning consequences." Then he quotes from James Whitcomb Riley, something I suspect no other Bishop in the Protestant Episcopal Church has done in a public address. The choice of a quotation from the Hoosier poet on the lips of Bishop Greer is a simple sign of a homespun quality about this manly man.

> The kind of man for you and me,
> He faces the world unflinchingly;

> And smites as long as the wrong resists
> With a knuckled faith, and force-like fists.
> He lives the life he is preaching of,
> And loves where most there is need of love.
>
> . . .
>
> And feeling still with a faith half glad
> That the bad are as good as the good are bad,
> He strikes straight out for the right; and he
> Is the kind of man for you and me.

These verses do not show Riley at his best but the preaching is there, and it is good.

Bishop Greer preached without manuscript and did not take "heads or outlines" into the pulpit. Such so-called aids to memory were hindrances to him. These lectures were delivered from the same plan, not read, but spoken, after careful preparation—the best of all methods of public address, if the speaker is willing to pay the price of painstaking study, meditation, writing, and mastering the subject. The Bishop was careful to distinguish between "preparing a sermon for Sunday, and preparing to preach on Sunday." Incidental to this comment, "you may use paper, twenty sheets or forty; but be careful to bear in mind that the paper is for the sermon, and not the sermon for the paper, and should not be enslaved by it."

Fortunate indeed were those who knew David Greer, called him friend, and heard him preach, for God did something for this man long before a solemn and elaborate human ceremony set him apart to a bishopric.

II. HERBERT HENSLEY HENSON

The Right Reverend Dr. Henson, Bishop of Durham, 1920-1937, liked to refer to himself as the "stormy petrel" of that ecclesiastical world which he so adorned and of which he was often a vigorous critic. Nor was he alone in this opinion; a goodly number of his contemporaries not only agreed with him in thus describing himself in ornithological terms, but went further and expressed themselves even more picturesquely. This was to be expected since the Bishop was noted for his independence as a liberal thinker, and a controversialist of rare ability, wielding a sharp tongue and, if possible, a sharper pen. There was "nothing soft about Herbert Henson," as one opponent put it.

Dr. Henson's rise in the Church was spectacular, due to the quality of his mind and his passion for preaching. Twelve years after his ordination he was made a Canon of St. Margaret's, Westminster Abbey; thus, at the age of thirty-seven he followed in the footsteps of Archdeacon Farrar, Canons Wilberforce and Robinson, and other illustrious churchmen. Next, he became, successively, Dean of Durham, Bishop of Hereford, and then Bishop of Durham, with Auckland Castle as his home. During these busy years he was a controversial and embattled personage who, much as he loved a debate, loved fair play more, and happily was able to retain the respect and admiration of all but the most relentless of his theological and political foes.[1]

I

From the beginning of his public life the Bishop kept a diary, and after his retirement he published his reminiscences, compiled from full and meticulously recorded memoranda, under the title *Retrospect of an Unimportant Life*, two volumes in one, Oxford University Press, 1943. As one whose library is lopsided with biographical volumes, and who has at least *minored* in this enchanting kind of literature, I rate Bishop Henson's autobiography as extraordinary and of absorbing interest. It is singularly personal, and written with a candor that is always refreshing and sometimes astonishing. It is the work of a scholar, philosopher, theologian, and powerful preacher, who moves among the political, social, and churchly great of his day, a spiritual and intellectual Philistine, and enjoying it hugely.

[1] "I think he [Henson] would do more good if he were more conciliatory and less combative. He insults the dominant party in the Church, and is contemptuous of the north-country Evangelicals, who are no doubt stupid and difficult."—Dean Inge's *Diary of a Dean*, p. 21.

Herbert Hensley Henson

Following a brief sketch of his home and earliest years, the first entry by date is May 19, 1885, and the last January 31, 1939. Both volumes are fully indexed, and the entries are frequently full and detailed, some covering many pages. Few works of this kind are so entertaining and penetrating. The reader is permitted to observe the processes of the author's thinking, likes and dislikes, frank opinions of royalty, nobility, prelates, salvationists, and nonconformists, and with salty anecdotes thrown in for good measure. Of vast interest to ministers everywhere is his racy shop talk; for instance, on the sermons he preached when he fell below his best, and on other occasions when he preached so ably as to set the fact down in his diary; again, the times when he felt he had failed and was embarrassed by the compliments of many who were sermon-tasters of seasoned judgment.

The Bishop was not an extempore speaker; his practice was to make elaborate preparation and read the manuscript. Thus, a Bishop Eden wrote Dr. Henson:

> You are one of the few preachers who take immense trouble, even over what others might think lesser opportunities, and you make them great by your historical knowledge, and mastery of language alike. I don't say this to flatter you; you know me too well to think that. But it makes me at least ashamed of the very inadequate efforts I have made, even on what were great occasions for me.

This "toiling terribly" over his sermons and lectures goes far to explain the size and character of the audiences which congregated to hear the Bishop preach. His was the sermonic stuff which made his hearers *think,* whether or not they agreed with his positions. Let it be said too that his preaching made some of his hearers furiously angry. For that matter so also did some of St. Paul's preaching.

Under the date of Saturday, September 25, 1920, and the place Stockholm, Bishop Henson takes two pages in his autobiography to tell about a "Swedish Bath" he took or, more accurately, *received.* Dare I include it here? I'll risk it, because, since Dr. Henson saw fit to relate the incident in his autobiography, the rather punctilious and learned Bishop seems much more human, and quite without a semblance of the perked up pride of high office which some affect . . .

Having for the space of one whole week been limited to an impossible pie-dish in which nothing more than an Apostolical feet-washing could be attempted, I was very ardently desirous of a more ample and effective ablution. Accordingly, to order a bath was my first proceeding on arrival in the Hotel. I was directed to a bathroom, where the bath, two-thirds filled with fairly hot water, had been duly prepared. I was somewhat disconcerted to find that there was no bolt for the door, but as I had been escorted thereto by two women, I assumed that I was in no real danger of being interrupted. Hardly, however, had I got into the water, before the door opened, and a vigorous young woman, armed with a lump of soap and a brush, such as floors are scrubbed with, entered, and before I could remember some intelligible word of protest, seized my foot, and began scrubbing my leg! As it was too late to save my modesty, I yielded to my fate, and was dealt with as thoroughly as ever an infant by its mother. The damsel never showed the faintest embarrassment but pursued her task without "turning a hair." After the scrubbing she indicated the shower bath, and when this had been undergone, proceeded to dry me, and "trim" my feet. Then I was suffered to resume my pyjamas, and she accompanied me back to my room, and was rewarded for her violences by a kronen. The whole performance seemed as natural and fitting as showing your tongue to a doctor, or stripping for his inspection; but it was a startling experience for a bashful bishop![2]

"A startling experience" is right, and with such an exciting introduction, we should be eager to learn about Bishop Henson's Yale lectures, given in 1909, at New Haven, at which time he was in his Canonry at St. Margaret's, Westminster, London. The Canon and his wife arrived in New York on April 21, 1909, with engagements at "New York, New Haven, Boston, New York, Boston, Cambridge, Mohonk, West Point, New York, Washington, Chicago, Minneapolis, Fargo, Bismarck, The Yellowstone Park, Seattle, and Victoria, B.C." Eighteen pages are devoted to this visit to our country, and they are crammed with illuminating comments on places, persons, events, and not a dull or drab page in the lot.

[2] *Retrospect of an Unimportant Life, 1863-1939*, Vol. 2, p. 49.

II

The Bishop's subject at Yale was on *The Liberty of Prophesying*. The subtitle in the published lectures reads: "With its just limits and temper considered with reference to the circumstances of the Modern Church." In the preface, the author frankly states: "I chose a subject which was apparently and acutely controversial, and I justified myself by pleading the needs of the existing situation." In addition to the eight lectures, three sermons are included which treat of the Christian ministry, the subjects as follows: "Divine Vocation," "Authority in Religion," and "Christian Teaching"; the latter preached before Harvard University, May 2, 1909.

Bishop Henson's lectures are solid, scholarly, and full of life. There is, too, an air of austerity about the discourses; a prophet is speaking, and the times are heavy with serious and vexatious issues. According to his habit the Bishop read the lectures, no doubt with impressive voice and mien. As a specimen of his style and vigorous reasoning, this partial paragraph from the opening lecture is characteristic:

> The suggestion that there may be degrees in the liberty permitted to the Christian preacher, greater here, less there, offends against the plainest verities of human nature. You must deal with every man as an indivisible unit, if you concede, as indeed you must concede, liberty of thought, you cannot reasonably attempt to prohibit liberty of speech. The indispensable assumption of the last prohibition is the rightness in principle of the first. A Christian minister may fairly be prohibited from preaching agnosticism or free love because it cannot be supposed that, even in the recesses of his own thought, he could be either an agnostic or an antinomian. The postulate of all subscription must be the correspondence of thought and speech. Accordingly, if you tolerate liberty of speech anywhere, you must tolerate it everywhere. There must not be one measure of liberty for the lecture hall and the theological treatise, and another for the pulpit and the parish magazine, however widely the specific exercise of liberty may, and indeed must, vary. In guarding against public scandal you must take care that you do no injury to private honor, for if once you wound private honor you will have opened the door to the worst of all public scandals. Moreover, if you conceive yourself

bound to make the attempt in the interest of the congregations, you will be greatly deceived, for the congregations also have moved far from the old moorings of traditional orthodoxy, and they will not long acquiesce in any treatment which ignores the fact.

The Bishop had some blistering things to say about "the baleful influence of the so-called religious press," devoting a section of his seventh lecture to the subject:

The preacher who would criticise conventional beliefs, and pursue a course adverse to the prevailing policy of his church, must sustain the opposition of the religious, that is, of the party, press. His words will be torn from their context; distorted into senses which were foreign to his mind; paraded before an excited and ignorant public without any of the reservations with which he had conditioned them. His explanations will be ignored: he may count himself fortunate if his personal character is not maligned. One of the gravest facts of our time is the power for evil of the "religious" press. No instrument for the enslavement of human understandings and the persecution of individuals can surpass what modern Roman Catholics call *la bonne presse*. . . . "Heresy hunts" can thus be quickly raised: and reputations created or destroyed. . . . It is a curious and depressing speculation why journalism which specifically concerns itself with religious affairs, and is indeed commonly the work of Christian ministers, should fall conspicuously below the modest level of morality attained by the journalism which is frankly secular.

The Lord Bishop of Durham was ever a fair target for criticism, whether from *The Church Times* or through numerous anonymous epistles about which he, in his autobiography, tells, if not gleefully, at any rate, gladly. On Thursday, December 29, 1927, he makes this entry in his Diary:

Some kind person thinks it worth while to send me a typewritten communication to the following effect:

"A *Christmas Wish*
for the
PRELATES

May the Almighty God send
Confusion in your deliberations,
And an early repentance for your
Nauseating prelatical pride and sin!
24th December, 1927."

This is but one of many tokens of the squalid fanaticism which is running loose in the nation.

Still of the same mind is this comment in his eighth and last lecture in which Dr. Henson said:

I think we grossly delude ourselves if we suppose that fanaticism is a spent force; and that the Church of the future will not continue the tradition of religious intolerance. On the contrary, I hold that the circumstances of the modern Church are, in some important respects, very unfavorable to religious liberty. Something has already been said of the baleful influence of the religious press, and of the social conditions which hamper the didactic work of the ministry. Here we may notice the peril to intellectual liberty implied in the emotionalism of urban populations, and in the application to religion of notions borrowed from commerce. It is often assumed that "business men" are naturally the friends of liberty, and, at least in England, popularity in a commercial center is supposed to be a sufficient certificate of religious tolerance. The truth seems to be that "business men" are extremely hostile to every form of ecclesiastical discipline which affects their own freedom of action, and to that extent may be regarded as the friends of liberty; but they have little sympathy with intellectual perplexities; they are ready to apply to religious questions the prompt and decisive methods of the city; to interpret clerical subscriptions in simple terms of legal contract; and to make success the criterion of spiritual efficiency; and to give little consideration to any teaching that cannot command popular acceptance. Commercial Christianity is apt to be morally lax, but intellectually rigid; it easily favors sensational preaching and aesthetic services, but it has little concern with thought and is actually hostile to discipline. The Christianity of the future will be more and more centered in great cities. The Church will express the tastes and reflect the standards of business men . . . and the liberty of prophesying will be straitly conditioned by the prevailing fashion. In this situation I apprehend large possibilities of oppression.

III

There are many references in Bishop Henson's autobiography to "Ralph," none other than Dean William Ralph Inge, of St. Paul's, London. The two were warm friends with a lot in common. Their thoughts ran pretty much in the same channels. Neither preached popular sermons, in the usual acceptation of the term.

Both were hard hitters in the pulpit, and their brethren quite generally held in wholesome respect the extra good brains of Henson, Inge, and company.

How did the Yale Divinity School receive Bishop (then, Canon) Henson's lectures? Here is the lecturer's answer to the question, as it appears in his autobiography:

The eight lectures were delivered between April 23rd and May 10th. The audience was mainly, but not exclusively, composed of students who, if they did not display emotion or enthusiasm (which, perhaps, could hardly have been expected when such a subject was treated with the cold detachment proper in an academic lecture-hall) were attentive and apparently interested. We left Yale with genuine regret, for the beauty of the place, the courtesy of the President and Professors, the cheerful friendliness of the students, and the considerate hospitality of our kind hosts left on our minds impressions which were pleasant and lasting.

On the same page, but at the end of another paragraph, Dr. Herbert Hensley Henson takes leave of his lectures at Yale with this rather plaintive reflection:

My lectures were well attended, and evoked no expressions of dissent, but, when published, their meager circulation showed that they were not generally acceptable.

Maybe so, but what prophet was ever popular in his own generation?

Note: On p. 113 of Bishop Henson's *Retrospect of an Unimportant Life, 1863-1939*, he gives his impressions of church life as he saw it in America. He introduces the paragraph with this explanation: "Indeed, we [Dr. Henson and his shipmate, Dr. James Denney] were not attracted by American Christianity as a whole, though of course we could not but know that impressions received in the course of a few weeks, or even a few months, could not be worth much. Yet they are not wholly without value. I can see much exaggeration, but also some justice in the following reflections recorded in my journals: 'There is no reverence anywhere—none in the vestry, none in the choir, none in the pulpit. The note of personal advertisement is everywhere audible; not rarely it is emphasized to the exclusion of every other note. In the midst of the service, the Minister makes lengthy announcements, which are incongruous to the point of indecency. Rivalry between denominations is naked and unashamed, and it kills every worthy ideal of religious work. "Religious Workers" are held together in a covenant of mutual admiration. Criticism is resented mortally. Mine ears ache with the superlatives of self-paid compliments to which they have listened. "Services" become ever shorter and "brighter," sermons ever more sentimental and 'sensational." Indeed it is a degraded race in sensationalism. It would seem that the spirit of commerce has established itself in the sanctuary. Religion appears to bring no discipline to the national character, and to carry no consecration to the national life.' There are other and nobler elements in American religion, and in any complete picture these would have to be included, but the features which arrested me when I saw America are still apparent. It is but just to add that they are nowhere more clearly discerned, or more freely denounced than in America itself. Nor are they unknown within Great Britain, where the tendency to approximate to American models grows stronger."

III. GEORGE WHARTON PEPPER

It was not until 1893, with the consent of Mr. Sage, the founder of the Lyman Beecher Lectureship, that the original articles were changed so that "if at any time they should deem it desirable to do so, to appoint a layman to deliver the course of lectures on the Lyman Beecher Foundation." Twenty-two years later, in 1915, George Wharton Pepper, of Philadelphia, the first layman to be invited, gave the Series with the appropriate title, A *Voice from the Crowd*.

Mr. Pepper, later a United States Senator from Pennsylvania, was eminently qualified for this assignment. An Episcopalian churchman of distinction, and serving his church on many important commissions, he was married in 1890 to Charlotte, daughter of Professor George Park Fisher, noted church historian and writer on other religious subjects. Mr. Pepper was 'a lawyer and engaged in a large and lucrative practice, but never too busy to serve his church, in the councils of which he stood high.

Mr. Pepper writes in the introductory note to his volume of lectures:

I received the invitation with a sense of gratification. I accepted it with a determination to do my best. The work of preparation has proved to be a profitable task. The delivery of the lectures was an interesting experience. Whether this volume contains anything which others may find either profitable or interesting is a matter about which I shall not allow myself to even speculate.

The Philadelphia lawyer gave both an interesting and profitable course of addresses, and evidently enjoyed himself hugely in telling the divinity students how the man in the pulpit looks to a man in the pew. Senator Pepper is a graduate of the University of Pennsylvania, the holder of many honorary degrees, and in his time has known many of the eminent men of his day, including James Russell Lowell and other Olympians of politics, the bar, and the pulpit.

I

Mr. Pepper plunged into his series with zest and his first lecture on "The Man in the Pew" was lively, candid, and not altogether complimentary to some preachers to whom he was obliged to listen. Trust a smart lawyer to see the weak link in the armor of his lawyer opponent or in that of the clergy. It is safe to say nobody grew drowsy as this alert layman spoke up in this fashion:

I suppose that a man in the church-going crowd ought to be grateful for this unlooked-for opportunity to express his views on preaching. I confess that I have felt moved at times to rise in my place and volunteer a few comments upon the sermon. Prudence, however, has restrained me. The lawyer is trained to sit silent while the other man is having his say. His patience is apt to be rewarded, for his turn comes by-and-by. The advocate learns by experience that it is best not to interrupt. I remember a case of importance in which a great lawyer was making his argument. His adversary made constant interruptions which, to my surprise, the speaker did not resent. Finally the court became impatient and the presiding judge rebuked the adversary and told him to await his turn. "Pray do not repress him," said the speaker, "his interruptions give me great satisfaction. If he sat silent, I should fear that I was missing my mark. When he wriggles I know that I have reached his vitals." Perhaps my self-control in the past is ascribable to fear that an interruption would indicate that I had been touched. At all events, I can have my say now without incriminating myself and I am glad that I have husbanded my little supply of ammunition.

Here is another choice passage, and it registers:

Speaking for myself, I am powerfully affected by the bearing of a man during service time. I find that, if he reads from the Bible, a great deal can be gathered respecting his inner self. There are all sorts of ways of reading the Scriptures. The dramatic rendering of a chapter, in which the reader speaks in different tones to represent the several dramatis personae, is happily a thing of the past. We are, however, unpleasantly familiar with the affected solemnity of the reader who employs a scripture voice, distinct from that which he uses on other occasions. Then there is the repulsive familiarity of the man who reads the Bible as he would any other book, reeling off, without difference of treatment, the most trivial incident and the most sacred experience. Far too seldom we hear a chapter read by a man who possesses the two primary qualifications for effective reading—a clear understanding of the significance of what he reads and an earnest intention that the people shall be the better for hearing it. We cannot all have good voices. Our elocution may be more or less imperfect. But that man wins my respect who has evidently prepared himself with care to read the selected passage and makes me feel that he is really striving for my edification. I can recall occasions in my life when the earnest, intelligent and reverent reading of particular chapters has marked an epoch in spiritual experience.

Lawyer Pepper welcomes the cheerful preacher and is repelled by the grim-faced, sanctimonious parson. When a lugubrious man appears in the pulpit and seems shrouded in gloom, this layman feels like shouting, "Cheer up. If you are going to preach the Gospel, please do not forget you are the bearer of tidings of great joy." In this connection he goes on to say:

Some time ago I was one of a great audience assembled to hear Mr. Sunday. Almost all those present were college students. Before he began to speak, the young faces had upon them a curious and unnatural look of depression. "Cheer up!" said the evangelist, "you're not in church." The effect was electric. The students became boys again. The speaker, by a single stroke, had broken down their reserve. I do not stop to argue the question whether the evangelist ought to have said it, or whether his implication was or was not fair to the clergy. I merely record the fact that several thousand young men, whether justly or unjustly, were obviously accustomed to associate preaching and gloom.

This from an Episcopalian is truly great. I can imagine the young preachers and the august faculty enjoying the novelty and the commonsense of this layman, who knows how to *lay it on*. No wonder the Senator's book passed through several editions. It is alive.

II

In quite a different mood Mr. Pepper discusses "The Vision of Unity." Here he is prophetic and a statesman in the realm of organized Christianity. Listen to this: "Can any Christian man seriously doubt the proposition that the persistent and pacific teachings of a united church would have made this war impossible? ... It is only through the realization of such a fundamental unity among the communions of Christendom that the influence of Christianity can be restored."

In regard to the divisions among Christians Mr. Pepper had five suggestions to make to the preacher of unity:

1. Be cheerful and good tempered. When the several phases of the subject are considered sympathetically, there is much, very much, that is hopeful.

2. Try to detect the spiritual dangers to which one's own apprehension of truth is particularly subject. Scolding the man in the pew because other men stay outside the building does less harm than commending the congregation for being what they are and rehearsing to them the shortcomings of those who are different.

3. Avoid formulating schemes of unity and be wary about arrangements with well-meaning but impetuous ministers who are often ready to take some action which is incomprehensible to the majority of disciples in their own communion.

4. While the men of this generation may be led to a better understanding of the views of separated brethren, they are in most instances likely to die without modifying their own. In other words the primary aim of the preacher of unity is to compete for the allegiance of the next generation.

5. The preacher of unity, while not shunning to declare to his people the whole counsel of God, should be careful not to attempt a disclosure of what has not yet been revealed to him. One of the things one admires about Saint Paul is his effort to distinguish between what is surely the mind of God and what is merely a private opinion of his own. As far as religious differences are concerned, it

is a safe assumption that if the view of truth taken by another communion seems absurd to you, you do not really understand it.

Senator Pepper's autobiography entitled *Philadelphia Lawyer* is chock full of good stories and lively anecdotes about the great and near great. Students of Lincoln lore will relish an account of Judge Craig Biddle's impressions of the Gettysburg speech as he listened to it on that memorable November 19, 1863. The home of Pepper's father-in-law, Professor George Park Fisher, was often host to such celebrities as Edward A. Freeman, the English historian; George Adam Smith of Aberdeen; John Brown of Bedford (the biographer of John Bunyan); Dr. John Watson (Ian Maclaren); James (afterward Lord) Bryce; and Dean Stanley of Westminster, London. At one of these gatherings in the Fisher home, Dr. Fisher told this story about Wendell Phillips. That eloquent orator was once busily reading on a railroad train when a stranger poked a religious tract into his hands, remarking briskly, "My business is to save souls from hell"; to which, without looking up, Phillips replied, "Go there and attend to it."

Senator Pepper is eighty-three as this is written, his interest in church, books, and public affairs unabated. And his preacher stories are as delightful as they are myriad, since in his day he has known most of the famed preachers of America and many of Great Britain. Henry Ward Beecher, Phillips Brooks, John Watson —these he knew and many others. It is worth a journey to Philadelphia just to listen to the Senator reminisce on the mighty men of the Christian pulpit.

IV. JAMES EDWARD FREEMAN

Shortly before World War II, Bishop Freeman was the preacher at a Union service in Central Woodward Church, Detroit, to which I had the honor of ministering for twenty-six years. After the service he went home with me and was the center of a group of ministerial friends whom I had asked to meet him. Complying with a request to give us some of his recollections about Woodrow

Wilson, he poured forth a steady stream of incidents and anecdotes about the President, with whom he was on intimate terms. It was midnight when the company scattered to their homes and the Bishop taken to his hotel.

When Warner Brothers decided to picturize Hartzel Spence's *One Foot in Heaven*, Bishop Freeman and I served on the sponsoring committee, which was charged with some responsibility in passing on the material to be used on the screen. One of the committee meetings was held in the Bishop's home in Washington, and no host could have exceeded him in delightful hospitality. Our business completed, we readily wooed the Bishop into a reminiscent mood, and the result was a full hour of biographical miscellanea, topped off with some capital stories. As a raconteur he had few equals among the clergy.

I

Bishop Freeman came into the ministry by way of the business world, and is one of three men who gave the Lyman Beecher Lectures, not college bred. His biographer states that Bishop H. C. Potter heard Freeman make a political speech which so pleased the New York prelate that he pressed the claims of the Church on the young businessman, persistently, and successfully too, for in 1895, the ordination of his protégé took place at Christ Church, New York City.

The progress of the Reverend James E. Freeman in the ministry was rapid and substantial, serving churches at Yonkers, New York, Minneapolis, Minnesota, and Washington, D.C., becoming Bishop at the capital of the nation just twenty-eight years after his ordination to the priesthood. Most self-educated men are alert mentally, of studious habits, and have a capacity for hard work; and this was true of Freeman. The combination of a popular eloquence, excellent administrative ability, plus captivating social gifts help to account for the success of Bishop Freeman in all of his parishes and, especially, at Washington, D.C.

An imposing presence and a resonant voice mean much to a public speaker, and nature was generous with the Bishop on both counts. He was one of those men in the Episcopacy who looked every inch the part. There is something about a long-tailed coat, either frock or cutaway, that sets a large man apart, puts him on a pedestal, so to speak, and the Bishop was well aware of this fact. He carried himself with a kind of conscious regality, yet was one of the friendliest of dignitaries to meet and to entertain.

II

Bishop Freeman was the Yale lecturer for 1928, and his theme, *The Ambassador*. The discourses were characteristic of the Bishop, popular in style, with liberal quotations, usually apt, and numerous anecdotes of an entertaining nature. With the possible exception of Bishop Mouzon, who was the lecturer a year later, Bishop Freeman was the most lavish with poetical effusions of all the lecturers in the Course; three of the eight discourses close with familiar favorites, and one, the fourth, concludes with a choice selection from Masefield which is little known.

The Bishop followed pretty closely the conventional pattern, speaking on the minister's *Credentials, Fitness, Assignment, Equipment, Loyalties, Technique, Perils,* and *Opportunities.* The discourses are helpful, and pitch a high yet attainable ideal for the clergy, and reveal a plentiful supply of sanity, sense of values, and excellent advisory material. The lecturer's favorite authors and preachers play a not inconspicuous part in the discussion, particularly, and naturally, Phillips Brooks, for whom he had an almost idolatrous esteem and affection. Physically, the men had something in common, and Bishop Freeman's biographer pushes their similarities still further, unwisely, I think. In speaking on the minister's fitness for his task the Bishop quotes a tidbit from Dr. R. S. Storrs' *Preaching Without Notes*, which deserves a wider hearing. The doctor describes a class of three men with whom a professor of theology was vainly struggling. They were a curious mixture of various and utterly diverse types: one was a skeptic, another a dyspeptic, and the third a Swedenborgian. Storrs adds a touch of grim humor, that the professor resigned and entered the more alluring field of politics; but he failed to say what became of the precious trio.

My favorite lecture in the Bishop's series is the one on the

Equipment of the preacher. It is pertinent, persuasive and practical, warm and friendly. Moreover, it reveals a fine grasp of the subject, with no fooling. The Bishop cites:

The similarity of style and manner, the widespread use of a tone of expression in the conduct of corporate worship, and even in preaching, the stilted and formal methods in approach to individuals, whether in the sanctuary or out of it, all these witness to the undue influence of a too precise and formal method of training that subordinates the student's personality, rendering it artificial and unresponsive to what are peculiarly and uniquely his own gifts and qualities of mind and heart. Someone has aptly said, "we are born originals and die copies."

Truly eloquent was the lecturer when he soliloquized:

A personality that like some beneficent influence brings refreshment and inspiration to a disillusioned world, that leaves behind a trail of light, that gives the tired soul its peace, the cloudy noon its sun, is the personality that from its oft-repeated communings with the Master rises to duties that await, with strength renewed, with soul aflame, with life ordained. So beautiful and pervasive was the Christian character of his son that Charles Wagner, the French preacher, wrote this word concerning him at the time of his death: "Thou hast sown with rays of white light the pathway to the grave, and left at the gates of death a gleam as of dawn."

III

One of my clerical friends, himself a bishop now, in referring to Bishop Freeman, pronounced him "vain." Granted, but what of it? So was George Washington. So were others who served acceptably in public affairs, some of them nobly. The Bishop was a lovable human being, a man's man, and a golfer who, when he once made a hole in one, was as proud as Lucifer of the shot. He wrote pretty fair poetry, was the master of a sonorous pulpit style, and the friend of many men of the cloth as well as of the eminent in politics and business. Give him a congenial group and a favorite subject and, he was, in his own way, as interesting a table talker as old Dr. Sam Johnson or Samuel Taylor Coleridge. A broad churchman, orthodox yet liberal, urbane and companionable. There was one phrase often on his lips which deserves to live:

An insular church is an insolent church.

V. EDWIN DuBOSE MOUZON

Bishop Mouzon, to date, is the only lecturer in the Beecher Course from the deep South. He was born in Spartanburg, South Carolina, educated at Wofford College, that State, held several important pastorates, was professor of theology, Southwestern College, Georgetown, Texas, and elected Bishop in the Methodist Church, South, in 1910. The Bishop was active in the movement for the reunion of his church in America, served as chairman of the committee "On Unification of American Methodism," but did not live to see the consummation of this movement which occurred at Kansas City, April 26, 1939.

In his autobiography *I Was Made a Minister*, the late Bishop Edwin Holt Hughes, writing of the unification events in which he had an important part, says: "Edwin DuBose Mouzon, as majestic in mind as he was in appearance, passed to heavenly counsel in the chariot whose quick transit gave no chance for pain. Impressive as he was in bearing, he was really a shy man in his social life. In my close relations with him I never knew him to boast of anything he had said or done. He had given incalculable service." The reference in the last sentence is to Bishop Mouzon's long and enthusiastic work in behalf of the reunion of American Methodism.

I

Bishop Mouzon brought to Yale Divinity School in 1929 something of the Southern oratory for which he was noted. It is doubtful if his lectures read as well as they sounded when he delivered them at Yale. He loved poetry, and his discourses are bejeweled with quotations from his favorite bards. Speaking on the theme *Preaching with Authority*, the Bishop followed pretty much the general pattern adopted by many of his predecessors in the course. Thus he discussed: I. Authority and Authorities; II. Perils of Traditionalism and Values in Tradition; III. Authority and the Bible; IV. The Basis of Authority in History; V. The Basis of Authority in Experience; VI. Authority from the Cross; VII. The Authority of the Church; and VIII. Preachers Having Authority. The style is discursive, with numerous authorities cited, and gives the impression of a speaker more at home in extempore speech than with manuscript. To this reviewer the final lecture is the best and possibly the most appealing to the student body who heard it at Yale. The Bishop was troubled by the belittling criticisms of preaching he had read and heard, and made a sturdy rebuttal of the indictment. He argued:

> The sermon is the distinguishing characteristic of worship in Protestant churches. It is also its most outstanding feature. Recently, however, a popular writer has ventured to tell us that "the sermon has been the great blight upon the Protestant church." On the contrary, we affirm that the sermon has been the source of our deepest and widest influence. . . . No form and ceremony; no choir, singing either the ancient hymns of the Church or the songs of the present day; no imitation of the sacramentarian ritual which our fathers left behind will serve to take the place of power made vacant by preachers who have lost their gospel.

For one, I enjoyed the Bishop's sturdy defense of Reginald John Campbell, who was under a steady fire for a time because of his New Theology. In 1910, when the fire was at its hottest, I heard Dr. Campbell at The City Temple preach an evening sermon from Psalm 17:15, "I shall be satisfied, when I awake, with thy likeness." I had come early and was given a seat well up toward the front. As I looked into the serene face of the preacher, his head crowned with beautiful white hair, I thought it the *orthodoxest* face I had ever seen. Possibly because of that evening in City Temple, listening to him preach from so precious a scripture, my interest in the Bishop's tribute to Campbell and his apt quotation from that preacher's autobiography, A *Spiritual Pilgrimage*, has something to do with my quoting this passage from Bishop Mouzon:

> The older preachers will call to mind the stir R. J. Campbell made some years ago with his New Theology. Certain honest souls were greatly perturbed and more solid theologians were quite uneasy about this new voice in the theological world. But one day fears touching

the essential soundness of the preacher were set at rest. For R. J. Campbell gave his personal testimony. And here follows what he said: "I cling to the Jesus of history as being one with the Christ of faith. . . . I feel that I know Jesus as Jesus. . . . Jesus Christ is central for my spiritual life: I worship him, and trust my soul to him. I admit that this is a purely subjective argument, but it is one that is justified by results, and there is abundance of testimony in favor of it. Millions have lived and died before and since Bernard of Clairvaux wrote his famous lines—

> " 'Jesus, the very thought of Thee
> With sweetness fills the breast;
> But sweeter far Thy face to see,
> And in Thy presence rest'—

millions who could say the same thing. He is very real to spiritual experience, this Jesus, so real that not all the theorizing in the world is going to displace him. . . . Take away from your faith in Christ the belief that that Christ has once been manifested in one supreme, transcendent personality, and you have immeasurably weakened its force. The human heart does cry out for a high priest who has been 'touched with the feeling of our infirmities'—

> " 'Whose feet have toiled along our pathways rough,
> Whose lips drawn human breath.'

I thoroughly agree with the wise saying that if we had never had such a Christ, a Christ after the flesh, we should be craving for one now as the one great need of our earthly life."[1]

I say frankly: If a man has this faith I care little as to what else he may believe or may not believe. The one essential is Christ; the one Saviour is Christ. This is the gospel we are to preach. With this gospel we shall be preachers having authority.

II

References to Phillips Brooks are of unending fascination to preachers everywhere. Next to Henry Ward Beecher, he is the oftenest quoted by lecturers in this Series. One of Bishop Mouzon's finest passages has to do with this noble servant of the Lord. Being so largely of an autobiographical nature makes it all the more

[1] *A Spiritual Pilgrimage*, pp. 216-217.

appealing. The lecturer had been listing the preachers who had helped shape his life and ministry. He had instanced Frederick William Robertson, of Brighton, who is the third most quoted preacher in this Lectureship, and then follows this impressive passage:

Phillips Brooks was elected Bishop in 1891. I had just come into the ministry. Brooks was elected on the thirtieth of April. Then the controversy broke out around him. The months dragged on and it began to look as if the bishops would not confirm his election. Not until July the tenth was the matter finally settled. The entire Church in America was interested in the discussion precipitated by the call to the bishopric of this broad-minded and large-hearted preacher. But it was said that he had not been properly baptized; it was well known that he did not believe in the doctrine of apostolic succession, and that he was not bound by ancient traditions. And worst of all, there came the inevitable accusation that he was not sound in the faith.

The attention of a young man just beginning to look around him in the world and see how the main currents were running was irresistibly drawn to this man, Phillips Brooks, big enough to be the Bishop of all the churches in the country. Then I read his *Lectures on Preaching*. I almost date time from reading those lectures. He had put himself into them. Always modest and seldom saying anything about the sacred privacies of the soul in its dealings with God, he had opened up his heart and had revealed himself to me in those notable lectures. "The lectures constitute the confessions of a great preacher." There was never a more satisfactory description of preaching than that given by Phillips Brooks. Said he: "Preaching is the communication of truth by man to men. It has in it two elements, truth and personality. Neither of these can it spare and still be preaching. . . . Truth through Personality is our description of real preaching. The truth must come really through the person, not merely over his lips, not merely into his understanding and out through his pen. It must come through his character, his affections, his whole intellectual and moral being. It must come genuinely through him."

There was the secret of Phillips Brooks. His sermons came through him. He spoke out of a great experience. This made him a preacher having authority. This gave him such influence with all men, and in particular with one young man who was listening for the sound of an authentic voice and who recognized here a preacher with soul wide open to all the winds that blow from heaven.

It whets our interest in Bishop Mouzon's work at Yale to know the kind of a man and preacher he was. Bishop Ivan Lee Holt, who knew him intimately and admired him greatly, says of this friend of many years:

> Bishop Edwin D. Mouzon was a man of commanding presence, tall and handsome. He carried a tenderness of love for the innate beauty in every relationship of life—in the home, the Methodist conference, the University campus. The scope of his activities was exceedingly broad, and the service that he rendered in all places was marked by distinction. Vision, conviction, sincerity and courage characterized him everywhere. He commanded the attention of the masters of thought as was evidenced by his being called to deliver the Fondren Lectures at Southern Methodist University, the Cole Lectures at Vanderbilt University, and the Lyman Beecher Lectures on Preaching at Yale University. His personality commanded admiration, attention and respect. He engaged in no conversation and listened to none that was below the level of his own life and thought. One could know not only what he believed but why he believed it.
>
> He had extraordinary ability in the pulpit and was regarded as one of the great preachers of Methodism. He was welcomed as a preacher on any occasion. What concerned him most was the proclamation of that truth which exalted Christ as Lord and Savior.
>
> For twenty-seven years he was a member of the Board of Missions of the Methodist Episcopal Church, South, journeying to Brazil to set up there the Autonomous Methodist Church of Brazil. He was completely dedicated to the cause of unifying American Methodism and for twenty years he was the outstanding leader in that movement in the South. He served as Bishop in Arkansas, Oklahoma, Texas and North Carolina. He was living at Charlotte, North Carolina, at the time of his death. By all standards of measurement he will live on as one of Methodism's truly great Bishops and as a leader in every important movement in his church. He was never a bystander, and he never stood on the side lines. He was an active participant, and it was a contagious joy to follow him.

In closing his final lecture Bishop Mouzon made a plea for three qualities without which no man should try to preach. First, there must be sincerity. "The preacher is a communicator. His convictions pass in some strange way over into the minds of his hearers. . . . If he is a man of strong faith, his faith will flow down into others." Second, moral purity. "Only the holy can know the Holy. . . . Only the pure in heart shall see God. 'If thine eye be evil, thy whole body shall be full of darkness.'" Third, complete surrender to Jesus Christ. "'No man having put his hand to the plow, and looking back, is fit for the Kingdom of God.' For the Kingdom of God is never for backward-looking men; it is only and always for those whose faces are turned toward the future. Christ calls for full committal to the interest of His Kingdom. Thus would we stand—in sincerity, in moral purity, in surrender!

> 'With parted lips and outstretched hands
> And listening ears Thy servant stands,
> Call Thou early, call Thou late,
> To thy great service dedicate.'"

VI. HENRY KNOX SHERRILL

Henry Knox Sherrill! What a good name, in keeping with the character of this beloved Churchman. Dr. Sherrill, who was elected Presiding Bishop of the Protestant Episcopal Church in 1947, was the Lyman Beecher lecturer in 1948, speaking on *The Church's Ministry in Our Time*. The book which contains his lectures is next to the smallest of the Series, consisting, with the index, of but 162 pages, while that of Principal L. P. Jacks, of Oxford, published in 1934, is the smaller by 19 pages, and no index. And of the two small volumes Sherrill's is the more helpful.

It is held quite generally by teachers of homiletics that a prerequisite to a great sermon is a great text. Bishop Sherrill chose a great text to stand at the head of his first lecture, which was on "The Spiritual State of the World," to wit: St. Luke 21:25, 26, which reads:

And there shall be signs in the sun, and in the moon, and in the stars; and upon the earth distress of nations, with perplexity; the sea and the waves roaring; men's hearts failing them for fear, and for looking after those things which are coming on the earth: for the powers of heaven shall be shaken.

It is an interesting pastime as well as a serious study for men of the ministry to speculate as to how the famous preachers would handle certain passages of Scripture. It will be recalled that Dr. Jowett followed for years this practice. He would ask himself, "How would Dale deal with it? By what road would Bushnell come up to it? Where would Maclaren take his stand to look at it?" Very good. Now take Bishop Sherrill's text quoted above, a portentous one, too. How would Buttrick regard it? What would Scherer do with it? In what unique way would Niebuhr manage it? These are fascinating conjectures, but the question now is what did Bishop Sherrill do with St. Luke 21:25, 26. Here is the answer:

These are words which are often taken as figurative. Whether that interpretation be true or not they are a realistic description of our times. "Men's hearts are failing them for fear and for looking after those things which are coming on the earth." We live in an apocalyptic day which may well prove to be a turning point in history. What is the meaning of the signs of the times? Are we witnessing the death throes of a civilization or are these portents the birth pangs of a new and nobler society which is to be? The answer is not easy to reach. We are necessarily children of our own generation. As a result it is well nigh impossible to judge objectively. We cannot see the woods for the trees. One can read of the rise and fall of Greece and of Rome with complete objectivity. We can assess the spiritual value attained by the world in the destruction of Jerusalem in the sixth century B.C. and the captivity of so many thousands. But how different to have been one of the company who sat down by the waters of Babylon and wept! How few there were who had any understanding of the message and the significance of Jesus of Nazareth or of St. Paul in their generation. In modern times the misinterpretation of both Washington and Lincoln, while they lived, is astounding to those of a later day. To view the events of today with wisdom is extremely difficult because we lack perspective and are bound to see them somewhat out of focus. We are not spectators of a drama enacted upon a stage. We are in the cast ourselves. We, and our children, our security, our hopes, yes—and our fears, are deeply involved.

. . . The skein is too tangled and reaches far back into the past. There is the burden of sin not only of ourselves but of preceding generations. The whole human family to a greater or lesser degree is involved in the causes of war. Caught in the web of their own weaving men already talk and prepare for the next war. What is the cause of this sickness? Some will say economic rivalry, others the selfish desire for power, others ideological differences. Certainly extreme nationalism is one strong reason. All of these factors and many more must be dealt with realistically and overcome. The United Nations is of course an essential step in this direction but no schemes of organization, no matter how hopeful, will solve the problem and cure our ills. The true cause rests in the minds and hearts of men. As Professor Toynbee has written, "In demonstrating that the broken down civilizations have not met their death from an assassin's hand, we have found no reason to dispute the allegation that they have been victims of violence and in almost every instance we have been led by the logical process of exhaustion to return a verdict of suicide. In tragic life, God wot, no villain need be! Passions spin the plot. We are betrayed by what is false within."[1]

Bishop Sherrill is an able Churchman. Now, not every Christian is a Churchman in the sense in which the word is employed here. Many Christian ministers stress the importance of the individual Christian instead of the corporate body of Christians which is the Church, but a genuine Churchman never fails to exalt the Church, sees it as fundamental in developing the individual and primary in furthering the Gospel. This is elementary to a million ecclesiastical Watsons, but not so to millions of church people other than those of the Episcopal communion. Thus Bishop Sherrill discusses earnestly "The Spiritual State of the Church" in lecture II:

The Churches face many and powerful adversaries but that has always been true in every age. The greatest dangers we face as Christians are not from without but from within. If the fellowship of the Church could clearly and heroically manifest the mind and the spirit of Christ, then there would be no question as to the impress which would be made upon our so-called civilization. The influence of the Church is limited because clergy and people, take it by and large, are very fallible human beings. (In one sense this is as it should be.) The Church is not an organization of proved saints, a kind of ecclesiastical club of the self-righteous. The Church is made up of a very large constituency from every walk of life, the good and the not-so-good, the rich and the poor, those who follow the Master and reveal them-

---

[1] Arnold Toynbee (Abridged by D. C. Somervell), *A Study of History*, p. 275. Copyright, 1946, by Oxford University Press.

selves in all that they are as of the company who have been with Jesus, and others who like St. Peter before the Crucifixion, follow him afar off, and some apparently not at all. As we shall see, one of the thrilling opportunities before us is to mold this vast concourse of people into the Body of the Christ who lived and died that he might draw all men unto himself. Anything less than total humanity within the Church would be indeed a limited and narrow brotherhood. But this very fact makes the achievement of high purpose exceedingly difficult. Within the life of the Church, as in the world, it is the few who have caught the vision who are willing to bear the heat and burden of the day and who are truly attempting to live the Christ life. I have had a medium-sized parish and a large church. These past seventeen years I have had the opportunity to observe many parishes of various communions. The evidence is always the same. It is the few upon whom the life and work of the Church depends. This is not to say that the Church does not help many outside of this number. There are cares, pleasures, riches, burdens which seem to make poor ground in which the seed may grow. Any clergyman will do well to recognize this simple fact—else he will beat his wings against the cage to no effect. Numbers, buildings, organizations, budgets—these have their place. But these are of small effect compared to the company of faithful people. But the matter is more complicated even than this. Among the company of the faithful will be found many who with all their earnestness are smallminded and exceedingly difficult as fellow workers. I have often said that the chief fault to be found with devoted Church people is not that some of them are downright wicked, it is that they are so petty in their outlook. We need to remind ourselves again and again that Christ was crucified in large measure by the respectable, narrow Church people of his time. So we are faced by the reality that here at home in the United States, at least one half of the population has no connection with any form of the Church; that of the half who are at least nominal members, only a small portion have really grasped the meaning of Christian discipleship, and that many of these, including perhaps ourselves, present peculiar personalities and problems.

I

It is not given to all ministers to speak helpfully to their comrades of the Cross on the subject of the ministry. Some of the ablest have not been at their best in addressing their brethren on the ties that bind them in a majestic fraternity. Spurgeon was superb at this; Joseph Parker was not. To do this sort of thing and do it well requires an understanding heart, a sense of mission, and a true humility. Bishop Sherrill possesses these priceless, precious qualities, and in his final lecture he talks to us as Phillips Brooks talked to weary, discouraged, and frustrated fellow ministers in his day, and as he talked their strength was strangely renewed and their lagging spirits soared as on eagles' wings. There follow a few passages from the Bishop's final words on "The Minister":

The minister must be able to face the facts courageously, with no special privilege of position or of sentiment, even as the Master met his generation, for we must recall that he held no position and even at times had no place to lay his head. All of this calls for quality in the minister of today with extraordinary gifts of faith and of wisdom.

The primary task of the clergyman as of the Church is to testify to the living God. This should be true of men in every walk of life but it is the special vocation of the clergyman. He is in the ministry, we trust, because he has been called by God. This does not mean that he has had a vision like those described in the Bible as vouchsafed to the prophets and apostles. Indeed the call may be more convincing because it has come through judgments, continued prayer for guidance, the advice of family and friends and sometimes the pressure of events.

The prospective minister who tries to save time by neglecting seminary training is similar to a woodsman who has so much to do that he has no time to sharpen his axe. In the seminary too there is the understandable urge to be at the actual practical tasks of the ministry as soon as possible.

It may not be fair for lay people to have a double standard for the clergyman and themselves, but nevertheless it is an unconscious tribute to the inherent worth of his calling. The laity expect to see in him what they know in their hearts they should be. A minister must always bear in mind the admonition of St. Paul, "If meat maketh my brother to offend, I will eat no flesh." In all that he does he must bear in mind the effect upon the weakest of the brethren.

A true pastor shares all these experiences year in and year out with his people. As I look back upon my years as a pastor, I have forgotten many of the administrative plans we had, the committee meetings I attended, but as long as I live I shall treasure the memory of opportunities of serving people personally and of trying, however inadequately, to bring to them the messages of the love of God in Christ. The comment is made, that parish calls are a waste of time because only casual gossip takes place. If this be true it is the minister's own fault. It is possible to direct the conversation into helpful and sometimes deep channels.

There are few great preachers or great sermons. But there is no reason that there cannot be countless helpful preachers and sermons. When we try to be some one other than ourselves, we fail. A former teacher of mine said that he had seen a great many Phillips Brookslets in his day. Similarly today one can hear many preachers who have modeled themselves on some outstanding preacher. The voice, the delivery, the style are obviously if imperfectly there. But it is all second-hand and unnatural. Whatever else a preacher may be, he must first of all be himself.

II

At the General Convention of the Episcopal Churches in America, held at San Francisco in September, 1949, Dr. Sherrill, as the Presiding Bishop, preached the sermon at the Opening Service. The text was Acts 2:11, "We do hear them speak in our tongues the wonderful works of God," and the preacher was probably never more persuasive or powerful than on this occasion. A single paragraph from the body of the discourse exhibits something of the plan and spirit of the sermon as a whole:

As we meet on this opening day of the General Convention, it is well for us to keep this event of Pentecost in mind. The world today presents many perplexing and tragic factors which I do not intend to recount here. They are, or should be apparent to all. The most distressing aspect is that we seem to be caught in a web of our own weaving. The mistakes, the sins of the past plague us now and for the future. The principal characters change but the basic difficulties remain with no permanent solution in view. The cycle seems to be constantly repeated. It is no wonder that the cry expressed in many forms arises, "Who shall deliver us from the body of this death?" We have no reason to object because the path is difficult for nowhere did the Master promise an easy favored road. Indeed, the statement was "In the world ye shall have tribulation." He asked His disciples "Are ye able to drink of the cup I drink?" Always he called to the heroic in man. The tragedy of today is deeper than the circumstances we confront. It lies even more in the fact that, take it by and large we have forgotten our dependence upon God, that of ourselves we have no power to help ourselves. The answer to the world's need is not to be found alone in the resources of the human spirit but in the power of God working in and through human life. Before we can overcome the circumstances without we must look within to the life of the spirit. Unless we are strong there we shall inevitably be carried along by an uncontrolled tide of events. But if we are filled by the Spirit of God we can move into our pagan and disorganized society, as did the Christians of the first century.

A fellow clergyman who greatly admires and is devoted to Bishop Sherrill, wrote of him in this intimate and affectionate manner:

He is not by nature an intellectual, though he reads much, as his lectures reveal. By nature he is a man of affairs and a Christian statesman, following in the footsteps of the great Bishop William Lawrence of the Diocese of Massachusetts. His preaching is simple, straightforward, earnest and basically ethical in its emphasis.

His administrative and energizing gifts have been shown in his long term as President of the Massachusetts General Hospital, as a very active member of the Corporation of Yale University and in many other undertakings of that sort. While he is vigorous and hard hitting and demands much of those who work with him and of those who would follow his leadership, he has been remarkably successful in winning the affectionate loyalty of those who work with him. This was true in the Diocese of Massachusetts, and it is increasingly evident in his role as our Presiding Bishop. He has lifted our goals as a Church to far more sacrificial heights and if we move ahead it will be largely as a result of his leadership.

He has a splendid record as a parish parson, as the rector of Trinity Church in Boston, as Bishop of Massachusetts and now as the Presiding Bishop of our Episcopal Church. In all those roles he has shown the same selfless devotion to the Church's task, indefatigable industry, courage in attacking large and difficult problems, a strong social and practical concern.

I was told at Yale that the finest and most enduring contribution that Bishop Sherrill brought to the Yale Divinity School in 1948 was *himself*.

XI

★ MEN OF LETTERS ★

*The peace of great books be for you,
Stains of pressed clover leaves on pages,
Bleach of the light of years held in
   leather.*   —CARL SANDBURG

I. HENRY VAN DYKE

Dr. van Dyke was the first minister to lecture in the Yale Series who, in addition to being eminent in the pulpit, was a successful author. He published many books, and his beautiful story *The Other Wise Man* touched and delighted millions. Over the years volumes of sermons, essays, poetry, and fiction, most of them artistically stamped and bound, streamed from his publishers, to find a ready sale. Following a brilliantly successful ministry at the Brick Presbyterian Church, New York City, Dr. van Dyke became professor of literature in Princeton University, and during the administration of Woodrow Wilson was United States Minister to the Netherlands, a responsible position for which he was admirably fitted.

A famous fisherman was this Presbyterian scholar and litterateur, and as much at home on a camping trip or fishing lark as in his library or classroom. Physically he was a small man, perhaps the smallest to lecture in the Series, as Phillips Brooks was the largest. As if to compensate for the smallness of his stature, he carried himself like a West Pointer, and if there was on public occasions an air of pomposity about Dr. van Dyke, socially there was seldom a more companionable person. Independent in thought and habits, he went his lordly way unruffled by criticism. Thus, when a woman wrote him with concern because she had learned he sometimes smoked, he replied: "Dear Madame: It is not true that I sometimes smoke. I always smoke."

In addition to his other distinctions and honors, Dr. van Dyke was Moderator of the Presbyterian General Assembly, U.S.A., and took a militant part in the long-drawn-out conflict between the "Modernists" and the "Fundamentalists" among his fellow Presbyterians. A liberal, the doctor was always ready to give a reason for the hope within him, nor was he ever far removed from the accepted theological positions of the fathers of his faith. And here, as everywhere else, the Princeton professor chose his own broad path quite indifferent to criticism, and in controversial matters, always the able adversary.

I

Dr. van Dyke took for the subject of his Yale lectures *The Gospel for an Age of Doubt*. The book which followed sold rapidly and went into six editions, which may have established a record in the history of the Lectureship. In the preface to the sixth edition, which came off the press in 1899, the author takes notice of some criticisms provoked by his discussion of the Atonement and also of the fact that some of his readers accused him of arraigning the present age as one of irreligion and infidelity, a charge he disclaims, saying:

In calling the present "an age of doubt," I do not mean that it is the only age in which doubt has been prevalent, nor that doubt is the only characteristic of the age. I mean simply that it is one of those periods of human history in which the sudden expansion of knowledge and the breaking-up of ancient moulds of thought have produced a profound and wide-spread feeling of uncertainty in regard to the subject of religion.

The van Dyke lectures are, as would be expected, scholarly and flawlessly written. They mirror closely a mind that was at home with theology, literature, philosophy, and science; a mind which while not unyielding, was firmly established in certain convictions and also open to modifying influences and reshaping interpretations in the realm of creedal statements. The manner of the lecturer was possibly professorial but not hurtfully so. In the book there is ease of movement, strength of statement, and nicety of phrasing.

The chapter headings are appealing. Thus: I. An Age of Doubt; II. The Gospel of a Person; III. The Unveiling of the Father; IV.

The Human Life of God; V. The Source of Authority; VI. Liberty; VII. Sovereignty; VIII. Service. To those who know Dr. van Dyke chiefly as a literary man, the theological sections of his lectures may come as a surprise, although this should not be the case, since Presbyterians are better schooled in theology than some other Christian bodies. Recall the noted theologians that communion has produced in this country—not to speak of Scotland or the Continent of Europe, such as Hodge, the Alexanders, Schaff, and Warfield, to mention but a few. Dr. van Dyke was schooled under the theological masters, both of the old world and the new, and he has a sure footing in their field and walks therein freely and forcefully.

In the preface to the sixth edition of his Lyman Beecher Lectures, van Dyke disposes of a number of criticisms which vied with praise of the volume, in this impressive personal manner:

> After years of doubt and inward conflict I have arrived at great peace and comfort in the unreserved acceptance of these teachings of Jesus. I do not believe that all things that happen are determined beforehand. The soul is free. The evil that men do is all their own; God has not foreordained it. His only predestination is to good, and if men will accept their divine destiny, God will help them to fulfil it. Election is not the arbitrary choice of a few to receive blessings from which the many are excluded. It is the selection of certain races and men to receive great privileges to fit them for the service of all mankind in the divine kingdom. This is my faith in regard to these questions. I have made no secret of it. The recent agitation concerning ministerial honour in creed subscription seemed to require that it should be frankly confessed. If such a faith were inconsistent with any ecclesiastical obligations, I should be prompt to renounce them. But it is evident that there is no inconsistency. A man may hold this faith and preach it, as a loyal Christian, in the fellowship of the Presbyterian Church.

So spake a stouthearted exponent of the Higher Calvinism.

II

Dr. van Dyke has nothing to say in these lectures on the technique of preaching; that was not in the province of his general theme. Still, there is much for the student of preaching to learn in his handling of his material, subject matter, attitudes, and most of all, in the brotherly spirit in which he discussed moot questions and issues. For there are clergymen who, when they enter the controversial arena, seem to forget the rules of the game and are the poorest of sportsmen.

A study of *The Gospel for an Age of Doubt* discloses helpful preaching aids which are something more than simply hints or suggestions. Take the subject of the second lecture, "The Gospel of a Person." Therein lies but half-hidden the seeds of sermons waiting to come into fullness of growth under the warmth of a fertile mind. But deeper still in this lecture than mere homiletic values is the emphasis the speaker lays upon the preacher's spiritual preparation to proclaim this "Gospel of a Person." Who of us in the great business of preaching does not need the high counsel which follows:

If we are to preach Christ we must know Christ, and know Him in such a sense that we can say with St. Paul that we are determined not to know anything save Jesus Christ and him crucified. We must study Him in the record of His life until His character is more real and vivid to us than that of brother or friend. We must imagine Him with ardent soul, until His figure glows before our inward sight, and His words sound in our ears as a living voice. We must love with His love, and sorrow with His grief, and rejoice with His joy, and offer ourselves with His sacrifice, so truly, so intensely that we can say, as St. Paul said, that we are crucified by His cross and risen in His resurrection.

There are passages in the eighth lecture, entitled "Service," which I think "jangle out of tune" with the content of some other lectures, which took strong grounds on the social responsibility of wealth. For Dr. van Dyke was not enamored with the "social gospel" and made no attempt to conceal his lack of sympathy with the preaching of that gospel. Dr. van Dyke could not honestly say as Frederick W. Robertson of Brighton said: "My tastes are with the aristocrats, my principles with the mob." Neither could Dean Inge and many other thinkers who ranked high in the Church. The extracts that follow should be examined in the light of the context, that full justice be done their author, who could "take" as well as "give."

Jesus does not preach an equality which is synonymous with life on a dead level. He does not preach equality at all. He preaches fraternity. And fraternity implies differences,—older and younger, stronger and weaker, higher and lower. The elder brother is the heir; all that the father has is his; but his sin lies in holding fast to his inheritance selfishly, in shutting out his younger brother, in forgetting and denying that he is a brother at all. . . . Let us try to think distinctly. It is said nowadays that Christianity means communism, and that it is the duty of all Christians to give away everything that they possess. It is strange that Christ never proclaimed this duty except to one man, and that man was not a Christian. Of course it must be admitted at once that this would be the duty of all Christians if it could be shown that it would be for the real good of their fellow-men. But this never has been shown. On the contrary, communism has always turned out badly. It was tried in Jerusalem, in a limited way, when the early Christians sold all that they had and made a common purse; but it led, in less than ten years, to confusion and strife, and sank the Jerusalem church into a condition of pauperism and dependence upon the other churches, which had avoided the well-meant but dangerous experiment.

There is a contemporaneousness about it that is startling. It leads one to believe had Dr. van Dyke lived a half dozen more years he would have been at odds with the "New Deal." He continues:

Tell the Lady Bountiful that she is not called to discard her ladyhood but to give herself with all her refinements, with all her accomplishments, with all that has been given to her of sweetness and light, to the ennobling service of humanity. Tell the Merchant-Prince that he is not called to abandon his place of influence and power, but to fill it in a princely spirit, to be a true friend and father to all who are dependent upon him, to make his prosperity a fountain of blessing to his fellow-men, to be a faithful steward of Almighty God.

This too is controversial, and fairly well mirrors the economic conservatism then in the saddle, but be it remembered that one of the excellencies of the Yale Lectureship is that it has called to its forum able men of widely different views in theology, economics, and sociology, believing that in so doing the "full Gospel" would be proclaimed; and an examination of the Series as a whole demonstrates the wisdom of that policy.

Of a lofty literary quality, stimulating in thought, urbane in spirit, the Yale discourses of Dr. Henry van Dyke provide to this day a table spread with wholesome food attractively garnished: some succulent delicacies, several interesting side dishes tartly spiced, and topped off with a delicious dessert. What more could a man hungry for an intellectual treat desire!

II. JOHN WATSON

Two of the Yale lecturers, Dr. John Watson (Ian Maclaren) and Dr. Henry van Dyke, had won fame quite apart from their successful ministerial careers. Both were authors of books which were widely circulated; both were Presbyterians, both Moderators of their respective Assemblies; and both were liberals in theology. Dr. Watson's *Beside the Bonnie Brier Bush* had had a phenomenal sale in this country, and the author's first visit to America was the occasion of numerous ovations during his triumphant lecture tour.

Born in England, a graduate of Edinburgh University and New College, also in Edinburgh, he was in the eighteenth year of his long and fruitful ministry at Sefton Park Church, Liverpool, and but forty-eight when he gave his Yale lectures on *The Cure of Souls*. Much was expected of this famous Scotsman, and he lived fully up to his vast reputation.

In the long list of lectures in this Series, Dr. Watson's are distinctive, and rate with Beecher's and Burton's in raciness combined with practical advice, and possibly disclosed a wider scholarship than either Beecher's or Burton's. The lectures were delivered without manuscript, and with no little zest. They were saturated with a shy, delicious humor which reached its peak in the last of the nine addresses, entitled "The Minister's Care of Himself." Little was lost of the charm and pith of the delivery when the lectures appeared in printed form almost simultaneously with their presentation.

Something should be said of Dr. Watson's oratory. The famous

John Watson

impresario, Major J. P. Pond, who managed so many celebrities on their lecture tours, said of Watson:

> His voice is excellent because its tones express the feelings to be conveyed. It is skillfully used with fine inflections and tonal shadings which give emphasis and delicacy to its delivery. His mobile mouth easily lends itself to vocal changes. He is not an orator in the usual sense of the word, but he is a speaker who readily holds an audience to the last moment.

Some of his American hearers found Dr. Watson difficult to understand readily because of the Scottish accent which hung over his speech like the mists that enshroud Ben Nevis.

It is interesting to note just here what Sir W. Robertson Nicoll wrote in his *Life of the Reverend John Watson, D.D.*:

> Before commencing his work with Major Pond, Watson delivered at Yale University the Lyman Beecher course of lectures on Preaching. These discourses were afterwards published in a volume called *The Cure of Souls*. They contained much autobiographical matter slightly disguised. Watson delivered his lectures to the Yale students extempore, and delighted them with his humor, while he moved them by his seriousness. Yale University, from which he received the degree of Doctor of Divinity, is one of the first Universities in America, and Watson was greatly impressed by its stately surroundings and by the ability and courtesy of its professors.
>
> I have before me Major Pond's program of Watson's lectures. It includes ninety-six engagements between October 1 and December 16, 1896. The welcome of America was so generous, frank, and universal, that to find a parallel men had to go back to the days of Charles Dickens. Pond, a man of unrivalled experience, said that he saw more happy faces while accompanying him than any other man was privileged to see in the same length of time. During every one of his ninety-six lectures Watson had as large audiences of men and women as could be crowded into the largest public halls in the principal cities of the United States and Canada. For the most part, he gave readings from his own books, but whether he gave readings or lectures the result was the same.[1]

Now back to the lectures. Dr. Watson began with the "Genesis of the sermon." The sermon, he said, is the result of six processes,

[1] Pp. 177-178.

and he listed the headings, thus: 1. *Selection;* 2. *Separation;* 3. *Illumination;* 4. *Meditation;* 5. *Elaboration;* 6. *Revision.* Under each of these headings the Doctor poured forth a steady stream of counsel, suggestion, and analysis, couched in clean-cut, polished sentences, with an undercurrent of humorous "asides." Thus,

If you mean to write a manuscript, then a day will suffice; if you mean to think a sermon, then it may be ten years. . . . It is one thing for the preacher to woo and win a single idea, and to set up house with it in undisturbed company, and another to have all his wife's relations landed on him. . . . A very impressive word of the new scientific coinage: What can yon sempstress make of it? Rich people have many pleasures, she has only her church.

To Watson, making a sermon is an art, a discipline, a joy, and a sacrifice.

Dr. Watson holds tenaciously and with a bright ebullience in his lecture on "The Technique of the Sermon," that the art of public speech has six canons, to wit: 1. *Unity;* 2. *Lucidity;* 3. *Beauty;* 4. *Humanity;* 5. *Charity;* 6. *Delivery.* Then says Watson: "The last and greatest canon of speaking is *Intensity,* and it will be freely granted that the want of present day preaching is spiritual passion." The young preacher of today, and for that matter the seasoned one as well, may study these six points with profit to himself and to his congregation. And the last, which the lecturer does not number, but uses as a climax, deserves long and serious reflection if it is to sink into the mind of the reader. Reading an essay from the pulpit may require beauty and lucidity but not necessarily *intensity.* This quality is missing in much of the preaching of our generation. But no really great preacher of the Gospel has been deficient in passion, fervor—in short, intensity.

Many must have rejoiced as they listened to Watson deal with "The Machinery of a Congregation," as many have read it with relish in book form. The home of the congregation, he holds, should be beautiful, comfortable, and convenient. He avers that there are churches so conservative that they not only retain the former habits of thought, but the very air of the past, so that one entering after a long absence recognizes the fragrance, since nothing refreshes memory like smell, and is again with his mother in the family pew, while the old minister, after preaching an hour, is giving out his third head. Were the air of one of the hermetically sealed churches bottled, and analyzed by some of those awful scientific inventions that are making darkness as light, it might be possible to write the history of the congregation with a likeness of the minister. Bad air, so Dr. Watson believed, is an auxiliary of Satan, and accounts for one man sleeping, for another fidgeting, for another detecting a personal attack in the sermon, for someone smelling heresy. It was carbonic gas he really sniffed. Watson gave it as his opinion that fresh air and orthodoxy go together as well as good temper and charity.

The lecture on "The Minister's Care of Himself" is simply immense. That it is covertly autobiographical may be safely assumed. Watson is for a sane mind in a sound body. "Suppose two men be both saints, you need not expect equally good stuff from each in the way of thought if one be sound in body and the other unsound."

In the losing battle of the preacher to find time for preparation, the lecturer schedules a hectic week, describing each day's obstacles to completing the sermon. Suppose we pass over all but Saturday, the preacher's last stand against the enemies of his sermonic preparation. Here is the way Watson tells the tragic story:

But *Saturday*! This will make up for all. Alas! his wife goes off guard, and a picturesque foreigner from the East takes possession of the study. The minister, courteous as one ought to be to distant strangers, lays himself out to extricate the visitor's meaning, and after an hour's patient exploration discovers that his caller comes from an unknown place, that he represents himself, that he wishes to build something, that he is determined to preach in the minister's church tomorrow for a collection. When the man from Mesopotamia has been induced to depart, it is vain to take up the sermon till evening. So far as I know, these details are not exaggerated and they are given at length for a serious purpose . . . no man is wearied or harassed by an enterprise of the first order. He is done to death by petty details, by useless talk, by religious faddists, by unnecessary correspondence.

When the reader closes Watson's volume of lectures after having read the others in the Course, he feels like saying, "This is the most entertaining of the lot."

John Watson loved America, and America was kind to him. His third and last visit to our shores, in 1907, was a repetition of the others, lecturing and preaching to crowded houses, dined and honored day after day, with little time for rest. Then in Mount Pleasant, Iowa, after a short and painful illness, he died on May 6 in a hotel. With Dr. John Watson's passing, at the age of fifty-seven, there went out of this life a buoyant spirit, richly gifted and fully committed to the High calling.

When the sorrowing wife brought him home for burial, Liverpool put on mourning, and the demand for a public funeral was too powerful to resist. All denominations and all parties joined in the tribute. It was estimated that the mourners and spectators would not have fallen short of sixty thousand. Some thirty thousand were present at Southdown Cemetery, where the last prayer was said and the pipers of the Scottish Volunteers played "Lochaber No More." Memorial sermons were preached by Professor James Stalker and the Reverend R. C. Gillie of Eastbourne.

The tired traveler had come home to rest in peace among his own.

XII

AFTER EIGHTY YEARS
★ 1871–1951 ★

Time is but the stream I go a-fishing in.
—Thoreau

AFTER EIGHTY YEARS
1871–1951

On April 12, 1871, the Lyman Beecher Lectureship at Yale University was officially born. At that time the state of the Union (37 States) was not altogether salubrious but was improving. The South was in the throes of the Reconstruction Era, and the wounds caused by the dreadful war were still raw and bleeding in Dixie. Ulysses S. Grant was rounding out his first term as President, and the nation was slowly "rousing herself like a strong man after sleep and shaking her invincible locks."

In literary New England the poetical foursome was still regnant. The pens of Longfellow, Emerson, Whittier, and Lowell were active although most of their best work was done. Mark Twain, Bret Harte, and Herman Melville were becoming names of moment, and W. D. Howells was pushing his way into print. Thomas A. Edison was engaged in important experiments in his "big little laboratory"; Woodrow Wilson, a boy of fifteen, was dreaming dreams and seeing visions in a Southern Presbyterian manse, while Theodore Roosevelt, two years Wilson's junior, was taking stock of his frail physique and resolving to overcome the handicap.

Religiously, Protestantism was aggressive, ardently revivalistic, and militantly denominational. The evangelism of the frontier was crude but effective. The foreign missionary enterprise was swinging into a vigorous stride and the Sunday schools were growing in numbers and power. Henry Ward Beecher, Phillips Brooks, and

Richard Salter Storrs were the unrivaled preachers in pulpit eminence, as was also Dwight L. Moody in noble and effective evangelistic zeal. In religious journalism Henry M. Field, H. Clay Trumbull, and Theodore Tilton were making reputations. In Illinois that "Son of Thunder," Peter Cartwright, was to live only a little more than a year. The motto, "In God We Trust," was graven on the bronze two-cent piece and also upon $20 and $10 gold pieces; likewise upon the silver dollar, half dollar, and quarter dollar pieces. The Bible was freely read in thousands of public schools. America felt herself to be a Christian nation and proud to proclaim that distinction.

Training for the Christian ministry was a paramount purpose in the foundation of Yale College in 1701. The original charter contains these words: "wherein Youth may be instructed in the Arts & Sciences who through the blessings of Almighty God may be fitted for Publick employment in Church or Civil state." In 1746 a Professorship of Divinity was established, which in 1822 developed into a separate department, later known as the Yale Divinity School. Thus the Lyman Beecher Foundation of 1871 was a logical outcome in the prospect and plans of the institution for thorough training in the ministerial vocation. It is time now to survey and assess this pre-eminent Lectureship which has reached the ripe old age of fourscore years.

I

Preaching Trends in the Lifetime of the Series

During the eighty years since the Lyman Beecher Lectureship on Preaching was established, society has been shaken to its foundations by revolution and drenched in the blood of two world wars. The power and integrity of organized Christianity has been attacked, not only by individuals but also by political and economic systems frankly and blatantly atheistic. A conflict between Communism and Christianity is raging, and an evil called secularism is at work sapping the vitality of the Church and other Christian institutions. Things we believed could not be shaken are tottering, and the principles of democracy which spring from New Testament teachings are battling for existence. Manifestly these ominous and disastrous facts have changed the emphasis upon doctrines once held fundamental, and produced a new apologetic for the Church and a restatement of theological concepts generally.

1

The first decade of the Yale Lectures, with the exception of those given by Henry Ward Beecher, put the emphasis on sound doctrine, by which is meant that the primary purpose and duty of the preacher is to expound the orthodox teaching on such fundamentals as the Incarnation, the Atonement, the fact and nature of sin, and the redemptive nature of the Gospel. The workmanship of the lecturers in this respect was forthright and competent.

There is a lofty kind of dogmatism in the lectures of Hall, Taylor, Robinson, Simpson, and Crosby, a serenity of assurance in those of Phillips Brooks, and a noble manner of dogmatic statement in the chapters of Dr. Dale. There is plenty of doctrine in the lectures of both Beecher and Brooks, but it is not put forth with an air of finality. Beecher and Brooks were liberals with a difference of evaluation. Neither of these men proclaimed the great doctrines of the Church with offensive militancy; rather they set forth the basic doctrines stoutly and without equivocation, yet in a spirit of amity. Dr. Taylor, in his fourth lecture avers: "In truth, gentlemen, there is nothing more absurd than this clamor against doctrine, for they who raise it do not seem to see that there is, beneath the cry itself, a doctrine to the effect that it makes no matter what a man believes, if only he says that he is resting upon Christ."

It is only fair to these splendid conservatives who gave doctrine so important a place in their lectures, to say that they were careful never to divorce it from the fruits of the Spirit, namely, "love, joy, peace, long-suffering, kindness, goodness, faithfulness, meekness, self-control, against which there is no law."

It was not until 1888, when Dr. Washington Gladden gave his lectures on *Tools and the Man*, that the claims of the social implications of the Gospel received major emphasis. Dr. Gladden, a Congregationalist, had attained a national reputation by his successful pastorates in important centers, his largest and last being the First Congregational Church of Columbus, Ohio, where he served successfully for forty-three years. A student of government and economics as well as a competent theologian, his voice was heard throughout the land proclaiming righteousness and social justice. For the first time in the Series there appeared the names of Adam Smith, Karl Marx, Thomas Malthus, Henry George, Jeremy Bentham, Baron Montesquieu, Josiah Strong, and others—prophets of economic and social change. Dr. Gladden championed the poor, the underprivileged, and the disinherited, and did so in the name of Christ their Saviour. Twenty-one years later he returned to Yale to deliver a second series, on *Social Salvation*.

In 1906 Charles Reynolds Brown presented a significant set of lectures on *The Social Message of the Modern Pulpit*, and Henry Sloane Coffin in 1918 spoke on *In a Day of Social Rebuilding*. Dr. Peter Taylor Forsyth[1] in 1911, Bishops Charles D. Williams, Francis J. McConnell, and Garfield Bromley Oxnam, in 1921, 1930, and 1944 respectively, kept the fires burning on the altar of the Christianizing of the social order. The impression made on those who heard the lectures or read them in book form was deep and lasting. These and other prophets of social change quickened the social thinking of thousands of ministers, and this new note was heard in thousands of sermons.

A reaction was bound to come, and it came by way of protests in pulpit and in print from conservative quarters, that the old and true Gospel was being neglected and in some instances repudiated. Thus the pulpit pendulum which had swung in some instances far to the left in social justice swung back, but not wholly to the right; rather, near the center, possibly to a point a little left of center, where it still oscillates.

There has been a return to theology discernible in the later Lyman Beecher lectures, also in many books, and in the pulpits of the leading denominations. Morrison's *What Is Christianity?* (1939) and Niebuhr's *Faith and History* (1945) are sharply in this trend; also H. H. Farmer's *God and Men* (1946). The Neo-orthodoxy has had its influence, and the writings of Karl Barth, Kierkegaard, Brunner, and others of this school have had an

---

[1] The more ethically we construe the Gospel the more are we driven upon the holiness of God. Forsyth in *Positive Preaching and the Modern Mind*, p. 373.

effect on American preaching, but scarcely equal to that of Reinhold Niebuhr's gloomy but powerful theological thought. The impact of his writings on the younger, seminary-trained ministers is notably strong and influential.

Psychology is having its day with the pulpit as this is written. The ministry to individuals has been and is a growing interest. Albert E. Day's *Jesus and Human Personality* (1934), reveals this influence, and so do myriad sermons preached every Sunday by a host of university-trained ministers. The magazine article by Dr. Fosdick two decades ago on "Does the Protestant Ministry Need a Confessional?" was as startling as an unexpected thunderclap. It must have turned the minds of multitudes in the ministry from mass society to the individual's need of personal solicitude on the part of his pastor.

The ministry of healing comes properly up for discussion here. Dr. Weatherhead's Yale lectures in 1949 exploited the possibilities of this field, and drew capacity audiences of ministers eager to hear him. This was to be expected, for his success in City Temple Church, London, has been remarkable. In one of his lectures in the series he informed the audience that he had associated with him in this work of healing, a Christian psychologist, a Christian psychiatrist, a Christian surgeon, and a Christian doctor of medicine. Dr. Weatherhead is himself a trained psychologist, and is well informed in the domain of psychiatry. Thus he employs hypnosis in his clinical ministry, but was quick to tell his hearers that no minister should use this method unless he has been trained in that field. Some of his own experiences in dealing with the mentally and morally sick were dramatically told, and during the narration of the cases the audience showed intense interest. On a lesser scale perhaps, yet still notable, the works of John Sutherland Bonnell, minister of the Fifth Avenue Presbyterian Church, Norman Vincent Peale of the Marble Collegiate Church, New York City, and Roy Burkhart, in his Community Church, Columbus, Ohio, are cited here as worthy of study.

That there is a danger in the ministry of healing for the untrained and the inexpert must be apparent to thoughtful ministers. "Counseling," as it is now called—the consoling, understanding ministry to individuals, in a kind of Protestant confessional—that has long been an important part of the pastoral task; but the employment of psychotherapy on the part of the Christian minister in dealing with his troubled parishioners is quite another matter. At its best it can be but an adjunct and not the major concern or responsibility of the Christian ministry. Dr. Weatherhead would agree with this conclusion, and has, I believe, so expressed himself.

It was not to be expected that the earlier lecturers would sound the ecumenical note in major. Denominationalism was strong and strident, but there were exceptions. Dr. Nathaniel Judson Burton, in his Yale lectures on preaching, so far back as 1884, smote the ecumenical lyre a resounding rap when he declared:

> I have heard many fine arguments to show the great value of denominations; but in my judgment, all real values could be better served in a Catholic, or universal church. I did not know that once, but I have known it for some years. We must not undertake to defend ourselves from the possible debasement incident to Form by any external abridgement of form.

The later lecturers in the Series occasionally sound this note of "ecumenicity," and it reaches major proportions in Dr. C. C. Morrison's *What Is Christianity?*; and an ample discussion of this theme in the Beecher Series may be confidently expected as the movement gains momentum. That it is gaining in the preaching of the younger clergy is happily true. It has been my privilege to hear a prayer offered by the pastor of a good church in Texas, of such extraordinary ecumenical content, that I feel moved to report it to a wider audience. The minister, a middle-aged man of unusual ability, began by asking God's blessings upon the Holy Father at Rome, the College of Cardinals, and all the parish priests; upon the Archbishop of Canterbury and the Church of England; upon the nonconformists of Great Britain; upon the president of the World Council of Churches meeting in Amsterdam even as the minister prayed; upon the president of the Federal Council of the Churches of Christ in America, and the United Churches of Canada; upon the patriarchs and metropolitans of the Eastern Orthodox Churches; on all of Protestantism of whatever name; upon the Salvation Army; upon the Jewish synagogues and temples where he thought the spirit of the ancient Hebrew prophets should prevail; and finally, he prayed for his brother-minister who was just about to preach on "The Unity for Which Christ Prayed," and that preacher happened to be the writer. Could such a prayer have been offered on a like occasion, say, ten years ago? I doubt it!

2

A professor of theology, and highly esteemed, who heard many of the Lyman Beecher lectures, writes:

> In general I have the feeling that preaching in the twenties centered on the ethical and social, avoided the theological, was sometimes humanist, commonly topical rather than textual. There was still a large degree of optimism as to man's capacity to erect the New Jerusalem in this green and pleasant land. And if there was some misgiving, it did not go beyond what a wit said of Tennyson, that he sounded like an archangel assuring the universe that it would muddle through. The change came about partly in response to external circumstance: the failure of the League of Nations, the depression of 1929, and the rise of the totalitarian powers. Coincidentally came the impact in the realm of ideas of neo-orthodoxy. At the same time, I wonder whether the majority of the lecturers were quickly responsive to the altered situation. The only one to my knowledge who responded swiftly was Reinhold Niebuhr.

The sharp turn in the present trend in preaching is, I observe, more in evidence in the theological seminaries and in the current preaching of the younger seminary-trained ministers than it is in the Yale lecturers of the past few years, with a few notable exceptions. It is interesting to find Dr. Andrew W. Blackwood of Princeton Theological Seminary saying in a recent paper on *What Is Right with Preaching Today?*:

> Preaching stands higher in the esteem of churchmen today than at any time in the past forty years. Forty years ago I was ordained as a minister of the Gospel. . . . If I felt inclined to look on the dark side of the picture I could point out ways in which we still fall short. . . .
>
> These trends ought to interest all of us who teach the finest of the fine arts, that of preaching the Gospel. You who deal with matters of delivery and we who concern ourselves with the preparation of sermons ought to look on these trends from much the same point of view.

You will understand that I approach them as a teacher of homiletics and not as a professor of public speaking. . . .

At many a divinity school today, note the rediscovery of the preacher. In the eyes of professors and students the preacher has become the most important person in the Protestant Church. His work in the pulpit is becoming the most important part of his calling from God. Forty years ago no professor of homiletics could have made such statements. During these two decades I have witnessed at least the beginnings of a renaissance. Early in my career I watched professors and students as they sought to discover substitutes for the primacy of preaching. Of late many of our seminary professors, though by no means all, have begun to put the first thing first. However, they still find it difficult to keep the young graduate from trying to manage an ecclesiastical merry-go-round.

The rediscovery of preaching has begun to affect every department of the seminary. For example, think of theology. Compare the methods of teaching dogmatics forty years ago with the ways of presenting doctrine today. Listen to Professor H. H. Farmer, of Cambridge, England. As a foremost teacher of theology he is addressing students for the ministry. His book, *The Servant of the Word*, stands second to no recent work about preaching. The scholar opens his book and his introductory chapter with these words:

"If one were asked to indicate in the briefest possible way the most central and distinctive trends in contemporary Christian theology, one would be tempted to answer, 'The rediscovery of the significance of preaching.'"

Professor Farmer makes clear that the trend has not yet begun to show itself everywhere in the Church. But in the seminary world he can point to C. H. Dodd as a foremost biblical scholar. This professor at Cambridge University shows that everywhere in the New Testament preaching stands first. His book, *The Apostolic Preaching and Its Development*, has led many of us to think of the apostles first of all as preachers. This amounts to the rediscovery of a truth well known to the fathers at the Reformation, but not to seminary students forty years ago.

The Right Reverend Sabapathy Kulandran, Bishop of the Jaffna Diocese of South India, is not so sanguine about the American pulpit as is Dr. Blackwood, but he is hopeful. In his *The Message and the Silence of the American Pulpit*, he writes:

The late Archbishop William Temple has rightly said that what is really important is not that there is a God, but what sort of a God

After Eighty Years

he is. The Church must see that its proclamation is the one important thing in all the world and that all its attributes and activities follow out of it. A Church without this conviction has no hope for the future and no logic in the present.

What signs are there that the Protestant Church in America is coming to this realization? Are there signs of the possibility of the Church here attaining to a faith that will be historic without being antiquated, modern without being modernistic, fundamental without being fundamentalist, lasting without being stale? No one who has had contact with the leading theological seminaries of America will deny that there is something happening there. A professor on one of the theological faculties that once had a reputation for a most devastating liberalism put the change that was taking place rather piquantly when he said that whereas in his university twenty years ago every day it was a case of "Here beginneth the Scripture lesson for the morning, John Dewey, chapter . . . , verse . . ." now there was a dawning consciousness that Mr. Dewey himself was also perhaps a child of his time. There is a breath stirring. In some institutions it is a strong and perhaps even a mighty wind. It is a wind that will soon sweep with a refreshing force over the land. It is heartening to note that it has already begun to blow outside. Many pulpits and studies have begun to feel its effects. Biblical categories of thought are coming back to their own. Already many voices may be heard engaged in a profound grapple with the great issues of all time and eternity from the standpoint of God's ultimate revelation in Jesus Christ. It is not too much to expect that the number of these voices will go on increasing, and that the movement that they represent will gain ground steadily and almost irresistibly.

It is earnestly to be hoped that the Christian Church in America will realize that there is nothing humiliating in constantly going back to its sources. Dr. George Macleod of Scotland, in a historic sermon at the Madras Conference, compared the need and naturalness of doing this with the situation in which King David, when in battle, had wanted water from the well by the gate at Bethlehem, where he had played as a boy. It was good even for a man who had become king to look back to his beginnings. It is good for any man, however great, to refer back occasionally to the ideals of his youth to see whether he has after all done very well, judged by his own aims. Progress that loses contact with the base may merely lead to the predicament of the babes in the wood. No movement ever gets away from its sources without sealing its own fate. Edmund Burke speaks of those great and important things of life in which no discoveries are to be made, and "which were understood long before we were born, altogether as well as they will be after the grave has heaped its mould on our presumption, and the silent tomb imposed its law on our pert loquacity."

The Christian faith makes certain affirmations about these stretches of reality that lie beyond the immediate. Those stretches of reality present many acute problems. The Christian faith asserts that these problems have been solved because of certain things that happened. Everything it says is on the assumption that the significance it gives to these events as a solution to the problems of reality is true. An attitude that can be silent on these themes takes it for granted that they can be ignored. What can be ignored is unimportant: it may or may not be true. As far as the Christian faith is concerned, to be indifferent in these matters is not to be neutral; it is to deny the very thing that the Christian faith is trying to assert. What the Christian faith is trying to assert is not merely that these affirmations are true in the sense that it is true that Shakespeare wrote *Hamlet* or that Galileo invented the telescope. It is trying to say that they are so important that every human being should know them, that life should be lived only on the assumption of their truth. The long silence of the American pulpit on these themes has deprived many people of contact with that power and the source of that new outlook on life which Christianity came to give. It has also deprived the American pulpit of that peculiar and distinctive basis which alone can make a message Christian.

To the extent that the American pulpit assimilates the truths so ably voiced by Bishop Kulandran, to that extent shall the preaching trends in our nation reach and maintain a higher level of redemptive power.

3

Something needs to be said here about the trend in pulpit speech across the years. Naturally there have been changes in public speaking since the Lyman Beecher Lectures began. The Golden Age of Oratory to which Henry Ward Beecher, Richard S. Storrs, and Matthew Simpson belonged, has passed and is not likely to return. To be sure, there are echoes of the older oratorical style in the South, and occasionally in the North; for example, the powerful eloquence of Frank W. Gunsaulus of Chicago, whose long, periodic sentences sometimes rivaled those of a Beecher or a Rufus Choate. Newell Dwight Hillis, in Beecher's old pulpit, perfected a style of preaching richly adorned with the flowers of literature, which was much admired and widely imitated. His delivery was fluent, and at times volcanic. Charles E. Jefferson of New York City was the master of a crisp, terse manner of speech, a spirited laconic eloquence, also much admired, and difficult to imitate because to achieve anything like its texture exacts an immense amount of preparation. It looked easy, which it was not.

Frederick F. Shannon, successor of Dr. Gunsaulus at Central Church, Chicago, was a poet-preacher of singular winsomeness. Slight of stature, he seemed to expand physically in the full tide of his inspired utterance. Dr. Harry Emerson Fosdick's sermons are distinguished by a touch of grandeur and a sustained stateliness, yet are never stiff or artificial. Dr. Joseph Fort Newton's chastely beautiful English, quite flawless in diction, has been a source of delight to congregations on both sides of the Atlantic. Dr. Leslie D. Weatherhead's manner of speech is a marvel of simplicity, freighted with arresting illustrative material, delivered with suavity and charm.

Dr. Reinhold Niebuhr's pulpit and platform style is unique both in content and presentation. He speaks rapidly, incisively, sometimes with facial contortions, and an opulency of vocabulary. Frequently he startles his hearers with an explosive epigram, and is seemingly of inexhaustible resources. Such noted preachers as Drs. Scherer, Buttrick, Sockman, and Sizoo, are artists in sermonic arrangement, and of impressive delivery. They speak right on in clear, luminous sentences and out of close preparation. Dr. Preston Bradley of Chicago is noted for an oratorical skill akin to the eloquence of a Bryan, and is not afraid of long, rolling sentences packed with pithy comments. To date no preacher of today has tried to reproduce the spectacular grandiloquence of Dr. T. DeWitt Talmage, which is well. Dr. Talmage drew vast crowds, and his published sermons circled the globe, but no teacher of homiletics has approved of his pulpit style.

In the South, as has been remarked, the oratorical style so popular in earlier days still persists and, in some instances, with distinction. Consider the noble eloquence of Dr. George W.

Truett, who in voice, presence, and evangelistic passion won pulpit eminence, not only among Baptists but throughout the South generally. In Louisville, Kentucky, many years ago, Dr. Carter Helmn Jones, Baptist, and Dr. Edward L. Powell, of the Disciples of Christ, were the two outstanding pulpit orators of that city. Dr. Jones was fascinating in his vivid, pictorial sermons, impeccably phrased; and Dr. Powell, powerful in his impassioned declamatory discourses. Utterly different in pulpit manner, both drew capacity audiences to their churches and made many converts.

On the whole, the trend of public speaking is toward the conversational style, in which Wendell Phillips was the unrivaled master in the Golden Age of American Oratory, and Dr. Charles E. Jefferson at a later period. When this method of delivery is perfected, the result is a high order of preaching to which it is a pleasure to repair. This style of public address gives freedom to the speaker and admits readily of the exercise of the dramatic art. Likewise, it favors the introduction of the element of surprise, always a valuable asset to pulpit power.

If there are fewer orators of the first rank in the ministry of today when compared with the pulpit of seventy-five years ago, there is an unrivaled number of ministers who preach with distinction, both in content and delivery, for which, in Pauline language, we should thank God, and take fresh courage.

4

The coming of the radio has produced a new and favorable factor in public speech, exacting as it does, brevity, conciseness, and careful enunciation. Speaking over the air has also put a premium on the skillful manipulation of manuscript, correct pronunciation, and concern for every detail in preparation and delivery. Then, too, making a recording of a speech, and the opportunity of the speaker to have it played back to him is of inestimable value to the orator.

That the radio pulpit has become of importance in this nation and others, consider the preaching over the air of such masters of the sermonic art as Drs. Fosdick, Scherer, and Sockman, in New York City, Preston Bradley in Chicago, and C. S. Lewis in England, to list but a few eminent speakers who took to the air. Dr.

Fosdick's radio ministry was so notable as to deserve further consideration here.

During his broadcasts of nearly twenty years under the auspices of the Federal Council of the Churches of Christ in America, Dr. Fosdick's name became one of the best known on the airways. He began his broadcasting over the network of the National Broadcasting Company in 1928, when the development of network broadcasting across the nation was just beginning. He continued this ministry through 1946, giving up his broadcasting only when he retired from his pastorate at Riverside Church. When the Blue network and the Red network of the National Broadcasting Company were separated in ownership, Dr. Fosdick's program was transferred to the facilities of the newly-formed American Broadcasting Company.

During eight months of each year Dr. Fosdick's voice was heard every Sunday afternoon by a vast audience. He appealed particularly to the more thoughtful listener, especially the listener who was not satisfied with the more conventional religious message. The correspondence which came to Dr. Fosdick from his listeners was almost overwhelming. Each year there were at least 100,000 individual requests for copies of messages which he had delivered over the year. Not a week went by when he did not receive thoughtful letters from people seeking personal counsel from him concerning their problems of faith and conduct.

Dr. Fosdick never "talked down" to his radio audience, or sought to be merely "popular." He always dealt with the profound subjects of spiritual life. Those who were in close touch with the diverse programs offered by the National Broadcasting Company believe that no one who used their facilities continuously had a stronger appeal to the more educated and cultured groups of the American public.

The opportunity to go on the air has compelled many a preacher who has been careless and diffuse in utterance, to choose his words with discrimination, and delete what is not essential to the clarity and unity of his message. Voice, pitch, range, and the nice shadings of expression—all these are involved in speech before a microphone. Thus it comes about that Hamlet's advice to his players is still pertinent:

Speak the speech I pray you, as I pronounce it to you, trippingly on the tongue; and if you mouth it as many of your players do, I had as lief the town crier spoke my lines.

Nevertheless the radio has its limitations. What a great American preacher[2] said about the impossibility of transferring great oratory to the printed page holds good in the realm of the radio:

The kindling eye, the play of emotion on the mobile countenance, the curling of the lip, the pointed finger or sudden thrust of the hand, the erect and quivering frame, the blood mounting to the temples, the momentary pause, the rush of rapid, eager speech, all that belongs to an intense and vital personality grappling with great thoughts, moved by strong passions, urged forward to high endeavor, cannot be transferred to plates of metal and traced upon paper.

From this summary of homiletical history since 1871, it is evident that even as theology is ever in a state of flux, the trend of preaching across the years has yielded naturally to many components of change, yet withal has never lost the essential factor, which is the proclamation of the spiritual and moral verities through human personality aflame with faith. Manner, form, emphasis, and verbal vestment are as variable as the seasons, yet, come time and change, the man who goes into a pulpit prepared, humbled, and excited by a sense of mission, will never want for hearers. To paraphrase one of Dr. Fosdick's penetrating comments:

Vital preaching, like good music, needs no defense but rendition.

II

Representative Character of the Lectureship

The Lyman Beecher Lectureship on Preaching was established by men of vision and catholicity of spirit. Nothing was further from their minds than to permit the Course to take a sectarian slant or favor palpably one communion over another. Beginning with a liberal Congregationalist, he was followed by a conservative Presbyterian, both "markedly successful." In the lifetime of the Lectureship no one school of theology has predominated, although the trend has been liberal and liberating.

[2] The Reverend Adolphus Julius Frederick Behrends (1839-1900).

The resolution adopted April 12, 1871, by the Corporation of Yale College stipulated that "the Lyman Beecher Lectureship on Preaching was to be filled from time to time, upon the appointment of the corporation, by a minister of the Gospel, of any evangelical denomination, who has been markedly successful in the special work of the Christian ministry." In 1893 the article was amended in order to open the Lectureship to a layman "if at any time they should deem it desirable to do so."

In a Lectureship of this nature, confined as it is to the ministerial vocation, some sameness in subject matter was to be expected, and some repetition inevitable. The marvel is that there has not been more. Variety of style and of method in handling similar topics, plus contrasts in the personalities of the speakers, have spared the Lectureship the dead hand of monotony.

In the myriad pages of this library on preaching, Liberal stands side by side with Conservative; college presidents and professors lock arms; army chaplains and philosophers rub shoulders with editors and publicists; and a lawyer destined to become a United States senator mingles freely with poets, essayists, and novelists. Orators, rhetoricians, theologians, and ecclesiastics are of the congenial company; big, husky men physically, and men slight and frail of body combine to make the aggregation one of talent and of personality extremely fascinating.

1

Listing each lecturer according to his denominational affiliation at the time of his appearance in the Course, up to 1949, the result is as follows: Congregationalists, 29; Presbyterians, 16; Episcopalians, including the Church of England, 9; Methodists, 9; Baptists, 5; Unitarians, 2; Disciples of Christ, 1; Lutheran, 1; Evangelical and Reformed, 1. Twenty-three of the lecturers were either born or educated in the British Isles. Twenty-nine of the ministers in the Course held pastorates in New York City, and fifteen were born in New England. Geographically, with a single exception, not a state west of the Mississippi is represented by a native son; only two from the deep South and none from the Southwest or the Northwest. Bishop Oxnam was born in California, while Charles Reynolds Brown, who resided in Oakland, California, when he first participated in the Series, was a West Virginian by birth.

This heavy representation from the East is easily accounted for, since the preponderance of pre-eminent ministers was, and still is, centered in that section. Then, too, Congregationalism, which founded and fostered both Yale Divinity School and the Lyman Beecher Series, is at its best culturally and numerically in New England. It is reasonable to expect that some of the future selections to this Lectureship will be drawn from other regions of the United States. Such procedure would be to the good of the Lectureship and also to the credit of the Divinity School, which attracts students from every section of America.

It may be assumed that all the men who have appeared in this Yale Lectureship were "markedly successful"; that is to say, they had occupied important churches, professorial positions, or the presidencies of colleges—successful men in their attainments, varying only in degree and in natural or acquired gifts. This was to be expected. There is never a premium put on mediocrity. But a question emerges. Are there not rural and small-town ministers also "markedly successful"? One can recall a few men who, in such fields, have made conspicuous success, as for example the late Reverend George B. Gilbert, author of *Forty Years a Country Preacher*, or the Reverend A. W. Hewitt, who wrote *Highland Shepherds* and other widely-read books the scenes of which center about his New England pastorates. There are other names which might be mentioned but these will suffice. It would add to the representative character of this historic Lectureship, and also to its greatening, if at least occasionally a lecturer were chosen from a field, humble perhaps in the sight of men, but surely not in the sight of God. For one, I think so, and so must a host of faithful pastors who cannot in the very nature of things hope to become ministers of large, prominent, and wealthy congregations.

2

A fair balance between liberal and conservative has been maintained through the lifetime of the Series; unconsciously so, I imagine, since the caliber of the men has meant more to those who have had the responsibility of choosing the speakers than their denominational badge. This should be expected since Yale stands for the open mind and the venturesome spirit of the pioneer and pathfinder. Grant this, and is it not remarkable that in a Course that has existed for three-quarters of a century no extremist of any pattern misused or exploited the Yale platform? This is something to remember and to cherish, for it is not always so.

Many types of great preachers have graced the Yale Lectureship; practically every phase of the ministerial task has been presented by men conspicuous for their success in pulpit, parish, classroom, or study. But no one conspicuous as an evangelistic force has as yet honored the Course, although the importance of evangelism has been accented by many of the speakers who, in some instances, devoted entire lectures to the subject, notably, Bishop McDowell, in 1932. But these men were not themselves especially noted as preachers of vast evangelistic zeal. Consider what richness of mind and heart the late Dr. George W. Truett of Dallas, Texas, could have brought to this Course on Preaching. In the judgment of those in a position to know, Dr. Truett was one of the most powerful preachers of his kind in America during the past forty years. A man of distinguished appearance, an orator of parts, austere at times, yet of vast compassion, such a man would have brought to Yale, and through his published lectures, to the country, a contribution which would have enriched the Lectureship and set many a student hearer afire with apostolic zeal.

For all this writer knows, Dr. Truett, or someone of his type, was considered and may have declined the honor. But the stricture holds good and cannot be tossed aside as unimportant. However, in fairness to the faculty of Yale Divinity School, it needs to be repeated just here that those who compose it are fully aware of the heavy and delicate responsibility that is theirs annually in choosing just one lecturer from scores of able men on both sides of the Atlantic. In addition to scholarship, character, and personal availability, denominational and geographical considerations are involved—these and the place of the man in the public eye at the time. How readily there comes to mind a host of "markedly successful" men, the equal of many and the superior of some who were chosen, yet who are missing from The Glorious Company.

Recall such names as these: Richard Salter Storrs, the peer of Beecher oratorically, and in some gifts his superior; Newell Dwight Hillis, in the colorful heyday of his fame; S. Parkes Cadman, eminent, magnetic, and versatile; Joseph Fort Newton, a "preachers' preacher," of diction chastely beautiful; William A. Cameron, noted Baptist preacher of Toronto, a sermonic genius; the inimitable William A. Quayle; Joseph M. M. Gray, brilliant, scholarly, prophetic; John A. Hutton, powerful preacher of England, and editor of *The British Weekly*; Joseph R. Sizoo, a master of pulpit discourse; Gaius Glenn Atkins, possessor of a literary style of haunting loveliness, and a lifelong student of preaching; Charles F. Aked, British-born, but rounding out a quarter of a century in the United States of America, a preacher of extraordinary literary excellence; Lynn Harold Hough, of scintillating sermonic brilliance; and David Swing, the poet-preacher. So one might go on and on, for not only these just named, but others also who were of an elect company mighty in word and deed.[3]

Some of these men, and others not mentioned here, were invited and declined, notably the Reverend Dr. Charles E. Raven of Cambridge, England. He was unable to fill the engagement after accepting, on account of World War I. Joseph Fort Newton is another who was invited, and his going to City Temple, London, meant "No" for answer. In England, the great Alexander Maclaren was asked and declined; also Charles H. Spurgeon, who replied, "I sit on my own gate and whistle my own tunes and am quite content." In some cases death prevented men from lecturing who had been asked; two examples of this lamentable fact are William Temple, Archbishop of Canterbury, and H. R. L. ("Dick") Sheppard, during his last years as rector of the Church of St. Martin's-in-the-Fields, London.

No Negro has yet given the Beecher lectures. Perhaps this was too much to expect in the past, but what about *now*? A large section of the world of sport has lifted the color ban, and millions of devotees have approved the action. Other doors once closed to the Negro are now open. There are at least a half-dozen ministers and educators of the Negro race whose brilliance, scholarship, and consecration are such as to rate them "markedly successful." It is good to know that Dr. Howard Thurman recently gave *The*

---

[3] To this list belongs also that master of drollery, wit, and wisdom, the Will Rogers of our ministerial fraternity, Halford E. Luccock, who is equally at home in pulpit or classroom, and likewise greatly beloved and admired.

Ingersoll Lecture on Immortality, and that Professor Edgar Sheffield Brightman of Boston University said: "Dr. Thurman's lecture is one of the most brilliant and satisfying, both intellectually and spiritually, in the entire Series."

3

An analysis of the Lectures from 1872 to 1949 should prove valuable. For instance, 29 lectures deal with the technique of preaching, based on the experience of the lecturer; 5 present enchanting studies of great preachers; 3 are concerned with the sources of sermonic material; 3 treat of some educational phase of the ministry; 4 have to do with the freedom and authority of the minister; 5 deal with the thought currents of the age; 4 treat theology at length; 4 stress the social aspects of the gospel; 5 deal with prophetic preaching; 9 direct their thinking to some objectives of the ministry; and one devoted his series to the healing ministry of the Christian faith. That there is some overlapping of subject matter was unavoidable, nor is this important. Repetition has scriptural authority.

It has been noted with concern by some students of the Series that in the later lectures the technique of preaching does not receive the close attention which it did in the lectures up to, say, 1900. There are certain marked exceptions; for example, the especially fine treatment of *The Art of Preaching,* by Charles Reynolds Brown, in 1923, the spirited series of J. Edgar Park in 1936, and Paul E. Scherer in 1943. That future lecturers will return to the homiletical art from time to time is desirable, since each generation of preachers is in need of instruction in the preparation and delivery of sermons by masters of the spoken word. The quotation that follows, from one of the ablest of young American preachers, is to the point:

I must concede also that my seminary failed in training us to preach. It was not an unqualified failure. The seminary gave us experience before some of the greatest preachers in America, experience that was invaluable and which I have never forgotten. It gave us a familiarity with the literature of homiletics. But there was not enough on how to write a sermon, what to read for preaching resources, how to use different kinds of material. And most woefully lacking was any close relationship between homiletics and the basic courses in philosophy, theology and ethics. The theology professor cannot turn his department into a preaching workshop, but the homiletics man ought to see to it that students are taught something about the art of transacting spiritual business with their people in these great matters of faith. That was never done for me so that I could go ahead with any confidence that my preaching was getting anywhere near the mark. Over the years I have reaped a rich harvest from the seeds that were sown in seminary study, but the processing of that harvest for delivery to parish people was not made easier.[4]

If the academic degrees of the lecturers in the Yale Series, those earned through prescribed courses of study together with those of an honorary character, were listed here, at least two pages would be required to marshal the imposing array of letters. Masters of Arts would vie with Bachelors of Divinity, and Doctors of Law, Literature, Science, Philosophy, and Divinity would pass by in proud phalanx. Yet be it known that three of the men who appeared in this noble Course were neither college graduates nor trained in seminaries, to wit: Bishop Simpson, H. Clay Trumbull, and Bishop Freeman. If all the books written by the Yale lecturers on preaching were collected in one place, the result would be a library of above 1,000 volumes, mostly, but not altogether, on religious subjects. Biography, fiction, poetry, autobiography, history, and textbooks would be represented in generous measure.

A critical appraisement of the Yale lecturers and their contributions to the Course and to the world is a task at once too difficult and too delicate to assay save in a general fashion. On the whole, the Series stands up creditably—with only one huge disappointment registered—a record seldom equaled and probably never surpassed. A few of the published lectures are "thin" both physically and otherwise. A dozen, perhaps, fall below the high level. But it must be borne in mind that in delivery the lectures that do not read so well may have sounded pretty good. It is probably true that a few of the men were less themselves than when on familiar platforms and in their own pulpits. This was certainly true of Bishop Simpson, who was a chained eagle, manu-

[4] Robert E. Luccock in *The Christian Century*, April 26, 1950.

script-bound, at New Haven. Yet even so handicapped, he delivered a creditable series.

In bestowing recognition and honors on the brave men who served the nation on land and sea and in the air, the United States government issues three grades of medals, in increasing scale of distinction. I make bold to rank the lecturers in the Lyman Beecher Series on Preaching after the manner of our beloved Republic in honoring her heroic sons. Thus: to 15 per cent of the lecturers whose discourses were published, *The Distinguished Service Medal*; to 70 per cent, *The Distinguished Service Cross*; and to 15 per cent, *The Congressional Medal of Honor*, which must be presented by the President of the United States.

III

THE LIGHTER SIDE OF THE LECTURESHIP

1

The lighter side of this long-lived Lectureship is as much in evidence as the scholarly, literary, and theological. A commentator on the Book of Proverbs refers to that sparkling collection as belonging to the "lighter Jewish literature." The accuracy of this descriptive phrase is not questioned, yet Proverbs has long been classed as belonging to the wisdom literature of the Bible. These two descriptions alike stand up because they are both true. Humor, wit, entertaining anecdotes, and that royal sport of verbal badminton popularly known as repartee, are shown to advantage in scores of these lectures.

"The idea that preachers are dull dogs is quite erroneous," writes Arthur Porritt. Quite as erroneous, let us say, as the notion that the Scots as a people are "close," the English devoid of a sense of humor, and the Irish invariably witty. Generalizations are commonly a hazard. The French have a proverb, "No general statement is true, not even this one." Sydney Smith (1771-1845), a clergyman of the Church of England, was one of the wittiest men of his day, and rates six columns in *Bartlett's Familiar Quotations* (Eleventh Edition) as against three for Charles Darwin. This fact may have no other significance than that a witty parson fared better in a popular anthology than a world-famous naturalist. Laurence Sterne, a fellow clergyman of Smith, who preceded him by a generation or so, was also a wit, but of the Rabelaisian school. Not even Dean Inge was really "gloomy," although his wit was often razor-edged.

2

The notion that divinity students supply the acid test for those who preach or lecture is true only in part. They enjoy good preaching as do the rest of us, and are impatient with mediocrity; and who is not? They are sharply critical of a display of learning on the part of a celebrity, and abhor bombastic rhetoric, to which, mercifully, they are not often subjected. Seminarians are hard to stampede and easy to bore. That they are sometimes uncharitable in their criticisms is of course true. The theological student who described the great Dean Inge's lectures as a "dud," was more picturesque than polite. Likewise, ecclesiastical "brass" fails utterly to awe the theologues, some of whom served in the World Wars. Sartorially the theologues, as they move about the campus or sit in classrooms, are anything but clerical. Hatless and happy, they are a sprightly company.

Actually, the divinity students at Yale are enthusiastic about the Beecher Lectures, and look forward eagerly to Convocation Week and the coming of another competent lecturer on the Art of Preaching. It is a familiar scene, and a happy one, to see the students thronging about a speaker at the end of his lecture, congratulating him and plying him with questions. Most preachers and lecturers covet the privilege of addressing a student body, assuming they are prepared and have left nothing to chance. Practically all of the lecturers have participated in the "Questions and Answers" sessions and enjoyed the experience, except Dr. J. H. Jowett, who seemed to feel that he was "heckled." There is reason to believe that this renowned preacher did not get as much pleasure from delivering his Yale discourses as did those who heard him. Under date of April 17, 1912, he thus wrote to a friend:

I am here for ten days delivering the Yale lectures on preaching. I accepted the invitation to give them long before Fifth Avenue was on the horizon. These lectures have been a nightmare to me, and I am glad I am rid of them, this week. When you are with a subject for a long time you are apt to get a bit sick of it. Your counsels begin to seem very stale. I only hope they are fresher to the students than they are to me. I have just dipped into the pool of my experiences and I am giving the men some of my findings.[5]

Here is a human side of a famous preacher quite conscientiously disclosed.

The Divinity School entertains its guests in the Course, as would be expected, with every gracious and hospitable consideration. A restful place is provided for them, for which an appropriate name would be "The Prophets' Chamber." It is conveniently situated on the left side of the main entrance to the "Quad," and attractively appointed. Here the honored guest may welcome members of the faculty and other friends and, if he wishes, snatch a few winks of sleep between engagements. Another pleasant feature of Convocation Week is mealtime in the refectory, where faculty and students meet on common ground, while the hum of conversation, flow of wit, and echoes of mirth provide an enjoyable interlude. In this connection it is pleasant to relate that when Dean and Mrs. Inge were at the Divinity School in 1925, they partook of the bountiful hospitality of Dean and Mrs. Charles Reynolds Brown. It is a joy to recall a memorable visit I myself had with the Browns in 1947, at which time they told me that of the many noted guests they had welcomed to their home, the Inges were among the most delightful. This is pleasing to know, for as reported elsewhere in this book, the Dean's lectures at Yale were a lamentable disappointment.

3

In regard to the popularity and sale of the Yale volumes on preaching, of the earlier ones, except those of Beecher, Brooks, Burton, and Broadus, not much is known. Beecher's three single volumes have been reprinted in one volume, which sells steadily. Burton's inimitable *In Pulpit and Parish*, which was brought out in a new edition, is in demand. Dr. Broadus' *On the Preparation and Delivery of Sermons* has had an amazing history. First published in 1870, it passed through various editions and was trans-

[5] Arthur Porritt, *John Henry Jowett*, p. 154.

lated into several languages. This remarkable work contains the substance of the lectures which Broadus gave at Yale in 1889 from notes, and never published separately. In the eighty years of its history, this book, now in a new and revised edition, has reached an all-time high in sales. John Watson's (Ian Maclaren) *The Cure of Souls* had a wide circulation on both sides of the Atlantic. Henry van Dyke's *The Gospel for an Age of Doubt* went through several editions. Of the later volumes, Silvester Horne's *The Romance of Preaching* sold widely, while Harry Emerson Fosdick's *The Modern Use of the Bible* tops all the others, selling approximately 80,000 copies.

Of equal interest is the fact that *all* of the books in the Yale Series are now in demand, and some of them very hard to find, since, with the exception of the volumes named above, the majority of the books are out of print and can be procured only through secondhand book shops specializing in such material. Throughout the United States of America and Canada ministers perseveringly collect the volumes in this library on preaching, and whenever the mail brings a book catalogue they are apt to drop everything and eagerly scan the lists for a Yale Series rarity. Accurate figures are not available but it is doubtful if as many as ten complete sets of the Lyman Beecher Lectures on Preaching are on the shelves of private libraries.

The youngest lecturer to appear in the Series was George Harris, Congregationalist, minister of High Street Church, Portland, Maine; Central Church, Providence, Rhode Island; professor in Andover Seminary; and president of Amherst College. He was thirty-seven when he was one of six who gave the Lectures in 1881. The oldest was Principal Lawrence P. Jacks of England, who was seventy-three when he spoke at Yale in 1933. Dr. Charles H. Parkhurst was seventy when he was in the Course. So also was John Brown, minister of Bunyan Meeting House at Bedford, England. Twenty-two of the speakers were in their "fiery forties" when they entered the lists at New Haven.

The attendance at the Lectures has been uniformly good, taxing the capacity of the chapel at times, but in only one instance were policemen present to handle the crowds which waited, eager to see and hear the lecturer. That was in 1924, when Dr. Fosdick

After Eighty Years 409

was the speaker. This information comes from one who stood with the mass of people impatiently waiting for the doors of the chapel to open. In consulting Dr. Fosdick on this subject, he said he had forgotten the incident, if indeed he ever knew of it. He attributed the huge attendance to the fact that the Conservative-Modernist controversy was raging, which at that particular time centered around him, and the wide newspaper publicity given the wrangle. In part Dr. Fosdick may have been right in this explanation, but controversy or not, the chapel would have been filled to hear the minister of Riverside Church.

Something should be said here of the financial side of the Lectureship. Whether that side is the lighter, is open to debate, but light or heavy, it is part of the story. The human interest in salaries, wages, fees, honoraria, and the like, is astonishingly widespread and not confined to any one business, trade, activity, or profession. Now it can be told that a number of the brethren of the cloth are curious as to the size of the honoraria paid the lecturers in the Beecher Foundation. Not only so, but they cherish an exaggerated idea as to the emolument received by their brother-ministers in this Course. Many will be surprised to learn that the honorarium is but $500 to those who reside in America, and $800 to guests from overseas, plus, of course, entertainment at the Divinity School. As fees go today, considering the drudgery of preparation and the nervous force expended in delivery, the sum paid the speakers seems a mere bagatelle. In 1872, when the Lectureship began, $500 was *five hundred dollars*, which alas! it was not when this was written. The initial sum of $10,000 given by Mr. Henry Sage to found the Lectureship could readily earn 6 per cent interest then, perhaps even so today, but the purchasing power of the dollar has shrunk.

No one perhaps is more painfully aware of the fact that on its face this honorarium seems not in keeping with the grandeur that is Yale's and the glory that was Founder Sage's, than the faculty and dean of the Divinity School. They have no good reason to be embarrassed, for there are compensations other than pecuniary. The enormous prestige of the Foundation and the prestige which accrues to those who appear in the Course cannot be fairly appraised in monetary terms. The likelihood is that were the records available, it would be disclosed that not a single lecturer quibbled over the fee paid him by the Divinity School. It is a good deal like a young man who, in the hope of marrying a charming girl, is so elated over winning her hand that it never once occurs to him to look her father up in Dun and Bradstreet before he proposes. To paraphrase an oft-quoted saying of Jesus: *What shall it profit a preacher if he gain huge fees and lose the soul of his majestic mission?*

It is altogether fitting that the late dean of Yale Divinity School, Dr. Charles Reynolds Brown, whose name is to many of us a synonym for that institution, should here pronounce the benediction. In a very real way too, this brilliant preacher and very great gentleman embodied the ideals and spirit of the Lyman Beecher Lectureship on Preaching, two courses of which he himself gave, and was so intimately associated with the famous Foundation for more than a quarter of a century. The paragraphs which follow and the verses he so loved close his autobiography entitled *My Own Yesterdays*:

I have seen many changes in these forty years, some of them good, and some of them depressing. I firmly believe that the challenge of those forces which are drawing people away from religion these days can be met. I am not a pessimist, and I do not believe that the Lord God Almighty has cut out for Himself a piece of work which will prove too hard for Him. If we do our part, with anything like a decent measure of fidelity, we shall see Him coming off more than conqueror. I expect to be there to witness His triumph and to join in the Hallelujah Chorus, "Blessing and honor and glory and power be unto Him, for the Lord God Omnipotent reigneth." All the kingdoms of this world, business, politics, education, recreation, and the rest, shall become the kingdoms of Christ.

I have given forty-one years of my own life to the Christian ministry. It has been hard work throughout, but a glad experience. If I had my life to live over, I would do it again, hoping to do it much better because of what I have learned through my blunders and failures and by the exceeding grace which has been given me from above. If any word which I have written here serves to make that high calling seem more interesting and alluring in the eyes of any young man of promise, I shall thank God and take courage and sing the Long Meter Doxology through again three times without stopping.

After Eighty Years

> "So let the way wind up the hill or down
> Though rough the road, the journey will be joy;
> Still seeking what I sought when but a boy,
> New friendships, high adventure and a crown.
> I shall grow old but never lose life's zest,
> Because the road's last turn will be the best."

Thus endeth the long lesson:

> What flaws! What faults!—on every page
> When *Finis* comes.[6]

[6] Henry Austin Dobson.

APPENDIX 1

Who's Who in the Lyman Beecher Lectureship on Preaching
[Compiled by the Rev. Hal Earl Norton, D.D.]

HENRY WARD BEECHER. Born June 24, 1813, Litchfield Connecticut. Graduated Amherst College, 1834, Lane Theological Seminary, 1837. Ordained to ministry of Presbyterian Church, 1838. Pastor, First Presbyterian Church, Lawrenceburg, Indiana, 1837-1839; Second Presbyterian Church, Indianapolis, Indiana, 1839-1847; transferred to Congregational ministry, 1847; pastor, Plymouth Church, Brooklyn, New York, 1847-1887. Lyman Beecher Lectures on Preaching; First Series in 1872, "Personal Elements in Preaching"; Second Series in 1873, "Social and Religious Machinery of the Church"; Third Series in 1874, "Methods of Using Christian Doctrines in Preaching." Died March 3, 1887.

JOHN HALL. Born July 31, 1829, County Armagh, Ireland. Graduated College of Belfast, 1846, Theological School of same, 1849. Ordained to ministry of Irish Presbyterian Church, 1850. Missionary to West of Ireland 1849-1853; pastor, First Presbyterian Church, New York City, 1867-1898. Lyman Beecher Lectures on Preaching in 1875, "God's Word Through Preaching." Died September 17, 1898.

WILLIAM MACKERGO TAYLOR. Born September 23, 1829, Kilmarnock, Scotland. Graduated University of Glasgow, 1849, United Presbyterian Divinity Hall, Edinburgh, Scotland, 1852. Ordained to ministry of United Presbyterian Church, 1852. Pastor, United Presbyterian Church, Kilmauris, Scotland, 1852-1855; United Presbyterian Church, Liverpool, England, 1855-1872; transferred to Congregational ministry, 1872; pastor, Broadway Tabernacle, New York City, 1872-1892; emeritus of same, 1892-1895. Lyman Beecher Lectures on Preaching, in 1876, "The Ministry of the Word," in 1886, "The Scottish Pulpit." Died February 8, 1895.

PHILLIPS BROOKS. Born December 13, 1835, Boston, Massachusetts. Graduated Harvard College, 1855; Virginia Theological Seminary, 1859. Ordained to ministry of Episcopal Church, 1859. Rector, The Church of the Advent, Philadelphia, Pennsylvania, 1859-1862; Holy Trinity Episcopal Church, 1862-1869; Trinity Episcopal Church, Boston, Massachusetts, 1869-1891; Bishop of Massachusetts, 1891-1893. Lyman Beecher Lectures on Preaching in 1877, "Lectures on Preaching." Died January 23, 1893.

ROBERT WILLIAM DALE. Born December 1, 1829, London, England. Graduated Spring Hill College, Birmingham, England, 1853; Theological Department of same, 1853. Ordained to ministry of Congregational Church, 1854. Co-pastor, Carr's Lane Congregational Church, Birmingham, 1853-1859; pastor of same, 1859-1895. Lyman Beecher Lectures on Preaching in 1878. Died March 15, 1895.

MATTHEW SIMPSON. Born June 21, 1811, at Cadiz, Ohio. Studied medicine under Dr. James McBean, 1830-1833. Ordained to ministry of Methodist Episcopal Church 1835. Pastor, St. Clairsville Circuit, Ohio, 1833-1834; Smithfield and East Liberty Churches, Pittsburgh, Pennsylvania, 1834-1835; East Liberty Church, Pittsburgh, 1835-1836; Williamsport Church, 1836-1837. Professor, Allegheny College, Meadville, Pennsylvania, 1838-1839; president, De Pauw University, Greencastle, Indiana, 1839-1848; editor, *The Western Advocate*, 1848-1852; Bishop, 1852-1884. Lyman Beecher Lectures on Preaching in 1879, "Lectures on Preaching." Died June 18, 1884.

HOWARD CROSBY. Born February 27, 1826, New York City. Graduated New York University, 1844, private study 1844-1851. Professor, New York University, 1851-1859; Rutgers University, 1859-1863. Ordained to ministry of Presbyterian Church, New Brunswick, New Jersey, 1861-1863; Fourth Avenue Presbyterian Church, New York City, 1863-1891. Lyman Beecher Lectures on Preaching in 1880, "The Christian Preacher." Died March 29, 1891.

JOSEPH TUTHILL DURYEA. Born December 9, 1832, Jamaica, New York. Graduated Princeton University, 1856; Princeton Theological Seminary, 1859. Ordained to ministry of Presbyterian Church, 1859. Pastor, Second Church, Troy, New York, 1859-1862; Collegiate Marble Reformed Church, New York City, 1862-1867; Classon Avenue Church, Brooklyn, New York, 1867-1879; transferred to ministry of Congregational Church, 1879; Central Congregational Church, Boston, Massachusetts, 1879-1888; First Congregational Church, Omaha, Nebraska, 1888-1895; First Dutch Reformed Church, Brooklyn, New York, 1895-1898. Lyman Beecher Lecture on Preaching in 1881, title unknown and unpublished. Died May 17, 1898.

GEORGE HARRIS. Born April 1, 1844, East Machias, Maine. Graduated Amherst College, 1866; Andover Theological Seminary, 1869. Ordained to ministry of Congregational Church, 1869. Pastor, High Street Congregational Church, Portland, Maine, 1869-1872; Central Congregational Church, Providence, Rhode Island, 1872-1883. Professor, Andover Theological Seminary, 1883-1889; president, Amherst College, 1889-1912; emeritus same 1912-1922. Lyman Beecher Lecture on Preaching in 1881 not published and title unknown. Died March 1, 1922.

SAMUEL HERRICK. Born April 6, 1841, Southampton, New York. Graduated Amherst College, 1859; Princeton Theological Seminary, 1863. Ordained to ministry of Presbyterian Church, 1863. Pastor, Wappinger's Falls, New York, 1863-1864; transferred to ministry of Congregational Church, Broadway Congregational Church, Chelsea, Massachusetts, 1864-1871; Mount Vernon Street Church, Boston, Massachusetts, 1871-1904. Lyman Beecher Lecture on Preaching in 1881 not published and title unknown. Died December 4, 1904.

LLEWELYN DAVID BEVAN. Born September 11, 1842, Llanelly, Wales. Graduated University College, London, 1863; student New College, London, 1858-1865; LL.B., University College, London, 1866. Ordained to ministry of Congregational Church, 1865. Assistant, King's Weigh House Chapel, London, 1865-1869; pastor, Tottenham Court Road Chapel, Whitfields, 1869-1876; Professor, New College, London, 1871-1876. Transferred to ministry of Presbyterian Church, pastor, Brick Presbyterian Church, New York City, 1876-1882; Highbury Quadrant Chapel, London, 1882-1886; Collins Street Independent Church, Melbourne, Australia, 1886-1910. Principal, Parkin College, Adelaide, Australia, 1910-1919. Lyman Beecher Lecture in 1881, title unknown. Died August 9, 1919.

EZEKIEL GILMAN ROBINSON. Born March 23, 1815, South Attleboro, Massachusetts. Graduated Brown University, 1838; Newton Theological Institution, 1842. Ordained to ministry of Baptist Church, 1842. Pastor, Cumberland Street Baptist Church, 1842. Norfolk, Virginia, 1842-1845; Old Cambridge Baptist Church, Cambridge, Massachusetts, 1845-1846. Professor, Covington Baptist Seminary, Covington, Kentucky, 1846-1848. Pastor, Ninth Street Baptist Church,

Cincinnati, Ohio, 1848-1853. Professor, Rochester Theological Seminary, 1853-1860; president same, 1860-1872; president, Brown University, 1872-1889; professor, University of Chicago, 1892-1894. Lyman Beecher Lectures in 1882, "Lectures on Preaching." Died June 13, 1894.

NATHANIEL JUDSON BURTON. Born December 17, 1824, Trumbull, Connecticut. Graduated Wesleyan University, Connecticut, 1850; Yale Divinity School, 1854. Ordained to ministry of Congregational Church, 1853. Pastor, Pilgrim Congregational Church, New Haven, Connecticut, 1853-1857; Fourth Congregational Church, Hartford, Connecticut, 1857-1870; Park Congregational Church, Hartford, Connecticut, 1870-1887. Lyman Beecher Lecture in 1881; Lyman Beecher Lectures in 1884, "In Pulpit and Parish," second edition; the original edition, "Yale Lectures on Preaching and Other Writings." Both editions contain the 1881 Lyman Beecher lecture, but not designated in either. Died October 13, 1887.

HENRY MARTIN STORRS. Born January 20, 1827, Ravenna, Ohio. Graduated Amherst College, 1846. Taught school, Gordonsville, Virginia, 1846-1848. Graduated Andover Theological Seminary, 1851; studied Yale Divinity School, 1851-1852. Ordained to ministry of Congregational Church, 1852. Pastor, Lawrence Street Congregational Church, Lawrence, Massachusetts, 1852-1855; First Orthodox Congregational Church, Cincinnati, Ohio, 1855-1867; South Congregational Church, Brooklyn, New York, 1867-1872. Secretary, American Home Missionary Society, 1872-1882. Transferred to ministry of Presbyterian Church, 1882; pastor First Presbyterian Church, Orange, New Jersey, 1882-1894. Lyman Beecher Lectures in 1885, "The American Preacher." Lectures unpublished. Died December 1, 1894.

WASHINGTON GLADDEN. Born February 11, 1836, Pottsgrove, Pennsylvania. Graduated Williams College, 1859. Ordained to ministry of Congregational Church, 1859. Pastor, First Methodist-Congregational Church, Brooklyn, New York, 1860-1861; First Congregational Church, Morrisania, New York, 1861-1866; First Congregational Church, North Adams, Massachusetts, 1866-1871. Religious Editor, *New York Independent*, 1871-1875. Pastor, North Congregational Church, Springfield, Massachusetts, 1875-1882; pastor, First Congregational Church, Columbus, Ohio, 1882-1918. Lyman Beecher Lectures on Preaching, First Series, in 1887, "Tools and the Man," Second Series, in 1902, "Social Salvation." Died July 2, 1918.

Appendix 1

HENRY CLAY TRUMBULL. Born June 8, 1830, Stonington, Connecticut. Attended Williston Academy. Engaged in business, 1851-1858. Secretary, Connecticut Sunday School Association, 1858-1862. Ordained to ministry of Congregational Church, 1862. Chaplain, Tenth Connecticut Volunteers, 1862-1865. Secretary, American Sunday School Union for New England, 1865-1875. Editor, *Sunday School Times*, 1875-1903. Lyman Beecher Lectures in 1888, "The Sunday School." Died December 8, 1903.

JOHN ALBERT BROADUS. Born January 24, 1827, Culpeper County, Virginia. Graduated University of Virginia, 1850. Taught privately, Fluvana, Virginia, 1850-1851. Ordained to ministry of Baptist Church, 1850. Pastor, Charlottesville Baptist Church, Charlottesville, Virginia, 1851-1859. Assistant professor, University of Virginia, 1851-1853; professor, Baptist Seminary, Greenville, South Carolina, 1859-1877. Pastor, Cedar Grove and Williamston, Baptist Churches, South Carolina, 1863-1864; secretary, Sunday School Board, 1864-1866; professor, Baptist Seminary, Louisville, Kentucky, 1877-1889; president of same, 1889-1895. Lyman Beecher Lectures in 1889 "Preaching and Ministerial Life"; published in revised edition, *On the Preparation and Delivery of Sermons*. Died March 15, 1895.

ADOLPHUS JULIUS FREDERICK BEHRENDS. Born December 18, 1839, Nymwegen, Holland. Came to United States, 1844. Graduated Denison University, 1862; Rochester Theological Seminary, 1865. Ordained to ministry of Baptist Church, 1865. Pastor, Warburton Avenue Baptist Church, Yonkers, New York, 1865-1873; First Baptist Church, Cleveland, Ohio, 1873-1876. Transferred to ministry of Congregational Church, 1876; pastor, Union Congregational Church, Providence, Rhode Island, 1876-1883; Central Congregational Church, Brooklyn, New York, 1883-1900. Lyman Beecher Lectures in 1890, "The Philosophy of Preaching." Died May 22, 1900.

JAMES STALKER. Born February 21, 1844, Crieff, Scotland. Graduated University of Edinburgh, 1869; New College, Edinburgh, 1873. Studied, Universities of Halle and Berlin, 1874. Ordained to ministry of Free Church, 1874. Pastor, St. Brycedale Free Church, Kirkcaldy, 1874-1887; Free St. Matthew's Church, Glasgow, Scotland, 1887-1902. Professor, Free Church College, Aberdeen, 1902-1924; professor emeritus of same, 1924-1927. Lyman Beecher Lectures in 1891, "The Preacher and His Models." Died February 5, 1927.

ANDREW MARTIN FAIRBAIRN. Born November 4, 1838, Inverkeithing, Scotland. Studied University of Edinburgh, 1857-1860. Graduated Theological College, Edinburgh, 1860. Ordained to ministry of Evangelical Union Church, 1860. Pastor Bathgate Evangelical Union Church, 1860-1872; transferred to ministry of Congregational Church, 1872; pastor, St. Paul's Congregational Church, Aberdeen, 1872-1877. Principal, Airedale College, Bradford, England, 1877-1886; Mansfield College, Oxford, England, 1886-1909. Lyman Beecher Lectures in 1892, "The Place of Christ in Modern Theology." Died February 12, 1912.

ROBERT FORMAN HORTON. Born September 18, 1855, London, England. Graduated New College, Oxford, England, 1875. Fellow and Lecturer, New College, 1875-1883. Ordained to ministry of Congregational Church, 1880. Pastor, First Congregational Church, Hampstead, England, 1880-1930; pastor emeritus of same, 1930-1934. Lyman Beecher Lectures in 1893, "Verbum Dei." Died April 1, 1934.

DAVID HUMMELL GREER. Born March 20, 1844, Wheeling, West Virginia. Graduated Washington and Jefferson College, 1862. Taught school, studied law, engaged in business, 1862-1864. Graduated Theological Seminary, Gambier, Ohio, 1866. Rector, Christ Church, Clarksburg, West Virginia, 1866-1868. Ordained to ministry of Episcopal Church, 1868. Rector, Trinity Episcopal Church, Covington, Kentucky, 1868-1871. Engaged in travel, 1871-1872. Rector Grace Episcopal Church, Providence, Rhode Island, 1872-1888; St. Bartholomew's Episcopal Church, New York City, 1888-1904. Bishop Coadjutor, New York, 1904-1908; Bishop of same, 1908-1919. Lyman Beecher Lectures in 1895, "The Preacher and His Place." Died May 19, 1919.

HENRY VAN DYKE. Born November 10, 1852, Germantown, Pennsylvania. Graduated Princeton University, 1873; Princeton Theological Seminary, 1877. Ordained to ministry of Presbyterian Church, 1879. Transferred to ministry of Congregational Church, 1879. Pastor, Congregational Church, Newport, Rhode Island, 1879-1882. Transferred to ministry of Presbyterian Church, 1882. Pastor, Brick Presbyterian Church, New York City, 1883-1900. Professor, Princeton University, 1900-1923. U.S. Minister to Netherlands and Luxemborg, 1913-1917. Lyman Beecher Lectures in 1896, "The Gospel for an Age of Doubt." Died April 10, 1933.

Appendix 1 419

JOHN WATSON. Born November 3, 1850, Manningtree, England. Graduated University of Edinburgh, 1870; New College, Edinburgh, 1874. Ordained to ministry of Free Church, Presbyterian, 1874. Pastor, Logiealmond Presbyterian Church, 1874-1877; Free St. Matthew's Presbyterian Church, Glasgow, Scotland, 1877-1880; Sefton Park Presbyterian Church, Liverpool, England, 1880-1905. Lyman Beecher Lectures in 1897, "The Cure of Souls." Died May 6, 1907, Mount Pleasant, Iowa.

WILLIAM JEWETT TUCKER. Born July 13, 1839, Griswold, Connecticut. Graduated Dartmouth College, 1861; Andover Theological Seminary, 1866. Ordained to ministry of Congregational Church, 1867. Pastor, Franklin Street Congregational Church, Manchester, New Hampshire, 1867-1875. Transferred to Ministry of Presbyterian Church, 1875. Pastor, Madison Square Presbyterian Church, New York City, 1875-1879. Transferred to ministry of Congregational Church, 1880. Professor, Andover Theological Seminary, 1879-1893. President, Dartmouth College, 1893-1909; president emeritus of same, 1909-1926. Lyman Beecher Lectures in 1898, "The Making and the Unmaking of the Preacher." Died September 29, 1926.

GEORGE ADAM SMITH. Born September 19, 1856, Calcutta, India. Graduated University of Edinburgh, 1875; New College, Edinburgh, 1879. Studied in Leipzig and Tübingen, 1880. Ordained to ministry of Free Church, Presbyterian, 1880. Assistant pastor, West Brechin Presbyterian Church, 1880. Tutor, Free Church College, Aberdeen, Scotland, 1880-1882. Pastor, Queen's Cross, Presbyterian Church, Aberdeen, 1882-1892. Professor, Free Church College, Glasgow, Scotland, 1892-1909. Principal, University of Aberdeen, 1909-1935; principal emeritus of same, 1935-. Knighted in 1916. Lyman Beecher Lectures in 1899, "Modern Criticism and the Preaching of the Old Testament." Died March 3, 1942.

JOHN BROWN. Born June 19, 1830, Bolton, England. Graduated London University, 1853. Ordained to ministry of Congregational Church, 1855. Pastor, Park Chapel Congregational Church, Manchester, 1855-1864; Bunyan Congregational Church, Bedford, 1864-1903. Lyman Beecher Lectures in 1900, "Puritan Preaching in England." Died January 16, 1922.

GEORGE ANGIER GORDON. Born January 2, 1853, Oyne, Scotland. Came to United States, 1871. Graduated Bangor Theological Seminary, 1877. Ordained to ministry of Congregational Church, 1877.

Pastor, Congregational Church, Temple, Maine, 1877-1878. Graduated Harvard College, 1881. Pastor, Second Congregational Church, Greenwich, Connecticut, 1881-1884; Old South Congregational Church, Boston, Massachusetts, 1884-1927. Lyman Beecher Lectures in 1903, "Ultimate Conceptions of Faith." Died October 25, 1929.

LYMAN ABBOTT. Born December 18, 1835, Boston, Massachusetts. Graduated University of City of New York, 1853. Practiced law with brothers 1853-1860. Ordained to ministry of Congregational Church, 1860. Pastor, First Congregational Church, Terre Haute, Indiana, 1860-1865. Secretary, Freedmen's Union Commission, 1865-1869. Pastor, New England Congregational Church, New York City, 1867-1869; Presbyterian, Cornwall-on-the-Hudson, 1870-1887; Plymouth Congregational Church, Brooklyn, New York, 1887-1898. Editor, *Outlook*, 1876-1922. Lyman Beecher Lectures in 1904, "The Christian Ministry." Died October 22, 1922.

FRANCIS GREENWOOD PEABODY. Born December 4, 1847, Boston, Massachusetts. Graduated Harvard College, 1869; Harvard Divinity School, 1872. Ordained to ministry of Unitarian Church, 1874. Pastor, First Parish Unitarian Church, Cambridge, Massachusetts, 1874-1880. Professor, Harvard Divinity School, 1881-1913; dean of same, 1901-1905; professor emeritus of same, 1913-1936. Lyman Beecher Lectures in 1905, "Jesus Christ and the Christian Character." Died December 28, 1936.

CHARLES REYNOLDS BROWN. Born October 1, 1862, Bethany, West Virginia. Graduated University of Iowa, 1883. Engaged in business, 1883-1886. Graduated Boston School of Theology, 1889. Ordained to ministry of Methodist Episcopal Church, 1891. Pastor, Wesley Methodist Church, Cincinnati, Ohio, 1889-1892. Transferred to ministry of Congregational Church, 1892. Pastor, Winthrop Congregational Church, Charlestown, Massachusetts, 1892-1896; First Congregational Church, Oakland, California, 1896-1911. Dean, Yale Divinity School, 1911-1928; dean emeritus of same, 1928-. Lyman Beecher Lectures on Preaching, First Series, in 1906, "The Social Message of the Modern Pulpit," Second Series, in 1923, "The Art of Preaching." Died November 28, 1950.

PETER TAYLOR FORSYTH. Born May 12, 1848, Aberdeen, Scotland. Graduated University of Aberdeen, Scotland, 1869. Studied in Göttingen, Germany, and New College, London, 1869-1872. Ordained to ministry of Congregational Church, 1872. Pastor, Shipley Congregational Church, Yorkshire, England, 1872-1876; St. Thomas Square Congregational Church, Hackney, England, 1876-1885; Cheetham Hill Congregational Church, Manchester, England, 1885-1888; Clarendon Park Congregational Church, Leicester, England, 1888-1894. Emmanuel Church, Cambridge, 1894-1901. Principal, Hackney College (now New College), London, 1901-1921. Lyman Beecher Lectures in 1907, "Positive Preaching and the Modern Mind." Died November 11, 1921.

WILLIAM HERBERT PERRY FAUNCE. Born January 15, 1859, Worcester, Massachusetts. Graduated Brown University, 1880; Newton Theological Institution, 1884. Ordained to ministry of Baptist Church, 1884. Pastor, State Street Baptist Church, Springfield, Massachusetts, 1884-1889; Fifth Avenue Baptist Church, New York City, 1889-1899. President, Brown University, 1899-1929. Lyman Beecher Lectures in 1908, "The Educational Ideal in the Ministry." Died January 31, 1929.

HERBERT HENSLEY HENSON. Born November 8, 1863, London, England. Graduated All Souls' College, Oxford, 1884. Fellow, All Souls' College, Oxford, England, 1884-1891. Ordained to ministry of Episcopal Church, 1888. Graduated theological course, Oxford, 1896. Head of Oxford House, Bethnal Green, 1887-1888. Vicar at Barking, Sussex, England, 1888-1895. Chaplain, St. Mary's Hospital, Ilford, England, 1895-1900. Rector, St. Margaret's Episcopal Church, London, England, 1900-1912. Dean of Durham, 1912-1918. Bishop of Hereford, 1918-1920. Bishop of Durham, 1920-1939. Canon, Westminster Abbey, 1940-1941. Retired, 1941. Lyman Beecher Lectures in 1909, "The Liberty of Prophesying." Died September 27, 1947.

CHARLES EDWARD JEFFERSON. Born August 29, 1860, Cambridge, Ohio. Graduated Ohio Wesleyan University, 1882. Superintendent of Schools, Worthington, Ohio, 1882-1884. Graduated Boston School of Theology, 1887. Ordained to ministry of Congregational Church, 1887. Pastor, First Congregational Church, Chelsea, Massachusetts, 1887-1898; Broadway Tabernacle Congregational Church, New York City, 1898-1930; pastor emeritus of same, 1930-1937. Lyman Beecher Lectures in 1910, "The Building of the Church." Died September 12, 1937.

FRANK WAKELEY GUNSAULUS. Born January 1, 1856, Chesterville, Ohio. Graduated Ohio Wesleyan University, 1875. Ordained to ministry of Methodist Episcopal Church, 1877. Pastor, Harrisburg Methodist Church, Harrisburg, Ohio, 1875-1876; Worthington Methodist Church, Worthington, Ohio, 1876-1877; Main

Street Methodist Church, Chillicothe, Ohio, 1877-1879. Transferred to ministry of Congregational Church, 1879. Pastor, Eastwood Congregational Church, Columbus, Ohio, 1879-1881; First Congregational Church, Newtonville, Massachusetts, 1881-1885; Brown Memorial Presbyterian Church, Baltimore, Maryland, 1885-1887; Plymouth Congregational Church, Chicago, Illinois, 1887-1899; Central Congregational Church, Chicago, Illinois, 1899-1919; pastor emeritus of same, 1919-1921. President, Armour Institute, 1893-1921. Lyman Beecher Lectures in 1911, "The Minister and the Spiritual Life." Died March 17, 1921.

JOHN HENRY JOWETT. Born August 25, 1863, Halifax, England. Graduated University of Edinburgh, 1887; Mansfield College, Oxford, England, 1889. Ordained to ministry of Congregational Church, 1889. Pastor, St. James Congregational Church, Newcastle-on-Tyne, 1889-1895; Carr's Lane Congregational Church, Birmingham, England, 1895-1911. Transferred to ministry of Presbyterian Church, 1911. Pastor, Fifth Avenue Presbyterian Church, New York City, 1911-1918. Transferred to ministry of Congregational Church, 1918. Pastor, Westminster Chapel, London, England, 1918-1923. Lyman Beecher Lectures in 1912, "The Preacher: His Life and Work." Died December 19, 1923.

CHARLES HENRY PARKHURST. Born April 17, 1842, Ashland, Massachusetts. Graduated Amherst College, 1866. Principal, Amherst High School, 1867-1869. Studied theology in Germany at Halle, 1869-1870. Professor, Williston Academy, 1870-1872. Theology in Germany again, 1872-1874. Ordained to ministry of Congregational Church, 1874. Pastor, Lenox Congregational Church, Lenox, Massachusetts, 1874-1880. Transferred to ministry of Presbyterian Church, 1880. Pastor, Madison Square Presbyterian Church, New York City, 1880-1918; pastor emeritus First Presbyterian Church, New York City, 1918-1933. Lyman Beecher Lectures in 1913, "The Pulpit and the Pew." Died September 8, 1933.

CHARLES SILVESTER HORNE. Born April 15, 1865, Cuckfield, England. Graduated University of Glasgow, 1885; Mansfield College, Oxford, 1888. Ordained to ministry of Congregational Church, 1889. Pastor, Kensington Congregational Church, London, 1889-1903; Whitefields Congregational Church, London, 1903-1914. Member House of Commons, 1910-1914. Lyman Beecher Lectures in 1914, "The Romance of Preaching." Died May 2, 1914.

Appendix 1 423

HON. GEORGE WHARTON PEPPER. Born March 16, 1867, Boston, Massachusetts. Graduated University of Pennsylvania, 1887; Law School of same, 1889. Admitted to Bar, 1889. United States Senator from Pennsylvania, 1922-1927. Lyman Beecher Lectures in 1915, "A Voice from the Crowd."

WILLIAM DeWITT HYDE. Born September 23, 1858, Winchendon, Massachusetts. Graduated Harvard College, 1879; Andover Theological Seminary, 1882. Ordained to ministry of Congregational Church, 1883. Pastor, Auburn Street Congregational Church, Paterson, New Jersey, 1883-1886. President, Bowdoin College, 1886-1917. Lyman Beecher Lectures in 1916, "The Gospel of Good Will." Died June 29, 1917.

WILLIAM FRASER McDOWELL. Born February 4, 1858, Millersburg, Ohio. Graduated Ohio Wesleyan University, 1879; Boston School of Theology, 1882; Ph.D. Ohio Wesleyan University, 1893. Ordained to ministry of Methodist Episcopal Church, 1882. Pastor, Methodist Episcopal Church, Lodi, Ohio, 1882-1883; First Methodist Church, Oberlin, Ohio, 1883-1885; First Methodist Church, Tiffin, Ohio, 1885-1890. Chancellor, University of Denver, 1890-1899. Secretary, Methodist Board of Education, 1899-1904. Bishop, Methodist Episcopal Church, North, 1904-1932; retired from same, 1932. Lyman Beecher Lectures in 1917, "Good Ministers of Jesus Christ." Died April 26, 1937.

HENRY SLOANE COFFIN. Born January 5, 1877, New York City. Graduated Yale University, 1897. Studied in New College, Edinburgh, Scotland, 1897-1899. Graduated Union Theological Seminary, 1900. Ordained to ministry of Presbyterian Church, 1900. Pastor, Bedford Park Presbyterian Church, New York City, 1900-1905; Madison Avenue Presbyterian Church, New York City, 1905-1926. Professor, Union Theological Seminary, 1904-1926; president of same, 1926-1945; president emeritus of same, 1945-. Lyman Beecher Lectures in 1918, "In a Day of Social Rebuilding."

JOHN KELMAN. Born June 20, 1864, Dundonald, Scotland. Graduated University of Edinburgh, 1884; New College, Edinburgh, 1887. Ordained to ministry of Free Church, 1887. Assistant pastor, Queen's Cross Free Church, Aberdeen, 1887-1891; pastor, Peterculter Free Church, Aberdeen, 1891-1897; New North Free Church, Edinburgh, 1897-1907; Free St. George's Church, Edinburgh, 1907-1919; Fifth

Avenue Church, New York City, 1919-1924; Frognal Church, Hampstead, England, 1924-1925; pastor emeritus of same, 1925-1929. Lyman Beecher Lectures in 1919, "The War and Preaching." Died May 3, 1929.

ALBERT PARKER FITCH. Born March 6, 1877, Boston, Massachusetts. Graduated Harvard University, 1900; Union Theological Seminary, 1903. Ordained to ministry of Congregational Church, 1903. Pastor, First Congregational Church, Flushing, New York, 1903-1905; Mount Vernon Congregational Church, Boston, Massachusetts, 1905-1909. President, Andover Theological Seminary, 1909-1917. Professor, Amherst College, 1917-1923; Carleton College, 1924-1927. Transferred to ministry of Presbyterian Church, 1928. Pastor, Park Avenue Presbyterian Church, New York City, 1928-1933; pastor emeritus of same, 1933-1944. Lyman Beecher Lectures in 1920, "Preaching and Paganism." Died May 22, 1944.

CHARLES DAVID WILLIAMS. Born July 30, 1860, Bellevue, Ohio. Graduated Kenyon College, 1880; Bexley Hall, 1884. Ordained to ministry of Episcopal Church, 1884. Rector, Fernbank and Riverside Episcopal Churches, Ohio, 1884-1889; St. Paul's Episcopal Church, Steubenville, Ohio, 1889-1893. Dean, Trinity Cathedral, Cleveland, Ohio, 1893-1906. Bishop of Michigan, 1906-1923. Lyman Beecher Lectures in 1921, "The Prophetic Ministry." Died February 14, 1923.

WILLIAM PIERSON MERRILL. Born January 10, 1867, Orange, New Jersey. Graduated Rutgers College, 1887; Union Theological Seminary, 1890. Ordained to ministry of Presbyterian Church, 1890. Pastor, Trinity Presbyterian Church, Chestnut Hill, Pennsylvania, 1890-1895; Sixth Presbyterian Church, Chicago, Illinois, 1895-1911; Brick Presbyterian Church, New York City, 1911-1938; pastor emeritus of same, 1938-. Lyman Beecher Lectures in 1922, "The Freedom of the Preacher."

HARRY EMERSON FOSDICK. Born May 24, 1878, Buffalo, New York. Graduated Colgate University, 1900; Union Theological Seminary, 1904. Ordained to ministry of Baptist Church, 1903. Pastor, First Baptist Church, Montclair, New Jersey, 1904-1915. Professor, Union Theological Seminary, 1908-1946. Pastor, Riverside Baptist Church, New York City, 1926-1946; pastor emeritus of same, 1946-. Lyman Beecher Lectures in 1924, "The Modern Use of the Bible."

WILLIAM RALPH INGE. Born June 6, 1860, Crayke, England. Graduated King's College, Cambridge, 1883. Assistant Master, Eton School, 1884-1888. Tutor, Hertford College, Oxford, 1889-1904. Vicar, All Saints, London, 1905-1907. Lady Margaret Professor of Divinity, Cambridge University, 1907-1911. Dean, Saint Paul's, London, 1911-1934; retired from same, 1934. Lyman Beecher Lectures in 1925, "The Preaching of the Kingdom of God," unpublished.

RAYMOND CALKINS. Born August 10, 1869, Buffalo, New York. Graduated Harvard College, 1890. Master, Belmont Boy's School, Belmont, California, 1890-1891. Professor, Grinnell College, 1891-1893. Instructor, Harvard College, 1893-1895. Graduated Harvard Divinity School, 1895. Ordained to ministry of Congregational Church, 1896. Assistant pastor, First Congregational Church, Pittsfield, Massachusetts, 1896-1903; pastor, Pilgrim Memorial Congregational Church, Pittsfield, Massachusetts, 1897-1903; State Street Congregational Church, Portland, Maine, 1903-1912; First Congregational Church, Cambridge, Massachusetts, 1912-1940; pastor emeritus of same, 1940-. Lyman Beecher Lectures in 1926, "The Eloquence of the Christian Experience."

JOHN ROBERT PATERSON SCLATER. Born April 9, 1876, Manchester, England. Graduated Emmanuel College, Cambridge, England, 1898; Westminster Theological School, Cambridge, 1902. Pastor, Green Hill Church, Derby, 1902-1907. Ordained to ministry of Presbyterian Church, 1902. Pastor, New North Presbyterian Church, Edinburgh, 1907-1923; Parkdale Presbyterian Church, Toronto, Canada, 1923-1924; Old St. Andrews Presbyterian Church, Toronto, Canada, 1924-. Lyman Beecher Lectures in 1927, "The Public Worship of God." Died 1949.

JAMES EDWARD FREEMAN. Born July 24, 1866, New York City. Engaged in Railroad Business, 1879-1894. Studied Theology under Bishop H. C. Potter. Ordained to Ministry of Episcopal Church, 1895. Assistant Rector, St. John's Episcopal Church, Yonkers, New York, 1894-1895; Rector, St. Andrew's Episcopal Church, Yonkers, New York, 1895-1910; St. Mark's Episcopal Church, Minneapolis, Minnesota, 1910-1921; Epiphany Episcopal Church, Washington, D. C., 1921-1923. Bishop, of Washington, D. C., 1923-1943. Lyman Beecher Lectures in 1928, "The Ambassador." Died June 6, 1943.

EDWIN DU BOSE MOUZON. Born May 19, 1869, Spartanburg, South Carolina. Graduated Wofford College, 1889. Ordained to Ministry of Methodist Episcopal South Church, 1889. Pastor, Bryan Methodist Church, Bryan, Texas, 1889-1890; Austin Methodist Church, Austin, Texas, 1890-1891; Caldwell Church, Caldwell, Texas, 1891-1893; Galveston Methodist Church, Galveston, Texas, 1894-1895; Flatonia Methodist Church, Flatonia, Texas, 1895-1896; Abilene Methodist Church, Abilene, Texas, 1896-1897; Fort Worth Methodist Church, Fort Worth, Texas, 1898-1901; Central Methodist Church, Kansas City, Missouri, 1901-1904; Travis Park Methodist Church, San Antonio, Texas, 1904-1908. Professor, Southwestern University, 1908-1910. Bishop, 1910-1937. Lyman Beecher Lectures in 1929, "Preaching with Authority." Died February 10, 1937.

FRANCIS JOHN McCONNELL. Born August 18, 1871, Trinway, Ohio. Graduated Ohio Wesleyan University, 1894; Boston School of Theology, 1897. Ordained to Ministry of Methodist Episcopal Church, 1894. Pastor, West Chelmsford Methodist Church, West Chelmsford, Massachusetts, 1894-1897; Newton Upper Falls Methodist Church, Upper Falls, Massachusetts, 1897-1899; Ipswich Methodist Church, Ipswich, Massachusetts, 1899-1902; Harvard Street Methodist Church, Cambridge, Massachusetts, 1902-1903; New York Avenue Methodist Church, Brooklyn, New York, 1903-1909. President, De Pauw University, 1909-1912. Bishop, 1912-1934. Lyman Beecher Lectures in 1930, "The Prophetic Ministry."

GEORGE ARTHUR BUTTRICK. Born March 23, 1892, Seaham, England. Graduated Lancaster College, 1915. Came to United States, 1915. Ordained to Ministry of Congregational Church, 1915. Pastor, Union Congregational Church, Quincy, Illinois, 1915-1918; First Congregational Church, Rutland, Vermont, 1918-1921. Transferred to Ministry of Presbyterian Church, 1921. Pastor, First Presbyterian Church, Buffalo, New York, 1921-1927; Madison Avenue Presbyterian Church, New York City, 1927-. Lyman Beecher Lectures in 1931, "Jesus Came Preaching"; single lecture in 1940, "Preaching the Whole Gospel."

ERNEST FREMONT TITTLE. Born October 21, 1885, Springfield, Ohio. Graduated Ohio Wesleyan University, 1906; Drew Theological Seminary, 1908. Pastor, Christiansburg Methodist Church, Christiansburg, Ohio, 1908-1910. Ordained to ministry of Methodist Episcopal Church, 1910. Riverdale Methodist Church, Dayton, Ohio, 1910-1913; University Methodist Church, Delaware, Ohio, 1913-1916; Broad Street Methodist Church, Columbus, Ohio, 1916-1918; First

Methodist Church, Evanston, Illinois, 1918-. Lyman Beecher Lectures in 1932, "Jesus After Nineteen Centuries"; single lecture in 1940, "The Church and the Glory of God." Died August 3, 1949.

LAWRENCE PEARSALL JACKS. Born October 9, 1860, Nottingham, England. Graduated University London, 1886. Ordained to ministry of Unitarian Church, 1887. Assistant to Stopford Brooke, Bedford, 1887; pastor, Renshaw Street Chapel, Liverpool, 1888-1894; Church of the Messiah, Birmingham, 1894-1903. Professor, Manchester College, Oxford, 1903-1915; principal of same, 1915-1931; principal emeritus of same, 1931-. Editor, *The Hibbert Journal*, 1902-1948; editor emeritus of same, 1949-. Lyman Beecher Lectures in 1933, "Elemental Religion."

ALBERT EDWARD DAY. Born November 18, 1884, Euphemia, Ohio. Graduated Taylor University, 1904. Ordained to ministry of Methodist Episcopal Church, 1908. Pastor, Bellefontaine Methodist Circuit, Bellefontaine, Ohio, 1904-1905; West Liberty Methodist Church, West Liberty, Ohio, 1906-1908; Bradford and Gettysburg, Methodist Churches, Ohio, 1908-1910; St. Paris Methodist Church, St. Paris, Ohio, 1910-1912; Hyde Park Methodist Church, Cincinnati, Ohio, 1913-1916; Williams Street Methodist Church, Delaware, Ohio, 1916-1919; First Methodist Church, Canton, Ohio, 1919-1925; Christ Methodist Church, Pittsburgh, Pennsylvania, 1925-1932; Mount Vernon Place Methodist Church, Baltimore, Maryland, 1932-1937; First Methodist Church, Pasadena, California, 1937-1945. Director, New Life Movement, Methodist, 1945-1948. Pastor, Mount Vernon Place Methodist Church, Baltimore, Maryland, 1948-. Lyman Beecher Lectures in 1934, "Jesus and Human Personality."

WALTER RUSSELL BOWIE. Born October 18, 1882, Richmond, Virginia. Graduated Harvard College, 1904; Virginia Theological Seminary, 1908. Ordained to ministry of Episcopal Church, 1909. Rector, Emmanuel Episcopal Church, Greenwood, Virginia, 1908-1911; St. Paul's Episcopal Church, Richmond, Virginia, 1911-1923; Grace Episcopal Church, New York City, 1923-1939. Professor, Union Theological Seminary, 1939-. Lyman Beecher Lectures in 1935, "The Renewing Gospel."

JOHN EDGAR PARK. Born March 7, 1879, Belfast, Ireland. Graduated Royal University, Dublin, 1902. Came to United States, 1902. Graduated Princeton Seminary, 1904. Ordained to ministry of Presbyterian Church, 1903. Stated Supply Sterling Pond and Stark, New

York, 1903-1904. Transferred to ministry of Congregational Church, 1904. Pastor, West Parish, Congregational Church, Andover, Massachusetts, 1904-1907; Second Congregational Church, Newton, Massachusetts, 1907-1926. President, Wheaton College, Norton, Massachusetts, 1926-1944; president emeritus of same, 1944-. Lyman Beecher Lectures in 1936, "The Miracle of Preaching."

WILLARD LEAROYD SPERRY. Born April 5, 1882, Peabody, Massachusetts. Graduated Olivet College, Michigan, 1903; Oxford University, England, 1907. Ordained to ministry of Congregational Church, 1908. Assistant pastor, First Congregational Church, Fall River, Massachusetts, 1908-1913; pastor of same, 1913-1914; Central Congregational Church, Boston, Massachusetts, 1914-1922. Professor, Andover Seminary, 1914-1922. Dean, Harvard Divinity School, 1922-. Lyman Beecher Lectures in 1938, "We Prophesy in Part."

CHARLES CLAYTON MORRISON. Born December 4, 1874, Harrison, Ohio. Graduated Drake University, 1898. Studied University of Chicago, 1902-1905. Ordained to ministry of Disciples, 1892. Pastor, Christian Church, Clarinda, Iowa, 1892-1893; Christian Church, Perry, Iowa, 1894-1898; Monroe Street Christian Church, Chicago, Illinois, 1898-1902; First Christian Church, Springfield, Illinois, 1902-1906; Monroe Street Christian Church, Chicago, Illinois, 1906-1908. Editor, *The Christian Century*, 1908-1947; Contributing Editor of same, 1947-. Lyman Beecher Lectures in 1939, "What Is Christianity?"

ARTHUR HOWE BRADFORD. Born November 19, 1883, Montclair, New Jersey. Graduated Yale College, 1905; Union Theological Seminary, 1909. Ordained to ministry of Congregational Church, 1909. Assistant pastor, South Congregational Church, Springfield, Massachusetts, 1909-1912; pastor, Rutland Congregational Church, Rutland, Vermont, 1913-1918; Central Congregational Church, Providence, Rhode Island, 1918-. Lyman Beecher Lecture in 1940, "Preachers Must Listen."

WYATT AIKEN SMART. Born October 22, 1883, Newberry, South Carolina. Graduated Vanderbilt University, 1904; Union Theological Seminary, 1907. Ordained to ministry of Methodist Church, South, 1907. Pastor, Trinity Methodist Church, Lynchburg, Virginia, 1907-1909; Park View Methodist Church, Portsmouth, Virginia, 1909-1913; First Methodist Church, Charlottesville, Virginia, 1913-

1914. Professor, Emory University, 1914-. Lyman Beecher Lecture in 1940, "Old Wine in New Bottles."

EDWIN McNEILL POTEAT. Born November 20, 1892, New Haven, Connecticut. Graduated Furman University, 1912; Southern Baptist Seminary, 1916. Ordained to ministry of Baptist Church, 1914. Missionary to China, 1918-1926. Professor, Shanghai University, 1926-1929. Pastor, Pullen Memorial Church, Raleigh, North Carolina, 1929-1937; Euclid Avenue Baptist Church, Cleveland, Ohio, 1937-1944. President, Colgate, Rochester Seminary, 1944-1948. Pastor, Pullen Memorial Baptist Church, Raleigh, North Carolina, 1948. Lyman Beecher Lecture in 1940, "The Dilemma of Civilization."

ELMORE McNEILL McKEE. Born March 28, 1896, Ridgewood, New Jersey. Graduated Yale University, 1919; Yale Divinity School, 1921. Studied University of Edinburgh, Scotland, 1921-1922. Ordained to ministry of Episcopal Church, 1922. Assistant rector, St. John's Episcopal Church, Waterbury, Connecticut, 1922-1924; rector, St. Paul's Episcopal Church, New Haven, Connecticut, 1924-1927. Chaplain, Yale University, 1927-1930. Rector, Trinity Episcopal Church, Buffalo, New York, 1930-1936; St. George's Episcopal Church, New York City, 1936-1946. American Friends Service, 1946. Lyman Beecher Lecture in 1940, "Leadership Uncensored."

RALPH WASHINGTON SOCKMAN. Born October 1, 1889, Mount Vernon, Ohio. Graduated Ohio Wesleyan University, 1911. Intercollegiate Secretary, Y.M.C.A., 1911-1913. Graduated Union Theological Seminary, 1915. Ordained to ministry of Methodist Episcopal Church, 1917. Associate pastor, Christ Methodist Church, New York City, 1915-1917; pastor of same, 1917-. Lyman Beecher Lectures in 1941, "The Highway of God."

MORGAN PHELPS NOYES. Born March 29, 1891, Warren, Pennsylvania. Graduated Yale University, 1914. Ordained to ministry of Congregational Church, 1917. Served in Y.M.C.A., 1917-1919. Graduated Union Theological Seminary, 1920. Assistant pastor, Madison Avenue Presbyterian Church, New York City, 1919-1920. Transferred to ministry of Presbyterian Church, 1920. Pastor, Dobbs Ferry Presbyterian Church, Dobbs Ferry, New York, 1920-1925; First Presbyterian Church, Brooklyn, New York, 1925-1932; Central Presbyterian Church, Montclair, New Jersey, 1932-. Lyman Beecher Lectures in 1942, "Preaching the Word of God."

PAUL EHRMAN SCHERER. Born June 22, 1892, Mt. Holly Springs, Pennsylvania. Graduated College of Charleston, South Carolina, 1911; Mt. Airy Lutheran Seminary, Philadelphia, Pennsylvania, 1916. Ordained to ministry of Lutheran Church, 1916. Assistant pastor, Holy Trinity Lutheran Church, Buffalo, New York, 1918-1919. Professor, Mt. Airy Seminary, Philadelphia, Pennsylvania, 1919-1929. Pastor, Holy Trinity Lutheran Church, New York City, 1920-1945. Professor, Union Theological Seminary, New York City, 1945-. Lyman Beecher Lectures in 1943, "For We Have This Treasure."

GARFIELD BROMLEY OXNAM. Born August 14, 1891, Sonora, California. Graduated University of Southern California, 1913; Boston University School of Theology, 1915. Ordained to ministry of Methodist Church, 1916. Pastor, Popular Methodist Church, Popular, California, 1916-1917; Church of All Nations, Methodist Episcopal, 1917-1927. Secretary, Los Angeles Missionary Society, 1917-1927. Professor, University of Southern California, 1919-1923; Boston University School of Theology, 1927-1928. President, DePauw University, Greencastle, Indiana, 1928-1936. Elected Bishop, Methodist Church, 1936. Lyman Beecher Lectures in 1944, "Preaching in a Revolutionary Age."

REINHOLD NIEBUHR. Born June 21, 1892, Wright City, Missouri. Graduated Elmhurst College, 1910; Eden Theological Seminary, 1913; Yale Divinity School, 1914. Ordained to ministry of Evangelical Synod, 1915. Pastor, Detroit Evangelical Church, Detroit, Michigan, 1915-1928. Union Theological Seminary, 1928-. Lyman Beecher Lectures in 1945, "Faith and History."

HERBERT H. FARMER. Born November 27, 1892, London. Graduated Cambridge University, 1914; Post Graduate Degree M.A. Idem, 1918; graduated Westminster College, Cambridge, 1917. Ordained to ministry of Presbyterian Church, 1919. Pastor, Stafford Presbyterian Church, Stafford, England, 1919-1922; New Barnet Presbyterian Church, London, 1922-1931. Riley Professor Christian Doctrine, Hartford Seminary Foundation, Hartford, Connecticut, 1931-1935. Barbour Professor of Systematic Theology, Westminster College, Cambridge, England, 1935-. Stanton Lecturer in the Philosophy of Religion, Cambridge University, 1937-1940. Lyman Beecher Lectures in 1946, "God and Men."

HAROLD COOKE PHILLIPS. Born November 26, 1892, Westmoreland, Jamaica, B.W.I. Graduated Denison University, 1919; Union Theological Seminary, 1922. Ordained to ministry of Baptist

Church, 1922. Pastor, First Baptist Church, Mt. Vernon, New York, 1922-1928; First Baptist Church, Cleveland, Ohio, 1928-. Lyman Beecher Lectures in 1947, "Bearing Witness to the Truth."

HENRY KNOX SHERRILL. Born November 6, 1890, Brooklyn, New York. Graduated Yale College, 1911; Episcopal Theological School, Cambridge, Massachusetts, 1914. Ordained to ministry of Episcopal Church, 1915. Assistant minister, Trinity Episcopal Church, Boston, Massachusetts, 1914-1917. Chaplain, A.E.F., France, July, 1917–January, 1919. Rector, Church of Our Savior, Brookline, Massachusetts, 1919-1923; Trinity Episcopal Church, Boston, Massachusetts, 1923-1930. Bishop, Episcopal Church, Massachusetts, 1930. Lyman Beecher Lectures in 1948, "The Church's Ministry in Our Time."

LESLIE D. WEATHERHEAD. Born October 14, 1893, London, England. Graduated, Manchester University, Manchester, England, 1926; Richmond Theological College, 1915. Ordained to ministry of Methodist Church, 1916. Chaplain, World War I, 1916-1919. Pastor, English Methodist Church, Madras, India, 1919-1922; Manchester Methodist Church, Manchester, England, Brunswick Methodist Church, Leeds, 1925-1936; City Temple Methodist Church, London, 1936-. Lyman Beecher Lectures in 1949, "The Minister's Relation to the Community."

APPENDIX 2

Bibliography

THE LYMAN BEECHER LECTURES ON PREACHING[1]

1871–1872 Henry Ward Beecher, *Yale Lectures on Preaching*, first series. New York: J. B. Ford & Co., 1872.
1872–1873 Henry Ward Beecher, *Yale Lectures on Preaching*, second series. New York: J. B. Ford & Co., 1873.
1873–1874 Henry Ward Beecher, *Yale Lectures on Preaching*, third series. New York: J. B. Ford & Co., 1874. A one-volume edition, *Yale Lectures on Preaching*, was published by the Pilgrim Press, Chicago.
1874–1875 John Hall, *God's Word Through Preaching*. New York: Dodd, Mead & Co., 1875.
1875–1876 William Mackergo Taylor, *The Ministry of the Word*. New York: Anson D. F. Randolph & Co., 1876.
1876–1877 Phillips Brooks, *Lectures on Preaching*. New York: E. P. Dutton & Co., 1877.
1877–1878 Robert William Dale, *Nine Lectures on Preaching*. New York: A. S. Barnes & Co., 1878.
1878–1879 Matthew Simpson, *Lectures on Preaching*. New York: Nelson & Philips, 1879.
1879–1880 Howard Crosby, *The Christian Preacher*. New York: Anson D. F. Randolph & Co., 1880.
1880–1881 Joseph Tuthill Duryea, George Harris, Samuel E. Herrick, Nathaniel Judson Burton, and Llewelyn David Bevan. Lectures not published.
1881–1882 Ezekiel Gilman Robinson, *Lectures on Preaching*. New York: Henry Holt & Co., 1883.
1882–1883 No lectures.
1883–1884 Nathaniel Judson Burton, *Yale Lectures on Preaching and Other Writings*. Boston: The Pilgrim Press, 1887. Re-

[1] Compiled by the Reverend Hal Earl Norton, D.D., Minister, First Baptist Church, Grinnell, Iowa.

printed by the Macmillan Co., 1925, under the title *In Pulpit and Parish*.

1884–1885 Henry Martin Storrs, *The American Preacher*. Not published.

1885–1886 Willian Mackergo Taylor, *The Scottish Pulpit*. New York: Harper & Brothers, 1887.

1886–1887 Washington Gladden, *Tools and the Man*. Boston: Houghton Mifflin Co., 1893.

1887–1888 Henry Clay Trumbull, *The Sunday School*. Philadelphia: John P. Wattles, 1888.

1888–1889 John Albert Broadus, *On the Preparation and Delivery of Sermons*. New York: Harper & Brothers, 1897.

1889–1890 Adolphus Julius Frederick Behrends, *The Philosophy of Preaching*. New York: Charles Scribner's Sons, 1893.

1890–1891 James Stalker, *The Preacher and His Models*. New York: A. C. Armstrong, 1893.

1891–1892 Andrew Martin Fairbairn, *The Place of Christ in Modern Theology*. New York: Charles Scribner's Sons, 1893.

1892–1893 Robert Forman Horton, *Verbum Dei*. New York: The Macmillan Co., 1893.

1893–1894 No lectures.

1894–1895 David Hummell Greer, *The Preacher and His Place*. New York: Charles Scribner's Sons, 1895.

1895–1896 Henry van Dyke, *The Gospel for an Age of Doubt*. New York: The Macmillan Co., 1896.

1896–1897 John Watson (Ian Maclaren), *The Cure of Souls*. New York: Dodd, Mead & Co., 1896.

1897–1898 William Jewett Tucker, *The Making and the Unmaking of the Preacher*. Boston: Houghton Mifflin Co., 1898.

1898–1899 Sir George Adam Smith, *Modern Criticism and the Preaching of the Old Testament*. New York: A. C. Armstrong, 1901.

1899–1900 John Brown, *Puritan Preaching in England*. New York: Charles Scribner's Sons, 1900.

1900–1901 No Lectures.

1901–1902 Washington Gladden, *Social Salvation*. Boston: Houghton Mifflin Co., 1902.

1902–1903 George Angier Gordon, *Ultimate Conceptions of Faith*. Boston: Houghton Mifflin Co., 1903.

1903–1904 Lyman Abbott, *The Christian Ministry*. Boston: Houghton Mifflin Co., 1905.

1904–1905 Francis Greenwood Peabody, *Jesus Christ and the Christian Character*. New York: The Macmillan Co., 1908.
1905–1906 Charles Reynolds Brown, *The Social Message of the Modern Pulpit*. New York: Charles Scribner's Sons, 1906.
1906–1907 Peter Taylor Forsyth, *Positive Preaching and the Modern Mind*. London: Hodder & Stoughton, 1907.
1907–1908 William Herbert Perry Faunce, *The Educational Ideal in the Ministry*. New York: The Macmillan Co., 1908; reprinted 1919.
1908–1909 Herbert Hensley Henson, *The Liberty of Prophesying*. New Haven: Yale University Press, 1909.
1909–1910 Charles Edward Jefferson, *The Building of the Church*. New York: The Macmillan Co., 1910.
1910–1911 Frank Wakeley Gunsaulus, *The Minister and the Spiritual Life*. New York: Fleming H. Revell, 1911.
1911–1912 John Henry Jowett, *The Preacher: His Life and Work*. New York: Harper & Brothers, 1912.
1912–1913 Charles Henry Parkhurst, *The Pulpit and the Pew*. New Haven: Yale University Press, 1913.
1913–1914 Charles Silvester Horne, *The Romance of Preaching*. New York: Fleming H. Revell, 1914.
1914–1915 George Wharton Pepper, *A Voice from the Crowd*. New Haven: Yale University Press, 1915.
1915–1916 William DeWitt Hyde, *The Gospel of Good Will*. New York: The Macmillan Co. 1916.
1916–1917 William Fraser McDowell, *Good Ministers of Jesus Christ*. New York: The Abingdon Press, 1917.
1917–1918 Henry Sloane Coffin, *In a Day of Social Rebuilding*. New Haven: Yale University Press, 1918.
1918–1919 John Kelman, *The War and Preaching*. New Haven: Yale University Press, 1919.
1919–1920 Albert Parker Fitch, *Preaching and Paganism*. New Haven: Yale University Press, 1920.
1920–1921 Charles David Williams, *The Prophetic Ministry for Today*. New York: The Macmillan Co., 1921.
1921–1922 William Pierson Merrill, *The Freedom of the Preacher*. New York: The Macmillan Co., 1922.
1922–1923 Charles Reynolds Brown, *The Art of Preaching*. New York: The Macmillan Co., 1922.
1923–1924 Harry Emerson Fosdick, *The Modern Use of the Bible*. New York: The Macmillan Co., 1924.

Appendix 2

1924–1925 William Ralph Inge, *The Preaching of the Kingdom of God in History*. Lectures not published.
1925–1926 Raymond Calkins, *The Eloquence of the Christian Experience*. New York: The Macmillan Co., 1927.
1926–1927 John Robert Paterson Sclater, *The Public Worship of God*. New York: Doubleday & Co., 1927.
1927–1928 James Edward Freeman, *The Ambassador*. New York: The Macmillan Co., 1928.
1928–1929 Edwin Du Bose Mouzon, *Preaching with Authority*. New York: The Macmillan Co., 1929.
1929–1930 Francis John McConnell, *The Prophetic Ministry*. New York and Nashville: Abingdon-Cokesbury Press, 1930.
1930–1931 George Arthur Buttrick, *Jesus Came Preaching*. New York: Charles Scribner's Sons, 1931.
1931–1932 Ernest Fremont Tittle, *Jesus After Nineteen Centuries*. New York and Nashville: Abingdon-Cokesbury Press, 1932.
1932–1933 Lawrence Pearsall Jacks, *Elemental Religion*. New York: Harper & Brothers, 1934.
1933–1934 Albert Edward Day, *Jesus and Human Personality*. New York and Nashville: Abingdon-Cokesbury Press, 1934.
1934–1935 Walter Russell Bowie, *The Renewing Gospel*. New York: Charles Scribner's Sons, 1935.
1935–1936 John Edgar Park, *The Miracle of Preaching*. New York: The Macmillan Co., 1936.
1936–1937 No lectures.
1937–1938 Willard Learoyd Sperry, *We Prophesy in Part*. New York: Harper & Brothers, 1938.
1938–1939 Charles Clayton Morrison, *What Is Christianity?* New York: Harper & Brothers, 1940.
1939–1940 George Arthur Buttrick, Edwin McNeill Poteat, Arthur Howe Bradford, Elmore McNeill McKee, Wyatt Aiken Smart, and Ernest Fremont Tittle, *Preaching in These Times*. New York: Charles Scribner's Sons, 1940.
1940–1941 Ralph Washington Sockman, *The Highway of God*. New York: The Macmillan Co., 1942.
1941–1942 Morgan Phelps Noyes, *Preaching the Word of God*. New York: Charles Scribner's Sons, 1943.
1942–1943 Paul Scherer, *For We Have This Treasure*. New York: Harper & Brothers, 1944.

1943-1944 G. Bromley Oxnam, *Preaching in a Revolutionary Age.* New York and Nashville: Abingdon-Cokesbury Press, 1944.
1944-1945 Reinhold Niebuhr, *Faith and History.* New York: Charles Scribner's Sons, 1949.
1945-1946 Herbert H. Farmer, *God and Men.* New York and Nashville: Abingdon-Cokesbury Press, 1947.
1946-1947 Harold Cooke Phillips, *Bearing Witness to the Truth.* New York and Nashville: Abingdon-Cokesbury Press, 1949.
1947-1948 Henry Knox Sherrill, *The Church's Ministry in Our Time.* New York: Charles Scribner's Sons, 1949.
1948-1949 Leslie D. Weatherhead, *The Minister's Relation to the Community.*

BIBLIOGRAPHY

ABBOTT, LYMAN. *Signs of Promise.* New York: Ford, Howard & Hulbert, 1889.
——— *Silhouettes of My Contemporaries.* New York: Doubleday & Co., 1921.
ALLEN, A. V. G. *Phillips Brooks,* One volume edition. New York: E. P. Dutton & Co., 1907.
ATKINS, GAIUS GLENN (Ed.). *Master Sermons of the Nineteenth Century.* New York: Harper & Brothers, 1940.
BAXTER, BATSELL BARRETT. *The Heart of the Yale Lectures.* New York: The Macmillan Co., 1947.
BEECHER, HENRY WARD. *A Summer Parish,* Sermons preached at the "Twin Mountain House," White Mountain, New Hampshire. New York: J. B. Ford & Co., 1875.
BLACKWOOD, ANDREW WATERSON. *The Protestant Pulpit.* New York and Nashville: Abingdon-Cokesbury Press, 1947.
BRASTOW, LEWIS O., D.D. *Representative Modern Preachers.* London & New York: Hodder & Stoughton and George H. Doran, 1904.
———. *The Modern Pulpit.* Cincinnati and New York: Jennings & Graham and Eaton & Mains, 1906.
BROADUS, JOHN A. *Sermons and Addresses.* New York: Fleming H. Revell, 1896.
BROOKS, PHILLIPS. *The Candle of the Lord and Other Sermons* (Autographed Copy). New York: E. P. Dutton & Co., 1887.

Appendix 2

BROWN, CHARLES R. *My Own Yesterdays*. New York and London: The Century Co., 1931.
BROWN, JOHN. *John Bunyan*. London, Glasgow and Birmingham: Hulberts, Ltd., 1928.
BURNETT, CHARLES T. *Hyde of Bowdoin*. Boston: Houghton Mifflin Co., 1931.
BUTLER, G. PAUL (Ed.). *Best Sermons* (1949-50 edition), Fifty-two selections. New York: Harper & Brothers, 1949.
BUTTRICK, GEORGE A. *The Parables of Jesus*. New York: Harper & Brothers, 1928.
———. *Prayer*. New York and Nashville: Abingdon-Cokesbury Press, 1942.
CALKINS, RAYMOND. *The Romance of the Ministry*. Boston: Pilgrim Press, 1944.
CROOKS, GEORGE R. *The Life of Bishop Matthew Simpson*. New York: Harper & Brothers, 1891.
DALE, A. W. W. *Life of R. W. Dale of Birmingham*, by his son. London: Hodder & Stoughton, 1898.
DAVIES, D. R. *Reinhold Niebuhr, Prophet from America*. New York: The Macmillan Co., 1948.
FOSDICK, HARRY EMERSON. *Living Under Tension*. New York: Harper & Brothers, 1941.
———. *On Being a Real Person*. New York: Harper & Brothers, 1943.
———. *On Being Fit To Live With*. New York: Harper & Brothers, 1946.
GIBSON, VAN R. *Grand Man of God—James Edward Freeman*. Yonkers, N. Y.: Llewellyn Publications, 1944.
GLADDEN, WASHINGTON, *Present Day Theology*. Columbus, Ohio: McClelland & Co., 1913.
———. *Recollections, An Autobiography*. Boston: Houghton Mifflin Co., 1909.
GORDON, GEORGE A. *My Education and Religion*. Boston: Houghton Mifflin Co., 1925.
HALL, THOMAS C. *John Hall, Pastor and Preacher*, a biography by his son. New York: Fleming H. Revell, 1901.
HENSON, HERBERT HENSLEY. *Retrospect of an Unimportant Life, 1863-1939*, two volumes in one. New York: Oxford University Press, 1942.
HOYT, ARTHUR S. *The Pulpit and American Life*. New York: The Macmillan Co., 1921.

HUGHES, EDWIN HOLT. *I Was Made a Minister—The Story of a Dedicated Life.* New York & Nashville: Abingdon-Cokesbury Press, 1943.
INGE, W. R. *Diary of a Dean.* New York: The Macmillan Co., 1950.
———. *Outspoken Essays.* New York: Longmans, Green & Co., 1921.
JACKS, L. P. *The Confessions of an Octogenarian.* New York: The Macmillan Co., 1942.
JEFFS, ERNEST H. *Princes of the Modern Pulpit.* New York and Nashville: Abingdon-Cokesbury Press, 1931.
JOHNSON, E. H. (Ed.). *Ezekiel Gilman Robinson—An Autobiography.* New York: Silver Burdett Co., 1896.
JONES, EDGAR DEWITT. *American Preachers of Today.* Indianapolis: Bobbs-Merrill, 1933.
JONES, E. WINSTON. *Preaching and the Dramatic Arts.* New York: The Macmillan Co., 1948.
KLEISER, GRANVILLE (Compiler). *The World's Great Sermons,* Volume VII. New York: Funk & Wagnalls, 1908.
LICHLITER, MCILYAR H. *The Heritage of Washington Gladden,* dedicatory sermon. Columbus, Ohio: *First Church News,* Dec., 1931.
LUCCOCK, HALFORD E. *In the Minister's Workshop.* New York and Nashville: Abingdon-Cokesbury Press, 1944.
MARRIOTT, SIR JOHN ALBERT PEEL. *Robert Forman Horton.* London: George Allen & Unwin, 1937.
MCCONNELL, FRANCIS JOHN. *Evangelicals, Revolutionists and Idealists.* New York & Nashville: Abingdon-Cokesbury Press, 1942.
NEWTON, JOSEPH FORT. *Some Living Masters of the Pulpit.* New York: Harper & Brothers, 1923.
NICHOLAS, L. NELSON. *Broadway Tabernacle History.* New York: Tuttle, Morehouse & Taylor, 1940.
NICOLL, SIR W. ROBERTSON. *Princes of the Church.* London & New York: Hodder & Stoughton, George H. Doran, 1921.
———. *"Ian Maclaren," Life of the Rev. John Watson.* New York: Dodd, Mead & Co., 1908.
PARKHURST, CHARLES H. *My Forty Years in New York.* New York: The Macmillan Co., 1923.
PEPPER, GEORGE WHARTON. *Philadelphia Lawyer, An Autobiography.* Philadelphia: J. B. Lippincott, 1944.
PORRITT, ARTHUR. *More and More of Memories.* London: George Allen & Unwin, 1947.
———. *The Best I Remember.* New York: George H. Doran, 1927.

PORRITT, ARTHUR. *John Henry Jowett*, New York: Harper & Brothers, 1924.
ROBERTSON, A. T. *Life and Letters of John A. Broadus*. Philadelphia: American Baptist Publication Society, 1901.
SCHERER, PAUL. *Facts That Undergird Life*. New York: Harper & Brothers, 1938.
SCLATER, J. R. P. *The Enterprise of Life*. London: Hodder & Stoughton, 1911.
SELBIE, W. B. *The Life of Andrew Martin Fairbairn*. London: Hodder & Stoughton, 1914.
———. *The Life of Charles Silvester Horne*. London: Hodder & Stoughton, 1921.
SLATTERY, CHARLES LEWIS. *David Hummell Greer*. New York: Longmans, Green & Co., 1921.
SMITH, GEORGE ADAM. *The Forgiveness of Sins and Other Sermons*. New York: Eaton and Mains, 1904.
SOCKMAN, RALPH W. *Recovery of Religion*. New York and Nashville: Abingdon-Cokesbury Press, 1938.
SPERRY, WILLARD L. *Those of the Way*. New York: Harper & Brothers, 1945.
STALKER, JAMES. *Imago Christi, The Example of Christ*. New York: American Tract Society, 1889.
STOWE, LYMAN BEECHER. *Saints, Sinners and Beechers*. Indianapolis: Bobbs-Merrill, 1934.
TITTLE, ERNEST FREMONT. *The Foolishness of Preaching*. New York: Henry Holt & Co., 1930.
TUCKER, WILLIAM JEWETT. *My Generation*. Boston: Houghton Mifflin Co., 1919.
VAN DYKE, TERTIUS. *Henry van Dyke, Teacher, Preacher, Diplomat, Dreamer, Doer*. New York: Harper & Brothers, 1935.
WATSON, JOHN (Ian Maclaren). *The Inspiration of Our Faith*. New York: A. C. Armstrong & Son, 1908.
WEATHERHEAD, LESLIE D. *The Eternal Voice*. New York and Nashville: Abingdon-Cokesbury Press, 1940.
———. *His Life and Ours*. New York and Nashville: Abingdon-Cokesbury Press, 1933.
———. *The Significance of Silence*. New York and Nashville: Abingdon-Cokesbury Press, 1945.
WILKINSON, WILLIAM CLEAVER. *Modern Masters of Pulpit Discourse*. New York: Funk & Wagnalls, 1905.

INDEX

Abbot, Lyman, xxviii-xxix, 227-31, 420
Agape, 297
Alexander, W. L., 308
Allen, A. V. G., 22-24
Amusements, worldly, 14
Apostles, 60-61, 392
Appleget, Thomas B., 202
Art of sermon construction; *see* literary style
Atkins, Gaius Glenn, 10 n., 20, 25, 159, 402
Atonement, 134, 149; *see also* Cross, the
Aubrey, Edwin E., 117-19
Auden, W. H., xxx
Augustine, 259
Authority in religion, 263, 365

Barber, George, 29 n.
Barbour, Clarence A., 203
Barry, F. R., 271
Barry, F. W., 343
Barth, K., 98, 112, 129, 388
Baxter, Richard, 310
Beecher, Harriet, xxviii
Beecher, Henry Ward, xiv, xvi, xxvi, 3-10, 15 n., 20, 31, 65-66, 92, 225, 227, 230-31, 237, 365, 385, 387, 413
Beecher, Lyman, xxvii-xxix
Behrends, Adolphus Julius Frederick, 15 n., 108-13, 398, 417
Bell, Wilbur Cosby, 342
Bernard of Clairvaux, 365
Bevan, Llewelyn David, 415
Bible, 17, 47, 60-61, 93, 103, 125-26, 132, 182, 270, 316-17, 331-32
 criticism of, 126
Bibliography of lectures, 432-39
Binney, Thomas, 311
Blackwood, Andrew W., 391-92

Blake, William, 246
Bonnell, John S., 389
Books, preachers' use of, 29-30, 93, 182, 205-7, 279-80
Bowie, Walter Russell, 339-42, 427
Bradford, Arthur Howe, 253, 255-57, 428
Bradford, John, 309
Brastow, Lewis O., 32, 75
Broadus, John Albert, 40, 50-56, 407, 417
Broadway Tabernacle, 15-16, 69
Brooks, John Graham, 204
Brooks, Phillips, 19-25, 92, 227, 243, 365-66, 385, 387, 413-14
Brougham, Lord, 180
Brown, Charles Reynolds, xx, xxix, 137-38, 235, 237-41, 313-14, 388, 407, 410, 420
Brown, John, 308-13, 419
Browning, Robert, 127, 299
Bruce, A. B., 117
Brunner, E., 98, 112, 129, 388
Bryan, William Jennings, 340
Bunyan, John, 308, 310, 312
Burke, Edmund, 393-94
Burkhart, Roy, 389
Burns, Robert, 48, 182
Burritt, Elihu, 32
Burton, Nathaniel Judson, 44-50, 390, 416
Bushnell, Horace, 222, 224, 288
Buttrick, George Arthur, xx, 80, 247-252, 253, 426

Cabot, Richard C., 188
Cadman, S. Parkes, 163, 401
Calkins, Raymond, 329-34, 425
Call to the ministry, 183, 276, 372
Calvinism, 65
Cambridge Platonists, 309
Campbell, R. J., 134, 364-65

441

Index

Candlish, Robert Smith, 307
Carlyle, Thomas, 282
Cartwright, Peter, 386
Catholicism, Roman, 136, 215, 229
Centrality of Christ, 116, 118, 249, 291, 336, 365, 368, 378
Certainty in religion, 30, 167-68, 330-331, 342
Chalmers, Thomas, 305, 307
Channing, W. E., 65-66
Chaplain, army, 90
Christ, Work of, 62, 72, 100, 118, 124, 133, 178, 205, 336, 365
Christian Century, The, 223, 232
Christian Science, 300
Christology, 98-99, 116
Church, 8, 71-72, 130, 136, 144, 156-157, 172, 234-36, 270-71, 343, 370-71
  and state, 43-44, 94
  unity of, 219, 236, 358, 390
Churchill, Winston, 204
Clarke, William Newton, 104
Coffin, Henry Sloane, xx, 155-59, 247, 268, 388, 423
Colet, John, 309
Combs, G. H., 327
Commager, H. S., xiv
Communism, 142, 379, 386
Conduct of worship, 230, 243, 290, 293
Confessional, the, 215, 389
Controversy in preaching, 23, 233
Conversion, 111-12, 205, 234, 322
Cornell University, xxv
Counseling, 291-92, 390
Crisis, the contemporary, 209-10, 369-70, 373, 376, 386
Crosby, Howard, 15 n., 36-40, 387, 414
Cross, the, 25, 62, 124, 134, 149, 159, 178, 250, 256, 278, 378
Crothers, Samuel McChord, 214

Dale, Robert William, 26-31, 119, 311-12, 318, 387, 414
Dargan, E. C., 50, 52
Davidson, A. B., 123 n.
Davies, D. R., 141-42, 144
Day, Albert Edward, 334-39, 427

Death, 66, 306, 342
Deism, 66-67
Delivery of sermons, 55; *see also* gestures, mannerisms
Denominationalism, 8, 108, 358, 390
Dobson, Henry Austin, 411
Doctrine, use of in preaching, 17, 22, 28, 54, 59, 98-99, 113, 186-87, 199, 258-59, 331, 387, 394
Dodd, C. H., 392
D'Orge, Jeanne, 273
Dostoevski, F., 253
Drinkwater, John, 341
Drummond, Henry, 125-26
Duryea, Joseph Tuthill, 414-15

Ecumenical movement; *see* unity, church
Eddy, Sherwood, 43
Education of minister, 37-38; *see also* preaching, preparation for
Education, religious, 7, 199, 223-25
Eloquence, xxix, 6, 75, 92-93, 316, 398; *see also* oratory
Ethical character of religion, 67, 152, 158, 185, 194
Evangelism, 78, 84, 110, 155 n., 234, 322, 401
Evolution, theory of, 33-34, 118, 269
Extemporary preaching, 17-18, 41; *see also* manuscript, use of

Fairbairn, Andrew Martin, 27-28, 79, 113-21, 194, 418
Faith, 149, 294-95, 322, 331, 365, 377
False prophets, 184
Farmer, Herbert Henry, 144-50, 388, 430
Faunce, William Herbert Perry, 197-203, 421
Field, Eugene, 78
Fifth Avenue Presbyterian Church, 11, 80
Fisher, George Park, 359
Fitch, Albert Parker, 95-101, 424
Flemming, Arthur S., xxx
Ford, Henry, 141
Forgiveness, 133, 250, 295-96

Index

Forsyth, Peter Taylor, 57, 116, 128-134, 145, 388, 420-21
Fosdick, Harry Emerson, 80, 101-7, 198, 252, 273-74, 395, 397, 424
Freedom of thought and speech, 264, 351, 353
Freeman, James Edward, xx, 359-62, 425
Friars, preaching, 309
Frivolity, danger of, 24, 29, 53, 184, 217-18, 263, 316
Fundamentalist controversy, 103, 325, 376

Gardner, C. S., 51
George, Henry, 218
Gestures, use of, 55, 74, 79, 289
Gibbon, Edward, xx-xxi
Gilbert, George B., 400
Gladden, Washington, xiv, 151-55, 192, 387, 416
God, nature of, 39-40, 47, 65-67, 116, 133, 144, 148-49, 269, 284-285, 299, 377
Good Will, power of, 206
Goodwin, Thomas, 310
Gordon, George Angier, 20 n., 63-68, 120, 241 n., 419-20
Gray, Thomas, 328
Greer, David Hummell, 343-47, 418
Gunsaulus, Frank Wakeley, 35, 74-79, 80, 394-95, 421-22
Guthrie, Thomas, 307-8

Habits and discipline of minister, 18, 29-30, 38, 62, 70, 73, 93, 174-175, 207, 286, 372, 378, 382, 403-4
Hadfield, J. A., 297
Hall, John, 10-15, 387, 413
Hall, Thomas C., 12
Hankey, Donald, 256
Hardy, Thomas, 257
Harris, George, 415
Harvard College, 191-92
Healing of sick, 294, 296, 300, 389
Hegel, 118
Henderson, Alexander, 308
Henson, Herbert Hensley, 347-55, 421

Herrick, Samuel, 415
Hewitt, A. W., 400
Hibbert Journal, The, 207-8, 211
Hillis, N. D., 80
Holt, Ivan Lee, 367
Holy Ghost, 59-61
Honorary degrees, 11, 31, 84
Horne, Charles Silvester, 313-18, 333, 422
Horton, Robert Forman, 57-63, 418
Housman, Laurence, 256
Hoyt, Arthur S., 40-41
Hughes, Edwin Holt, 164, 323-24, 363
Humanism, 98, 254
Humor, 24, 34, 49, 143, 240, 287, 405
Hutchinson, Paul, 169-70, 173 n.
Hyde, William DeWitt, 203-7, 423

Illustrations, use of, 320
Imagination, use of, 47
Immortality, 66, 210
Incarnation, the, 125
Inge, William Ralph, 135-39, 348 n., 353-54, 378, 406, 425
Inspiration, 30, 35, 59-61, 88, 248, 277, 332

Jacks, Lawrence Pearsall, 207-11, 427
Jefferson, Charles Edward, 45, 63, 69-74, 80, 252, 395, 421
Jeffs, Ernest H., 57, 79, 80, 81, 83, 84, 139 n.
Jenkins, Burris A., 270
Jerome, Jerome K., 204
Jesus, teachings of, 195-96, 336, 341
Jewell, Bishop, 309
John the Baptist, 261-62
Johnson, Samuel, 215
Jones, J. D., 313
Jowett, John Henry, 79-85, 406-7, 422
Judas, 196
Justification by faith, 54

Kelman, John, 89-95, 423-24
Kennedy, Charles Rann, 204
Kenyon, Helen, xxx

Index

Ker, John, 308
Kierkegaard, S., 129
Kingsley, Charles, 190-91
Kleiser, Grenville, 39
Knox, John, 304-5
Kulandran, S., 392-94

Latimer, Hugh, 309
Lawrence, Gertrude, 255
Lawrence, William, 374
Leighton, Archbishop, 308
Lemmon, Clarence E., 144
Liberalism, 33-34, 36, 65-66, 98, 104-105, 110, 113, 129, 141-43, 258, 263, 269, 393
Lichliter, McIlyar H., 154-55
Lincoln, Abraham, 31, 76-77, 92, 272
Literary style, 38, 72, 73, 102, 131, 176, 182, 212, 250, 275, 328, 382, 395
Liturgy, 230, 243
Love of God, 67, 133, 149, 297-98
Luther, Martin, 54
Lyman Beecher Lectureship:
  academic status of lecturers, 404
  age of lecturers, 408
  audience for, 4, 289, 406, 408-9
  classification of, xix-xx
  denominational affiliations of lecturers, 399
  estimate of, xix, 221, 242, 275, 385-98, 404-5
  geographical distribution of lecturers, 399-400
  honoraria received by lecturers, 409-10
  origin of, xxiii-xxiv, xxvi, 355
  scope and character of, xviii, 398-404
  publication of lectures, 407-8
  who's who of lecturers, 413-31

Maclaren, Alexander, 311-12
Maclaren, Ian; see Watson, John
Macleod, George, 393
Maier, Walter A., 260
Man, nature of, 147-48, 157
Mannerisms, 49, 55, 79, 290, 307, 357

Manuscript, use of, 14, 17-18, 41-42, 73, 83, 179, 228, 232, 325, 335, 347, 382
Marriott, Sir John, 58, 62
Martineau, James, 331
Masefield, John, 204
Maurice, F. D., 332
McConnell, Francis John, 152, 163-168, 388, 426
McDowell, William Fraser, 319-24, 423
McKee, Elmore McNeill, 253, 257-258, 429
McLeod, Norman, 308
McMillan, John, 183 n.
Melville, Herman, 285
Memoriter preaching, 17-18, 41
Merrill, Boynton, 68
Merrill, William Pierson, 324-29, 424
Minister, the, and secular activities, 18, 70, 86-87, 94, 160, 286, 346
  as pastor, 7, 83, 215, 272-73, 292, 372-73
  as priest, 229
  perils of, 330, 337-38, 371
  qualifications of, 17, 46, 184-86, 276-77, 292, 346
  rights and duties of, 12-13, 81, 199, 292, 320, 322, 334, 344, 372, 410
Ministry, prophetic; see prophetic ministry
Miracles, 61, 300
Moody, Dwight L., 23, 122 n., 386
Morgan, Campbell, 134, 247
Morrison, Charles Clayton, xx, 42, 78-79, 223, 232-36, 388, 390, 428
Mouzon, Edwin DuBose, 363-68, 425-26
Mozley, J. K., 129
Music, 6
Mysticism, 168

Nationalism, 154, 162, 370
Neo-orthodoxy, 98, 112, 388
"New Deal," the, 379
Newspapers, 57, 87, 231, 263
Newton, Joseph Fort, 70, 75, 76, 80, 83, 139, 395, 402

Index

Nicoll, Sir W. Robertson, 27, 30-31, 122-23, 127, 147, 317, 381
Niebuhr, Reinhold, 98, 102, 112, 129, 140-44, 152, 174, 388, 395, 430
Norton, Hal Earl, xx, 432
Noyes, Morgan Phelps, 266-73, 429

Oman, John, 146
Oratory, 21, 35, 75, 92-93, 131, 199, 381, 394-96
Orozco, 177-78
Oxnam, Garfield Bromley, 173-79, 388, 430

Palmer, George Herbert, 204
Paradox, use of, 143
Parish administration, 34, 160, 371
Park, John Edgar, 211-16, 427-28
Parker, Joseph, 134
Parkhurst, Charles Henry, 15 n., 85-88, 422
Pastoral work, 7, 83, 215, 272-73, 292, 372-73
Pastorate, length of, 190
Paul, 54, 71, 149, 185, 234-35, 333, 372
Peabody, Francis Greenwood, 67-68, 151, 191-97, 216, 420
Peale, Norman Vincent, 389
Peel, Albert, 62
Pepper, George Wharton, 355-59, 423
Personality, 21, 82, 99, 144, 148, 169, 188, 264, 337, 362, 366
Phelps, Austin, 53
Phillips, Harold Cooke, 281-88, 430-431
Phillips, Wendell, 45, 359, 396
Pilgrims, the, 43-44
Pilgrim's Progress, The, 310-11
Plymouth Church, 3, 9, 225-26
Politics and religion, 43, 86-87, 94
Pope, Liston, xxix
Porritt, Arthur, 61, 68, 70-71, 84, 115, 121, 134, 180
Poteat, Edwin McNeill, 253-55, 429
Potter, H. C., 360
Power of God, 374
Prayer, 61-62, 230-31, 293-94, 296

Preaching, and good taste, 53, 316
 and doctrine, 17, 22, 28, 54, 59, 98-99, 113, 186-87, 199, 258-59, 331, 387, 394
 and humor, 24, 34, 49, 240
 and modern science, 13, 33-34, 200-201, 389
 and politics, 43, 94, 161, 170, 218, 257
 and social reform, 86-87, 152, 379
 from the Bible, 17, 104-5, 127, 132, 182, 316-17, 393
 from manuscript, 14, 17, 41-42, 73, 83, 232, 347, 382
 from memory, 17-18
 nature of, 21, 189, 320
 preparation for, xxix, 29-30, 38, 62, 70, 73, 82, 93, 207, 244, 264-265, 279, 286-87, 372, 378, 382-383, 403-4
 qualifications for, 37, 46, 186, 188, 357, 366
 value of, xv-xvi, 30, 81, 88, 169, 238-39, 315, 327, 332, 345, 364, 391-92, 398, 410
Priestly function of minister, 229
Property, 139, 152, 161, 163, 164-165, 379
Prophetic ministry, the, 59-61, 131, 160-61, 166-68, 173, 183, 217-218, 219, 248, 277, 326
Protestantism, 234-36, 263, 385
Psychotherapy, 295-96, 299-300, 336, 340, 389-90
Publication of lectures, 407-8
Puritan preachers, 308-13
Puritanism, 14, 199

Quayle, William A., 307, 332, 402

Radio, influence of the, 396-98
Rainy, Robert, 308
Rauschenbusch, Walter, 192
Redemption, 99, 131-33, 249-50, 254, 270
Religious education, 7, 199, 223-25
Religious experience, 330
Religious press, 352
Revelation, 125, 393
Riis, Jacob A., 204

Riley, James Whitcomb, 346-47
Ritschl, 118-19
Riverside Church, the, 101, 107
Robertson, Frederick W., 23, 156, 366, 378
Robinson, Ezekiel Gilman, 40-44, 387, 415-16
Robinson, John, 315-16
Robinson, William, 123, 128-30, 133-34, 145-46
Rutherfurd, Samuel, 305

Sacraments, the, 130, 243
Sage, Henry W., xv, xxiii-xxiv
Sandburg, Carl, 255, 375
Sarolea, Charles, 204
Scarlett, William, 25 n.
Scherer, Paul Ehrman, 273-81, 396, 430
Schleiermacher, 111, 127, 133
Schweitzer, Albert, 170
Science and the preacher, 13, 33-34, 299
Sclater, John Robert Paterson, 89, 241-47, 425
Scottish preachers, 303-8
Sectarianism, 8, 108, 219
Selbie, W. B., 115-16
Sermons, book, 205-7
  conversational type of, 106
  length of, 240
  nature and qualities of, 5-6, 22, 30, 88, 92-93, 111, 131, 143-44, 183 n., 238-39, 286, 327, 364
  sources of, 73, 82, 93, 244, 264-65, 279, 382
Sex, 298
Seymore, Charles, 289
Shakespeare, William, 278-79
Shaw, G. B., 136 n.
Sheppard, Dick, 280, 402
Sherrill, Henry Knox, 368-74, 431
Simplicity in preaching, 73, 169, 187, 195, 290, 323, 331
Simpson, Matthew, 31-36, 323, 387, 414
Sin, 71, 112-13, 133, 249, 251, 295
Sincerity in preaching, 93, 161, 220, 277, 287, 290-91, 362, 367, 373, 382

Sinnot, Edmund W., xxx
Smart, Wyatt Aiken, 253, 258-60, 428-29
Smith, George Adam, 103, 121-27, 419
Social Gospel, the, 152-53, 218-19, 249, 378, 387
Social nature of religion, 67, 152, 158
Social reform, 86-87, 112, 152-53, 162, 164-65, 171, 218, 249, 258-59, 379, 388
Sockman, Ralph Washington, 260-66, 396, 429
South, Robert, 310
Spargo, John, 314
Sperry, Willard Learoyd, 216-21, 428
Spiritualism, 300
Spurgeon, Charles H., 311, 322, 402
Stalker, James, 180-87, 417
Stanley, Dean, 310
State and Church, 43-44, 94, 257
Storrs, Henry Martin, 416
Storrs, Richard Salter, 15 n., 16, 225, 361, 386
Suffering, problem of, 124, 254-55, 299
Sunday school, the, 223-25
Sunday School Times, The, 222-23
Sunday, William A., 84, 155 n.
Sympathy in preaching, 55

Taft, Charles P., xxx
Talmadge, T. DeWitt, 395
Tammany Hall, 85, 87
Taste, questions of, 53, 316
Taylor, William Mackergo, 15-19, 303-8, 387, 413
Teaching function of minister, 199-200
Teachings of Jesus, 195-96
Temple, William, 143, 402
Temptation, 180
Text, choice of, 29
Theology in preaching, 28, 39-40, 47, 331, 387-89
Thomas, Elbert D., 44 n.
Thoreau, H. D., 385
Thurman, Howard, 402
Time, minister's use of, 18, 70, 160
Titles of published lectures, 432-36

Tittle, Ernest Fremont, 169-73, 253, 426-27
Toynbee, Arnold, 370
Training of preacher, 18, 29-30, 38, 62, 70, 73, 93, 174-75, 383
Treat, Roger Eddy, 73-74
Truett, George W., 396, 401
Trumbell, Henry Clay, 222-27, 417
Truth in religion, 22, 28, 48, 167-68, 201, 283-86
Tucker, William Jewett, 187-91, 419
Tyng, Stephen H., 225-26

Unity, Church, 217, 219, 236, 358, 390
University degrees, 11, 31, 84

Van Dusen, Henry P., 96-97
Van Dyke, Henry, 15, 165, 325, 375-380, 418
Van Dyke, Tertius, 325
Voice, use of, 74, 357, 381
Von Hügel, Baron, 129

War, 90-91, 154, 156, 266, 272, 280, 370
Ward, Harry F., 152

Wardlaw, Ralph, 308
Watson, John, xxvii, 239, 380-84, 419
Wealth, 139, 152, 161, 163, 164-65, 379
Weatherhead, Leslie D., xiv, 198, 288-302, 335, 389, 395, 431
Weatherspoon, J. B., 51
Weigle, Luther, xxix, 98, 252, 289
Wesley, John, 295
White, Andrew D., xxv
Whittier, J. G., 301, 385
Whyte, Alexander, 286
Who's who in the Lectureship, 413-431
Wilde, Oscar, 102
Wilkinson, William Cleaver, 4, 10, 15, 21, 41, 42, 51
Williams, Charles David, 152, 159-163, 424
Wilson, Woodrow, 360, 375, 385
Wolfe, Paul Austin, 94-95
Woolman, John, 256
Word of God, the, 6, 60-61
Wordsworth, William, 254
Worship, public, 229, 243, 293
Wriston, Henry M., xxx